Elizabeth I and Ireland

The past generation has seen a veritable revolution in scholarly work on Elizabeth I, on Ireland, and on the colonial aspects of the literary productions that typically served to link the two. It is now commonly accepted that Elizabeth was a much more active and activist figure than an older scholarship allowed. Gaelic elites are acknowledged to have had close interactions with the crown and continental powers; Ireland itself has been shown to have occupied a greater place in Tudor political calculations than previously thought. Literary masterpieces of the age are recognised for their imperial and colonial entanglements. *Elizabeth I and Ireland* is the first collection to fully connect these recent scholarly advances. Bringing together historians of Ireland and England, and literary scholars of both vernacular languages, this is the first sustained consideration of the roles played by Elizabeth and by the Irish in shaping relations between the realms.

BRENDAN KANE is Associate Professor of History at the University of Connecticut.

VALERIE McGOWAN-DOYLE is Associate Professor of History at Lorain County Community College and Adjunct Faculty in Irish Studies/Humanities, John Carroll University.

Elizabeth I and Ireland

Edited by

Brendan Kane and Valerie McGowan-Doyle

CAMBRIDGE
UNIVERSITY PRESS

CAMBRIDGE
UNIVERSITY PRESS

University Printing House, Cambridge CB2 8BS, United Kingdom

Cambridge University Press is part of the University of Cambridge.

It furthers the University's mission by disseminating knowledge in the pursuit of education, learning and research at the highest international levels of excellence.

www.cambridge.org
Information on this title: www.cambridge.org/9781107040878

© Cambridge University Press 2014

First published 2014

A catalogue record for this publication is available from the British Library

Library of Congress Cataloguing in Publication data
Elizabeth I and Ireland / edited by Brendan Kane and Valerie McGowan-Doyle.
    pages   cm
Includes bibliographical references and index.
ISBN 978-1-107-04087-8 (hard-back : alk. paper)
1. Great Britain – History – Elizabeth, 1558–1603.   2. Great Britain – Foreign
relations – Ireland.   3. Ireland – Foreign relations – Great Britain.   4. Ireland –
History – 16th century.   I. Kane, Brendan Michael, 1968–   II. McGowan-Doyle,
Valerie.
DA355.E566   2014
941.505 – dc23   2014010673

ISBN 978-1-107-04087-8 Hardback

To Vincent Carey
Friend, mentor, and inspiration

In Memoriam
Nancy Comarella
Robin Worley

Contents

Illustrations

Contributors

CIARAN BRADY: Professor, Early Modern History and Historiography, Trinity College, Dublin.

Brady's many publications include *The Chief Governors: the rise and fall of reform government in Tudor Ireland, 1536–1588* (Cambridge, 1994) and the collection *British interventions in early modern Ireland* (Cambridge, 2005), coedited with Prof. Jane Ohlmeyer. His most recent book is *James Anthony Froude: an intellectual biography of a Victorian prophet* (2013).

MARC CABALL: Senior Lecturer, University College Dublin, School of History and Archives and current chairman of the COST (European Co-operation in Science and Technology) Domain Committee for Individuals, Societies, Cultures and Health.

Caball has published widely on the cultural history of early modern Ireland. Among his recent publications are: 'Responses to transformation: Gaelic poets and the plantation of Ulster', in Éamonn Ó Ciardha and Micheál Ó Siochrú (eds.), *The plantation of Ulster: ideology and practice* (2012), pp. 176–97, and '"Solid divine and worthy scholar": William Bedell, Venice and Gaelic culture', in James Kelly and Ciarán Mac Murchaidh (eds.), *Irish and English: essays on the Irish linguistic and cultural frontier, 1600–1900* (2012), pp. 43–57. He edited (with Andrew Carpenter), *Oral and print cultures in Ireland, 1600–1900* (2010).

ANDREW HADFIELD: Professor, English, University of Sussex.

Hadfield is the author and editor of a number of works, most recently, *Edmund Spenser: A Life* (2012), and *The Oxford Handbook of Early Modern Prose, 1500–1640* (2013). He is currently editing the works of Thomas Nashe and working on a study of lying in the early modern period.

PAUL E. J. HAMMER: Professor, History, University of Colorado.

Hammer is author of *The polarisation of Elizabethan politics: the political career of Robert Devereux, 2nd earl of Essex, 1585–1597* (Cambridge,

1999) and *Elizabeth's wars: government and society in Tudor England, 1544–1604* (2003). Among his present book projects is one on the Essex Rising of 1601.

MARK A. HUTCHINSON: Junior Research Fellow, Lichtenberg-Kolleg, University of Göttingen Institute of Advanced Study.

Hutchinson was formerly an IRC Government of Ireland Postdoctoral Fellow at University College Cork. He is interested in the influence of reformed theology, as well as early modern 'statist' thought, on Elizabethan government in Ireland. He recently contributed an article to the *Sidney Journal* in 2011. He is also working on a monograph that will examine Irish government policy from the 1550s to the 1590s, and the emergence of a modern notion of 'the state' within Irish government correspondence.

BRENDAN KANE (coeditor): Associate Professor, History, University of Connecticut.

Kane's *The politics and culture of honour in Britain and Ireland, 1541–1641* appeared with Cambridge University Press in 2010. He is currently working on a study of knowledge/power relations in early modern England and Ireland. With Thomas Herron he co-curated the exhibition *Nobility and newcomers in Renaissance Ireland* (Folger Shakespeare Library, 19 January–19 May 2013) and co-wrote the exhibition catalogue of the same name.

RICHARD McCABE: Professor, English, Merton College, University of Oxford, FBA.

McCabe's many publications include *Spenser's monstrous regiment: Elizabethan Ireland and the poetics of difference* (2002), *Incest, drama and nature's law* (Cambridge, 1993), and *The pillars of eternity: time and providence in* The Faerie Queene (1989). He also edited *Edmund Spenser: the shorter poems* (1999) and *The Oxford Handbook of Edmund Spenser* (2010). His current research addresses literary patronage in the early modern period and Renaissance tragedy.

VALERIE McGOWAN-DOYLE (coeditor): Associate Professor, History, Lorain County Community College, and Adjunct Faculty, Irish Studies/Humanities, John Carroll University.

McGowan-Doyle is the author of *The Book of Howth: Elizabethan conquest and the Old English* (2011) as well as several essays on the Old English in the late Tudor and early Stuart periods. Her current work addresses women and violence in early modern Ireland.

PETER McQUILLAN: Associate Professor, Department of Irish Language and Literature, University of Notre Dame.

McQuillan is author of *Modality and the Subjunctive Mood in Irish* (2002) and *Native and Natural: Aspects of the Concepts of Right and Freedom in Irish* (2004). He is now engaged on a study of Gaelic concepts of civility from the sixteenth to the eighteenth century.

LEAH MARCUS: Edwin Mims Professor of English, Vanderbilt University.

Marcus's many publications include *Puzzling Shakespeare: local reading and its discontents* (1988) and *Elizabeth I: collected works* (coedited with Janel Mueller and Mary Beth Rose; 1986). She is currently finishing a book entitled *How Shakespeare became colonial.*

HIRAM MORGAN: Senior Lecturer in History, University College Cork, and Director of CELT: Corpus of Electronic Texts of Ireland.

Morgan's many publications include *Tyrone's rebellion: the outbreak of the Nine Years War in Ireland* (1993) as well two edited essay collections, *Political ideology in Ireland, 1541–1641* (1999) and *The Battle of Kinsale* (2004). He has recently coedited *Great deeds in Ireland: Richard Stanihurst's De Rebus in Hibernia Gestis* (2013) and is currently completing a biography of Hugh O'Neill, earl of Tyrone, for the Royal Irish Academy.

B. R. SIEGFRIED: Nan Osmond Grass Professor of English Literature, Brigham Young University.

Siegfried's recent publications explore Irish influences on Elizabethan thought, including essays in the edited collections *Ireland and the Pale* (2011), *The foreign relations of Elizabeth I* (2011), *Sidney Studies Journal* special edition on the Pale (2011), and *Elizabeth I: always her own free woman* (2001). Gráinne Ní Mháille is the subject of her current book-length project.

Acknowledgements

This project began as a conference of the same name hosted by the University of Connecticut (12–14 November 2009). Robert Tilton was instrumental in convincing us to organise it and in encouraging a broad disciplinary approach. The other members of the organising committee were vital in bringing together just such an interdisciplinary programme: Kenneth Gouwens, Elizabeth Hart, Rachael Lynch, and Gregory Semenza. In the days of uncertainty over whether we could host such an ambitious conference in the midst of global financial downturn, the University of Connecticut Humanities Institute came to the rescue with the funding that allowed it to go ahead. We are immensely grateful to its director, Sharon Harris, for allowing both the conference and thus ultimately this collection to happen. Funding was also provided by the University of Connecticut's Departments of History and English, the Research Administration, the Office of the Dean of the College of Liberal Arts and Sciences, European Studies, the Renaissance Colloquium, and Irish Studies, and we thank the following for all their assistance in that process: Richard Brown, Mary Burke, Nancy Comarella, Clare Costley-King'oo, John Davis, 'Hap' Fairbanks, Wayne Franklin, Charles Mahoney, Jeffrey Ogbar, Shirley Roe, Gregory Semenza, Jeremy Teitlebaum, Robert Tilton, and Robin Worley. Thanks go to our plenary speakers, Marc Caball, Paul Hammer, Leah Marcus, and Hiram Morgan, and to those who gave presentations: Jean Brink, Ruth Canning, Vincent Carey, Kim Draggoo, Stephen Galbraith, Thomas Herron, Karen Holland, Mark Hutchinson, Stuart Kinsella, Eric Klingelhofer, Wayne E. Lee, Brian Lockey, Chris Maginn, Adam McKeown, Peter McQuillan, John Montano, Eoin O'Neill, Rory Rapple, Brandie Siegfried, and Natalie Sweet. We also wish to praise those who chaired panels, Mary Burke, Clare Costley-King'oo, Elizabeth Hart, and Donald McNamara. Rebecca Rondeau and Steve Rugens in Conference Services made it all work smoothly. Gratitude, finally, is owed to those who attended the conference, providing lively and productive discussion.

Special thanks are also due to Peter Lake for his support of the project from its inception.

We extend our deepest gratitude to the editors and staff at Cambridge University Press – in particular to Elizabeth Friend-Smith, Maartje Scheltens, Katy Mack, Joanna Breeze, Karen Anderson Howes, and Chloe Dawson for their tremendous assistance and patience – as well as to the anonymous readers for their close attention to the text and productive comments.

Intellectually, this collection is indebted to the path-breaking work on the topic of Elizabeth I and Ireland by Hiram Morgan and Vincent Carey.

The volume is dedicated to Vincent as small thanks for his many years of encouragement and intellectual inspiration. It is also dedicated in memoriam to two wonderful people without whom the conference would never have happened: Nancy Comarella, Graduate Program Assistant in History, and Robin Worley, Business Manager in English, both at the University of Connecticut. Beloved friends and colleagues, they are mourned and missed by all who knew them.

And, finally, with love and thanks we acknowledge our greatest supporters, Patrick, Maebh, Mary Clare, Sandy, Eoin, and Gavin.

Abbreviations

BL	British Library
Cal. Carew	*Calendar of the Carew manuscripts preserved in the archiepiscopal library at Lambeth, 1515–1624*, J. S. Brewer and William Bullen (eds.), 6 vols. (London, 1867–73)
CSPD	*Calendar of state papers, domestic*, R. Lemon and M. A. E. Green (eds.), 12 vols. (London, 1856–72)
CSPI	*Calendar of state papers relating to Ireland . . . 1509–1603*, H. C. Hamilton, E. G. Atkinson, and R. P. Mahaffy (eds.), 11 vols. (London, 1860–1912)
DIB	*Dictionary of Irish biography*, James McGuire and James Quinn (eds.), 9 vols. (Cambridge, 2009)
HMC, *Salisbury*	Historical Manuscripts Commission, *Calendar of manuscripts of the . . . marquess of Salisbury preserved at Hatfield House*, 24 vols. (London, 1883–1976)
Letters and memorials	Arthur Collins (ed.), *Letters and memorials of state*, 2 vols. (London, 1746)
LPL	Lambeth Palace Library
ODNB	*Oxford dictionary of national biography*, H. C. G. Matthew and Brian Harrison (eds.), 60 vols. (Oxford University Press, 2004)
Sidney SP	*Sidney state papers, 1565–1570*, Tomás Ó Laidhin (ed.) (Dublin, 1962)
SP	The National Archives, State Papers, Ireland
TNA	The National Archives, London

1 Elizabeth I and Ireland: an introduction

Brendan Kane and Valerie McGowan-Doyle

In 1562 Christopher St Lawrence, 7th baron Howth, was dispatched from Dublin to attend Elizabeth I at court. He was charged with an important task: to defend Lord Lieutenant Sussex's campaigns against the rebellious Shane O'Neill and the tax, or cess, he imposed on Irish residents to fund them. At stake in this visit were the greatest questions of governance across the realms, namely the completed conquest, defence, and financial upkeep of the Tudor monarchy's second kingdom. Howth must have seemed a natural choice for this vital mission. He was no mere administrative lackey but a noble descendant of the twelfth-century Anglo-Norman conquerors of Ireland, one of the self-identifying 'English-Irish' elites who held swathes of the island in the crown's interest. A local lord of ancient lineage and hereditary loyalty, Howth was also privy to the most intimate discussions of Sussex's administration. Yet in spite of the lieutenant's careful selection of this 'native' English noble to defend his administration and its policies, the initial meeting of emissary and monarch demonstrated that things which seemed clear in Dublin were not equally so in London: when presented with Howth, Elizabeth enquired whether Sussex's representative 'could speak the English tongue'.[1]

Howth's fraught first encounter with his prince highlights a number of issues key to an understanding of English–Irish relations in this crucial period of complementary centralisation and imperial expansion by the Tudor state. First, the sending of Howth to court raises the question of Elizabeth's role in determining Irish policy. The vital issues of defence and innovative taxation were argued not simply through means of letters to Secretary Burghley but through direct engagement with the queen. How active a prince was she in her Irish realm? Second, to what extent was Elizabeth aware of the cultural distinctions dividing her subjects in Ireland? Clearly she knew that Gaelic was spoken there. But did she think that being from Ireland equalled being Gaelic (or effectively 'Gaelicised')?

[1] *Cal. Carew*, V, p. 201.

Given Howth's self-identification as an Englishman (albeit one living in Ireland), and the queen's own closeness to the Old English magnate, the earl of Ormond, Elizabeth's question seems an odd one: was it a sign of ignorance of, or of sensitivity to, cultural distinction? Finally, then, this episode forces upon us the question of how prince and Irish subject – Gaelic, Old English, or New English – viewed their shared relationship. That Elizabeth suspected Howth might be a monoglot Irish speaker dismayed him, and helped spur his future, herculean literary/antiquarian efforts in defence of Old English identity.[2] But it also suggests that she would not have been surprised to see one of her Gaelic subjects attend court. In fact, earlier that year the great Ulster lord Shane O'Neill himself had spent several months at court, his entourage in tow.[3] Was there a place for the Gaelic Irish at the political table and in the Tudor political nation? Given that the queen did ask for and receive an Irish primer with matching phrases in English, Latin, and Irish, did attention to cultural distinctiveness affect her political style? The present collection addresses these, and many other, crucial yet under-studied questions related to English–Irish relations in the tumultuous years of Elizabeth I's reign over both kingdoms.

This project grows out of a desire to connect ground-breaking scholarly work, published over roughly the past two decades, on Elizabeth I, on Ireland, and on the colonial aspects of the literary productions that typically served to link the two. Taking the first of these subjects first, gone are the days when the queen could be written off the political stage as merely the flighty charge of practical-minded, male councillors, Burghley chief among them. The real debate among scholars seems, instead, to centre on the extent to which the queen's political agency and engagement were directed towards far-sighted matters of policy and statecraft or towards short-term advantage of a largely personal interest. Regarding the former, there has always existed a thread in the historiography that portrayed Elizabeth as an active figure in the development of church, state, and empire. The synthetic biographies of Elizabeth by

---

[2] Valerie McGowan-Doyle, *The Book of Howth: Elizabethan conquest and the Old English* (Cork, 2011).

[3] James Hogan, 'Shane O'Neill comes to the court of Elizabeth', in Séamus Pender (ed.), *Féilscríbhinn Torna: essays and studies presented to Professor Tadhg Ua Donnchadha* (Cork, 1947), pp. 154–70; Ciaran Brady, 'Shane O'Neill departs from the court of Elizabeth: Irish, English, Scottish perspectives and the paralysis of policy, July 1559 to April 1562', in S. J. Connolly (ed.), *Kingdoms united? Great Britain and Ireland since 1500: integration and diversity* (Dublin, 1999), pp. 13–28; Ciaran Brady, *Shane O'Neill* (Dundalk, 1996). For a selection of documents on O'Neill's visit to court, see SP 63/4/76 and SP 63/5/1, 42, 45.

Wallace MacCaffrey and David Loades, published ten years apart brought this general assessment to a wide audience: having surveyed the dauntingly expansive literature on the subject, they each concluded that time-worn notions of Elizabeth as merely weaker-vessel-in-chief were misguided.[4]

Innovative studies of gender and power produced complementary findings: Elizabeth was able to turn her gender to advantage in manoeuvring through the male-dominated world of high politics.[5] Natalie Mears's more recent work on Elizabeth and queenship has tacked differently in pursuit of monarchical authority. Largely eschewing a "feminist" approach, she highlighted instead the social networks and connections through which decisions were made. It was in private 'probouleutic groups', she argued, that major decisions in the regime were reached, with council meetings existing largely as *ex post facto* fora in which previously determined positions were formalised.[6] Not all scholars have been so convinced of the queen's agency, however – or at least not convinced that it was something directed towards effective governance. Christopher Haigh and Patrick Collinson, to take two prominent examples, have argued instead that Elizabeth was, in Natalie Mears's words, more 'vain and manipulative' than she was a clear-headed architect of state-building.[7] In short, she was more politically engaged than politically capable. That is not to say that she was weak and distant as a ruler, just that her definition of the political perhaps did not satisfy the standards of later commentators interested in *longue durée* state-formation.

A curious aspect of this vigorous debate on Elizabeth I and politics is the absence of Ireland from the discussion. Given that she was prince of two realms, the lack of attention paid to the western kingdom is a

---

[4] Wallace MacCaffrey, *Elizabeth I* (London, 1993); David Loades, *Elizabeth I* (London, 2003).

[5] Prominent examples include Carole Levin, *The heart and stomach of a king: Elizabeth I and the politics of sex and power* (Philadelphia, 1994); Anne McLaren, *Political culture in the reign of Elizabeth I: queen and commonwealth, 1558–1585* (Cambridge, 1999); Carole Levin, Jo Eldridge Carney, and Debra Barrett-Graves (eds.), *Elizabeth I: always her own free woman* (Aldershot, 2003); Susan Doran, *Queen Elizabeth I* (New York, 2003); Charles Beem and Dennis Moore (eds.), *The name of a queen: William Fleetwood's Itinerarium ad Windsor* (Basingstoke, 2013); and Ilona Bell, *Elizabeth I: the voice of a monarch* (Basingstoke, 2010). Important studies that demonstrate the powerful constraints upon, and challenges to, her exercise of power are Susan Doran, *Monarchy and matrimony: the courtships of Elizabeth I* (London, 1996); Julia Walker (ed.), *Dissing Elizabeth: negative representations of Gloriana* (Durham, NC, 1998); and Susan Doran and Thomas S. Freeman (eds.), *The myth of Elizabeth* (Basingstoke, 2003).

[6] Natalie Mears, *Queenship and political discourse in the Elizabethan realms* (Cambridge, 2005).

[7] *Ibid.*, p. 2.

significant oversight. Particularly puzzling in this regard is the fact that there exist excellent studies of Elizabeth and foreign policy,[8] which is to say that scholars focus either on the queen and domestic English governance or on her relations with other sovereign powers and skip over Ireland, which was a theatre of politics that uniquely displayed both domestic and international aspects. Indeed, recent work on Elizabeth and 'Elizabethan' political culture largely fails to consider Ireland. Outside the provocative and suggestive discussions in Mears's monograph, the standard work on Elizabeth and her western kingdom remains the Irish-focused chapters in Wallace MacCaffrey's study of war and politics in the latter part of the reign.[9] This oversight also affects recent, major editions of Elizabeth's works. As Leah Marcus points out in the present collection (pp. 40–59), she and her coeditors chose precious few letters related to Ireland when selecting items for their volume of Elizabeth's writings and speeches. More recently, Susan Felch and Donald Stump dedicated a section to Ireland in their coedited Norton Critical Edition of the queen's work. However, it addresses only the final years of the reign and the Nine Years' War (1594–1603). Moreover, the section's real concern is not with Ireland or the Irish but rather with the collapse of the relationship between the queen and her last great favourite, Robert Devereux, 2nd earl of Essex, who just happened to have been named to suppress the rebellion, which fatefully and famously he failed to do.[10]

This absence is all the more curious given developments within the Irish historiography favouring the power and agency of those in the western realm. It has long been accepted that Elizabeth's reign marked a turning point in Anglo-Irish relations – a point after which they hardened along confessional and ethnic lines.[11] Increasingly, however, scholars are keen to add that the 'losers' in that historical drama – to quote the title of a chronologically broader essay collection on the subject edited by Ciaran Brady[12] – were neither entirely powerless nor unified in matters of politics, culture, or faith. Sophisticated studies of 'faith and fatherland' ideology, of identity-formation, of intellectually and constitutionally

---

[8] Charles Beem (ed.), *The foreign relations of Elizabeth I* (Basingstoke, 2011). See, too, Susan Doran, *Elizabeth I and foreign policy* (New York, 2000), an introduction for A-level and first-year college students.

[9] Wallace MacCaffrey, *Elizabeth I: war and politics, 1588–1603* (Princeton, 1992), pp. 329–448. Encouraging, however, is the sophisticated treatment of queen and Irish affairs in Susan Brigden's textbook survey of the age, *New worlds, lost worlds: the rule of the Tudors, 1485–1603* (New York, 2000).

[10] Susan Felch and Donald Stump (eds.), *Elizabeth I and her age* (New York, 2009).

[11] The key text here remains Nicholas Canny, *The Elizabethan conquest of Ireland: a pattern established, 1565–1576* (Hassocks, 1976).

[12] Ciaran Brady (ed.), *Worsted in the game: losers in Irish history* (Dublin, 1989).

based forms of resistance, of political and social 'negotiation', of Irish–continental connections and interchange, and of the Old English and Gaelic nobility have transformed understandings of Ireland in this period of tremendous conflict and upheaval.[13] Recent work on Gaelic language and culture has been crucial to this increasingly nuanced knowledge of late sixteenth-century Ireland. It has been argued that the Gaelic literati (the so-called bards) were so conservative and insular in their worldview that they failed to register the severity of the cultural destruction posed by Tudor/Stuart centralisation until it was too late and that world collapsed around them.[14] A steadily growing body of interdisciplinary work is, however, now sketching out the place of the language, and the Gaelic Irish more generally, in the political, social, and confessional main events of the day.[15] In doing so, it is also placing Irish-language sources into closer comparison with English and Latin ones, thus bringing more of

[13] A small sampling of relevant works includes Hiram Morgan, *Tyrone's rebellion: the outbreak of the Nine Years War in Tudor Ireland* (Dublin, 1999); Nicholas Canny, *The formation of the Old English elite in Ireland* (Dublin, 1975); McGowan-Doyle, *The Book of Howth*; Jon Crawford, *Anglicizing the government of Ireland: the Irish privy council and the expansion of Tudor rule, 1556–1578* (Dublin, 1993); Michael Braddick and John Walter (eds.), *Negotiating power in early modern society: order, hierarchy and subordination in Britain and Ireland* (Cambridge, 2011), Brendan Kane, *The politics and culture of honour in Britain and Ireland, 1541–1641* (Cambridge, 2010); Colm Lennon, *Richard Stanihurst, the Dubliner, 1547–1618* (Dublin, 1981); Vincent Carey, *Surviving the Tudors: the 'wizard' earl of Kildare and English rule in Ireland, 1537–1586* (Dublin, 2002); David Edwards, *The Ormond lordship in County Kilkenny, 1515–1642: the rise and fall of Butler feudal power* (Dublin, 2003).

[14] The key text here is Michelle O Riordan, *The Gaelic mind and the collapse of the Gaelic world* (Cork, 1987). While heavily criticised, it is a learned and provocative study that remains of great value. See, too, T. J. Dunne, 'The Gaelic response to conquest and colonisation: the evidence of the poetry', *Studia Hibernica* 20 (1980), 7–30; and Nicholas Canny, 'The formation of the Irish mind: religion, politics and Gaelic Irish literature 1580–1750', *Past & Present* 95 (1982), 91–116.

[15] See for instance Marc Caball, *Poets and politics: reaction and continuity in Irish poetry, 1558–1625* (Notre Dame and Cork, 1998); Brendan Bradshaw, 'Native reactions to the westward enterprise: a case-study in Gaelic ideology', in K. R. Andrews, N. P. Canny, and P. E. H. Hair (eds.), *The westward enterprise: English activities in Ireland, the Atlantic and America 1480–1650* (Detroit, 1979), pp. 65–80; Breandán Ó Buachalla, 'James our true king: the ideology of Irish royalism in the seventeenth century', in D. G. Boyce, Robert Eccleshall, and Vincent Geoghegan (eds.), *Political thought in Ireland since the seventeenth century* (London, 1993), pp. 7–35; Mícheál Mac Craith, 'From the Elizabethan settlement to the Battle of the Boyne: literature in Irish 1560–1690', in Margaret Kelleher and Philip O'Leary (eds.), *The Cambridge history of Irish literature*, 2 vols. (Cambridge, 2006), vol. I, pp. 191–231; Patricia Palmer, *Language and conquest in early modern Ireland: English Renaissance literature and Elizaabethan imperial expansion* (Cambridge, 2001); Sarah McKibben, *Endangered masculinities in Irish poetry: 1540–1780* (Dublin, 2011); Pádraig Breatnach, *Téamaí taighde Nua-Ghaeilge* (Dublin, 1997); Brendan Kane, 'Languages of legitimacy? *An Ghaeilge*, the earl of Thomond and British politics in the Renaissance Pale, 1600–1624', in Michael Potterton and Thomas Herron (eds.), *Dublin and the Pale in the Renaissance, c. 1540–1660* (Dublin, 2011), pp. 267–79;

the multi-lingual character of early modern Anglo-Irish relations into scholarly view.[16]

In that burgeoning corpus, however, there is almost no discussion of Gaelic views of the monarch herself. Partly this is a product of the archive: the local literati left little comment on the queen. Survival rates of Irish sources are not excellent, however, and perhaps we might expect more direct discussion of the monarch if we had further examples to draw upon. Nevertheless, judging from what we do have, it seems safe to conclude that Gaelic intellectuals did not expend great effort writing to, or explicitly about, their putative monarch. Given the strict customs of patronage and performance in Irish literary production, it seems hardly surprising that, say, praise poems to local lords lacked quatrains dedicated to Elizabeth I.[17] This does not mean that the queen and, crucially, her court were of no concern to the authors of these works; it simply means that one must read with attention to form, genre, and patronage and pull out the threads related to that concern. Bards, we must remember, were no mere rhymers, but rather powerful political players in their own right; their stock-in-trade was commentary on nobility and courtly life. On the one hand, they often served as representatives of local lords in their dealings with the crown; on the other, their immense local authority caused great anxiety among state officials and spurred intense effort to disempower them.[18] What remains to be explored – and, indeed, what is in part investigated here – are the (typically) oblique commentaries and criticisms of queen and court that emerge from close reading of Irish-language texts. The bards and Elizabeth were well aware of each other's existence and, as the chapters that follow demonstrate, they were keenly attuned to the competing claims for authority that existed, tensely, between them.

The 'new' histories of Elizabeth, and of Ireland and the Irish, have now undoubtedly developed to the point where conversation between them is long overdue. From the English side of this historiographical divide, there are excellent studies of Elizabethan views of Ireland and the

---

James Kelly and Ciarán Mac Murchaidh (eds.), *Irish and English: essays on the Irish linguistic and cultural frontier, 1600–1900* (Dublin, 2012).

[16] Particularly relevant here are Jason Harris and Keith Sidwell (eds.), *Making Ireland Roman: Irish neo-Latin writers and the republic of letters* (Cork, 2009); David Edwards and Keith Sidwell (eds.), *The Tipperary hero: Dermot O'Meara's Ormonius* (Turnhout, Belgium, 2012); and John Barry and Hiram Morgan (eds.), *Great deeds in Ireland: Richard Stanihurst's De rebus in Hibernia gestis* (Cork, 2013).

[17] Generally on bardic culture and practice, see Pádraig Breatnach, 'The chief's poet', *Proceedings of the Royal Irish Academy* 83 C (1983), 37–79.

[18] Patricia Palmer, *Language and conquest.*

Irish.[19] Yet there exists no sustained consideration of the views of Elizabeth *herself* towards Ireland and the Irish. If indeed she was a politically active monarch, and the matter of Ireland crucial to English political calculations, then this is a vital subject of study. Conversely, while historians of Ireland have always been the more historiographically bilingual,[20] they too have largely ignored the queen's direct role in governing the realm. (Recent work by Hiram Morgan and Vincent Carey, which sets much of the agenda for the present volume, provides notable exceptions.)[21] Generally speaking, then, the term 'Elizabethan' is a frequently used and convenient label – for historians of England and Ireland alike – that gives historical contextualisation to developments in English–Irish relations over the last half of the sixteenth century. Yet missing in the scholarship is analysis of how the term applies to Elizabeth herself, and the role that she played in the conquest of Ireland. Moreover, if Gaelic Irish and Old English alike were more engaged with the state, be it through practical politics or written commentary and critique, then there needs to be greater consideration of their views of the person who claimed sovereignty over them. While there has been much recent attention paid to Irish views of the English living in their midst, there is almost no work that explores their views of the monarch to whom they were (at least nominally) subject.

Making sense of these connections requires analysis of literary productions in both vernaculars, Irish and English. Elizabeth never visited Ireland; few of her Irish subjects ever travelled to court. Necessarily, then, elucidating the reciprocal relationship between prince and subject is heavily reliant on the study of texts. As noted earlier, modern collections of Elizabeth's own writings have devoted limited attention to her commentaries on Ireland. But there are a great number and variety of

---

[19] For the classic expression, see D. B. Quinn, *The Elizabethans and the Irish* (New York, 1966); for a more recent one with a post-colonial influence, see John Montaño, *The roots of English colonialism* (Cambridge, 2011).

[20] This point is made succinctly by Nicholas Canny in the course of discussing the so-called New British History, an archipelagic approach that since the 1980s has done much to bring the provincial realms to the attention of historians of England: 'The impact of New British History has proven less dramatic for writing on the histories of Scotland and Ireland because, at a professional level, historians of those countries had already been keeping abreast of, and relating their findings to, historical writing on England.' Canny is addressing a later period, of course; attention to Ireland in work on the Elizabethan period has been even rarer. See Nicholas Canny, 'Writing early modern history: Ireland, Britain, and the wider world', *Historical Journal* 46 (3) (2003), 737.

[21] Hiram Morgan, '"Never any realm worse governed": Queen Elizabeth and Ireland', *Transactions of the Royal Historical Society*, 6th series, 14 (2004), 295–308; Vincent Carey, 'Elizabeth I and state terror in sixteenth-century Ireland', in Donald Stump, Linda Shenk, and Carole Levin (eds.), *Elizabeth I and the 'sovereign arts': essays in literature, history, and culture* (Tempe, AZ, 2011), pp. 201–16.

documents from which such a study might be constructed. As for the literary productions of her subjects, undoubtedly they possess a wealth of insight into this relationship. The masterpieces of luminaries such as Spenser, Sidney, and Shakespeare are now considered in the context of their authors' political entanglements and aspirations – not the least of which were imperial and colonial expansion into Ireland and beyond.[22] How might these and less well-known politically engaged works, many of which were dedicated to Elizabeth, elucidate this relationship? What do Irish-language sources, especially the highly politicised court poetry of the bards, have to say about queen and court? Our interest here is in literary analysis of the reciprocal representations of monarch and Irish subject and, more broadly, a desire to bring scholars of English and Irish literature together in pursuit of a common topic. As with historians of Ireland and England, contact between literary scholars of Irish and English might be strengthened, and done to the benefit of practitioners in both fields.

Indeed, the collection is intended not only as a study of Elizabeth I and Ireland, but also as an extended effort at cross-disciplinary and multilingual scholarly interaction. Some of the finest work on early modern Ireland and England is to be found in interdisciplinary collections;[23] given the size of the literature in all of these subfields, it is too great a task to expect one person to grasp and synthesise them all.[24] Certainly, the idea is to offer not consensus, but rather perspective and interpretation that might spark further discussion and research across discipline and subdiscipline. Having offered the above, very brief, survey of the four fields represented in the collection, we turn to the individual chapters. They draw out more fully the contexts of their particular approach, but in organising them we have chosen to order them not by discipline but in

[22] A small sampling of works in what is now a rich and expansive literature includes Richard McCabe, *The pillars of eternity: time and providence in* The Faerie Queene (Dublin, 1989); Christopher Highley, *Shakespeare, Spenser, and the crisis in Ireland* (Cambridge, 1997); Nicholas Canny, *Making Ireland British, 1580–1650* (Oxford, 2001); Andrew Hadfield, *Shakespeare, Spenser and the matter of Britain* (New York, 2004); Thomas Herron, *Spenser's Irish work: poetry, plantation and colonial reformation* (Ashgate, 2007); Willy Maley, *Salvaging Spenser: colonialism, culture and identity* (Basingstoke, 1997).

[23] See, among others, Brendan Bradshaw, Andrew Hadfield, and Willy Maley (eds.), *Representing Ireland: literature and the origins of conflict, 1534–1660* (Cambridge, 1993); Ciaran Brady and Jane Ohlmeyer (eds.), *British interventions in early modern Ireland* (Cambridge, 2005); Vincent Carey and Ute Lotz-Heumann (eds.), *Taking sides? Colonial and confessional mentalities in early modern Ireland* (Dublin, 2003); Patricia Coughlan (ed.), *Spenser and Ireland: an interdisciplinary perspective* (Cork, 1989); David Edwards (ed.), *Regions and rulers in Ireland, 1100–1650* (Dublin, 2004).

[24] Canny's *Making Ireland British* is arguably the exception to this claim, ranging as it does across history and literature in English and Irish. It also offers relatively substantial attention to the queen and her role in Irish policy.

a loose thematic structure – following particular themes as represented in the contributions as a way to think beyond discipline and about the collection's subject and, in doing so, hoping to spur readers to consider ways forward in all four fields, individually and collectively.

This book begins with consideration of the politics of monarchical representation in Ireland. Whereas representation of Elizabeth was essential in England, it became fundamentally problematic in Ireland. Richard McCabe draws upon New English, Old English, and Gaelic sources – English- and Irish-language – to demonstrate that the fracturing of the royal image in Ireland was a function of the irreconcilability of the two sovereignties over which Elizabeth ruled. He focuses on two of the principal arenas in which her image was fractured: religion, in which Elizabeth was supreme governor of the reformed church yet considered a heretic by Catholics; and the political realm in which, as McCabe argues, New English writers pressed Elizabeth to function as absolute monarch in Ireland in a way which she did not (indeed, could not) in England. Leah Marcus considers three other arenas central to representations of Elizabeth in England: gender, honour, and notions of divine election. As in McCabe's consideration of the realms of religion and political authority, all three of Marcus's chosen frameworks proved to be just as fundamentally problematic when applied in Ireland, where local contexts precluded the successful application of images used to great effect in England. Elizabeth's image as nurse-mother to her subjects, for instance, ran counter to New English denigration of the Old English for their use of Irish wet-nurses, a practice identified as both cause and reflection of their degeneration. Were this image to be pressed in Ireland, Elizabeth would represent the very mingling of English and Irish the regime sought to eradicate.

The essays by Peter McQuillan and Brandie Siegfried narrow focus to consider representations of Elizabeth and her court in two specific compositions from Irish-language authors. An understanding of Gaelic images of Elizabeth is as important to have as it is difficult to reconstruct. As noted earlier, attention to Irish-language sources has transformed the study of early modern Ireland. Yet among the numerous extant sources – primarily court poetry and annals – there is precious little direct mention of Elizabeth. This does not mean that the Gaelic intelligentsia was ignorant of, or silent on, their putative sovereign and her court. It does mean, however, that we must read very carefully for signs of its members' opinions of queen and administration. Siegfried assesses theories of sovereignty and the recognition of legitimate rule in Gaelic Counter-Reformation thought relative to this concept's expression in English law and English colonial thought. While the discourse of lineage figured prominently in both, each was underpinned by a very different perception of time, Aristotelian in the case of English thought and Augustinian in Gaelic. This difference is at the core of *Seanchas Búrcach* (also entitled *Historia et genealogia familiae de Burgo*) – a historical/geneaological production of the Anglo-Norman-descended, though deeply 'Gaelicised', Burkes of Galway – where it is employed in rejection of Elizabeth's legitimacy as sovereign. This work's rendering of Elizabeth as irreducibly foreign, 'that saxon queen', thus nullified her claim to lineage as the source of her legitimacy. McQuillan's essay meticulously parses and deconstructs Eochaidh Ó hEodhasa's poem, 'Ionmholta malairt bhisigh' ('A change for the better is laudable'), composed in the immediate aftermath of Elizabeth's death and the Nine Years' War. Ó hEodhasa was trained in the classic style of the *ollamh* to be a promoter of dynasties and arbiter of secular, political legitimacy. His stock-in-trade was the eulogistic poem, a highly politicised and engaged genre which Nicholas Canny has famously described as being the closest Gaelic Ireland comes to 'state papers'.[25] McQuillan sees in Ó hEodhasa's poem a deep awareness, and withering appraisal, of the queen and her court. While not contesting the legitimacy of Elizabeth's sovereignty, Ó hEodhasa nonetheless anticipates a more favourable climate under the newly installed James VI/I. The sophistication of that critique is deftly revealed in McQuillan's demonstration of Baldessare Castiglione's influence on Ó hEodhasa. Given the focus of English literary scholars on the discourse of civility versus savagery found in English-language texts, McQuillan's explication of Ó hEodhasa's intentions offers a salutary reminder that that discourse moved in both directions: Gaelic-language authors could think themselves as the ones in line with continental standards of civility and those in London degenerate.

A study of Elizabeth I and Ireland must pay particular attention to matters of religious change and resistance. The causes of reformed religion's inability to secure legitimacy in the minds of Irish subjects have been, and remain, an issue of particular concern to historians of Ireland.[26] Here, Ciaran Brady and Mark Hutchinson make substantial contributions to this debate in arguing that Elizabeth's intervention in Ireland actually impeded the progress of the Reformation at key stages. Standing out for both is the critical period of Sir Henry Sidney's governorship during the

---

[25] Canny, 'Formation of the Irish mind', 111.
[26] Brendan Bradshaw, 'Sword, word and strategy in the Reformation in Ireland', *Historical Journal* 21 (1978), 475–502; Nicholas Canny, 'Why the Reformation failed in Ireland: *une question mal posée*', *Journal of Ecclesiastical History* 30 (1979), 423–50; Karl Bottigheimer, 'The failure of the Reformation in Ireland: *une question bien posée*', *Journal of Ecclesiastical History* 36 (1985), 196–207.

early and middle years of her reign. Brady makes two crucial observations: first, that Elizabeth was not involved in Irish affairs on any regular basis, but, second, that when she was her interventions could have dramatic effect. Importantly, he recontextualises many of the issues recognised as central to Elizabethan politics in Ireland, such as fears of foreign invasion, early plantation efforts in Ulster, marriage and succession, female rule, and court politics, including patronage and factionalism, as a vehicle for reconsideration of the destabilising nature of the Elizabethan regime in Ireland and, more critically, Elizabeth's role in it. The Old English figure prominently in his study, in particular their increasing resistance to loss of office but more importantly their resistance to reformed religion. It was in fact, Brady argues, the question of reformed religion which moved Elizabeth to take a more direct role in Irish affairs, in this case by rejecting Sidney's attempts at further reformation. Hutchinson similarly argues that Elizabeth played a substantially interventionist role in matters of religion, again evident in her reluctance to further Irish church reform as Sidney wished. Differences in the extent to which reform should be pursued first surfaced in Sidney's instructions upon taking office in 1565, which authorised him only to enforce established Reformation statutes. Although the deputy's request to move beyond statute was denied, he moved ahead nonetheless. Here the appointment of Christopher Goodman as his chaplain in 1566 is particularly telling, for Goodman had already established a reputation as a reformer, even inviting John Knox to join him in Ireland. Hutchinson's narrower focus on specifics of the conflict between Elizabeth and Sidney on the extent of reform permits him to consider more systematically contemporary debates on the nature of man and one's capacity for reform. The Irish evidence, Hutchinson argues, permits us to see – where the English evidence does not – Elizabeth's position within this debate as it underpinned her reluctance to support an evangelical mission in Ireland.

Equally, any analysis of queen and Irish kingdom must consider the former's role in the so-called Tudor conquest. Valerie McGowan-Doyle considers the displacement of the Old English nobility from places of political influence, a development not yet contextualised within scholarly debates regarding the Tudor nobility or Tudor political culture more broadly.[27] Though Old English loss of standing with the Dublin

---

[27] See, for example, Lawrence Stone, *The crisis of the aristocracy, 1558–1641* (Oxford, 1965); G. W. Bernard, *Power and politics in Tudor England* (Aldershot, 2000); Linda Levy Peck, 'Peers, patronage and the politics of history', in John Guy (ed.), *The reign of Elizabeth I: court and culture in the last decade* (Cambridge, 1995), pp. 87–108. Influential works on Tudor political culture include Dale Hoak (ed.), *Tudor political culture* (Cambridge, 1995); Guy (ed.), *The reign of Elizabeth I*; John F. McDiarmid (ed.), *The monarchical*

administration has traditionally been viewed as a function of various viceroys' policies and attitudes, McGowan-Doyle argues both that
Elizabeth was aware of this development and that she played a role in it
by intervening decisively at pivotal points. Attention to issues of counsel
and the application of the rhetoric of counsel are instrumental in revealing Old English assumptions about their relationship to Elizabeth; they
are equally instrumental in revealing Elizabeth's rejection of their presumed rights as subjects and nobles. Hiram Morgan and Paul Hammer
both consider Elizabeth's involvement in the later years of her reign as
the crisis of the Nine Years' War unfolded. Hammer's consideration of
Elizabeth's anger over the earl of Essex's creation of knights reveals again
her very direct intervention in what was, as Hammer argues, an essential
element in Essex's ability to conduct military operations. Here her insistence on obedience to orders and a superficial knowledge of, but failure
to understand more deeply, the reality of conditions 'on the ground'
contributed both to this military crisis and to Essex's downfall. Morgan's
chapter similarly asserts a pivotal interventionist role for Elizabeth in the
crisis of the 1590s and challenges fundamentally the political judgement
she exercised in Irish affairs. Although she repeatedly blamed her officers for failures in Ireland, critical decisions taken by the queen, such as
dividing military command there, were responsible for aggravating the
course of events. This destabilising interventionism did not go uncom-
mented on by her subalterns, and Morgan's chapter offers an important
new assessment of the 1598 treatise, 'The supplication of the blood of the
English most lamentably murdered in Ireland, cryeng out of the yearth for
revenge', attributing this work critical of the regime to Edmund Spenser.
Collectively these three chapters demonstrate that the late Tudor reconquest of Ireland was as much Elizabeth's conquest as an Elizabethan
one.

That being the case, criticism of Elizabeth's problematic intervention
in the latter years of her reign figured prominently in New English literature of the period, as Andrew Hadfield's consideration of the work
of the soldier-poets Ralph Byrchensa, Lodowick Bryskett, and Edmund
Spenser further demonstrates. Elizabeth's gender was a fundamental concern for Byrchensa, precluding her having acquired any military experience and thereby rendering her unable to appreciate military realities

republic of early modern England: essays in response to Patrick Collinson (Aldershot, 2007);
G. W. Bernard, 'The Tudor nobility in perspective', in G. W. Bernard (ed.), *The Tudor
nobility* (New York, 1992), pp. 1–48; Jane Ohlmeyer, 'Making Ireland English: the early
seventeenth-century Irish peerage', in Brian Mac Cuarta (ed.), *Reshaping Ireland 1550–
1700. Colonization and its consequences: essays presented to Nicholas Canny* (Dublin, 2011),
pp. 131–47.

and thus to provide effective policy or leadership. Spenser argued for an equally deep divide in experience and perspective between Elizabeth's court and her military men in Ireland, thus questioning not only the queen's ability but critically also her advisers' ability to devise military or colonial policy. These criticisms frequently incorporated defence of viceroys, soldiers, and colonists, and justification for the greater use of violence in accomplishing completed conquest.

Brendan Kane broadens the consideration of Elizabeth and collective violence by comparing the queen's reactions to rebellion in both realms. To date, rebellions in England and Ireland have been kept largely separate in the literature; even those few studies that have explored the possibility of points of contact have concluded that risings in the two realms were of fundamentally different types: the former were 'law-and-order' problems, the latter signs of imperial reach and its resistance. Kane, however, questions this binary by pointing out that we have ignored the queen's own views of, and reactions to, rebellion in her two realms. He suggests that the different categories of rebellion suggested in the historical scholarship – 'Tudor' and 'Irish' – would have made limited sense to the monarch who saw them all as varieties of a cross-realm plague of subjects challenging her sovereignty. An important point raised by this chapter, too, is that Elizabeth enjoyed significant support from some among the Irish elites. Although many of the studies included here highlight the tensions between queen and Irish subject – Kane's too, of course, in its discussion of rebellion – his chapter nevertheless also reminds us that, without the support of key figures such as the earls of Ormond, Clanricard, and Thomond, the suppression of rebellion in the western kingdom would not have been possible.

Marc Caball also demonstrates points of contact and sympathy between queen and Irish subject, here working from the Irish perspective. He takes as his subject Seaán Ó Cearnaigh's 1571 Irish primer of religion, discussing it with a view to elucidating hitherto unacknowledged aspects of the Reformation in late sixteenth-century Ireland. His argument that the text is much more than simply an Irish translation of an English text opens up two vitally important windows on to early modern English–Irish relations. First, he demonstrates that Protestantism could work within a Gaelic cultural setting and that that reformist community was internally cohesive and supporting and not simply dependent upon English oversight and direction. Second, in doing so, he points to how acceptance of Elizabeth's legitimacy as head of both church and state allowed certain members of the Irish intellectual classes the opportunity to carve out and develop innovative religious and cultural forms in an Ireland that was a constituent part of the Tudor state.

In the vast literature assessing the Tudor period, the places accorded both Elizabeth I and Ireland might be said to mirror each other: they have been acknowledged as important to the story of the age, yet not seen as vital to the real decisions that drove it. As such, they were things to be studied largely in isolation. But as the scholarly developments briefly traced above reveal, neither queen nor Ireland and the Irish was as peripheral as generations worth of scholarship might suggest. As their respective roles in shaping this crucial period come increasingly to light, it is hoped that drawing out the points of contact linking them (be they co-operative, conflictual, or wherever between) will sharpen our understanding of the age and, perhaps, its legacies – ones that remain with us today. The subjects addressed in the chapters in this book represent a mere sampling of those relevant to an understanding of Elizabeth I and Ireland, but it is hoped that they prove sufficient to open up the subject and to promote dialogue across disciplines and specialisations.

2 Ireland's Eliza: queen or *cailleach*?

Richard A. McCabe

> Semiramiz Elizabeth, sister unto the queene, by her father's side, and a daughter to An Bullin...as next heire unto the crowne intred to be queene of England and began to reforme, or rather deforme, all that was don by queene Mary in matters of religion (though hitherto Catholicke herself) [and] not onely followed the footstepp of her father, in callinge herself supreame head of the churche (which since the worlds creation noe woman was soe stiled untill then) but alsoe to frame a newe religion, and to add somethinge to her fathers iniquitie, denied 5 sacraments of holy churche...
>
> *An Aphorismical Discovery of Treasonable Faction (c.* 1653)[1]

The anonymous author of *An Aphorismical Discovery* chose his exemplum carefully: Semiramis was reputed to be cruel, licentious, and emasculating, the malign alter ego of *The Faerie Queene*'s elusive Gloriana. But Ireland was a land of dual identities, a land in which Hugh O'Neill was earl of Tyrone, Richard Stanihurst was loyal Palesman and seditious seminarian, Miler Magrath was Protestant archbishop of Cashel and Catholic bishop of Down and Connor, and the royal persecutor of Catholics was once 'Catholicke herself' – a terrible fact that Spenser's elaborate allegory is constructed to disguise.[2] But when he undertook to view Queen Elizabeth 'in mirrours more then one' (*Faerie Queene,* 3 Proem 5) Spenser committed himself to looking in the 'glass' of her Irish polity and what was reflected there was as much banshee as fairy queen.[3]

---

[1] J. T. Gilbert (ed.), *A contemporary history of affairs in Ireland from AD 1641 to 1652,* 3 vols. (Dublin, 1879), vol. I, pt 1, p. 4.

[2] For the polemic use of Elizabeth's youthful conformity to Catholicism, see James E. Phillips, *Images of a queen: Mary Stuart in sixteenth-century literature* (Berkeley, CA, 1964), p. 95.

[3] All quotations are from Edmund Spenser, *The Faerie Queene,* A. C. Hamilton (ed.) (London, 2001), and *Edmund Spenser: the shorter poems,* R. A. McCabe (ed.) (Harmondsworth, 1999). Spenser's prose works are cited in the text by page from *The works of Edmund Spenser,* Edwin Greenlaw *et al.* (eds.), Variorum Edition, 11 vols. (Baltimore, 1932–58), vol. IX (1949).

Ireland reminded him that his Gloriana was once his Duessa and might ultimately become his Lucifera.

Iconography and iconoclasm

Spenser's experience was a common one. It was only to be expected that a counter-iconography should arise among those who disputed the queen's claim to Irish sovereignty, but less predictable was the effect that her role as 'queen of Ireland' was to have on Old and New English perceptions of the crown. The most serious defamation of Elizabeth to issue from Ireland was attributed to her lord deputy, Sir John Perrot, during his trial for treason. The changes levelled against Perrot were complex and entailed, *inter alia*, alleged conspiracy with Spain, but their Irish dimension testifies to official paranoia about the inefficacy of state propaganda. In the relative security of Ireland, it was feared, people spoke their real opinions and revealed their true attitude towards the queen. Perrot was even accused of complicity in the dissemination of bardic satires against Elizabeth and, in what became known as the 'treason of the picture', the alleged desecration of an image of the queen by the Gaelic chieftain, Brian O'Rourke.[4] Contrary accounts of this incident suggested that the picture being abused was not of the queen but of an old hag (the Gaelic '*cailleach*') who was being ritually humiliated in a traditional form of charivari. But given the contemporary appearance of grotesque caricatures of the queen on the continent, the authorities may well have suspected that the image was one of the queen as *cailleach*.[5] In Ireland she was often denigrated in precisely those terms.[6] The accusations against Perrot were probably fabricated, and he denied them vigorously, but the climate of discontent that had been generated among the New English was more than sufficient to lend them credence. Both of Perrot's predecessors in the office of lord deputy had notoriously difficult relationships with Elizabeth, as Sir Henry Sidney's *Memoirs* and Lord Grey's correspondence attest.[7]

---

[4] For a full account of the charges against Perrot, see Hiram Morgan, 'The fall of Sir John Perrot', in John Guy (ed.), *The reign of Elizabeth I: court and culture in the last decade* (Cambridge, 1995), p. 119; Roger Turvey, *The treason and trial of Sir John Perrot* (Cardiff, 2005), pp. 108–9, 112, 148–9, 155–6. See also Daniel Galloway, 'Brian of the Ramparts O' Rourke (1566–1591)', *Breifne* 2 (1962), 50–79.

[5] Sir Roy Strong, *Gloriana: the portraits of Queen Elizabeth I* (London, 1987), p. 34; Phillips, *Images of a queen*, p. 115.

[6] Natalie Mears, *Queenship and political discourse in the Elizabethan realms* (Cambridge, 2005), pp. 219, 242–3.

[7] See Richard A. McCabe, *Spenser's monstrous regiment: Elizabethan Ireland and the poetics of difference* (Oxford, 2002), pp. 11–14, 82–100.

The remarkable coalescence of extremes in the accusations against Perrot demonstrates the problems of representing Elizabeth in Ireland, let alone as queen of Ireland.

The iconography of 'England's Eliza' is familiar, that of Ireland's Eliza far less so. Although in other respects it affords a masterly analysis of the making of the royal image, for example, Kevin Sharpe's *Selling the Tudor monarchy* (2009) scarcely mentions Ireland.[8] This is perhaps understandable: the monarchy was much harder to 'sell' in Ireland because the monarch was perpetually absent and absence could easily be interpreted as neglect. In England, from the beginning of the reign to the end, magnificent progresses and pageants imprinted the presence of the queen on the national consciousness, but she never set foot in Ireland and only a tiny minority of her Irish subjects journeyed to the English court. In Ireland representation had to compensate for absence. In 1581, in a somewhat desperate response to this situation, Geoffrey Fenton, Ireland's future secretary of state, asked Sir Francis Walsingham, secretary of state and adviser to Elizabeth I, to send over a picture of the queen to hang 'by the cloth of state' in the Irish parliament.[9] The allegations against O'Rourke are best understood in this context; the image that Fenton planned to hang in state was the image supposedly dragged after a horse with the alleged approval of the queen's own deputy. In Tudor Ireland royal iconography and royal iconoclasm were oddly symbiotic. But for that very reason exclusive attention to negative representations of Elizabeth can be misleading.[10] There were times, as we shall see, when even turbulent Gaelic chieftains such as Shane O'Neill found it useful to promote positive views of the queen, times when the symbiotic became the parasitic. Elizabeth's Irish image was as nuanced as the situation was complex. Gaelic, Old English, and New English factions drew political benefit from exploiting one another's discontent. All attempted to fashion the absent queen to their own ends by misrepresenting her representation among the others – a game ruthlessly played out in the charges levelled against Perrot.

The uncertainty over the identity of the picture that O'Rourke is alleged to have desecrated is richly indicative of the problem of royal

---

[8] See Elkin Calhoun Wilson, *England's Eliza* (New York, 1966 [1939], reprint); Kevin Sharpe, *Selling the Tudor monarchy: authority and image in sixteenth-century England* (New Haven, 2009). For the problems of female regiment generally, see Mears, *Queenship*, and A. N. McLaren, *Political culture in the reign of Elizabeth I: queen and commonwealth, 1558–1585* (Cambridge, 1999), pp. 1–45.

[9] SP 63/82/18, cited in Christopher Highley, 'The royal image in Elizabethan Ireland', in Julia M. Walker (ed.), *Dissing Elizabeth: negative representations of Gloriana* (Durham, NC, 1998), p. 65.

[10] See, for example, Highley, 'The royal image in Elizabethan Ireland'.

absenteeism. Elizabeth's features were far less familiar in Ireland than in England. Although miniatures, cameos, medallions, and coins may well have been displayed, worn, and traded by those in the Irish service, formal portraits of the queen seem to have been rare even in the houses of the Old English. The long gallery of the earl of Ormond's manor house at Carrick-on Suir, featured a portrait in plaster over one of the fireplaces executed in close imitation of officially authorised English exemplars by Steven van der Muelen and Remigius Hogenberg.[11] But therein lay the problem. Here was no 'Irish' queen but an English import. Indeed, both the portrait and its location, a manor house ostentatiously built in the current English fashion to display the earl's 'civility' to the New English, exemplify the problems of political and cultural imposition that preoccupy the colonial tracts of polemicists such as Spenser and Richard Beacon. By displaying Elizabeth's official image, Ormond was making a statement about himself no less than the queen. That image, we need to remember, was available most readily, when available at all, in the woodcuts and engravings of books imported from London (single images intended for separate sale remained uncommon even in England until the late 1580s). But the London press was carefully controlled and standard authorities such as the Bishops' Bible (1562), Foxe's *Actes and Monuments* (1563), and Saxton's *Atlas of England and Wales* (1579) featured iconographic images of Elizabeth designed to convey specific religious or political messages. Current evidence suggests, however, that only a small fraction of such publications was imported into Ireland where the majority population for the most part neither read nor spoke English.[12] There are also indications that dedications to the queen were sometimes torn out of imported books, that verbal icons were defaced as well as painted ones.[13]

Those that survive are highly problematical. Drawn in 1566, just eight years into her reign and four years before her excommunication, the depiction of the queen in *The Great Parchment Book of Waterford* associates her with distinctly Catholic imagery relating to Marian devotion and the doctrine of purgatory. 'Hereby', comments Niall J. Byrne, 'is represented for the first time that duality of allegiance which would persist in the city for the following seventy-five years, whereby Waterford

---

[11] See Jane Fenlon, 'The decorative plasterwork at Ormond Castle – a unique survival', *Architectural History* 41 (1998), 76–8; further images are supplied in Fenlon, *Caisleán Urmhumhan* (Dublin, 1996).

[12] See Raymond Gillespie, 'Print culture, 1550–1700', in Raymond Gillespie and Andrew Hadfield (eds.), *The Irish book in English 1550–1800* (Oxford, 2006), pp. 17–33.

[13] Robert Dudley Edwards, *Church and state in Tudor Ireland; a history of penal laws against Irish Catholics 1534–1603* (Dublin, 1934), pp. 298–9.

would continue as a Roman Catholic City, while professing total loyalty to a Protestant monarch.'[14] That would be significant in itself, but I doubt if the image affords even so much assurance. In stark contrast to all the official portraits of the day, Elizabeth is depicted as a private person without orb, sceptre, or crown, a feature that might indicate lèse-majesté in any other context. The crown and royal arms figure separately in the upper left-hand corner of the folio, detached from the queen's person. The implication might well be that the city is loyal to the crown but to the current wearer only in so far as she conforms to the image of her sister and predecessor, the Catholic Mary – a distinction that James Fitzmaurice later pressed into the service of rebellion in 1579.

To the problems of visually or verbally representing the queen in Ireland must be added the even greater difficulties of representative personnel. In practical terms Elizabeth had no option but to act through a deputy, but the choice was fraught with dangers. The early Tudors learned the hard way that Old English deputies had agendas of their own, while Elizabeth's exclusive reliance on New English deputies risked alienating much of the Old English elite. To make matters worse, while the iconography of England's Eliza was exquisitely tuned to her gender, the public face of her rule in Ireland was necessarily male, and the continual conflicts between the queen and her deputies damaged the credibility of female regiment *per se.* Never willing to allow her deputy the independence that the job required, Elizabeth was often seen as failing to act decisively while at the same time impeding the action of decisive men. The royal image was thus constantly distorted by, and in, its own representatives.[15]

The argument of the present chapter is that official attempts to represent Elizabeth as 'queen of Ireland' ultimately fractured the royal image because the two 'sovereignties' to which she laid claim were ultimately irreconcilable. The Act for the Kingly Title (1541) that made the English monarch 'king' rather than 'lord' of Ireland, created 'subjects' of the indigenous population with all the legal benefits that such status entailed.[16] The implications were well expressed by Thomas Churchyard in 1579 when he claimed that the Irish were

---

[14] *The Great Parchment Book of Waterford: Liber Antiquissimus Civitatis Waterfordiae*, Niall J. Byrne (ed.) (Dublin, 2007), p. xviii. See also plates II–VIII. While problematical in many ways, the image also represents an early attempt to lend specifically Irish context to the image by supplying the name of Waterford in Gaelic, 'Portlárge'.

[15] McCabe, *Spenser's monstrous regiment*, pp. 7–27.

[16] See S. J. Connolly, *Contested island: Ireland 1460–1630* (Oxford, 2007), pp. 111–12; Brendan Bradshaw, *The Irish constitutional revolution of the sixteenth century* (Cambridge, 1979).

> our neighbors nere
> And ought with equall name,
> Like subiects live with us,
>   for since one Prince wee have,
> One minde & maner should we shew,
>   good order that doeth crave.[17]

But this was very much an expression of how things 'ought' to be rather than how they were. In theory, as Ciaran Brady points out, 'sovereignty' entailed 'good lordship' and the queen periodically intervened in Irish affairs to ensure fair play for her Irish 'subjects'.[18] But the consistent exercise of 'good lordship' required a level of impartiality that Elizabeth could not afford to maintain. The threat to England posed by the Irish situation was far too urgent. As everyone knew, Ireland had never been conquered effectively, and there was widespread sympathy for Catholic Spain among the indigenous population. Fears of invasion were persistent and well grounded. From the 1580s onwards, the New English colonial project, as espoused by figures such as Arthur Lord Grey and Sir Richard Bingham, frequently necessitated the suspension of the rule of law in acts of summary justice that would have been quite unthinkable at home.[19] Churchyard's graphic account of the methods adopted by Sir Humphrey Gilbert, ironically published the same year as the eirenic passage quoted above, demonstrates the stark disjunction between aspiration and reality.[20] It was an intractable situation. The activities undertaken in the queen's name by Gilbert and his peers alienated Elizabeth's supposed Irish 'subjects' while her periodic attempts to restrain such activities alienated her New English officers. But even should she somehow find a way to reconcile the aims of the Old and New English there was little chance of simultaneously satisfying the Gaelic Irish who generally assumed her partiality to one English faction or the other. In the Four Masters' *Annála Ríoghachta Éireann* or *Annals of the Kingdom of Ireland* (1633), she is never other than the 'Saxon queen', the queen of England in Ireland rather than queen of Ireland.

---

[17] Thomas Churchyard, *The miserie of Flanders, calamitie of Fraunce, missfortune of Portugall, unquietnes of Irelande, troubles of Scotlande: and the blessed state of Englande* (London, 1579), sig. D1v.
[18] Ciaran Brady, *The chief governors: the rise and fall of reform government in Tudor Ireland, 1536–1588* (Cambridge, 1994), p. 242.
[19] See David Edwards, 'Ideology and experience: Spenser's *View* and martial law in Ireland', in Hiram Morgan (ed.), *Political ideology in Ireland, 1541–1641* (Dublin, 1999), pp. 127–57.
[20] Thomas Churchyard, *A Generall Rehearsal of Warres* (London, 1579), sig. Q3v.

Ireland's Saxon queen

Few sections of the Irish community had quite so much to gain from the accession of Elizabeth as the house of Ormond. Thomas Butler, the tenth earl, was the queen's second cousin through Anne Boleyn and a lifelong favourite. He had been educated with the future Edward VI and saw service in the Wyatt rebellion. Although he had negotiated the reign of Mary with political aplomb (as his Irish critics often reminded him), his professed Protestantism under Elizabeth immensely strengthened his hand by removing one of the key objections to committing public office to the Old English. To the dismay of a succession of lord deputies, his extraordinary rapport with the queen secured his power base in Ireland, where he performed a delicate balancing act between the 'English' and 'Irish' elements of his public persona. It should not surprise us, therefore, that the single most fulsome eulogy of Elizabeth written in Gaelic came from a poet associated with the Butlers. The poem has been traditionally, if problematically, attributed to Flann Mac Craith, who also wrote the earl's elegy. But if the authorship is doubtful, the poem's associations are not. Perrot defended himself against accusations of complicity in the dissemination of Gaelic satires against Elizabeth by asserting that he had commissioned Gaelic eulogies.[21] None of these appears to have survived, but the assertion was clearly designed to indicate that Perrot was no less committed to the queen than Ormond was. So apparently unqualified is Mac Craith's poem in its praise of Elizabeth that nationalist commentators later condemned it as treacherous or read it as ironic. But it is, in fact, remarkably judicious in its wording and choice of topic:

> I n-ainm an áirdmhic doghnídh grása,
>   is éinmhic álainn óghMhuire
> doghéan aiste do phrionnsa Shacsan
>   cúmtha cneasta cóirighthe.[22]

> [In the name of the High Son, the Author of graces,
>   The Virgin Mary's beautiful only Son,
> I shall make for the Sovereign of England a poem
>   Well-fashioned, courteous, and orderly.]

One notices from the outset that Elizabeth is queen of England ('prionnsa Shacsan'), not Ireland. Her status within Ireland remains vague:

---

[21] Sir James Perrot, *The history of that most eminent statesman, Sir John Perrot*, R. Rawlinson (ed.) (London, 1728), p. 311.

[22] John C. MacErlean (ed. and trans.), *Duanaire Dháibhidh Uí Bhruadair: the poems of David O Bruadair*, 3 vols. (London, 1910–17), vol. III, p. 64.

'She holds Ireland in England's protection [i gcléith Sacsan] / Hard by the borders of Britain fair'. The contrast with an anonymous English poem written in Ireland around 1560 is striking:

> Triumphant Joys may *Ireland* sing,
> Of *Henry* the Eighth our gallant King:
> For He has left us an Off-spring,
> To be the Good Queen of Ireland.
> Let Bonefires shine in every place,
> Sing, and Ring the bells apace;
> And pray that long may live Her Grace,
> To be the Good Queen *of Ireland*.[23]

Here nothing is held in reserve and the author, whether Old or New English, was clearly a Protestant. By contrast, the prominence of the Virgin Mary in the second line of the Gaelic eulogy suggests a different orientation. In England Elizabeth was associated with Marian iconoclasm (of which her adoption of Marian iconography was a disconcerting offshoot) but here, as in *The Great Parchment Book of Waterford*, the two figures are made to seem both compatible and distinct.[24] Like many highly successful examples of political rhetoric, the poem seems to say more than it does. It takes a comparative approach to become aware of what is *not quite being said*. A phrase such as 'holds Ireland in England's protection' would never have come from the pen of Barnaby Rich, John Derricke, or Edmund Spenser. But the bard's subtlety of diction enables him to write a Gaelic eulogy of an English queen. Elizabeth is credited with uniting the houses of York and Lancaster in her person and is said to be beautiful, learned, and generous but, contrary to English practice, nothing is said of her virginity. That topos is reserved for the Virgin Mary. The latter half of the poem concentrates on Elizabeth's wide-ranging successes in war and foreign policy from Flanders to Brazil, in what is clearly the equivalent of a conventional bardic *caithréim* or battle-roll. The *caithréim* was designed to celebrate victory, not sympathise with loss, and this one functions accordingly whether it is dealing with the defeat of the Armada, the 'hacking off' of natives' limbs in Brazil, or 'piratical' ventures in the Atlantic:

> Do réir measta a bhfuil re gaisce
>   sna trí rannaibh ródacha
>   níl acht meascadh cur chum casta

[23] *Verse in English from Tudor and Stuart Ireland*, Andrew Carpenter (ed.) (Cork, 2003), p. 49.

[24] Helen Hackett, *Virgin mother, maiden queen: Elizabeth I and the cult of the Virgin Mary* (Basingstoke, 1995), pp. 1–3.

le rígh Sacsan slóighthilte
féach Éire aice i gcléith Sacsan.[25]

[In the judgement of all the great experts of war
    To be found in the three road-crossed continents,
It spells rout and confusion to try to encounter
    The host-mighty sovereign of Saxon-land.
Lo, she holds Ireland in England's protection.]

Yet the poem manages not to mention a single victory on Irish soil. For many Gaelic readers the most disturbing aspect of the *caithréim* would doubtless have been its celebration of the defeat of the Armada in which so many Catholics had invested their hopes. But the poem never engages with the significance of that defeat for Ireland or Catholicism generally – indeed there is no mention of Rome at all. Rather, the eulogy achieves a fine balance between conflicting sensibilities. Most notable in this respect is its commemoration throughout, and strategically at the close, of the queen's liberality, 'for the presents and gifts bestowed by her bounty, / And the help she had given her councillors'. Ormond is not mentioned, nor does he need to be. As was evident to all, he was the most highly favoured member of the Irish privy council. What the eulogy presents, then, is not so much an English-style sovereign as a Gaelic-style patron, an empress abroad, perhaps, but a protector at home. This is an image far removed from political reality, but hardly more so than Spenser's Gloriana or Sir Walter Raleigh's Cynthia.

The Elizabeth presented in poems such as Mac Craith's eulogy or 'Taghaim Tómás' – that of a generous patron and protector of Ireland, moderate in religion and well disposed to the native population – was one that the queen had actively cultivated.[26] As early as the mid 1560s she had, according to his own account of the matter, encouraged Christopher Nugent, 5th baron Delvin, to produce a Gaelic primer to instruct her in the language. 'It pleasyde your Majestie (whiche I take a speciall favour)', he wrote, 'to comaunde me delyver your Highnes the Iryshe caracters, with instructions for reading of the language.' There is no evidence to corroborate this – and dedications frequently enhance their authors' status by alleging a 'speciall' relationship with the dedicatee – but the nature of the claim being made is highly significant whether true or false. The project is presented as originating with the queen and, Nugent argues, there can be no more 'euydent' sign of her goodwill towards Ireland than

---

[25] Ó Bruadair, *Duanaire Dháibhidh Uí Bhruadair,* vol. III, p. 68.
[26] James Carney (ed.), *Poems on the Butlers of Ormond, Cahir, and Dunboyne* (Dublin, 1945), p. 74.

the desyer your Highnes hath to vnderstande the language of your people theare. For as speache is the spetiall mean whereby all subjectes learne obedience, and their Prynces, or Governors, understande their greeves and harmes; so the same beinge delyvered by an interpretor cann never carye that grace, or proper intellygence, which the tonge itselfe being understode expressith. This defect, founde out by your Majestye, bredd that gratious desyere formorly spoken of, which beinge an acte deservinge the praise of all men, so the same made knowen unto your subjectes, no doubt would greatlye increase their love and obedyence.[27]

The concluding sentence, with its implicit undertaking to publicise the queen's goodwill among his peers, indicates Nugent's awareness of the crucial role that self-representation played in fashioning the royal image.[28] Being seen to request the primer was more important than using it. 'In this generous acte', Nugent concluded, Elizabeth would be deemed to 'excell' all her predecessors.[29] Perceived 'generosity' was the key to the matter.

The fact that Nugent was both Old English *and* Gaelic-speaking emphasises the complexity of the situation confronting Elizabeth. Fulfilling the role of monarch to the Old English demanded a distinct set of skills and sensibilities that were often lacking in her official representatives. While New English politicians such as Sir William Herbert favoured the use of Gaelic for strictly polemical purposes, many were openly hostile to the language generally. The ethos that Elizabeth tried to create through Nugent was radically different and she promoted it in a number of ways.[30] In 1567, for example, she personally provided funds for the creation of a Gaelic 'carecter' or type 'to print the New Testament in Irish'. The apparent altruism was, of course, self-serving. Representing her rule as providential was central to Elizabeth's policy. The Bishops' Bible was already in preparation in England and appeared the following year (1568) with the queen's portrait on the title page. By underwriting the costs of the Gaelic Gospels she was attempting to promote the same sort of image in Ireland. To her intense, and frankly expressed, frustration, publication was delayed until 1602 when the New Testament finally issued from Trinity College Dublin, whose foundation in 1592 further reinforced the queen's role as promoter of humanist

---

[27] See J. T. Gilbert, *Facsimiles of the National Manuscripts of Ireland*, 5 vols. (London, 1882), vol. IV, pt 1, p. xxxv and document XXII.

[28] For the queen's self-fashioning, see Frances Teague, 'Queen Elizabeth in her speeches', in S. P. Cerasano and M. Wynne-Davies (eds.), *Gloriana's face: women, public and private, in the English Renaissance* (Detroit, 1992), pp. 63–78.

[29] Gilbert, *Facsimiles*, vol. IV, pt 1, p. xxxv and document XXII.

[30] Sir William Herbert, *Croftus sive de Hibernia Liber*, Arthur Keaveney and John A. Madden (eds.) (Dublin, 1992), pp. 97–9.

education and civility.[31] In the meantime there appeared Seaán Ó Cearnaigh's *Aibidil Gaoidheilge & Caiticiosma* (1571) ('Irish Alphabet and Catechism'), which proudly claims to have been published 'at the expense of our pious and all-powerful supreme prince Elizabeth' ['ar chosdas ar n-árd-phrionnsa dhiagha mór-chumhachdaigh Elízabed']. The queen was being presented quite consistently at this period as a loving monarch willing to expend her own resources to bring the word of God to her people in their own tongue. By requesting the primer and patronising the translation of the Gospels and the catechism, Elizabeth was attempting to develop the royal image in Ireland in a new way, one that was entirely consistent with recognising the Gaelic clansmen as her 'subjects'.

The celebrated reception of Shane O'Neill at court in 1562 formed part of the same strategy. Shane did homage to the queen in Gaelic asserting that,

as I have of long time desired to come into the presence of your Majesty, to acknowledge my humble and bounden subjection, so now, here upon my knees, I acknowledge you to be my Sovereign Lady, and confess that I have offended you and your laws, for which I have required and obtained your pardon. Because my speech, being Irish, is not well understood, I caused this my submission to be written both in English and Irish, and thereto have set my hand and seal.[32]

But Shane, no less than Elizabeth, was playing a double-handed game. The visitation, with all its extravagant professions of loyalty and love, served his purposes as much, if not more, than the queen's. He had previously accused the viceroy of blocking access to the monarch and professed unwillingness to deal with a mere representative.[33] Reception at court lent him status at home: if he was a pawn on Elizabeth's chessboard, she was a 'queen' on his. Privately he disparaged her by asserting that 'he never made peace with the queen, but by her own seeking', and the same pattern of humble submission and subsequent rebellion would be endlessly repeated throughout the reign.[34] John Derricke's *The Image of Ireland with a Discoverie of the Wood Karne* (1581) begins with a panegyric of the English crown from Arthur to Elizabeth and ends with the

---

[31] For Elizabeth's attitude to the Gaelic scriptures, see Bruce Dickins, 'The Irish broadside of 1571 and Queen Elizabeth's types', *Transactions of the Cambridge Bibliographical Society* 1 (1949), 49.

[32] James Hogan, 'Shane O'Neill comes to the court of Elizabeth', in Séamus Pender (ed.), *Féilscríbhinn Torna: essays presented to Professor Tadhg Ua Donnchadha* (Cork, 1947), p. 166; see also Ciaran Brady, 'Shane O'Neill departs from the court of Elizabeth: Irish, English, Scottish perspectives and the paralysis of policy, July 1559 to April 1562', in S. J. Connolly (ed.), *Kingdoms united? Great Britain and Ireland since 1500: integration and diversity* (Dublin, 1999), pp. 13–28.

[33] SP 63/4/21.   [34] SP 63/16/35.

submission of Turlough O'Neill, Shane's successor, to the lord deputy, Sir Henry Sidney:

> My prince's friend I vow myself to be,
> And loyal eke unto her noble grace,
> A friend to her a friend likewise to me,
> As time shall try the utmost of her case.
> And who that seeks her honour to deface,
> I do protest by all my force and might,
> My blood to gage but I'll maintain my right.[35]

The suggestion that Turlough would defend the queen's image from defacement should not be dismissed as mere poetic licence. He had previously written to Elizabeth professing the ancestral loyalty of his family to the crown, and he had praised Sir Henry Sidney as one who would not make 'rebels' of 'subjects'.[36] Derricke's licence consisted only in representing a recurrent ploy as a climactic act. The accompanying woodcut shows Turlough kneeling in English dress before Sidney and promising 'for ever to her noble grace, a subiect true to stand'. The image served no less potent a purpose in Gaelic polity than did defamation of the crown. It allowed O'Neill to 'civilise' his own public image among the Old and New English by appropriating Elizabeth's:

> This is the prince which to her realms
>   procureth rest and peace,
> This is the queen that causeth wars
>   and bloody broils to cease.
> This is the queen that little cares
>   to hazard life or blood.
> This is the queen that nothing spares
>   to do her people good.[37]

But this is emphatically not the queen that Spenser and like-minded colonists wanted. Hence the call, towards the end of *A View of the Present State of Ireland* for the appointment of a strong 'Lorde Liuetennante' with plenipotentiary powers to act as circumstances required 'beinge allwaies heare residente' (p. 228) – a clause necessitated by the queen's perpetual absence. But Elizabeth well understood that such 'representation' could easily promote displacement. Having lambasted the regal pretensions of the earl of Leicester's demeanour in the Netherlands, she had no intention of creating the sort of vice-regal post that Spenser suggested.[38] The poet's

[35] John Derricke, *The Image of Ireland with a Discoverie of the Wood Karne* (1581), David B. Quinn (ed.) (Belfast, 1985), p. 210.
[36] SP 63/53/61.   [37] Derricke, *The image of Ireland*, p. 180.
[38] See Jasper Ridley, *Elizabeth I* (London, 1981), p. 251.

candidate for the new office was none other than Leicester's protégé, the earl of Essex, but he was eventually appointed to the old one, albeit with exceptional resources, and ran into trouble with the queen almost immediately. The royal image, as Elizabeth deployed it, was very much an instrument of expediency. Although she was commonly taxed for pacifism or appeasement both in Ireland and on the continent, her letters to Essex during the Irish campaign tax him for lack of military determination. Her self-representation now (as previously during the Armada crisis) was of a decisive military ruler who needed generals adequate to her resolve. As she is at pains to point out, Essex's failure against Tyrone, despite the extraordinary manpower she had made available to him, damaged *her* international image. His reputation was a subordinate matter. 'We . . . have the eyes of foreign Princes upon our actions', she reminds him,

this one thing . . . doth more displease us than any charge or expense that happens, which is, that it must be the Queen of England's fortune (who had held down the greatest enemy she had) to make a base bush kern to be accounted so famous a rebel, as to be a person against whom so many thousands of foot and horse, besides the force of all the nobility of that kingdom, must be thought too little to be employed.[39]

It was a point that later commentators recognised, and it indicates the queen's level of concern with the wider effects that being queen of Ireland might have on the perception of her sovereignty generally. Far from granting Essex the sort of plenipotentiary powers that Spenser advocated, she was insistent that he consult her in all matters of policy before anything was finalised. His decision to parley with Tyrone 'half an hour together' caused her great concern since she was advised 'of the half-hour's conference only, but not what passed on either side . . . as we cannot tell, but by divination, what to think may be the issue of this proceeding'.[40] Despite protestations of trust she was clearly suspicious – as much, as it happens, of incompetence as of treachery – but Irish chroniclers saw an opportunity to exploit the missing half-hour to the disadvantage of both queen and minister. In a remarkable passage in his account of the Nine Years' War, written while events were still unfolding, Peter Lombard, the Roman Catholic archbishop of Armagh, has O'Neill address Essex as follows:

You know what a tyrant is your queen, that scarce anyone lives thoroughly safe under her, unless those who are either powerless or ignorant . . . You know also in what a slippery state is your country, with the imminence of the death of this

[39] *The letters of Queen Elizabeth*, G. B. Harrison (ed.) (London, 1968), pp. 264–5.
[40] *Ibid.*, p. 275.

aged woman, and how the strongest will become the future ruler... bide your time; attach yourself to those under whose protection you may at the proper time preserve yourself safe and sound.[41]

The passage is brilliantly calculated to cause the maximum damage. Elizabeth is not only a 'tyrant' but an 'aged woman' who has no future except in the pages of history. Soon power will shift and the game will change. The epitaph, of course, proved premature. The queen lived to see the Battle of Kinsale if not quite O'Neill's capitulation in its aftermath, but not before one final assault on the royal image when Essex, abandoning Ireland without leave, burst in upon her at Nonsuch before she had finished dressing – a form of 'treason' more devastating than O'Rourke's in revealing the essential disparity between sitter and 'picture'.[42]

The heretic queen

If Elizabeth's claim to be supreme governor of the Church caused difficulties even in England, it greatly exacerbated the problem of religious difference in Ireland. The vast majority of Elizabeth's Gaelic and Old English 'subjects' were Roman Catholic, and the queen's excommunication by Pius V in 1570 afforded a ready platform for rebellion. Whereas Mary Tudor was regarded as restoring the *status quo ante*, and Mary, queen of Scots, was mooted as a future deliverer, Elizabeth was commonly depicted as a pernicious heretic. In calling his fellow countrymen to arms in 1579, James Fitzmaurice Fitzgerald was therefore careful to assert that 'we are not at war against the legitimate and honourable crown of England, but against that she-tyrant who, by refusing to hear Christ in the person of His Vicar, and even by daring to subject the Church of Christ to the ruling of a woman in matters of faith, on which she has no right to pronounce, has deservedly forfeited her royal authority'.[43] Elements of proto-nationalism have been detected in Fitzmaurice's appeal to 'faith and fatherland' but his insistence on the legitimacy of the crown is equally significant in foreshadowing later attempts to cultivate rapprochement with Elizabeth's successor, the son of Mary, queen of Scots.[44] So far as Elizabeth was concerned, however, Fitzmaurice is adamant that

---

[41] Peter Lombard, *The Irish war of defence 1598–1600: extracts from the 'De Hibernia insula commentarius'*, M. J. Byrne (ed. and trans.) (Cork, 1930), p. 81.

[42] *Letters and memorials*, vol. II, p. 127.

[43] M. V. Ronan, *The Reformation in Ireland under Elizabeth 1558–1580* (London, 1930), p. 620.

[44] See Brendán Ó Buachalla, 'James our true king: the ideology of Irish royalism in the seventeenth century', in D. G. Boyce, Robert Eccleshall, and Vincent Geoghegan (eds.), *Political thought in Ireland since the seventeenth century* (London, 1993), pp. 7–35.

there could be no profit for Catholics, either spiritual or material, in serving such a person. From the theological viewpoint 'if any man die for the defence of Elizabeth, can she save him before the throne of God?' From a more worldly perspective, one had to consider how support of the childless Elizabeth would look to her (possibly Catholic) successor. Elizabeth was

a woman that is hated of all Christian princes for the great injuries which she has done them, hated of her own subjects, as well for the compelling them to forswear their Christian faith touching the supremacy of Christ's Vicar on earth, as also for not publishing the heir apparent to the Crown – a woman that leaves no issue of her own body either to reward them that should fight for her or to revenge them that shall fight against her – nay rather, a woman that is surely hated of her successor whosoever he be; and therefore they that seek to please her cannot but be unpleasant to the next heir of the crown, whose right she so tyrannously forbids to be published.[45]

This was a particularly shrewd piece of political argumentation designed to exploit the uncertainties of the succession, but it also posed a vigorous challenge to Elizabeth's official image as the virgin queen. According to Fitzmaurice, Henry VIII's heresy was punished in the lack of issue among his children, the curse falling even upon the virtuous Mary, 'a builder-up of God's house'.[46] Elizabeth was fated to be the last of the line, not virgin but barren.

Many of Fitzmaurice's letters and proclamations were inspired, if not drafted, by Nicholas Sander, who acted from July 1579 as spiritual counsellor to the insurgents and representative of the papacy – a papacy that had invested far less in the military enterprise than he would have wished. His *Rise and Growth of the Anglican Schism* (*De Origine ac Progressu Schismatis Anglicani*), posthumously published in 1585, sheds light on the methods used to undermine the royal image that Elizabeth's Protestant English supporters had crafted. Fitzmaurice's emphasis on the barrenness of Henry VIII's children is entirely drawn from Sander as, to a great extent, are the arguments against secular headship of the church.[47] Elizabeth was not, Sander contends, the 'sacrata virgo' whose birth is hailed by commentators such as John Foxe as a providential blessing, but the incestuous offspring of father (Henry VIII) and daughter (Anne Boleyn), illicit by the laws of nature and illegitimate by the laws of England.[48] Like her father, she had set up the monarchy as an object of worship, replacing

[45] Ronan, *The Reformation in Ireland*, p. 617.   [46] *Ibid.*, p. 616.

[47] Nicholas Sander, *Rise and growth of the Anglican schism*, David Lewis (ed. and trans.) (London, 1877), p. 229.

[48] It was alleged that Henry VIII had fathered Anne Boleyn during an illicit affair with her mother. The polemic advantage of this story for Catholics was that the man who

the cross with the royal arms, but her crime was aggravated by her gender: 'Elizabeth, on account of her sex, never could be a minister of the Word, without which the government of the Church becomes impossible.'[49] Attempts to lend an aura of spirituality to Elizabeth's claims are therefore dismissed as bogus, and evident similarities between the iconography of the virgin queen and that of the Virgin Mary are regarded as blasphemous.[50] As we have seen, Mac Craith's eulogy is careful to ensure that the two iconographies never converge and Sander's writings indicate why. According to him, English Protestants showed greater regard for Elizabeth's birthday than the Virgin Mary's and 'in the church of St Paul, the chief church of London . . . the praises of Elizabeth are said to be sung at the end of the public prayers, as the Antiphon of our Lady was sung in former days'.[51] Such were the arguments that underlie Fitzmaurice's proclamations. The iconoclasm of the English Reformation was being turned back upon its authors – a circumstance that lent peculiarly ironic resonance to alleged treasons of the picture.[52]

Ireland's empress

When Sir Henry Sidney accused some of the foremost Palesmen in 1577 of infringing the royal prerogative by opposing the imposition of cess, he was engaging in a contest for the queen's image that began with her accession.[53] The situation in 1558 was difficult for the Old English whose professions of loyalty were tinged with fears for the loss of the religious liberty they had regained under Mary. Their further discomfiture after Elizabeth's excommunication in 1570 could easily be manipulated by their New English opponents to suggest that they could never be true 'subjects'. But Old English petitions to the queen sought rather to portray the New English as driving a wedge between Elizabeth and her loyal Irish supporters. The queen was claimed by both parties. While Richard Stanihurst's contributions to the Irish sections of the first edition of Holinshed (1577) are dedicated to Sir Henry Sidney, their sympathies lie primarily with the hereditary Palesmen, and from their viewpoint it

divorced Catherine of Aragon on the grounds of kinship through marriage proceeded to wed his own natural daughter.

[49] Sander, *Rise and growth*, pp. 100, 172, 237–8.
[50] See Hackett, *Virgin mother, maiden queen.*   [51] *Ibid.*, pp. 284–5.
[52] For iconoclasm, see Ernest B. Gilman, *Iconoclasm and poetry in the English Reformation: down went Dagon* (Chicago, 1986); Eamon Duffy, *The stripping of the altars: traditional religion in England 1400–1580*, 2nd edn (New Haven, 2005).
[53] For the problem of cess, see Steven Ellis, *Tudor Ireland: crown, community and the conflict of cultures, 1470–1603* (London, 1985), pp. 268–73; Brady, *Chief governors*, pp. 145–58, 215–44; Connolly, *Contested island*, pp. 202–6.

was Sidney himself who had 'alienated the hearts of the subjects from loiall obedience' by insisting on the cess.[54] By contrast, the 'Supplie' of the Irish chronicles added by John Hooker to the 1587 edition is pervasively New English in sentiment and the Palesmen are heavily criticised.[55] Hooker is particularly sceptical of the claim that 'their intent was never to denie hir [Elizabeth's] roiall prerogative' in the matter of the cess 'but onlie to redresse certeine abuses'.[56] Sir Henry Sidney's eventual victory is accordingly represented as an example of productive co-operation between deputy and crown.[57] But Sir Henry Sidney's personal account of his relationship with the queen makes for very different reading:

I loathed, I say again, to tarry any longer in that land, chiefly for that I saw the queen make so little account of my service in killing that pernicious rebel [Rory Og O More]... It grieved me not a little that Her Majesty rejected those bills which I sent to be allowed to be made laws, whereof many had been devised by me, and by my instruction penned.[58]

By the time that Sidney finally received 'comfortable and thankful letters' from the queen 'signed with her own hand', he was 'fifty-four yeres of age, toothlesse and trembling' and five thousand pounds in debt. But Sidney had missed the point: Elizabeth wished to be represented in Ireland, not supplanted. If she did not press home her victory in the matter of the cess with anything like the rigour that Sidney desired, it was because she wished to ensure that loyalty was vested in her not him, or any of his successors. An accommodation with the Palesmen was quickly reached once the issue of the prerogative was agreed in principle. The outcome was inevitable. While in the very act of professing to accord the lord deputy 'all like pre-eminence as her Highness might have being here resident in the royal person', the Palesmen's representatives had petitioned for leave to visit the court and address her directly.[59] Initially their journey to London saw them imprisoned in the Tower, but in the longer term it facilitated the resolution they desired. By appealing beyond Sidney to Elizabeth, the Palesmen located the seat of power exactly where

---

[54] Raphael Holinshed, *Holinshed's chronicles: England, Scotland, and Ireland...*, 6 vols. (London, 1808), vol. VI, p. 394. For a full account of the disputes concerning cess, see Brady, *Chief governors*, pp. 215–44 (esp. pp. 237–40).
[55] See Richard A. McCabe, 'Making history: Holinshed's Irish *Chronicles*, 1577 and 1587', in David J. Baker and Willy Maley (eds.), *British identities and English Renaissance literature* (Cambridge, 2002), pp. 51–67.
[56] Holinshed, *Holinshed's chronicles*, vol. VI, p. 394. Hooker is citing the Palesmen's petition of 28 June 1578. See *Cal. Carew*, 1575–88, p. 133 (see also pp. 76, 83).
[57] Holinshed, *Holinshed's chronicles*, vol. VI, pp. 389–94.
[58] Sir Henry Sidney, *A viceroy's vindication? Sir Henry Sidney's memoir of service in Ireland, 1556–1578*, Ciaran Brady (ed.) (Cork, 2002), p. 102.
[59] *Cal. Carew*, 1575–88, p. 57.

the queen wished it to be. She understood the game better than many of its New English players.

But there was a price to pay for such expediency. The experiences of lord deputies from Sussex to Perrot damaged the queen's image among her own officers. According to E.C.S., the anonymous author of *The Government of Ireland under the Honourable, Iust, and wise Governor Sir John Perrot* (1626), Elizabeth 'repented, (no doubt)' for recalling Lord Grey but was 'unwilling to confesse errour, or to shew the power of such as had prevailed with her' in the decision.[60] According to Sir James Perrot, the lord deputy's illegitimate son, her failure to support her deputies in suppressing the Irish rebels occasioned the very loss of confidence in the monarchy that Elizabeth herself feared:

> Many men of noe meane understanding abroad, and some at home, have wondered how it came to passe that Queene Elizabeth, a princesse of soe greate fame, power, and magnanimitie, who contested with the greatest kinge of Christendom . . . should yet be soe incombred and soe much infested with theise hir rebellious subjectes of Ireland, that all hir other forayne enimies and home-bred conspirators were never able in all hir raigne halfe soe much to anoy hir State, distroy hir subjectes, or to consume hir treasure, as did theise meane (and in comparison of other nations) contemptible rebellious subjectes of Ireland.[61]

It is little wonder, then, that New English writers of the late 1580s and 1590s laboured the imperial theme. Far more was involved in their designation of Elizabeth as 'empress' than a flattering mode of address. At issue, as Rory Rapple demonstrates, was the notion of 'imperium' as essentially absolute and coercive.[62] The queen was increasingly seen among the New English as far too lenient to the Irish, far too willing to prevaricate, temporise, grant pardons, and come to terms. This is the leitmotif of Spenser's *View of the Present State of Ireland*. The writer's sympathies are with Lord Grey, Perrot's immediate predecessor, and the entire treatise is suffused with oblique criticism of the queen. All who in future adopt Grey's strong-arm tactics, it is suggested, will fail because the queen 'will not endure to heare suche tragedies made of her people and pore subiectes' (p. 159). The key word here, as in the Churchyard poem, is 'subiectes'. The queen's disposition to retrieve as 'subjects' those whom the New English would discard as 'rebels', or

---

[60] E.C.S., *The Government of Ireland under the Honourable, Iust, and wise Governor Sir John Perrot, 1584–1588* (London, 1626), pp. 2–3.

[61] Sir James Perrot, *The Chronicle of Ireland 1548–1608*, Herbert Wood (ed.) (Dublin, 1933), pp. 6–7.

[62] Rory Rapple, *Martial power and Elizabethan political culture: military men in England and Ireland, 1558–1594* (Cambridge, 2009), pp. 181–99. The case was strengthened by the resurgence of 'imperial monarchy' thinking in England after the execution of Mary, queen of Scots. See John Guy, *The Tudor monarchy* (London, 1997), pp. 101–3.

eradicate as 'salvages', drove a deep fissure between Dublin and London. Spenser dismissed the Act for the Kingly Title as an irrelevance on the grounds that it gave nothing to Henry VIII that he did not already possess by right of conquest 'but onelye the bare name of a Kinge' (p. 52). This is an extraordinary statement for someone who elsewhere invests such significance in royal titles. It could be made only in the context of Ireland where Elizabeth was expected to act as 'empresse', the title that precedes 'Queene of England, France and Ireland' in the dedications to the 1590 and 1596 editions of *The Faerie Queene*.

Deriving from the Latin 'imperium', the term 'imperial' had a wide range of connotations in the sixteenth century. As employed by Henry VIII, it denoted the integrity of English sovereignty independent of papal Rome, but it also retained strong associations with ancient Rome's policy of conquest and colonisation.[63] The Old English generally were insistent that Ireland was a separate kingdom because it underwrote their legal rights and political privileges, but the New English – many of whom, like Raleigh and Gilbert, proceeded to the Americas – not infrequently treated it as a colony. Richard Beacon's uncompromising New English tract, *Solon his Follie, or A Politique Discourse Touching the Reformation of Common-weales, conquered, declined or corrupted* (1594) is addressed to Elizabeth as the 'renowned Queene, and Empresse' who has acted to 'augment, strengthen, and honour your imperiall crowne of Englande, by the thorough reformation of this your Realme of Ireland'. The imperial title was additionally useful here because, as Beacon's formulation suggests, it implied the subordination of Irish affairs to those of England. While the 'subject of Irelande' is alleged to rejoice in the country's reformation, the main concern is the effect that Irish policy has on the 'imperiall crowne of England'.[64] From the New English viewpoint, this was the right set of priorities and the preferred image of Elizabeth's government in Ireland. Spenser's 'Brief Note of Ireland', written at the nadir of the settlers' fortunes during the Nine Years' War, is addressed to his 'moste mightie Empresse our Dred soveraigne'. The treatise urges her to show 'mercie' to the settlers by putting away 'clemencye' towards the Irish and returning to the Roman imperial mode (pp. 236, 241). Spenser did not live to see the outcome. In the posthumously published *Two Cantos of Mutabilitie* (1609) 'Diana' is represented as abandoning the colonists to their fate despite being the 'soveraine Queene profest / Of

---

[63] See Anthony Pagden, *Lords of all the world: ideologies of empire in Spain, Britain and France c. 1500–c. 1800* (New Haven, 1995), pp. 12–17; Walter Ullmann, "'This realm of England is an empire'", *Journal of Ecclesiastical History* 30 (1979), 175–203.

[64] Richard Beacon, *Solon his Follie, or a Politique Discourse touching the Reformation of Common-weales conquered, declined or corrupted*, Clare Carroll and Vincent Carey (eds.) (Binghamton, NY, 1996), pp. 1–4.

woods and forrests' (*Faerie Queene*, VII, vi. 38), and in that element of 'profession' lay the crux of the problem. Elizabeth's dual professions of sovereignty raised mutually exclusive expectations.

The New English wished it to be understood that executive power inhered not in the Irish parliament or the Gaelic and Old English aristocracies, but solely in the 'imperial' crown. Yet as agents of the crown they sought to appropriate what they elsewhere deemed exclusive and indivisible. It was a contradiction of which Elizabeth was all too well aware. She realised, that is to say, that her royal prerogative might provide a perfect cover for others' self-aggrandisement, that what was done in her name might radically undermine her interests. Underlying the imperial iconography of New English propaganda lay the insinuation that only through New English efforts could Elizabeth gain effective sovereignty of Ireland.[65] The common burden of such works as Sir William Herbert's *Croftus sive de Hibernia Liber* (*c.* 1591), Richard Beacon's *Solon his Follie* (1594), and Spenser's *View of the Present State of Ireland* (1596) is that the country should be governed not as an independent kingdom but an imperial dependency, and all three invoke the ancient Roman exemplum at various points.[66] The fact that all three also reference Machiavelli is indicative of the New English desire for Elizabeth to operate as a different sort of 'prince' in Ireland than in England, an absolutist one.[67] From this point of view, the Old English 'queen' and New English 'empress' were fundamentally incompatible. But Elizabeth was above all a political pragmatist and the iconography of pragmatism is necessarily changeable and ambiguous: *nunquam eadem* not *semper eadem*. Elizabeth was well aware that any commitment to the New English definition of 'imperium' entailed a limitation of her freedom to manoeuvre and, ironically, a diminution of her personal powers. While appearing to exaggerate the royal prerogative, New English rhetoric invariably seeks to appropriate Elizabeth to a New English agenda. Beacon's dedicatory epistle 'To her Most Sacred Majestie', for example, overtly constitutes a sort of prose poem celebrating her accomplishments in Ireland as manifesting a combination of Foxean providentialism and Spenserian 'magnificence':

If all the actes and monumentes of former ages, most mighty and renowned Queene, and Empresse, which might recommend this action of reformation unto all posterities, were committed to oblivion, yet the recordes and monumentes of your Majesties most happy governement, may sufficiently revive the same: where it is saide, that your Highnes hath atchieved unto that which is most rightly

---

[65] *Ibid.*, pp. 175, 177.
[66] See Herbert, *Croftus sive de Hibernia Liber*, pp. 75–81; Beacon, *Solon his Follie*, pp. 143–5.
[67] See Vincent Carey, 'The Irish face of Machiavelli: Richard Beacon's *Solon his Follie* (1594) and republican ideology in the conquest of Ireland', in Morgan (ed.), *Political ideology*, p. 90.

tearmed the greatest magnificence of a Prince, which doth not onely consist in high bloud, hauty progenie, aboundance of private riches and substance . . . but it restesth chiefely in populous and wel governed regions, & in beautiful Cities and Townes; [The act of attainder of Shane Oneile, Ann. 11. Elizab.] al which being impaired in your Realme of Ireland, by the iniquitie of former times, nowe as well the one as the other, by your Majesties most godly and careful course of governement, are recontinued, amended, and augmented.[68]

But the treatise that follows suggests, to the contrary, that the 'reformation' of Ireland remains to be accomplished in both religious and political terms. Indeed, as Beacon's marginal annotations indicate, the sentences describing the 'magnificence' of princely rule are adapted from the preamble to the Act of Attainder of Shane O'Neill (1569), and this well-signalled borrowing functions as a sort of cautionary palimpsest: a disturbing reminder that the aims of the attainder remained unfulfilled twenty-five years later.[69] What advertises itself as a celebration is actually an exercise in the ancient rhetorical art of *laudando praecipere.* Published just one year after Beacon, Spenser's portrayal of Cynthia in *Colin Clouts Come Home Againe* (1595) is indicative of the deepening sense of disappointment felt in New English circles. Colin Clout, the poet's persona, previously characterised as one of 'faire Eliza's' English subjects, is here made to visit the court as a stranger, a rhetorical device that powerfully encapsulates the sense of alienation that the colonists were experiencing. Colin's extravagant praise of Cynthia, while fulsome and extensive, lies inert in the political dynamic of the poem – he visits her, praises her, and leaves her, but she appears to do nothing to alleviate the corruptions of court or country (either country). It is as though the royal image had become an ideal without an application.[70]

Poems of royal triumph were dutifully produced in the aftermath of Kinsale, but following the queen's death more sober New English assessments began to appear.[71] The very title of Sir John Davies's *A Discoverie of the True Causes why Ireland was neuer entirely Subdued, nor brought vnder Obedience of the Crowne of England, vntill the Beginning of his Maiesties happie Raigne* (1612) is symptomatic of such revisionism. While Davies

---

[68] Beacon, *Solon his Follie*, p. 102. The reference in square brackets was originally supplied as a marginal annotation.

[69] For an analysis of the text and context of the attainder, see Ciaran Brady, 'The attainder of Shane O'Neill, Sir Henry Sidney and the problems of Tudor state-building in Ireland', in Ciaran Brady and Jane Ohlmeyer (eds.), *British interventions in early modern Ireland* (Cambridge, 2005), pp. 28–48.

[70] See Richard A. McCabe, 'Edmund Spenser: poet of exile', British Academy Chatterton Lecture on Poetry, in '1991 Lectures and Memoirs', *Proceedings of the British Academy* 80 (1993), 89–94.

[71] For poems celebrating the English victory, see Hiram Morgan (ed.), *The Battle of Kinsale* (Bray, 2004), pp. 379–414.

asserts that Elizabeth dealt adequately enough with the rebellions of Shane O'Neill and the earl of Desmond, he sees her as performing at best only a series of holding operations. To him, her policy seemed reactive, not proactive: even when faced with 'the extreame perill of loosing the Kingdome' to the earl of Tyrone her aim was merely 'to keep and retaine that *Soveraignetie*, which the Crowne of England had in *Ireland* (such as it was) and not to recover a more absolute Dominion'. Judged by Davies's definition of 'conquest' – 'to give Lawes to a conquered people' – Elizabeth was never successful in Ireland.[72] Fynes Moryson went further in asserting that the violent policies of Lord Grey and Sir Richard Bingham were justified by the circumstances and the queen's 'womanly' opposition to them ill advised. Although Spenser hints at the same conclusion, this is perhaps that first time that Elizabeth's gender is openly represented as inimical to the interests of the English crown in Ireland – and the passage remained in manuscript.[73] While outwardly respectful to a monarch 'of famous memory', the extensive review of Irish history that Moryson inserted into the first edition of his *Itinerary* (1617) criticises the queen for failing to 'countenance' a succession of lord deputies from Grey to Mountjoy and for 'appeasing' Tyrone, a dangerous 'foxe' who knew how to humour and manipulate the English court.[74] Mountjoy, to whom Moryson acted as private secretary, is seen as succeeding despite the queen, not because of her, and he achieves his greatest diplomatic coup by suppressing the news of her death until Tyrone had already submitted, a particularly cynical use of the royal image whose force was not lost on its victim.[75] The meticulous detail with which Moryson recounts the mechanisms of the subterfuge suggests that the queen was finally more useful to Mountjoy dead than living – when, that is to say, she was no more than an image and could neither contradict nor countermand her official representative.

The posthumous queen

To most of her Gaelic subjects, an image is all that Elizabeth had ever been, an image so often depicted, defaced, and over-painted that the

---

[72] Sir John Davies, *A Discoverie of the True Causes why Ireland was neuer entirely Subdued nor brought vnder Obedience of the Crowne of England, vntill the Beginning of his Maiesties happie Raigne* (London, 1612), pp. 97–8, 100, 286.

[73] Fynes Moryson, *Shakespeare's Europe: unpublished chapters of Fynes Moryson's Itinerary*, Charles Hughes (ed.) (London, 1903), pp. 259–60.

[74] Fynes Moryson, *An itinerary, containing his ten yeeres travell through the twelve dominions of Germany, Bohmerland, Sweitzerland, Netherland, Denmarke, Poland, Italy, Turky, France, England, Scotland & Ireland*, 4 vols. (Glasgow, 1907–8), vol. II, pp. 165, 179, 193, 206, 333; vol. III, p. 311.

[75] *Ibid.*, vol. III, pp. 295–304.

features became unrecognisable. She never achieved in Ireland the effect that was crucial to her English success: familiarity. Rather, it was her very absence that facilitated both the strongest professions of loyalty and defiance. In Lughaidh Ó Clérigh's *Beatha Aodha Ruaidh Uí Dhomhnaill* (*The Life of Red Hugh O'Donnell*) Elizabeth is the Protestant Saxon Prince ['Prionnsa Saxan'] against whom Red Hugh O'Donnell defines his own brand of patriotic, pious heroism. Her iconography is part of his. She is the inveterate enemy of the Irish – 'taking their patrimony from them and perverting them from the Roman Catholic faith, which St Patrick had preached to their elders and ancestors' – and he their defender. She is presented as acting violently out of 'wrath and anger' or falling into 'anxiety and great grief' at the success of her opponents. Her followers are devious and cunning or, when Irish, treacherous.[76]

Much of Ó Clérigh's account of the Nine Years' War was later decanted into the Four Masters' *Annála Ríoghachta Éireann* (1633), where it supplies a tense subtext to the compilers' more overt efforts at rapprochement with the Stuart crown. Elizabeth's accession is noted in a single sentence in the entry from 1558: 'Queen Elizabeth was made sovereign over England on 17 November' ('Queene Elizabeth do oirdneadh ós Saxaibh an 17 November').[77] Her status in relation to Ireland is left conspicuously vague by contrast to James, who is said in the entry for 1603 to have been appointed 'in the place of the queen [as king] over England, France, and Ireland' ('King Séamus iar na oirdneath i nionadh na bainríogna ós saxaibh, Frainc, agus uar Éirinn').[78] While Old English families, and notably the Geraldines, are represented as owing loyalty 'to their Sovereign' because her ancestors had granted them their ancestral lands and titles, her Gaelic opponents are praised and elegised with bardic fervour.[79] Such unresolved dichotomies fracture the Four Masters' account of Elizabethan Ireland and create a conflicted image of the queen, sovereign to some, enemy to others, and hostile to the faith of the majority of both.

If the Four Masters were influenced by their patron, Feargal O'Gara's loyalty to the crown, Philip O'Sullivan Beare's *Historiae Catholicae*

---

[76] Paul Walsh (ed. and trans.), *Beatha Aodha Ruaidh Uí Dhomhnaill: the life of Aodh Ruadh O Domhnaill*, 2 vols. (London, 1948–57), vol. I, 123, 131, 195.

[77] John O'Donovan (ed. and trans.), *Annála Ríoghachta Éireann: Annals of the Kingdom of Ireland by the Four Masters*, 2nd edn, 7 vols. (Dublin, 1856), vol. V, p. 1569.

[78] *Ibid.*, vol. VI, p. 2337.

[79] *Ibid.*, vol. V, p. 1797; vol. VI, p. 2375. For the ambivalent rhetoric of the Four Masters, see Richard A. McCabe, 'Fighting words: writing the "Nine Years' War"', in Thomas Herron and Michael Potterton (eds.), *Ireland in the Renaissance, c. 1540–1660* (Dublin, 2007), pp. 120–1. For comparison, see Fearghal Óg Mac an Bhaird's fine elegy, 'Teasda Éire san Easbáinn', in Pádraig Breatnach, 'Marbhna Aodha Ruaidh Uí Dhomhnaill (1602)', *Éigse* 15 (1) (1973), 31–50.

Iberniae Compendium (1621) hones its image of Elizabeth to the prejudices of its dedicatee, Philip IV of Spain. Constructed here is a black legend of inhuman cruelty designed to reflect on Elizabeth much as Bartolomé de Las Casas's account of the Spanish Americas had reflected on Charles V and Philip II. Ironically, the single-minded ruthlessness that O'Sullivan Beare attributes to Elizabeth is the very quality that many of her more radical New English ministers would have wished her to display. In his opinion, the likes of Grey and Bingham worked with the entire approval of their monarch who was herself the 'instigator' of their crimes.[80] Her motivation was simple, the spread of heresy, and she would not stop short of genocide:

> The queen and her councillors and magistrates directed all their zeal and plots to despoil the Irish of their goods, to gradually overthrow them and take away their lives... and so the destruction and annihilation of the whole island and Catholic faith were imminent. This was the state of things when the great war began.[81]

This made it possible to present the ensuing conflict as a struggle for survival against a 'tyrant' determined to enforce her will 'by fear, terror, punishment and violence', and the image proved highly influential.[82] The anonymous author of 'An Síogaí Rómhánach' ('The Roman Sprite'), an *aisling* or dream-vision of around 1650 that surveys Irish history from the Reformation to the Confederate Wars, presents Elizabeth as a pestilential whore who brought indiscriminate carnage to the country and procured the murder of Mary Stuart.[83] But, as Marc Caball has demonstrated, much of the bardic poetry written during Elizabeth's reign was in any case implicitly hostile to her claims to sovereignty and celebrated figures, such as O'Rourke, who were subsequently executed for treason.[84]

In England, after the euphoria of the Stuart succession had abated, the myth of 'Good Queen Bess' quickly took root and history was embellished or supplanted by legend.[85] But no such developments occurred in Ireland. 'Here', as Wallace MacCaffrey observes, 'the Queen's limitations as a ruler were acutely felt. Her pragmatic short-term vision

---

[80] Philip O'Sullivan Beare, *Ireland under Elizabeth: chapters towards a history of Ireland in the reign of Elizabeth... by Don Philip O'Sullivan Beare*, Matthew J. Byrne (ed. and trans.) (Dublin, 1903), pp. 1–2, 21–5, 37–8.

[81] *Ibid.*, pp. 33, 48–9.   [82] *Ibid.*, p. 43.

[83] Cecile O'Rahilly (ed.), *Five seventeenth-century political poems* (Dublin, 1977), p. 21.

[84] Marc Caball, *Poets and politics: reaction and continuity in Irish poetry, 1558–1625* (Notre Dame and Cork, 1998), pp. 25–31, 43–5, 48–50.

[85] See Susan Doran and Thomas S. Freeman (eds.), *The myth of Elizabeth* (Basingstoke, 2003); Michael Dobson and Nicola J. Watson, *England's Elizabeth: an afterlife in fame and fantasy* (Oxford, 2002).

could not be brought to focus on longer-term needs. Her preoccupation with immediate problems and her obsession with cutting costs made it impossible to attract her interests to long-range planning.'[86] According to Richard Bellings, secretary to the Confederation of Kilkenny, it was only under James I that the Irish had become 'free subjects' with equivalent rights to their English counterparts guaranteed by 'the Common Law'. The fault of the Stuarts, as he saw it, lay in not making a clear enough break with Elizabethan policy. The worst anti-Catholic laws were passed under Elizabeth, and although her successors did not enforce them rigorously, 'because they still stood unrepealed, what the Prince did was less noted than what the law might do'.[87] The increasing sense among all parties that Elizabeth's legacy was poisoned attests to her fundamental failure to establish a coherent image as 'queen of Ireland'. In 'An Síogaí Rómhánach' a 'fairy' speaker is used to demolish the reputation of Spenser's 'Faerie Queene' and offer a sort of '*cailleach*' in her place. In England, through her speeches, proclamations and public appearances Elizabeth successfully cultivated the notion that she somehow embodied the nation. But absence cannot convey embodiment, and the concept of Irish nationality was as yet inchoate. Sharpe's *Selling the Tudor monarchy* demonstrates the power of political iconography, but Tudor Ireland displays its limitations. Successive attempts to adapt English strategy to the Irish situation, to hang a royal portrait under the cloth of state in lieu of an absentee, merely emphasised the sense of distance, difference, and alienation. In Ireland to hang the portrait was to invite 'treason of the picture'.

---

[86] Wallace MacCaffrey, *Elizabeth I* (London, 1993), p. 421.
[87] Richard Bellings, *History of the Irish Confederation and the War in Ireland, 1641–1643*, J. T. Gilbert (ed.), 10 vols. (Dublin, 1882), vol. I, pp. 2–3.

3   Elizabeth on Ireland

Leah S. Marcus

In 2000 and 2002, my coeditors Janel Mueller and Mary Beth Rose and I published a volume entitled *Elizabeth I: collected works*. In that edition, we tried to offer a representative sample of Elizabeth I's letters, along with speeches, poems, and other writings. But we included only a handful of Elizabeth's letters about Ireland – seven letters as opposed to twenty-three about Scotland, most of which were addressed either to Mary, queen of Scots, or to James VI.[1] This is a remarkable imbalance if we consider that Ireland was a country Elizabeth actually reigned over while Scotland was an independent kingdom with its own monarch. The imbalance derives in part from our scholarly orientation: we are all scholars of English literature as opposed to history, and all of us had a special interest in Elizabeth herself as a writer. That orientation carries over into the present chapter, which will be far more speculative than historians will necessarily find comfortable, and will consider Ireland from within the frame of Elizabeth's perspective.

In shortchanging Ireland in our volume of *Works* we were doubtless influenced by an anachronistic view of Britain as comprising its present territories and therefore including Scotland, but not most of Tudor Ireland. We were likewise influenced by the fact that James VI of Scotland went on to become James I of England. But we were, I suspect, also motivated by a desire to present Queen Elizabeth I in a positive light. The project of editing her writings was hatched during the heyday of second-wave feminism: we wanted to show that a woman could demonstrate all the skills and savvy that were usually attributed to men, and

---

[1] Elizabeth I, *Elizabeth I: collected works*, Leah S. Marcus, Janel Mueller, and Mary Beth Rose (eds.) (Chicago, 2000). This collection was, however, highly selective. There has never been a successful attempt to collect all of Elizabeth's letters. We do not know how many letters she actually wrote or dictated about Irish affairs: it is often extremely difficult to ascertain her authorship of diplomatic letters, since scores of letters were sent out over her name and signature without being her own compositions; moreover, given the charisma of the queen's signature for Anglophiles, her signed letters have had high market value and have scattered over the centuries into private collections of autographs, where they are often almost impossible to track down.

Elizabeth was for us a prime example. We avoided Ireland, perhaps, because the story of Elizabeth in relation to Ireland is not, by and large, a success story. Most of Elizabeth's biographers – especially the more hagiographic among them – have also had disproportionately little to say about Elizabeth in Ireland.

The final years of Elizabeth's reign were the years of the Nine Years' War in Ireland. As Elizabeth lay dying in March 1603, Hugh O'Neill, the earl of Tyrone, the chief of the confederates who had fought on the Irish side, was offering his submission to her agent, Charles Blount, Lord Mountjoy. So the story of Elizabeth in Ireland has a 'happy' ending, at least from a time-bound and English point of view: after much expense of men and money, Elizabeth could die knowing that the Irish war had been won. Given the coincidence in time between the end of the war and the end of the reign, we could easily read the late Tudor experience in Ireland along an upward, Whiggish trajectory, and view earlier episodes in the history of Tudor Ireland as part of a gradual, inevitable process of colonial conquest. But that is not the way Elizabeth's relationship to Ireland looked during most of her reign, nor did the queen, for the most part, buy into the aggressive colonising policies of her 'New English' subjects. Early in the reign, her lord deputy in Ireland, Thomas Radcliffe, the earl of Sussex, complained that the queen's Irish policy was like 'Penelope's web', in that what was woven by one governor would only be picked to pieces by the next, so that there was 'mere wearisome repetition rather than progress'.[2]

At least Sussex's formulation allowed the queen a considerable degree of agency: she was the Penelope who wove and unwove her web of Irish policy to put off the suitors who clamoured outside, drinking, revelling, and consuming her estate. In 1565 in letters of instruction for Sir Henry Sidney, Elizabeth picked up the same language, but without imputing to herself the same degree of agency: 'if we still advise, we shall never do; thus are we ever knitting a knot never tied; yea, and if our web be framed with rotten hurdles, when our loom is well-nigh done, our work is new to begin'.[3] In the queen's own formulation, she in relation to Ireland is at least potentially a Penelope with a defective loom – one 'framed with rotten hurdles'; the unravelling of her policies is not within her control but instead a function of the faltering structures within which she attempts to weave and over which she has only limited control. Ireland was Elizabeth's

---

[2] SP 63/4/66, fol. 147v; and Richard Bagwell's explication of the letter in *Ireland under the Tudors*, 3 vols. (1885–90; London, 1963), vol. II, p. 33.

[3] Cited in *Letters and memorials*, vol. I, p. 8. Brady dates this letter 6 January 1566 (old style).

Afghanistan. For most of her reign, she was all too painfully aware that she had accomplished little there except the heavy loss of her subjects' lives and the expenditure of millions of pounds.

In his recent article entitled, quoting Elizabeth herself, '"Never any realm worse governed": Queen Elizabeth and Ireland', Hiram Morgan offers a highly negative assessment of Elizabeth's record, stating flatly that 'Elizabeth was not a great monarch' and going on, following the biographer Wallace MacCaffrey, to list her failures in Ireland: she pinched pennies, she had no broad vision for the realm and limited herself to short-term policies, she vacillated and temporised. Her rule 'was not about creating an empire in Ireland or elsewhere, despite many aspirations in that direction emerging from sections of the intelligentsia, gentry and merchant classes'.[4] Occasionally she did support efforts at plantation in Ireland, and I do not think it is fair to blame her for their failures. From a post-colonial perspective that identifies Ireland as the first of England's many colonial projects that ran roughshod over the rights of conquered territories in order to create the British Empire, the queen's relative lack of enthusiasm for empire-building can be seen in a much more positive light, though she never went so far as to question England's right and responsibility to rule Ireland.

Hiram Morgan's assessment echoes some of the critique of frustrated New English settlers who were looking for a Hibernian Eldorado, hoping to plant Ireland in model agricultural tracts that would take on the attributes of settled, English rural life and also reap vast wealth for the investors. Some of the would-be New English colonists advocated that the existing Irish be extirpated from the areas to be settled by the English, but Elizabeth forbade this plan and supported Irish land claims when it could be demonstrated that the claimants had not been affiliated with rebels.[5] Viewed from a posture of post-colonial critique, Elizabeth's many failures to intervene in Irish affairs with the zeal and fiscal bounty that her critics demanded can appear realistic rather than short-sighted. Arguably, her basic instinct was to practise 'benign neglect' of Ireland unless her honour was directly at stake. Quite possibly, that instinct, if she had been able to follow it consistently, would have led to less bitterness and polarisation over the long term than her sporadic attempts at forced modernisation and military intervention. As she put the matter of colonisation and conquest more generally in a 1593 speech before Parliament,

---

[4] Hiram Morgan, '"Never any realm worse governed": Queen Elizabeth and Ireland', *Transactions of the Royal Historical Society*, sixth series, 14 (2004), 295.
[5] See Michael MacCarthy-Morrogh, *The Munster plantation: English migration to southern Ireland, 1583–1641* (Oxford, 1986), pp. 27–8.

It may be thought simplicity in me that all this time of my reign [I] have not sought to advance my territories and enlarged my dominions, for both opportunity hath served me to do it, and my strength was able to have done it. I acknowledge my womanhood and weakness in that respect, but it hath not been fear to obtain or doubt how to keep the things so obtained that hath withholden me from these attempts; only my mind was never to invade my neighbors, nor to usurp upon any, only contented to reign over my own and to rule as a just prince.[6]

It is a deep historical irony that this statement of distaste for political and military conquest came on the eve of the Nine Years' War in Ireland, in which Elizabeth was forced into precisely the role of conqueror that her speech implicitly condemned.

Unlike some of her subjects, Elizabeth had a fairly well-developed ability to interpret Ireland from a culturally relativist point of view. At a time when official policy was to confine the Irish churches to using either English or Latin, Elizabeth showed an interest in Gaelic. Tony Crowley's *War of words: the politics of language in Ireland* documents English attempts to impose their language on the Irish. As Edmund Spenser (assuming that he wrote *A View of the Present State of Ireland*) put the matter, 'it hath always been the use of the conqueror to dispose the language of the conquered, and to force him by all means to learn his'.[7] For most of the New English, Irish was not a language but instead an absence of language, mere gibberish, or even a form of silence.[8] Elizabeth, however, urged that the Scriptures be translated into Gaelic and arranged for Gaelic type to be supplied towards that effort. On several occasions, she preferred Irish churchmen with some knowledge of Gaelic.[9] According to Crowley, her interest in the language prompted Christopher Nugent, Lord Delvin, to compose his *Primer of the Irish language* (1584–5).[10]

Elizabeth had some grasp of Irish culture, or at least of the fact that the Irish possessed a distinct culture as opposed to an absence of culture. She was frequently inclined to pardon Irish rebels so long as she was not 'touched in her honour' and so long as her clemency was not mistaken for weakness. This inclination, which maddened many of her

---

[6] Elizabeth I, *Works*, Marcus *et al.* (eds.), p. 329.

[7] Cited from Edmund Spenser, *A View of the Present State of Ireland* (1596), Risa S. Bear (ed.) (Eugene, OR, 1997), scholarsbank.uoregon.edu/xmlui/handle/1794/825, pt 2, p. 5; Tony Crowley, *War of words: the politics of language in Ireland 1537–2004* (London, 2005).

[8] See Patricia Palmer's enlightening study, *Language and conquest in early modern Ireland: English Renaissance literature and Elizabethan imperial expansion* (Cambridge, 2001).

[9] *Ibid.*, pp. 127–8.

[10] Crowley, *War of words*, pp. 17–18. Arguably, Patricia Palmer underplays the queen's own interest in the Irish language: according to her account, as opposed to Crowley's, Nugent wrote the primer in an 'attempt to interest Queen Elizabeth in Irish', not in response to her specific request (*Language and conquest*, pp. 80–1).

contemporaries, stemmed at least in part from her recognition that what appeared to be a total breakdown of order from the vantage point of England might instead be the usual skirmishing for hegemony on the part of Irish chieftains. After the death of Sir Ross MacMahon, chief of Monaghan, in 1589, for example, Elizabeth was inclined to pardon his brother Hugh Roe (despite his having rescued prisoners, stolen cattle, and burned houses as part of his effort to become MacMahon) on grounds that he had committed 'such march offences as are ever ordinarily committed in that realm'.[11] She was also more tolerant of Irish than of English Catholics on grounds that Catholicism was engrained in the culture. In 1586, before the Armada invasion of 1588 hardened attitudes, she declared that Protestants and Catholics of Ireland should be treated equally.[12] In this chapter, however, I will not be interested in defending Elizabeth's policies in Ireland. I will instead attempt to contextualise them by considering some of her most controversial written statements about that kingdom in light of broader motifs of her reign, especially gender, honour, and her strong sense of divine election.

Gender

Elizabeth I was a woman ruler who successfully evaded the woman's destiny of marriage and consequent dilution of her authority as monarch. The story of Elizabeth's efforts early in her reign to silence those in Parliament and elsewhere who demanded that she marry and produce an heir is a tale that has often been told and is documented in several memorable speeches. In 1566, in response to a joint delegation of Lords and Commons imploring her to marry, she upbraided them,

> though I be a woman, yet I have as good a courage answerable to my place as ever my father had. I am your anointed queen. I will never be by violence constrained to do anything. I thank God I am indeed endued with such qualifies that if I were turned out of the realm in my petticoat, I were able to live in any place of Christendom.

She went on to deny their request that she at least specify a succession, saying,

---

[11] Cited from a 19 Nov. 1589 letter from the Lords of the Council in England to Sir William Fitzwilliam, Lord Deputy of Ireland, as quoted in E. P. Shirley, *The history of the County of Monaghan* (London, 1879), p. 82. For the whole episode, see *ibid.*, pp. 80–91.

[12] Emmet O'Byrne, *War, politics, and the Irish of Leinster, 1156–1606* (Dublin, 2003), p. 211.

as soon as there may be a convenient time and that it may be done with least peril unto you, although never without great danger unto me, I will deal therein for your safety and offer it unto you as your prince and head, without request. For it is monstrous that the feet should direct the head.[13]

This vehement language disappears after the 1560s, except in cases of unusual crisis, as in Elizabeth's Armada speech of 1588, in which she famously claimed 'I know I have the body but of a weak and feeble woman, but I have the heart and stomach of a king and of a king of England too.'[14] But, arguably, no sooner had she silenced the most vocal of protests by her English subjects about her incapacity for rule than her Irish subjects took up the chorus. Particularly after the 1570 papal bull excommunicating Elizabeth and relieving her Catholic subjects, whether English or Irish, from the duty of obeying her as head of the English church, the Irish protested her sovereignty on grounds that as a woman she was 'uncapax of all holy orders'. A proclamation by rebel James Fitzmaurice Fitzgerald in 1578 called her 'a she-tyrant who has deservedly lost her royal power by refusing to listen to Christ in the person of his vicar, and through daring to subject Christ's Church to her feminine sex on matters of faith, about which she has no right to speak'. The papal nuncio, Nicholas Sander, attacked her in similar terms, arguing that her childlessness was a divine judgement upon Henry VIII and his race for their apostasy and specifying that female rule was a continuation of the misrule practised in Eden when Eve mastered Adam.[15] It was held in Ireland that she could be a sorceress: she was commonly called 'Caliaghe' (*cailleach*), a word that literally meant only 'old woman' or 'hag', but also carried cultural associations with magic. In 1585, rebel members of the Burke sept were quoted as saying, 'What have we to do with that Caliaghe? How unwise are we, being so mighty a nation, to have been so long subject to a woman. The Pope and the King of Spain shall have the rule of us, and none other.'[16]

The issues in Ireland in the 1570s and afterwards were somewhat different from the issues of marriage and succession in England in the 1560s in that the Irish were always at least as outraged by Elizabeth's Protestantism as by her gender. But the misogyny was quite familiar. And the Irish confederates allied against Elizabeth in the 1590s used very similar language. When they petitioned Philip II of Spain to provide them with a new ruler, it hardly needs to be stated, that ruler was specified as

[13] Elizabeth I, *Works*, Marcus *et al.* (eds.), pp. 97–8.   [14] *Ibid.*, p. 326.

[15] Bagwell, *Ireland under the Tudors*, vol. III, pp. 51–2, 16, 18.

[16] LPL, Carew MS 692, p. 15v. See also Natalie Mears, *Queenship and political discourse in the Elizabethan realms* (Cambridge, 2005), pp. 241–3.

male: 'a man who is completely honourable and gifted, for Your Majesty's own benefit and that of the commonwealth of Ireland, a man who will not in the least disdain to rule over us, but also to be among us and to rule and advise our people with kindness and wisdom'.[17] It was not only in terms of her role as head of the established church that Elizabeth was disqualified for Irish rule. The Anglo-Norman law passed down among the Old English in Ireland from its Norman French conqueror, King Henry II, was closer to Brehon and Salic law than to English law in its view of female inheritance.[18] If the laws pertaining to individual inheritance were extrapolated to the kingdom of Ireland as a whole, female inheritance of the crown was illegal so long as there was any living male relative capable of assuming the inheritance.

Persistent myths of Elizabeth's reign had a way of turning ominous if mapped on to the political discord in Ireland. Elizabeth liked to refer to herself as a nurse-mother to her subjects – in one of her published devotions, for example, she called herself a 'true nourisher and nurse' of her people,[19] and her English subjects picked up the language in panegyric and imaginative literature.[20] But in Ireland the image of the nurse was tarnished by the prevalence of Irish nurses in Old English households: at least according to New English observers, the employment of Gaelic nurses was a primary cause of the decline and increasing hostility of the Old English settlers towards Elizabeth's government, since it was popularly believed that milk was refined blood, capable of transmitting family characteristics, so that a nurseling would absorb morals and customs along with the milk of its nurse.[21] As Spenser put the matter in his *View of the Present State of Ireland*, '[T]he chief cause of bringing in the Irish language amongst them was specially their fostering and marrying with the Irish, which are two most dangerous infections; for first the child that

---

[17] Cited from a letter preserved in the Spanish archives from Irish confederates O'Neill and O'Donnell to Philip II of Spain in Hiram Morgan, *Tyrone's rebellion: the outbreak of the Nine Years War in Tudor Ireland* (Woodbridge, UK, 1993), p. 210. See also Mears, *Queenship*, pp. 222–46.

[18] Steven G. Ellis, *Tudor Ireland: crown, community and the conflict of cultures, 1470–1603* (London, 1985), pp. 41, 103–4. See also K. W. Nicholls, 'Irishwomen and property in the sixteenth century', in Margaret MacCurtain and Mary O'Dowd (eds.), *Women in early modern Ireland* (Edinburgh, 1991), pp. 17–31; Joseph R. Peden, 'Property rights in Celtic Irish law', *Journal of Libertarian Studies* 1 (1977), 81–95, esp. 91–3; Fergus Kelly, *A guide to early Irish law* (Dublin, 1988; 1995, reprint); Andrew Lyall, *Land law in Ireland* (Dublin, 1994); and Christine Kinealy, *A new history of Ireland* (Stroud, UK, 2004), pp. 72–3.

[19] Elizabeth I, *Works*, Marcus et al. (eds.), p. 149.

[20] See, for example, Michelle Ephraim, 'Jewish matriarchs and the staging of Elizabeth I in *The History of Jacob and Esau*', *Studies in English Literature 1500–1900* 43 (2003), 301–21.

[21] On mother's milk as refined blood, see Leah S. Marcus, *Childhood and cultural despair: a theme and variations in seventeenth-century literature* (Pittsburgh, 1978), p. 144.

sucketh the milk of the nurse must of necessity learn his first speech of her' along with her 'manners and conditions' with the result that 'the speech being Irish, the heart must needs be Irish'.[22]

Of course it would be possible, from an Irish perspective, to interpret the queen as offering herself as a pure and healthy 'nurse mother' to be substituted in imaginative terms for the corrupting Gaelic nurses. But it would be equally possible to regard the queen's language as itself devalued simply by the pervasiveness and rancor of the controversy over English–Irish mixing in the nursing of children. To the extent that her image as 'nourisher and nurse' of her people was projected on to Ireland, the queen could be imagined as fostering the very mingling of English and Irish blood that a long line of English laws had attempted to prevent. One of the most visible of Elizabeth's symbolic Irish nurselings was Hugh O'Neill, the earl of Tyrone, who frequently called himself 'a ward of your majesty' and 'raised from nothing by Her Majesty', but who went on to be the chief among confederates in the Nine Years' War.[23] Late in the war, possibly continuing the nurse metaphor, Elizabeth termed O'Neill 'the most ungrateful viper to us that raised him' – instead of a docile nurseling, a viper at her breast.[24]

Similarly, Elizabeth liked to describe herself as married to her realm, as in her 1561 conversations with the Scottish ambassador, William Maitland, laird of Lethington: 'I am married already to the realm of England when I was crowned with this ring, which I bear continually in token thereof.'[25] But by bardic tradition Ireland was traditionally portrayed as a woman, even a mythic goddess figure, who offered the crown to the king along with her body in marriage. As Natalie Mears points out, Irish bards, even when they were praising Elizabeth, never referred to her as queen of Ireland but only as queen of England, though later poems felt no compunction about referring to James I as king of Ireland.[26] This curious omission could be based in part on the fact that James I, unlike Elizabeth, claimed descent via the kings of Scotland from the ancient kings of Ireland, but it is based just as strongly in the traditional gendering of Ireland, by which the ruler could not be a woman without creating what would then have appeared an anomaly – a same-sex marriage in the imagined union of Ireland and her monarch.[27]

---

[22] Spenser, *View*, pt 2, pp. 5–6.   [23] Morgan, *Tyrone's rebellion*, pp. 93–4.

[24] Cited from Elizabeth I's letter to Charles Blount, Lord Montjoy (31 Oct. 1602), in Fynes Moryson, *An History of Ireland from the Year 1599, to 1603* (Dublin, 1735), vol. II, p. 225.

[25] Elizabeth I, *Works*, Marcus *et al.* (eds.), p. 65.   [26] Mears, *Queenship*, p. 207.

[27] In addition to the discussion in Mears, see Breandán Ó Buachalla, 'Poetry and politics in early modern Ireland', *Eighteenth-Century Ireland* 7 (1992), 149–75, esp. 163–5; Bart Jaski, *Early Irish kingship and succession* (Dublin, 2000), pp. 57–72; and James M. Smith,

Then too, intermarriage between English settlers and the Gaelic Irish, though it did occur in practice, had been illegal from the Statutes of Kilkenny (1366) until 1541, when Henry VIII assumed direct rule over Ireland. It continued to be discouraged by English officials under Elizabeth because it tended to Irishise the English rather than the reverse.[28] Spenser complained in the *View* that an Englishman marrying an Irish woman would inevitably 'bring forth an evil race, seeing that commonly the child taketh most of his nature of his mother'.[29] The very language of Elizabeth's expression of loving unity with her people, in so far as it was applied to her Gaelic subjects, could be interpreted as violating cultural taboo: if she was married to the Irish she was, on the level of public perceptions about myths of her rule, practising miscegenation by violating English prejudice against the mixing of English and Irish blood in Ireland. The queen's self-portrayal as married to her people served to create an emotional bond with her English subjects at least some of the time, but there was no way that the same rhetorical gesture of loving union could work in an uncomplicated way in Ireland. It would be fair to say that Elizabeth never managed to develop a set of publicly projected gender positions for herself that endeared her to the Irish in the same way that her various self-depictions as wife or nurse often endeared her to the English.

In England, Elizabeth had considerable ability to control her unruly subjects through her personal magnetism and sheer force of will. But in Ireland she was a distant figure, and her authority even over her own deputies, let alone her Old English or Gaelic subjects, was arguably more tenuous because of her gender. As Morgan acknowledges, 'If having to govern through men was one of the problems of female monarchy, having to govern an overseas territory through a succession of ambitious, macho proxies was an even greater undertaking.'[30] One of the few compensations for service in Ireland was freedom from direct servitude to a woman. Morgan contends, quite plausibly, that a central reason for Elizabeth's unwillingness to rescue her deputy Sir John Perrot from treason charges concocted against him by Lord Burghley and others in 1588 was

---

'Effaced history: facing the colonial contexts of Ben Jonson's "Irish Masque at Court"', *English Literary History* 65 (1998), 297–321.

[28] See Jane Ohlmeyer, *Making Ireland English: the Irish aristocracy in the seventeenth century* (New Haven, 2012), p. 6; and Brendan Bradshaw, *The Irish constitutional revolution of the sixteenth century* (Cambridge, 1979), pp. 266–81. As Bradshaw points out, the terms by which Henry VIII became king of Ireland implied that all the Irish 'as members of the kingdom... could claim the protection and privileges of subjects under the law', including intermarriage (p. 266).

[29] Spenser, *View*, pt 2, p. 6.   [30] Morgan, '"Never any realm worse governed"', 298.

that some of her courtiers shared with the queen Perrot's reaction to one of her orders: 'Stick not so much upon her Majesty's letter, she will command what she will but we will do what we list... Ah now silly woman, now she will now curb me, she shall not rule me now... God's wounds, thus is to serve a base bastard piss-kitchen woman; if I had served any prince in Christendom, I had not been so dealt withal.'[31] Similarly, much of Elizabeth's rage and helplessness over the earl of Essex's insubordination as her deputy in the Irish wars during the late 1590s surely arose from her observation that once her favourite had crossed the seas to Ireland he acted with reckless autonomy and became deaf to her commands. Her godson, Sir John Harington, reported that, when the earl of Essex returned suddenly from Ireland without her permission in September 1599, Harington found the queen in a state of enraged disapproval: 'She chafed much, walked fastly to and fro, looked with discomposure in her visage; and I remember, she catched my girdle when I kneeled to her, and swore, "By God's Son, I am no Queen, that MAN is above me! – Who gave him command to come here so soon? I did send him on other business."'[32]

Honour

As Brendan Kane has shown in his recent book on *The Politics and Culture of Honour in Britain and Ireland*, the repeated Tudor protests about royal honour in relation to Ireland were far more than empty language.[33] In 1540, when Henry VIII's advisers tried to convince him to recast Ulster from a lordship into a kingdom in its own right, Henry initially resisted the change on grounds that it would be detrimental to his honour. He worried over 'whether it be either honour or wisdom for Us to (take) upon Us that title of a King, and not to have revenues there, sufficient to maintain the state of the same' and 'what dishonour it may be to Us' should he now give royal Irish lands and English aristocratic titles for purposes of pacification to Irish chieftains, in effect ceding 'our own inheritance to those which have unjustly intruded and usurped the same'.[34] If the Irish refused to become obedient subjects as a result of the new policy of surrender and regrant, by which they were to cede their Irish titles in

---

[31] Cited *ibid.*, 302, from Morgan's earlier 'The fall of Sir John Perrot', in John Guy (ed.), *The reign of Elizabeth I: court and culture in the last decade* (Cambridge, 1995), p. 121.

[32] Sir John Harington, *Nugae Antiquae*, Henry Harington (ed.), 3 vols. (1779; Hildersheim, 1968, reprint), vol. II, p. 134.

[33] Brendan Kane, *The politics and culture of honour in Britain and Ireland, 1541–1641* (Cambridge, 2010).

[34] Cited *ibid.*, p. 3.

favour of English ones, Henry would be shamed in the eyes of the world. As a ruler of the kingdom of Ireland, which he was from 1541 onwards, he was much more vulnerable to challenges to his honour than had he remained a mere 'lord' of Ireland, because every act of rebellion was now, in a manner of speaking, a wound to his 'body politic'.

Elizabeth I was arguably even more vulnerable to Irish denigrations of her honour if only because of her status as a self-declared virgin queen. Throughout her life, she made the most of her descent from the powerful Henry VIII. She resembled him in appearance, in personal charm, and in the range of her talents, and she made a point of associating herself with him. During the reign of Mary Tudor, court observers noted of Elizabeth, 'She prides herself on her father and glories in him; everybody saying that she also resembles him more than the queen does.'[35] As monarch, Elizabeth made a habit of standing proudly in front of a full-length portrait of her father, as though encouraging her subjects to see her father in her. On one bizarre occasion she was reported to have asked Richard Topcliffe, 'Be not these the arms, legs, and body of King Henry?' to which he diplomatically answered 'Yea.'[36]

For Sir John Harington, Elizabeth's rage at Essex on his return from Ireland 'left no doubtings whose daughter she was'.[37] Occasionally, she invoked her father's rigour as a way of emphasising her relative mildness despite her capacity for more draconian measures. In a 1573 letter to Sir William Fitzwilliam and the council of Ireland, for example, she reproved Fitzwilliam and the council for pardoning one of Fitzwilliam's adherents who had committed a murder:

If this had been in our father's time – who removed a deputy thence for calling of one of the Council dissenting from his opinion, 'Churl'– you may soon conceive how it would have been taken. Our moderate reign and government can be contented to bear this, so you will take this for a warning, and hereafter have before your eyes not the will or pleasure of our deputy or any other councillor, but first God's honor and then justice and our service.[38]

---

[35] *Calendar of state papers and manuscripts relating to English affairs, existing in the archives and collections of Venice, and in other libraries of northern Italy*, G. C. Bentinck *et al.* (eds.), 38 vols. (London, 1864–1947), vol. VI, 2, p. 1059. See also Leah S. Marcus, 'Erasing the stigma of daughterhood: Mary I, Elizabeth I, and Henry VIII', in Lynda Boose and Betty S. Flowers (eds.), *Daughters and fathers* (Baltimore, 1989), pp. 400–17.

[36] The episode, reported at second hand from Father Thomas Portmort, one of Topcliffe's Catholic prisoners, may well be apocryphal, but at the very least it is a record of popular perceptions (cited from a letter of Richard Verstegan (*c.* 1592) in *The letters and despatches of Richard Verstegan (c. 1550–1640)*, Anthony G. Petti (ed.) (London, 1959), p. 97).

[37] Harington, *Nugae Antiquae*, vol. II, pp. 78–9.

[38] Elizabeth I, *Works*, Marcus *et al.* (eds.), p. 220.

Increasingly over the decades, in her speeches and proclamations Elizabeth I associated her rule with male as opposed to female epithets: she was a 'prince' or even, as in the Armada speech, a ruler with the 'heart and stomach of a king'. In her 'Golden Speech' of 1601, she referred to her 'kingly dignity' and repeatedly called herself a 'king' – not so much her father's daughter as her father's son.[39] By this late point in the reign, her English subjects were accustomed to her androgynous language of rule and had by and large assimilated its message, noting that in her 'Stately and Majestic comportment' she carried 'more of her Father than Mother' and that she had 'too stately a stomach to suffer a commander'; she was 'king and queen both'.[40]

In parallel with the development of these male epithets for rule, however, Elizabeth retained and elaborated her early public self-definition as a virgin queen. Peter Stallybrass has shown how her rhetoric associated her personal physical intactness, and the power of virginity in general, with the invulnerability of the isle of Britain (Scotland, which was a separate kingdom, excepted): as the queen was defined as permanently impervious to sexual conquest, so the island nation was immune to invasion. This connection between the queen's physical body and the impregnable geographical body of Britain was cause for particular celebration after the Armada victory of 1588, in which the would-be Spanish invaders were repelled as though by supernatural intervention. In the Ditchley portrait (c. 1592), the queen reifies the connection between the land and her royal person by standing upon a map of England and facing a fair-weather sky, with the clouds of war banished behind her.[41]

The political fiction of a connection between the intact virginity of the queen and the impregnability of the realm was plausible enough to be credible in England, particularly if one discounted the frequent 'violating' incursions by the Scots across the northern border. But the fiction carried little credibility if extended to the queen's body of Ireland. In the aftermath of the Armada, Spanish forces were washed up on Irish beaches by the thousands, and a few of them ended up fighting for rebel Irish chieftains. After 1588 there were repeated threats of Spanish armadas destined for Ireland, culminating in Philip III's actual landing

---

[39] *Ibid.*, p. 339.

[40] Cited from Paul Johnson, *Elizabeth I: a biography* (New York, 1974), p. 111; and Sir Robert Naunton, *Fragmenta regalia*, Edward Arber (ed.) (1870; New York, 1966, reprint), p. 15. See also Marcus, 'Shakespeare's comic heroines, Queen Elizabeth I, and the political uses of androgyny', in Mary Beth Rose (ed.), *Women in the Middle Ages and the Renaissance: literary and historical perspectives* (Syracuse, NY, 1985), pp. 135–53.

[41] Peter Stallybrass, 'Patriarchal territories: the body enclosed', in Margaret W. Ferguson, Maureen Quilligan, and Nancy J. Vickers (eds.) *Rewriting the Renaissance: the discourse of sexual difference in early modern Europe* (Chicago, 1986), pp. 123–42.

of more than 3,000 men at Kinsale in 1601.[42] As it happened, neither the actual invasion nor the persistent rumours of other possible armadas to Ireland amounted to a significant military threat, but they were always unnerving and very damaging to Elizabeth's honour because they not only demonstrated her incapacity to keep order in her kingdom of Ireland but also violated, on the level of cultural imaginary, her proud reputation for a 'virginal' political intactness.

As Carole Levin has shown, even in England there were frequent, if largely surreptitious, rumours about the queen's sexual dalliances and even secret pregnancies and births.[43] But in Ireland the queen was called 'sorceress' and 'old hag' (*cailleach*) relatively openly by those who opposed her rule. Irish opponents set up images if the queen in order to show their contempt. In 1586, for example, Brian O'Rourke obtained a wooden portrait of a woman with a pin in her belly, labelled it 'Queen Elizabeth', railed against it, and had his galloglasses dishonour it in specifically sexual terms: 'stroak [or possibly *struck*] it in all the parts with their weapons'.[44] Many such episodes, as Mears argues, were not so much anti-woman as anti-Protestant. Still, Elizabeth's much-praised sexual intactness made such symbolic violations particularly satisfying for rebels who wished to dishonour her. When it came to Ireland, Elizabeth I was not so much a virgin queen as a leaky vessel easily breached and assaulted. Her projected regal identity in Ireland was dishonoured in specifically sex-linked ways by her inability to keep order and secure the realm.

Divine election

One of Elizabeth's persistent strategies in accounting for her political and military successes was to turn the tables on the various strains of gender rhetoric I have examined thus far and portray herself as indeed *uncapax* as a mere woman, but then go on to argue that her very weakness was a testimony to God's working through her to accomplish his will. This language is pervasive in Elizabeth's published devotions, where she habitually refers to herself as God's 'handmaid',[45] and also in her speeches. In her Golden Speech, for example, she protested, after referring to some of

---

[42] See William Palmer, *The problem of Ireland in Tudor foreign policy, 1485–1603* (Woodbridge, UK, 1994), pp. 120–38.

[43] Carole Levin, 'Queens and claimants: political insecurity in sixteenth-century England', in Janet Sharistanian (ed.), *Gender, ideology, and action: historical perspectives on women's public lives* (New York, 1986), pp. 41–66.

[44] Mears, *Queenship*, p. 243.

[45] For examples, see Elizabeth I, *Works*, Marcus et al. (eds.), pp. 136, 138–9.

the successes of her reign, 'Shall I ascribe anything to myself and my sexly weakness? I were not worthy to live then, and of all most unworthy of the mercies I have had from God.'[46] Writing during the reign of James I, Sir John Davies echoed Elizabeth's habitual rhetoric. Asking how it could be that Elizabeth had succeeded in subduing Ireland while many kings before her had failed, Davies asked, 'who can tell whether the Divine Wisdom, to abate the glory of those kings, did not reserve this work to be done by a queen, that it might rather appear to be His own immediate work?'[47]

Similar language surfaces in Elizabeth's own composition, her 'Song on the Armada Victory', which credits God with the miraculous defeat of the Spaniards and calls upon him:

> Look and bow down Thine ear, O Lord.
> From Thy bright sphere behold and see
> Thy handmaid and Thy handiwork,
> Amongst Thy priests, offering to Thee
> Zeal for incense, reaching the skies;
> Myself and scepter, sacrifice.[48]

Why does she term her victory a sacrifice? As I have argued elsewhere, Elizabeth viewed the death of her favourite, the earl of Leicester, in the summer of 1588 as the price she personally had to pay for victory over Spain. Contemporaries noted that few in England mourned the loss of Leicester. While the rest of the nation celebrated her glorious achievement in defeating the Armada, the queen herself kept in isolation and grieved.[49] In the queen's 'Song' she herself is the national Hebraic 'sacrifice' demanded by God in return for the Armada victory in that she alone has been stricken by the loss of Leicester, with whom she had been on intimate terms since her youth.

We do not have the queen's own verses to confirm the idea, but I would argue that Elizabeth similarly viewed the loss of her later favourite, the earl of Essex – who was undone by his escapades in Ireland, led by desperation into open rebellion against the queen, and executed in 1601 – as the personal price she had to pay for her victory over the Irish confederates in the Nine Years' War. The year that commenced with

---

[46] *Ibid.*, p. 340.

[47] Sir John Davies, *A discovery of the true causes why Ireland was never entirely subdued and brought under the obedience of the crown of England until the beginning of His Majesty's happy reign* (1612), James P. Myers Jnr (ed.) (Washington, DC, 1988), p. 110.

[48] Elizabeth I, *Works*, Marcus et al. (eds.), pp. 410–11.

[49] See Leah S. Marcus, 'Elizabeth on Elizabeth: underexamined episodes in an overexamined life', in Kevin Sharpe and Steven N. Zwicker (eds.) *Writing lives: biography and textuality, identity and representation in early modern England* (Oxford, 2008), pp. 209–32.

the execution of Essex was the year in which the Irish war began to turn decisively in England's favour. Though she acquiesced in Essex's execution, she mourned his loss as she had earlier mourned Leicester, but arguably with a greater sense of personal guilt since Essex was executed by her warrant whereas Leicester had died of natural causes. The French ambassador reported that she frequently expressed 'sighs and tears in her eyes' on the subject of the earl of Essex's death. A correspondent of one of James VI's courtiers reported from London, 'Our queen is troubled with a rheum in her arm, which vexeth her very much, besides the grief she hath conceived for my lord of Essex's death. She sleepeth not so much by days [as] she used, neither taketh rest by night. Her delight is to sit in the dark, and sometimes with shedding tears to bewail Essex.'[50] Modern biographers have tended to distrust this evidence, as coming from foreign sources, but the queen's godson Sir John Harington is considerably more vivid on the topic of Elizabeth's state of mind after Essex's death. Even in 1602, Harington reported, the queen was still tormented by it:

It was not many days since I was bidden to her presence; I blest the happy moment and found her in most pitiable state. She bade the archbishop ask me if I had seen Tyrone. I replied with reverence that I had seen him with the Lord Deputy. She looked up with much choler and grief in her countenance and said, 'Oh, now it mindeth me that *you* was *one* who saw this man *elsewhere*' [i.e., Harington was one of the troops who had accompanied Essex to Ireland], and hereat she dropped a tear and smote her bosom . . . This sight moved me to think on what passed in Ireland, and I trust she did not less think on *some* who were busier there than myself.[51]

By the '*some*' who had been busy in Ireland Harington of course meant Essex. It is not only that Elizabeth was still in mourning for him only months before her own death: she was smiting her bosom – beating her breast – which suggests guilt as well as grief. Once more, we can speculate, she perceived herself as making a huge personal sacrifice for the good of the nation. The death and disgrace of her favourite Essex were the price of her victory in Ireland.

Returning to our topic of the queen's habitual association of victory with self-abnegation, we will note that she used the same rhetoric, albeit much more notoriously, in her personal headnote to a letter of 12 December 1580 during the Desmond wars, congratulating Arthur Lord Grey de Wilton on his slaughter of Irish forces after his victory over the garrison at

---

[50] Cited from contemporary letters recorded in Thomas Birch (ed.), *Memoirs of the reign of Queen Elizabeth*, 2 vols. (London, 1754), vol. II, pp. 505–7.

[51] Harington, *Nugae Antiquae*, vol. II, pp. 77–8.

Smerwick: 'The mighty hand of the Almighty's power hath showed manifest the force of his strength in the weakness of feeblest sex and minds this year to make men ashamed ever after to disdain us, in which action I joy that you have been chose the instrument of his glory which I mean to give you no cause to forethink.'[52] There were some 600 foreign forces slaughtered that day, and it is likely that the garrison had surrendered before the massacre. Perhaps the queen sent her words of exultation to Grey before she fully understood the circumstances of the bloodshed. Or perhaps this is one of the occasions on which we can see how ruthless Elizabeth, like her father Henry VIII, was willing to be when 'touched in her honour' and convinced of the rightness of her cause as the instrument of God.[53]

Beginning at least as early as 1588, Elizabeth developed a practice of composing and uttering public prayers to celebrate military victory. There are at least two public prayers associated with the Armada victory in addition to a third prayer that may have been more private.[54] The first of these is grandly headed in Sir Thomas Egerton's copy 'A godly prayer and thanksgiving worthy the Christian Deborah and Theodosia of our days'. It praises God for deploying all four of the elements against the Spanish ships to 'daunt our foes and confound their malice'; it includes the expected gesture of sexual self-abnegation in the furtherance of divine plan: 'I most humbly, with bowed heart and bended knees, do render my humblest acknowledgments and lowliest thanks; and not the least for that the weakest sex hath been so fortified by Thy strongest help that neither my people might find lack by my weakness nor foreigners triumph at my ruin.'[55] The second Armada prayer takes the shape of a poem, the first stanza of which was briefly discussed above; the other two stanzas go on to praise the 'wonders in my days' performed by God by means of wind and water that 'scatter[ed] all mine enemies' just as he guarded the ancient Israelites during the Exodus by a 'fiery Pillar and day's Cloud'. This poem or 'Song' was, according to the antiquarian Sir Henry Spelman's copy, incorporated into London's public celebration of the Armada victory: 'made by her majesty and sung before her at her coming from Whitehall to Paul's [Cathedral] through Fleet Street in Anno Domini 1588'.[56]

As Elizabeth's sense of divine mission grew after the Armada victory, she began to compose her own prayers to call down divine blessing upon

---

[52] SP 63/79/13.

[53] See Vincent P. Carey, 'Atrocity and history: Grey, Spenser and the slaughter at Smerwick (1580)', in David Edwards, Pádraig Lenihan, and Clodagh Tait (eds.), *Age of atrocity: violence and political conflict in early modern Ireland* (Dublin, 2007), pp. 79–94.

[54] Elizabeth I, *Works*, Marcus et al. (eds.), pp. 423–4, 410–11.

[55] *Ibid.*, p. 424.   [56] *Ibid.*, pp. 410–11.

her forces as they departed into combat. We have several copies of a prayer made by Elizabeth on the eve of the Cadiz expedition in 1596. One copy is headed 'A prayer made by her majesty herself on the behalf of her army sent into Spain under the conduct of the right honourable Robert, earl of Essex, and th'earls Lord Howard, lord high admiral of England, and lords generally of the same'. This prayer, significantly, does not refer to Elizabeth's 'weakest sex' but concentrates on articulating the purpose of the expedition – not 'malice of revenge nor quittance of injury, nor desire of bloodshed, nor greediness of lucre hath bred the resolution of our now-set-out army, but a heedful care and wary watch that no neglect of foes nor our surety of harm might breed either harm to us or glory to them'.[57] A copy of the prayer was sent to Essex the night before his departure for Cadiz; copies were also distributed to the fleet, and the prayer was issued in a printed version for use in parish churches. All of the publicity paid off. No doubt Elizabeth considered the prayer to have been efficacious, for the Cadiz expedition was very successful.

But the winning combination of Essex, Elizabeth, and God failed the next year. The queen composed and issued a similar public prayer on the sailing of the Azores expedition of 1597, also commanded by Essex, in which she called upon God to grant victory: 'So shall Thy name be spread for wonders wrought; and the faithful encouraged to repose in Thy unfellowed grace.'[58] The Azores expedition foundered and Elizabeth ordered the Cadiz prayer removed from a printed collection of prayers being assembled by Archbishop John Whitgift.[59] She was learning, finally, that God was not always on her side to exalt the 'weakest sex' to victory over the strongest.

So far as I know, Elizabeth herself wrote no public prayers associated with Essex's expedition to Ireland in 1599 – just a long series of adamant and largely futile letters protesting the earl's 'blemish[ing] of our honour'.[60] In a letter dated 19 July, Elizabeth complains to Essex,

We will add this one thing that doth more displease us than any charge or expense that happens: which is that it must be the queen of England's fortune (who hath holden down the greatest enemy she had) to make a base bush kern to be accounted so famous a rebel as to be a person against whom so many thousands

---

[57] *Ibid.*, pp. 425–6.   [58] *Ibid.*, p. 427.

[59] See Tucher Brooke, 'Queen Elizabeth's prayers', *Huntington Library Quarterly* 2 (1938), 69–77; and a letter from Cecil to Whitgift (11 Jul. 1597) in LPL, MS Fairhurst 3740, fol. 195.

[60] Elizabeth I, *Works*, Marcus *et al.* (eds.), p. 397. The government did issue a public prayer for Essex's expedition, 'A Prayer for the good successe of her Maiesties forces *in Ireland*' (London, 1599; STC 16530), but this prayer refers to the queen in the third person and shows no sign of Elizabeth's authorship.

of foot and horse, besides the force of all the nobility of that kingdom, must be thought too little to be employed.

The 'base bush kern' is no doubt Hugh O'Neill, the earl of Tyrone, whom later in the letter she calls 'a wretch whom we have raised from the dust', in reference to her managing of his wardship.[61] How was it possible that she could destroy a whole Armada and be foiled by a mere Irish ruffian? The closest thing to a prayer that we have in relation to the Irish expeditions to suppress the Nine Years' War is Elizabeth's famous 'Kitchenmaid' letter of 3 December 1600, to Essex's much abler successor, Charles Blount, Lord Mountjoy.

According to Richard Bagwell, who was writing in the late nineteenth century, there are a number of Kitchenmaid letters, presumably all addressed from the queen to Mountjoy as 'mistress Kitchenmaid'.[62] Only one of these letters made it into the Carew papers now at Lambeth Palace Library, and to my severe frustration I have not managed to locate the rest, though one of the letters Bagwell had in mind may have been Elizabeth's later letter to Mountjoy dated 15 July 1602 and reproduced by Fynes Moryson. This missive included a postscript in Elizabeth's hand praising Mountjoy's continuing success in cleaning up Tyrone's routed troops as the acts of 'a Queen's kitchen-maid' and 'a Traitor's scullion'.[63]

What set off the series of Kitchenmaid letters was a letter by Mountjoy stating with dark wit that he had been spending quite some time in Tyrone's kitchen, which he meant to warm so well that Tyrone 'should keep the worse fires ever after' – that is, lack the materials required to cook anything because of his utter military defeat.[64] In what is almost certainly the first letter of the series, Elizabeth responded to Mountjoy, memorably and humorously,

> Mistress Kitchenmaid,
>
> I had not thought that precedency had been ever in question but among the higher and greater sort; but now I find by good proof that some of more dignity and greater calling may by good desert and faithful care give the upper hand to one of your faculty, that with your frying pan and other kitchen stuff have brought to their last home more rebels, and passed greater breakneck places than those that promised more and did less. Comfort yourself, therefore, in this: that neither your careful

---

[61] Elizabeth I, *Works*, Marcus *et al.* (eds.), pp. 391–3.
[62] Bagwell, *Ireland under the Tudors*, vol. III, p. 387 n. 1.
[63] Moryson, *An History*, vol. II, p. 178.   [64] *Ibid.*, p. 181.

endeavors, nor dangerous travails, nor heedful regards to our service, without your own by-respects, could ever have been bestowed upon a prince that more esteems them, considers and regards them, than she for whom chiefly, I know, all this hath been done, and who keeps his verdict ever in store for you – that no vainglory nor popular fawning can ever advance you forward, but true vow of duty and reverence of prince, which two afore your life I see you do prefer.[65]

In his earlier letter, as noted above, Mountjoy had borrowed a tactic from Elizabeth by reducing his warfare in Ireland to the menial task of warming up Tyrone's kitchen, much as the queen in her earlier devotions had termed herself the mere 'handmaid' of God, or in one of her speeches expressed the desire to be a simple milkmaid.[66] Elizabeth's Kitchenmaid letter to Mountjoy plays upon the *deposuit potentes et exaltavit humiles* theme that in her prayers and meditations she had so often articulated in relation to herself and the divine favour poured out upon her 'sexly weakness' as a simple servant of the Lord. Mountjoy also reverses the earlier insult of Sir John Perrot, who had fatally called Elizabeth a 'base bastard piss-kitchen woman', by taking that role upon himself. Elizabeth's letter implicitly contrasts the dutiful Mountjoy with the 'fawning' Essex, who had promised much and delivered little. Finally her wounded honour in Ireland was being restored, and by one who was willing to abject himself before her and carry out her orders rather than by one who refused to honour her wishes once he was out of her reach.

Elizabeth's Kitchenmaid letter also refers, via macabre indirection, to Mountjoy's successful military tactic of burning crops (which he himself had referred to as warming Tyrone's kitchen) and thereby depriving the Irish of food: the commander is not a kitchenmaid who prepares food as she rattles her 'frying pan and other kitchen stuff', but a kitchenmaid who denies food and starves rebels into submission. There may also be a reference to the Irish custom of 'kitchen fosterage' – an explicitly political form of fosterage by which not only a single child but the child's whole family was taken under the wing and fostered by another to create a web of strong alliances.[67] Ironically, Mountjoy's version of 'kitchen fosterage' works to cement loyalty by denying sustenance to a dependent group rather than by nurturing it. But the result, Elizabeth exults, is the same: rebels reduced to obedient subjects and royal honour restored.

---

[65] Elizabeth I, *Works*, Marcus *et al.* (eds.), pp. 399–400.   [66] *Ibid.*, p. 188.

[67] See Fiona Fitzsimons, 'Fosterage and gossiprid in late medieval Ireland: some new evidence', in Patrick J. Duffy, David Edwards, and Elizabeth FitzPatrick (eds.), *Gaelic Ireland* c. *1250*–c. *1650: land, lordship and settlement* (Dublin, 2001), pp. 138–49.

It is, I suppose, possible to imagine that the queen died happy, at least in relation to Ireland, in that she died confident that the long, costly drama of subduing the Irish was at last coming to a close. But, as I have tried to argue, it was only the most extreme version of Elizabeth as vehicle of divine retribution that could reduce the starvation of thousands of her subjects to the playful antics of a transgendered epistolary Kitchenmaid. Even as she playfully praised Mountjoy for his successes, she was privately mourning Essex: her exultation fuelled her sense of guilt and loss. The price of victory was, for her personally, extraordinarily high. And, despite her success at the very end of her life, her record in Ireland over the course of the reign was largely a chronicle of failure and frustration. For all her occasional fulminations against Irish rebels, her inability to rule successfully in Ireland stemmed from unwillingness to commit fully to tactics as ruthless as Mountjoy's – tactics that amounted at times to the cultural eradication long advocated by the New English in Ireland but that had usually been discouraged by Elizabeth herself. We know the long and fateful history that followed upon the victory of Mistress Kitchenmaid over Tyrone and the confederates. We can only speculate as to the altered history that might have been if Elizabeth had had less to celebrate in the end.

4 A bardic critique of queen and court: 'Ionmholta malairt bhisigh', Eochaidh Ó hEodhasa, 1603

Peter McQuillan

This chapter will look closely at a poem composed in the immediate aftermath of the Irish defeat in the Nine Years' War (1595–1603) by a member of the class of Irish hereditary professional poets, whose productions dominate the Irish literary scene between the thirteenth and early seventeenth centuries. The poem was written at a time of great national uncertainty but the poet deftly juxtaposes aesthetic, cultural, and political issues in order to position himself in relation to them. This is not particularly surprising given the symbiotic relationship between praise poetry and the political realities of lordship in Gaelic Ireland, but I will argue that the poet adapts this to his own particular purposes, and I will suggest not just an Irish, but also a European context for this. Explicit reference in the bardic corpus to Elizabeth I is, of course, extremely rare. Yet the situation addressed by the poem was the direct outcome of Elizabethan policy in Ireland. The poem hints at the precarious position of the Gaelic Irish elite in Ulster as well as the awkward choices facing it as a result of that conflict. It is also interesting in terms of the discourse of civility versus savagery so carefully detailed by scholars of English-language literature, suggesting as it does that Gaelic poets were no strangers to European standards of civility such as had been adopted at the English court.

Background to the poem

Following the defeat of the Irish at Kinsale in 1601, Red Hugh, the O'Donnell, departed Ireland for Spain to seek further military assistance against the English, committing his command in his absence to his brother, and *tanist* (his elective successor, Irish *tánaiste*), Rory O'Donnell (1574/5–1608). He left behind an unstable political situation as regards the lordship of Tyrconnell. There were rivals on the ground at home who attempted to establish themselves as the O'Donnell: Niall Garbh, Caffar Óg, and Shane McManus Óg, although all ultimately failed in their attempts and came to grief at the hands of the English authorities. On hearing of Red Hugh's death in Spain in August 1602, Rory made his peace with the English authorities by submitting to Lord Deputy Mountjoy in December of that same year. In 1603, O'Donnell was knighted by Lord Deputy Carey in Dublin and made earl of Tyrconnell. The political situation remained unstable, however. Of particular interest here is the role of Niall Garbh, Rory's cousin and brother-in-law but representative of a rival branch of the O'Donnells. The two branches had been struggling for power within the lordship since the 1540s. In 1603, Rory and Niall Garbh travelled to London to submit to the crown their respective claims to the earldom of Tyrconnell.[1] The adjudication was in favour of Rory as earl, although the judgement was not entirely to his satisfaction. Rory's absence in England provides the setting of the poem to be discussed herein.[2]

The poet is Eochaidh Ó hEodhasa (c. 1560–1612), of Ballyhose, Co. Fermanagh. His principal professional relationship was with the Maguires of Fermanagh, as he was appointed *ollamh* (court poet) during the chieftainship of Cú Chonnacht Maguire (died 1589), subsequently retaining his position under Cú Chonnacht's son Aodh (Hugh). In common with other poets, however, Ó hEodhasa composed eulogies for members of other aristocratic families such as O'Neill, O'Doherty, MacSweeney, and O'Rourke (Ulster), as well as Burke, MacDermot, and O'Conor (Connaught), and O'Byrne (Leinster). He also addressed Red Hugh O'Donnell, brother of Rory, in his poetry. On the new king's accession in 1603, Ó hEodhasa composed a notable poem of welcome for James I of England, Scotland, and Ireland.[3] I will have occasion to mention this poem briefly once more later.

Summary of the poem, 'Ionmholta malairt bhisigh'

The poet begins by commending a change for the better, in particular a change from which he himself has profited (stanza one). He then explains that he has renounced the recondite professional ('bardic') style of poetry for a more common sort which earns him more popular acclaim and less opprobrium (stanzas two and three). He will henceforth renounce any payment for his poetry if the meaning of even one stanza should elude

---

[1] *Annals of the Four Masters*, M1603.8, www.ucc.ie/celt/published/G100005F/index.html.
[2] John J. Silke, 'O'Donnell, Rory, styled first earl of Tyrconnell (1574/5–1608)', *ODNB*; John J. Silke, 'O'Donnell, Sir Niall Garbh (1568/9–1626?)', *ODNB*. For the political background to the O'Donnell lordship, see Darren McGettigan, 'The political community in the lordship of Tír Chonaill', in Robert Armstrong and Tadhg Ó hAnnracháin (eds.), *Community in early modern Ireland* (Dublin, 2006), pp. 91–102.
[3] Pádraig A. Breatnach, 'Ó hEodhasa, Eochaidh (c. 1560–1612)', *ODNB*.

a single member of his audience (stanza four). Since simple poetry is all that is demanded of him, he will, with his patron's permission, discharge his obligations (stanza five) in this manner. He avers that not even the most obtuse of the world will outdo him in ease and simplicity (stanza six), while reminding us that his abandonment of the true professional style will cause the prospective earl to laugh (stanza seven). The poet is in fact very circumspect about the idea that O'Donnell should be allowed to judge his new poetry at all (stanza eight); nonetheless, the lure of the profit to be accrued by the poet through the adoption of the more popular style remains (stanza nine). Ó hEodhasa ingratiates himself to the earl by praising his easy familiarity with the arcane style, the difficulty of which used to break the poet's heart; however, his absence in England had given the poet his chance (stanzas ten and eleven). Finally, the earl should know that if he opposes the poet's change of direction that many will in turn oppose *him* (stanza twelve).

Interpretations of the poem

This poem has traditionally been interpreted as reflecting the downturn in the fortunes of the professional poet class from the early seventeenth century onwards, caused largely by the downfall of their Gaelic aristocratic patrons.[4] As Osborn Bergin puts it, 'it was as if a poet laureate had to seek engagements at a music hall'.[5] Declan Kiberd sees the poem as hovering between a 'fastidious contempt for the mass mind', the poet's new audience, and the poet's acceptance of that audience.[6] For Marc Caball, the tone of the poem is 'assuredly one of ironic banter', a sophisticated professional poet vowing to outdo the idiots of the world in banality in order to reap the rewards of popularity.[7] All three of these readings place the poem within the context of bardic corporate decline in Ireland resulting from the endemic warfare of the sixteenth century, Tudor conquest and colonisation, and the spread of English common law. In a jurisdiction where the latter increasingly prevailed, as Caball points out, the politically legitimating function of professional poetry, the valorisation of one's lord through praise and genealogy, became largely redundant.[8] Two other, more recent interpretations have rather played down the specifically local

---

[4] For the text of the poem, see Osborn Bergin, *Irish bardic poetry: texts and translations* (Dublin, 1970), pp. 127–9; for a translation see pp. 270–1.

[5] *Ibid.*, p. 127.

[6] Declan Kiberd, 'Bardic poetry: the loss of aura', in *Irish classics* (Cambridge, MA, 2001), pp. 13–24, esp. pp. 15–17.

[7] Marc Caball, *Poets and politics: reaction and continuity in Irish poetry, 1558–1625* (Notre Dame and Cork, 1998), p. 94.

[8] *Ibid.*, p. 95.

political resonances of the poem. Mícheál Mac Craith speculates that it might have been part of a verse correspondence involving the poet, his patron, and the patron's wife, Brigid Fitzgerald, whom Rory married in 1604, in the artificial style of the *amour courtois*. The references to an easier style of composition in the present poem are then seen as perhaps reflecting Rory's interest in love poetry on the eve of his marriage.[9] While acknowledging that '[s]ocial, economic and political changes doubtless have their influence on all the material composed in any given period',[10] Michelle O Riordan prefers to see the poem as representing in Irish terms a more general European trend away from the medieval 'preceptive' arts and towards a greater engagement with vernacular literature.[11] The latter two interpretations, it seems to me, in broadening the scope of possible interpretations of the poem, do not necessarily negate the more traditional approaches, but are rather a potential enrichment of them. This is a point that I will be trying to expand upon in the discussion that follows.

A close reading of the poem

The poem opens in characteristically (for bardic poetry) aphoristic fashion: we are told that 'a change for the better is to be praised', whence the poet points to a particular change, as yet unspecified, beneficial to himself:

(1) Ionmholta malairt bhisigh:
tárraidh sinde 'san amsa
iomlaoid go suarrach sona,
do-chuaidh a sochar dhamhsa.

A change for the better is laudable:
We have achieved at this time
a contemptible fortunate exchange,
Its profit has redounded to me.[12]

---

[9] Mícheál Mac Craith, 'Eochaidh Ó hEoghasa agus an freagra fileata', in Pádraigín Riggs, Breandán Conchúir, and Seán Ó Coileáin (eds.), *Saoi na hÉigse: aistí in ómós do Sheán Ó Tuama* (Baile Átha Cliath, 2000), pp. 23–33. Unlike the formalised praise poetry of the professional poets, love poetry was also the preserve of amateurs.

[10] Michelle O Riordan, *Irish bardic poetry and rhetorical reality* (Cork, 2007), p. 251.

[11] *Ibid.*, p. 260. 'Preceptive' describes the later medieval approach to the art of poetry (*ars poetriae*) and is essentially prescriptive: based on the analysis of the discourse of poetry, precepts for future compositions are laid down for aspiring poets. These include how to find appropriate subject matter and how to treat it properly within the fixed confines of a *genre*. See *ibid.*, pp. 24–56; for a full history of European developments, see James J. Murphy, *Rhetoric in the Middle Ages: a history of rhetorical theory from Saint Augustine to the Renaissance* (Berkeley, CA, 1974), esp. pp. 135–93.

[12] Unless otherwise stated, translations in this chapter are mine.

As a general maxim, the opening line seems unassailable but, in the third line, there is a telling juxtaposition of two alliterating adjectives which, as O Riordan notes, creates for the poem 'the unstable or contradictory tone of irony from the outset'.[13] Whatever change 'for the better' this is, it has clearly left the poet with some qualms of conscience, or at least with feelings of unease. The combination of these adjectives is oxymoronic: the change in question is both contemptible (*suarrach*) and fortunate (*sona*), the latter because it has been to the poet's profit (*sochar*), the reasons for the former characterisation being as yet unclear. The close association of these three words is metrically reinforced – by alliteration (*suarrach sona*) and by assonance (*sona : sochar*).

Let us look a little more closely at the structure of this combination *suarrach sona*. Its syntax is elliptical. Possibly elided is the conjunction 'and' (Irish *agus*), so 'contemptible [and] fortunate', where the two elements are simply to be viewed as conjoined. Another possible ellipsis would be a concessive conjunction such as 'though' (Irish *giodh*). A concessive reading is appropriate here because a concessive clause characteristically expresses something that is contrary to the expectations raised by the main clause; the oxymoronic element consists therefore of an assumed incompatibility between the two elements (clauses).[14] So we could posit (i) '[though] contemptible, fortunate', or (ii) 'contemptible [though] fortunate', as the underlying pragmatic structure. But would these two concessive orderings differ appreciably from one another in terms of their interpretation? The difference in nuance between the two readings would be predicated on the poet's expectations of his audience/readership as follows (in each case the main assertion is in capital letters). The position of such clauses here is a function of the presentation and relative weighting of information. In the case of

(i) '[though] contemptible, FORTUNATE'

the poet assumes that the audience already accepts that the change is contemptible, against which background he asserts its fortunate aspect. In the case of

(ii) 'CONTEMPTIBLE [though] fortunate'

the poet asserts that the change is contemptible and the modifier 'fortunate' adds further information to this assertion. In other words, in (i) the content of the *though*-clause is old and therefore assumed information, while in (ii) it is new and therefore 'newsworthy'. The postposed

---

[13] O Riordan, *Irish bardic poetry*, pp. 251–2.

[14] Ekkehard König, 'Conditionals, concessive conditionals and concessives: areas of contrast, overlap and neutralization', in Elizabeth Traugott, Alice Ter Meulen, Judy Snitzer Reilly, and Charles A. Ferguson (eds.), *On conditionals* (Cambridge, 1986), pp. 229–46.

concessive therefore has a greater communicative dynamic than the pre-posed one.

The important point here, however, is that by simply juxtaposing the two words the poet leaves the matter open – is this change *primarily* contemptible or fortunate, or is neither being privileged over the other? This uncertainty has to do with the pragmatics of adverbial clauses and their positioning in language, as we have seen.[15] The poet invites us to make our own inferences, or simply to recognise the ambiguity.

There are other grammatical and lexical features of this stanza that contribute to the overall feeling of instability referred to by O Riordan, to a sense of obliquity and indirectness. First, the opening word of the poem, *ionmholta*, is based on the verbal stem *mol-* 'praise' but is a non-agentive adjectival form akin to a Latin gerundive, 'can/must be praised'. Any prospective agent, however, is left unspecified. Second, the first stanza contains two further important words semantically very close to each other, *malairt* and *iomlaoid*, both 'change' or 'exchange'. As O Riordan also notes, the noun *iomlaoid* is also potentially ambivalent as it can also mean 'mistake', while *malairt* and its derivatives can have connotations of fickleness and betrayal.[16] Third, the plural pronoun *sinde*, 'we, us', could be interpreted initially here either in its semantic form as plural (to include a second party) or as pragmatically singular (the 'royal we'), especially as the last line of the stanza contains a semantically singular pronoun *dhamhsa* 'for me'. We are left with the feeling that the poet is dissembling to some degree, is being less than candid. Presumably, the change is 'praiseworthy' because 'fortunate' but *he* does not expressly want to praise it himself (as agent) because it is also 'contemptible'. Then we wonder is the poet simply talking about a change that affects himself, or himself and someone else (again unspecified). Is the poet referring to a simple 'change' affecting only himself, or to something more complex, an 'exchange' which would imply a reciprocal process involving someone else? Is this exchange, if such, a betrayal of some sort? These features I believe all to be central to an exposition of the poet's intent, but I will defer detailed consideration of them until closer to the end of the chapter.

To return to our figure of condensed incongruity in stanza one, the paradox is explained in stanza two. The poet explains that the change is contemptible because he has reneged on the compositional practices of

---

[15] See Erich Poppe, 'The pragmatics of complex sentences', *Journal of Celtic Linguistics* 3 (1994), 1–34.

[16] O Riordan, *Irish bardic poetry*, p. 390 n. 7. For *malairt*, see *malart*, in *Dictionary of the Irish language: compact edition* (Dublin, 1983), p. 452.

professional poets but fortunate in that composition is now easier and results in more widespread acclaim:

> (2) Do thréig sind sreatha caola
> foirceadal bhfaobhrach bhfrithir
> ar shórt gnáthach grés robhog,
> is mó as a moltar sinde.

> We have abandoned the narrow sequences
> of sharp keen-edged instructions
> for a common sort of all-too-easy composition [*literally* 'web'];
> The more we are praised for it.

The alliteration in this stanza is especially effective. In line 2, *foirceadal bhfaobhrach bhfrithir* ('of sharp keen-edged instructions') suggests that *uaim* 'alliteration' (lit. 'stitching') is a feature of the high style. However, this effect is undermined in line 3 when an alliterating pair characterises the alleged new style and is preceded by the word *sórt* 'sort', which creates the effect immediately of a lower stylistic register (*sórt* **g**náthach **g**rés, 'a kind of common poetry'), perhaps enhanced here by the status of *sórt* as a foreign loanword.[17] The use of alliteration in two successive lines whose content is so different, the contrast between the hardness of one style and the softness or ease of the other, creates an ironic effect. In the last line of this stanza, there is a further non-agentive verb form: *moltar (sinde)* '(we) are praised', a parallel to the *ionmholta* of stanza one. As I have previously indicated, I will take up the issue of this verb *mol* 'praise' and its implications for the poem in more detail later on. Suffice to say for now that the use of non-agentive forms of this verb by a professional poet, whose central function was the production of eulogy in the validation of political lordship, is not without a certain irony. For all their gracefulness and urbanity, there is a certain obliquity and reticence, coyness even, about these opening stanzas that suggests to us that all is perhaps not as it seems.

In stanza three, the poet amplifies the argument of the preceding stanza, explaining that the high bardic style had merely earned him popular disdain, while the hyperbole of stanza four consists of the assertion that he will give up his claim to *any* payment (*énbhonn*) for his poetry should anyone fail to understand a *single* verse (*énrand*) of it:

> (3) Le dorchacht na ngrés snoighthe
> do bhínnse ag tuilliodh gráine:
> fa hí ughachta mhóráin
> nár dhíol róghráidh ar ndáinne.

---

[17] A relatively new loanword from English into Irish in the late sixteenth and early seventeenth centuries, judging by the examples in *Dictionary of the Irish Language*, p. 558.

With the darkness of hewn-out compositions
I used to earn opprobrium:
It was the opinion of many
that our poetry was not much to be loved.

(4) Maithim, giodh mór an sonas,
énbhonn feasda dá thoradh,
má théid énrand gan tuigse
dom dhánsa ó dhuine ar domhan.

I renounce, though great the good fortune,
a single penny as its reward,
if even a single verse of my poetry
should defy the understanding of anyone on earth.

His hyperbole serves to disarm any charge of cynicism against him by
his ostensibly renouncing payment in such circumstances. In fact, this
initiates a sequence of stanzas in which the juxtaposition of overstatement
and understatement sets the tone.

Stanza five is a counterpart of the second stanza, whose 'narrow rows
of instruction' have now been replaced by the facility of composition
'on the open road'.[18] A key phrase here is *dán bog* 'an easy poem', a
piece of understatement, which offsets the hyperbole of the preceding
stanza. Stanza five also brings the first explicit reference to the source
of the poet's potential problem in respect of this *malairt* or *iomlaoid*: his
patron, Rory O'Donnell, the new-fangled, or perhaps prospective, earl
of Tyrconnell. (Significantly, Rory is not expressly named in the poem.)
The poet would not presume to follow his new course without his lord's
approbation, despite the fact that this new course is what is more widely
in demand:

(5) Dán bog ar bhél na slighiodh,
ós é anois siorthior oraind,
cuirfeadsa dhíom na fiacha
go ccead d'iarla Chlann gConaill.

An easy poem where the roads open out,
since that is what is asked of us now,
I will discharge my obligations
with the permission of the earl of the clans of Conall.

As I will argue later, this reference to the 'earl of the clans of Conall' will
be of considerable significance in deciphering the poem's message.

Stanza six also contains a cryptic and very condensed reference to the
apologue of the thirty wise philosophers who, having predicted a shower

---

[18] As O Riordan points out, oppositions pervade the poem: easy–difficult; broad–narrow;
light–dark; soft–hard; see O Riordan, *Irish bardic poetry*, p. 252.

of rain that would make all caught out in it insane, hide themselves
accordingly in a cave. When they emerge, however, they find that no one
understands them and their wisdom anymore. In order to be understood
at all, therefore, they have to go 'out in the rain' (*fá uisce an cheatha*)
like everyone else. The moral here is that to survive in the world you
must become like everyone else; if everyone else loses his mind, you
must conform and lose yours too. The tone of this stanza is once again
hyperbolic, if the poet must write like a dunce then so be it:[19]

> (6) Mo gheallsa ar bhuga ar mhaoile
> ní bhérdaois daoithe an bheatha:
> do-chuaidh mé, maith an tuicsi,
> le cách fá uisge an cheatha.

> The dunces of the world will not best me
> in simplicity or dullness:
> I have gone, it is well understood,
> like everyone else, out into the rain.

O Riordan identifies this stanza as the structural turning point, after
which the poem becomes a 'mirror image' of itself, but one in which the
second half of the structure 'amplifies' or develops the first part.[20] Thus,
stanzas seven and eight revisit the concession of stanzas two and three,
except that now the concern is with the future (the earl's reaction to his
new style) and not the past (the general reaction to his old poetry). To
forestall this future, in the first line of the stanza, the poet has recourse to
the rhetorical strategy of pre-empting a potential reaction by anticipating
it (the figure of occupatio), which again constitutes a revisiting of the
oxymoron that is *suarrach sona* (see again stanzas one and four). He
acknowledges again the reality that is both contemptible and fortunate:
that he has forsaken the hard paths of erudition for ease and profit. The
possible price for this is his patron's derision:

> (7) Do thréig mé – gá mó sonas? –
> mo shlighthe docra diamhra:
> dá gcluine cuid dar ndáinne,
> beanfaidh gáire as an iarla.

> I have abandoned – what greater fortune? –
> My difficult, obscure ways:
> If he hears some of our poetry,
> it will make the earl laugh.

[19] See Mícheál Mac Craith, *Lorg na hIasachta ar na dánta grá* (Baile Átha Cliath, 1989), pp.
132–46, for a detailed discussion of the use of this apologue in both Irish and European
literary tradition.
[20] O Riordan, *Irish bardic poetry*, p. 256.

Stanzas eight and nine are linked by use of the word *eagla* 'fear' in relation to the earl's possible reaction. First, in stanza eight, again speaking hyperbolically, the poet refuses to allow his patron to sit on a 'tribunal' to judge him:

> (8) D'eagla mo chora as gárda
> ón mhéid dá ttárras loise,
> diúltaimse flaith ó gConaill
> do dhol oraind a ccoisde.

> For fear of dismissal from his retinue,
> From which I have attained glory,
> I refuse to allow the sovereign of the descendants of Conall
> to sit on a jury to try me.

> (9) Is iomdha tré dhán bhfallsa
> lán dom annsacht a mbliadhna:
> do thuillfinn tuilleadh ceana
> muna bheith eagla an iarla.

> Many, on account of false poetry,[21]
> are full of love for me this year,
> I would earn yet more affection
> were it not for fear of the earl.

While 'fear' (*eagla*) links the two stanzas, they are divided by the nomenclature used to refer to the subject, a device reminiscent of the last line of stanza five, except in this case the two elements are separated: the absent patron is referred to as *flaith* 'ruler, sovereign' (Gaelic term) and *iarla* 'earl' (foreign term). In stanza nine, the erudite earl is expressly opposed by the many, an adumbration of the concluding stanza. As well as flattering O'Donnell's supposed erudition, stanza ten refers for the first time to his absence from Ireland. This is important because, in the world delineated by the poem, it seems to allow the poet a certain latitude, it opens a ludic or 'playful' space which the poet can artfully exploit.[22] It allows him to balance the praise of his patron with his own impudence in either composing 'quickly' or striking a 'brave' pose (Bergin), depending on how we take the word *tapaidh*:

> (10) Mac Aodha, aigneadh fosaidh,
> fear ler robhog ar gcruaidhne,

---

[21] *Ibid.*, p. 257, takes the Irish *fallsa* (another loanword) as meaning 'lazy', a sense which it has dialectally in contemporary Irish. It seems more likely in the present context to take it as 'false', 'deceiving', as Bergin does. See *Dictionary of the Irish Language*, p. 294.

[22] Perhaps connecting the poem with the *mise-en-scène* of Castiglione's *Il Libro del Cortegiano* (*The Book of the Courtier*); this is discussed more fully in the conclusion to this chapter.

> ní cás dúinn dénamh tapaidh,
> ó tharla a Saxaibh uainne.

> The son of Hugh, a steady disposition,
> A man for whom our difficulty is too easy,
> It is no great matter for us to appear brave,
> [I have no difficulty about hasty composition][23]
> since he happens to be away from us in England.

The lord's absence is presented as sheer happenstance (another piece of understatement), and stanza eleven seems to underline the poet's newly found sense of ease and freedom, which is almost adventitious ('this custom which has come to us'). At the same time further overstatement (the old style used to break his heart) balances a previous understatement (that his new poetry is so simple):

> (11) Beag nach brisiodh mo chroidhe
> gach dán roimhe dá gcumainn:
> is mór an t-adhbhor sláinte
> an nós so táinig chugainn.

> It just about used to break my heart,
> every poem I would compose before now;
> it is a great source of good health,
> this custom which has come to us.

The final stanza recalls and amplifies stanza five – in terms of the prevailing aesthetic taste in poetry, O'Donnell now faces competition as arbiter:

> (12) Dá lochtaighe triath Bearnais
> énrand dá ndealbhthor linde
> budh iomdha ag cor 'na aghaidh–
> ionmholta malairt bhisigh.

> If the hero of Bearnas should find fault
> with a single verse crafted by us,
> there will be many speaking up against him,
> a change for the better is laudable.

There are now, therefore, two potential sources of favour for the poet: the lord-as-patron and, also, 'the many' who might oppose him. The poet's indirectness is again a feature of this stanza – he skilfully anticipates the earl's objection to his new artistic style before he makes it (occupatio); in addition, the argument is now construed as between the earl and the poet's *audience* not the poet himself. This point will be developed later.

---

[23] Translation in square brackets from O Riordan, *Irish bardic poetry*, p. 252; historically, her translation is the more probable, although the case is not closed.

I want now to look more closely at one aspect of the poem's rhetorical structure already hinted at in the previous section. The poet refers to the absent O'Donnell in various ways, but never by his personal name, rather using various titles or epithets at different points in the poem. On the one hand, he uses time-honoured, honorific Gaelic terms: *flaith*[24] *ó gConaill* 'prince / sovereign of the descendants of Conall'[25] in stanza eight; *triath Bearnais* 'the lord / hero of Bearnas' (a place name in Tyrconnell) in stanza twelve. On the other hand, he also employs the English term 'earl' in its Gaelicised form *iarla* on three occasions (stanzas five, seven, and nine).[26] The question then arises as to whether or not this juxtaposition of terms is simply adventitious or in some other way 'meaningful'.

I believe, in fact, that the key to the poet's overall purpose lies here. The juxtaposition of nomenclatures takes the poem's opening gambit, the compressed paradox of a change that is *suarrach sona* 'contemptible and fortunate', and transfers it from the aesthetic and cultural domain of the poet into the political world of the prince but, crucially, without being so tactless as to state it. We may recall here that Rory's absence, away in England, is a consequence of his investiture with the earldom of Tyrconnell and that he too faces his own 'change', his own *malairt* or *iomlaoid*, no less than the poet.

Let us consider now the first reference that occurs in the poem to O'Donnell as 'earl'. In stanza five, the poet seeks leave of the absent earl to compose in the easy style, referring to him as 'the earl of the clans of Conall':

> go gcead d'iarla Chlann gConaill

'With the permission of the earl of the clans of Conall', the poet seeks the permission of his patron, the Gaelic *tanist*-cum-Jacobean courtier to pursue his new artistic course. The English title of 'earl' normally goes with a territorial rather than a tribal designation. Here, it seems to me, is another figure of condensed incongruity, which recalls the poet's own dilemma of stanza one. The phrase *iarla Chlann gConaill* is itself, like the opening gambit *suarrach sona*, an oxymoron of sorts in its collocation of two seeming opposites. The poet seems to be hinting perhaps that both he and his patron are facing comparable situations, one in the aesthetic and the other in the political domain. However, while he articulates it

---

[24] A venerable word in Irish and indeed Indo-European tradition, cognate with English *wield* (originally 'rule') and with Slavonic *Vladimir* 'great ruler'. The fact that its adjectival derivative *flaitheamhail* means 'generous' says everything about the symbiotic relationship between political sovereignty and munificence in Gaelic Irish ideology.

[25] The eponymous ancestor of *síol gConaill* 'the seed of Conall', i.e. the O'Donnells.

[26] Actually not a contemporary borrowing from English *earl* but rather one of greater antiquity, from Old Norse *jarl*. See *Dictionary of Irish Language*, under *iarla*.

expressly in his own case, he is somewhat more oblique in the case of his lord.[27]

As the poem proceeds, these aesthetic and political domains emerge as homologous rather than simply analogous, the poet's stated dilemma increasingly implicating his patron. It may be noted, first of all, that where O'Donnell appears in his guise of the 'Gaelic Irish tanist', as in stanzas eight and twelve, his attitude towards the poet's new artistic path is assumed to be dismissive, even hostile. Rory as *flaith ó gConaill* 'the sovereign of the descendants of Conall' (stanza eight) should never be permitted to pass sentence on the poet, while in the phrase *triath Bearnais* 'the chief (or "hero") of Bearnas' (stanza twelve), he again anticipates O'Donnell's objection to the new literary fashion.

Of greater interest, I think, in terms of his ultimate purpose, is the poet's employment of 'English' nomenclature. In stanza seven, the poet conjectures that the 'earl' will laugh at the alleged banality of his new artistic departure. This has usually been taken to mean that O'Donnell will laugh in *disdain*; likewise, in the stanza immediately following, the poet confesses that his 'fear' of the earl's possible reaction is holding him back from taking full advantage of his new-found popularity. There is, however, an intriguing suggestion by Mícheál Mac Craith, who, as alluded to above, situates this poem in quite a different context from one simply of bardic corporate decline. As well as being a professional court poet, Ó hEodhasa was also a composer of love poems in the *amour courtois* style more accessible to amateur practitioners and connoisseurs alike (quite a few professional poets in fact turned their hand to this style of poetry). Rory was received in London by James I in July 1603, and on 29 September of the same year was invested with the title earl of Tyrconnell in Dublin. Lady Brigid Fitzgerald of Maynooth married Rory 'soon after 29 September 1603'.[28] Ó hEodhasa was *ollamh flatha* (or 'chief's poet') to Cú Chonnacht Maguire and composed a love poem, entitled 'Ní mé bhur n-aithne, a aos gráidh' ('Friends, I am not of your acquaintance') addressed to Lady Fitzgerald but putatively composed by his lord Cú Chonnacht. In reply, Brigid had a poem of rejection composed, 'A mhacaoimh dhealbhas an dán' ('O young man who composes the poem') in which she sees through the first poem's pretence.[29] It is within this context of the 'response in verse' genre, at that time very

---

[27] Such a combination is not unparalleled in the Irish poetry of his period. We find, for example, *iarla Ó gConaill* ('the earl of the descendants of Conall') in a poem of 1608; see Láimhbheartach Mac Cionnaith (ed.), *Dioghluim dána* (Baile Átha Cliath, 1938), p. 421, l. 37.

[28] Cathal G. Ó Háinle, 'Flattery rejected: two seventeenth-century Irish poems', *Hermathena* 138 (1985), 5.

[29] *Ibid.*, 10–27.

fashionable at the Jacobean court, that Mac Craith would situate our poem, largely on the basis of a couple of verbal echoes between it and the poem attributed to Brigid.[30] He opines that this verse correspondence began with 'Ionmholta malairt bhisigh' where the poet is in effect poking gentle fun at his patron for his new-found interest in easy love poetry (the *dán bog* of the poem, a phrase echoed in the 'Fitzgerald' reply) on the eve of his nuptials. Thus, 'a change for the better is laudable' applies also on this very personal level for Rory but this scenario for the poem also emphasises its Jacobean courtly context. The poet's 'fear of the earl' in this context is transformed into a kind of gentle irony.[31] In addition, Rory's 'laughter' in stanza seven is now born less of derision than of appreciation.

But only in his guise as the Jacobean earl, and this is where I diverge from Mac Craith somewhat, although I find his overall situation of this poem in this particular context very plausible. His parting comment is to the effect that this poem, along with the others associated with it in the correspondence referred to above, shows that the Gaelic nobility, despite the precarious situation of the early seventeenth century, could use poetry as a temporary respite from political intrigue.[32] While this might be true in general terms, I do not feel that it serves Ó hEodhasa's purpose in the poem under consideration here. What needs to be remembered, in the symbolic world delineated by the poem, is something that Mac Craith himself, more than any other scholar of recent times, has brought to attention. This is the fact that 'easy poetry' of the *amour courtois* type represents precisely English influence on Irish literature in the sixteenth and seventeenth centuries at its most quintessential.[33]

A predilection for 'easy poetry' is therefore not as innocent as it might seem in the circumstances – aesthetic preferences may well implicate political ones (the poet hints). The phrase *iarla Chlann gConaill* temporarily unites two opposite and irreconcilable political personae in a condensed figure as incongruous as the poet's own *suarrach sona* at the beginning of the poem. Thereafter, Rory's cultural and political personality is split: Gaelic chief and Jacobean earl, which is it to be? The lord's predicament is that of the poet, but the trick is that the poet, unlike in his own case, does not spell this one out: he intimates it, and therefore leaves it hanging. Artfully (but apparently artlessly) the poet leaves things open, the poem ends in a 'subjunctive' ('*if. . .* '), but he in fact intimates that he has a way out that his patron might not have ('*the many. . .* '). This is another dimension of the poet's 'indirection' – he presents his potential advantage obliquely: *he* is not saying it, but the

---

[30] Mac Craith, 'Eochaidh Ó hEodhasa', pp. 29–31.   [31] *Ibid.*, esp. pp. 29–31.
[32] *Ibid.*, p. 32.   [33] Mac Craith, *Lorg na hIasachta* (see n. 19).

'many' will adjudicate in his favour. Again, while this approbation ostensibly relates to aesthetic fashion, it also strikes a potentially chilling note for his patron on the political front (can *he* be so sure of the support of the 'masses'?)

Let me highlight a couple of further aspects of the poet's 'artlessness' in this respect. Imagine a member of the poet's audience questioning his intentions in juxtaposing Gaelic and English titles: was the poet actually suggesting anything along the lines that I have? In reply, the poet (tongue in cheek) points to the occurrences of *iarla* in the poem – *all are metrically required*. In each case, *iarla* provides an assonantal rhyme with another word in the stanza: an end rhyme in stanzas seven (*diamhra*) and nine (*bliadhna*), as well as an internal rhyme in stanza five (*fiacha*). This effectively disarms his interrogator: the poet's deployment of the lexical item in question is (apparently) as innocently motivated as that. The full significance of this point will become clearer later in this chapter.

Consider again the poem's opening two stanzas in relation to grammatical number, specifically the pronominal forms used (highlighted). In these two stanzas, all the pronominal forms are morphologically plural, except for the final word of the first verse, which is unambiguously singular:

> Ionmholta malairt bhisigh:
> tárraidh **sinde** 'san amsa
> iomlaoid go suarrach sona,
> do-chuaidh a sochar **dhamhsa**.

> Do thréig **sind** sreatha caola
> foirceadal bhfaobhrach bhfrithir
> ar shórt gnáthach grés robhog,
> is mó as a moltar **sinde**.

> A change for the better is laudable:
> **We** have achieved at this time
> a contemptible fortunate exchange,
> Its profit has redounded to **me**.

> **We** have abandoned the narrow sequences
> of sharp keen-edged instructions
> for a common sort of all-too-easy composition;
> The more **we** are praised for it.

The use of the first person plural pronoun to stand (ostensibly) for the singular is unremarkable in bardic poetry and occurs on a number of occasions in this poem. Consider also in this respect stanza ten (plural pronominal form again highlighted; in addition the plural possessive 'our'):

Mac Aodha, aigneadh fosaidh,
fear ler robhog *ar* gcruaidh*ne*,
ní cás **dúinn** dénamh tapaidh,
ó tharla a Saxaibh **uainne**.

The son of Hugh, a steady disposition,
One who finds *our* difficulty too easy,
It is no great matter for **us** to appear brave,
[I have no difficulty about hasty composition]
since he happens to be away from **us** in England.

The reason most of these forms are highlighted is that they are emphatic or contrastive forms, *we* (or '*I*') as opposed to *you* or anyone else. Again, these contrastive forms are typically metrically motivated, adding the required suffix gives the disyllable needed at the end of each line, for example (so *dhamh* 'to me' becomes *dhamhsa* 'to *me*'; *sind* 'us' becomes *sinde* '*us*'; and so on). Similarly, the plural or singular forms are used in accordance with the requirements of assonantal rhyme (*amsa : dhamhsa*, but *frithir : sinde*). So once again, the poet has an escape hatch if challenged as to his real intent – is he really just talking about himself or is he implicating his patron? I think, nonetheless, that stanza one might well read differently when reconsidered in the light of the poem's concluding stanza, where the poet hints that he may have the edge: 'a change has come to *us* which has resulted in profit for *me*', taking plural and singular forms at face value. This would represent a re-reading of this stanza based on the poem's conclusion. One might also approach stanza ten in a similar way except that here the plural form *uainne* 'from *us*', if taken as semantically plural, expressly *excludes* Rory as he is away in England. This re-reading would also connect with the final stanza where the poet hints that his allegiances might shift – in that case, *uainne* would be *inclusive* of 'the many'.

To interpret these plural forms as pragmatically singular, that is, as referring to the poet himself, would be unremarkable. Yet, it is clear as the poem unfolds that *two* people have experienced 'a change' 'for the better' (?); on the aesthetic level (the poet) and on the personal and political levels (the patron, he is getting married and has become / is becoming an 'earl').

Consider in addition the interpretation of the line *fear ler robhog ar gcruaidhne*, 'a man for whom our difficulty is too easy' (stanza ten, line two). This has traditionally been taken as a compliment to Rory's supposed erudition; could it also mean that he is too sanguine about the decision he himself faces and its ramifications?

As I have already indicated at the beginning of this chapter, the first stanza contains two further important words semantically very close to each other, *malairt* and *iomlaoid*, both meaning 'change', or 'exchange'. To investigate briefly some of the implications involved here with respect to these two items, let us backtrack somewhat to consider a poem composed sometime in the 1580s by Tadhg Dall Ó hUiginn (*c.* 1550–91) for Cormac O'Hara, lord of Leyney, Co. Sligo. The ostensible premise of this poem is that Cormac is so shrewd in his understanding of the poet–patron exchange that he cannot be deceived in his dealings with poets; he always gets the better of the deal.[34] The poem's opening is very much concerned with this idea of 'exchange', the 'bargaining' and 'bartering' between poet and patron (the relevant lexical items are highlighted). I present here the first four stanzas in their entirety as they give the reader a good sense of the honorific encomiastic style of this kind of poetry:

> (1) Maith an ceannaighe Cormac,
> mac Céin dá gclaon iobharshlat,
> glac thabhartach um cheann gcruidh,
> **malartach**[35] is fhearr aguibh.

> A good merchant is Cormac,
> Cian's son for whom the yew-branch bends;
> a generous hand in bestowing cattle,
> the best barterer amongst you.

> (2) Ré linn Chormuic ní cluintir
> fear a mheallta i **malairtibh**[36],
> bheith soimheallta is sé do-bheir
> dá ghné shoineannta shoilbheir.

> In Cormac's days never is anyone heard
> to cheat him in bargaining,
> that is what makes him of the pleasant,
> affable countenance easy to beguile.

> (3) Mac Céin na gcéimeann ndocrach –
> móide is maith an **malortach** –
> sduagh dhaoineach ó bheannaibh Breagh
> meallaidh gach aoinneach eisean.

> Cian's son, he of hardy achievements,
> the better bargainer is he–
> beloved hero from Bregia's hills –
> that each one coaxes [i.e. praises] him.

---

[34] As I intend to show elsewhere, however, there is more than one sting in the tail of this poem. All original citations and translations of Tadhg Dall's poetry in this essay are from Eleanor Knott (ed. and trans.), *The bardic poems of Tadhg Dall Ó hUiginn (1550–1591)*, 2 vols. (London, 1922–6).

[35] The agentive noun based on *malairt*.   [36] Dative plural form of *malairt*, 'in exchanges'.

(4) Féach an fearr **iomlaoid** oile
ná an mhoirn shuthain shíorroidhe
téid don fhlaith ionfhuair fhaoilidh,
ar mhaith ndiombuain ndíomhaoinigh.

Behold, is there any better exchange than the lasting,
enduring honor that goes
to the pleasant, kindly chieftain
in return for vain, transitory wealth?[37]

While the opening three stanzas emphasize the more 'commercial' or mercenary aspects of this process (the conceit of patron as 'merchant'), the key to an understanding of the traditional ideology of exchange between the Irish poet and his chief lies in stanza four. This verse rehearses the well-worn theme of the transitory nature of material reward as opposed to the immortality of fame, but the important word here is Irish *moirn* (or *muirn*) 'favour, affection, esteem', which is one of the lexical items that indexes the special relationship deemed appropriate between the two parties.[38] Another such item in the affective vocabulary between poet and patron is *díoghrais* 'love, zeal, fervour, devotion', which occurs in stanza ten in the same kind of context as *muirn* above. In the third line, the phrase *díoghrais molta* 'the fervour of praise' is a common expression among the poets to express the degree of their devotion to their addressee, the Gaelic lord. Note here that we have the same element *mol-* 'praise' as in opening word of Ó hEodhasa's poem, *ionmholta*:[39]

(10) Maith an ceannaighe an fear fuair
air bhréig ndiomolaidh ndiombuain
díoghrais molta bhuain bhaluidh,
i n-uair obtha dh'ealadhuin.

A good merchant is he who got in return
for a worthless, transitory figment
the sincerest of fragrant, lasting panegyric
at a time when art was being rejected.

The ideas represented by *muirn* and *díoghrais* are central to the reciprocity of exchange that is the ideal between poet and patron in early modern Ireland (often referred to as a *connradh*, 'contract, compact'). They apply

---

[37] For the text, see Knott (ed. and trans.), *The bardic poems of Tadhg Dall Ó hUiginn*, vol. I, p. 220; for the translation, see vol. II, p. 146. In the translation of stanza three, the bracketed gloss is my own.

[38] See Pádraig A. Breatnach, 'The chief's poet', *Proceedings of the Royal Irish Academy* 83 C (1983), 44–5.

[39] *Ibid.*, 45. In fact, the two words can be collocated, as in *díoghrais mhuirne*, 'devotion of affection', 'the best of affection'.

just as much to the lord's engagement as to the versifier's; witness the same Tadhg Dall's address to Cathal O'Conor, where he compares the 'honour' (this is how the editor translates *muirn* here) that he had received with the esteem bestowed on some of the great poets of the past:

> **Muirn** Mheic Liag i Leith Mogha,
> i n-aimsir Bhriain Bhóromha,
> gér mhaith rí fionntolcha Fáil,
> níorbh ionchomtha í is m'anáir.

> Mac Liag's honor in Leath Mogha,
> In the time of Brian of Bóromha,
> Though good was the king of Fál's fair height,[40]
> It is not fit to set beside mine.

For the poet, therefore, it is through *mol(adh)* 'praise' that his esteem (*muirn, díoghrais*) is expressed and it is through this expression that he reciprocates in the exchange (*malairt, iomlaoid*) between himself and his patron (the latter's *muirn* is realised through the material rewards that he confers on the poet, the 'transitory figment' of Ó hUiginn's previous poem above).

The first two stanzas of Ó hEodhasa's poem lean heavily on the ideas of 'exchange' and of 'praise', but it is interesting to take another look at what the poet might be trying to do with them here. I indicated earlier in this chapter that their use here indicated a certain 'indirection' on the poet's part.

The associations of *malairt* and *iomlaoid* in bardic ideology are with the workings of the poet–patron 'exchange', the wheels of which are greased by the poet's application of *mol* 'praise'. Within these terms, the poet would appear to be acclaiming a more fundamental 'change' than simply a shift in aesthetic and literary taste, one that in fact subverts the entire mechanism of reciprocity between him and his lord. In other words, the *malairt* is not simply in favour of a style of poetry that is easier to master and produce but one which implies a new audience. This is further suggested in the course of the poem by the poet's references to the 'many' who now prefer his poetry and these references reach their culmination in the final stanza, as we have seen.

Given the centrality of praise to the entire bardic endeavour (*díoghrais molta* 'the favour/fervour of praise'), it is worth looking at how the poet uses this. As already indicated, the form *ionmholta* ('laudable, praisewor-thy') is oblique in that it gives no indication of agency (i.e. 'by whom?'). Also noteworthy is the other non-agentive form of this verb in the last line

---

[40] I.e., Ireland. For the text, see Knott (ed.), *The bardic poems of Tadhg Dall Ó hUiginn*, vol. I, p. 96; for the translation, see vol. II, p. 64.

of stanza two in relation to the new style: 'the more *we are praised* for it'. Given that within the bardic paradigm the central function of the poet is to *bestow* praise, what we have here is an inversion of that paradigm. This suggests that for the poet, in a changing world, favour now potentially lies elsewhere than with his lord. In the concluding section, I will suggest a European context for this, and for the poem in general.

Conclusion

In another poem composed around this same time, Eochaidh Ó hEodhasa welcomes James VI of Scotland on his accession to the throne of England as James I of England, Ireland, and Scotland. We thus have a further composition of his, contemporaneous with the one under discussion here, acclaiming a change for the better: James is the bright sun who will dispel the mists of (Tudor) oppression for Ireland.[41] It has been argued that a section of this paean of welcome for James indicates the poet's familiarity with aspects of the writings of Machiavelli.[42] To conclude here, I would like to suggest that Ó hEodhasa may also have been acquainted with the ideas of one of Machiavelli's Italian contemporaries.

In *Il Libro del Cortegiano* (*The Book of the Courtier*), published in 1528 and set at the court of Duke Federigo of Urbino, Baldessare Castiglione (1478–1529) presented a new standard of conduct for the Italian nobility. He based this on decorum and refinement in addition to a regard for secular learning and the arts, rather than on the traditional medieval standards of military prowess. Gunpowder had rendered the traditional martial values of Europe's military elite largely redundant, and the military reputation of Italy's aristocracy had taken a beating at the hands of the invading French and Spanish armies in the early sixteenth century.[43] Castiglione's book has been described as the most influential manual on the behaviour appropriate to a nobleman to appear in early modern Europe and was translated into English by Sir Thomas Hoby in 1561 as *The Courtyer*. Numerous reissues were printed in Italian, French,

---

[41] Pádraig A. Breatnach (ed. and trans.), 'Metamorphoses 1603: dán le Eochaidh Ó hEodhasa', *Éigse* 17 (1977–8), 169–80; Breandán Ó Buachalla, 'Na Stíobhartaigh agus an t-aos léinn: cing Séamus', *Proceedings of the Royal Irish Academy* 93 C 4 (1983), 81–134; Ó Buachalla, 'James our true king: the ideology of Irish royalism in the seventeenth century', in D. G. Boyce, Robert Eccleshall, and Vincent Geoghegan (eds.), *Political thought in Ireland since the seventeenth century* (London, 1993), pp. 7–35.

[42] Clare Carroll, 'The Janus face of Machiavelli, adapting *The Prince* and the *Discourses* in early modern Ireland', in Clare Carroll, *Circe's Cup* (Cork, 2001), pp. 91–103.

[43] Theodore K. Rabb, *The last days of the Renaissance: the march to modernity* (New York, 2006), pp. 55–62.

Latin, and English throughout the sixteenth and early seventeenth centuries.[44]

Castiglione's principal concern is the relationship between the courtier and his prince, especially the strategies available to the former for self-preservation and self-promotion in an autocratic world.[45] Central to these strategies is the cultivation of a quality which Castiglione refers to as 'grace', a standard of conduct, 'a rhetoric of performance',[46] calculated to please his prince and thus win his preferment. As Eduardo Saccone points out, both the end of this process (the prince's favour) and the means to that end (the courtier's grace) are referred to by the Italian word *grazia*. For the courtier, therefore, 'grace' is both the reward itself and the quality by which he achieves that reward.[47]

Grace, therefore, establishes a reciprocal relationship between the courtier and his prince, and Italian lexical structure reflects this reciprocity.[48] As such, *grazia* recalls the structure of Irish *muirn* and *díoghrais* discussed earlier, except that the Irish professional poets traditionally saw the favour of their lord as a right based on the corporate entitlements due to them as a class rather than involving any *savoir gré* on their part.[49] In fact, one of the classic expositions of this position is an earlier poem by Ó hEodhasa himself, addressed to his then patron Hugh Maguire sometime after the latter had become lord of Fermanagh in 1589.[50] A look at the first stanza of this poem will suffice here:

> Mór an t-ainm ollamh flatha;
> measdar giodh maith ealatha
> nach faláir d'fhior an anma
> cion tar anáir n-ealadhna.

---

[44] Anna Bryson, *From courtesy to civility: changing codes of conduct in early modern England* (Oxford, 1998), p. 36. For an accessible collection of essays on various aspects of Castiglione's treatise, see Robert W. Hanning and David Rosand (eds.) *Castiglione: the ideal and the real in Renaissance culture* (New Haven, 1983). Useful, too, is Peter Burke, *The fortunes of The Courtier: the European reception of Castiglione's Cortegiano* (State College, PA, 1995).

[45] Daniel Javitch, '*Il Cortegiano* and the constraints of despotism', in Hanning and Rosand (eds.), *Castiglione: the ideal*, pp. 17–28.

[46] To paraphrase Wayne A. Rebhorn, *The emperor of men's minds: literature and the Renaissance discourse of rhetoric* (Ithaca, NY, 1995), p. 122.

[47] Eduardo Saccone, '*Grazia, sprezzatura, affettazione* in the *Courtier*', in Hanning and Rosand (eds.), *Castiglione: the ideal*, pp. 45–68.

[48] Jorge Arditi, *A genealogy of manners: transformations of social relations in France and England from the fourteenth to the eighteenth century* (Chicago, 1998), pp. 86–121.

[49] It was not simply 'patronage' as such in the sense of material support afforded to artists by the wealthy: Breatnach, 'The chief's poet', 37–40; Breatnach, 'Moladh na féile; téama i bhfilíocht na scol', *Léachtaí Cholm Cille XXIV: an dán díreach* (Maigh Nuad, 1994), pp. 61–76.

[50] Text and translation are from Breatnach, 'The chief's poet', 38–9.

Great is the title chief's poet;
it is held that though art is worthy,
a man bearing the title has a claim on honour
that goes beyond the respect due to art

As Pádraig Breatnach points out, the phrase *anáir ealadhna* 'the respect of [due to] art' is a reference to this traditional sense of bardic entitlement. By 1603–4, the world is changing for poet and patron: the cost of the endemic warfare of the late sixteenth and early seventeenth centuries, the spread of English common law, confiscation, and plantation have all weakened the Gaelic aristocracy, thereby undercutting the economic basis for the poets' survival, as well as weakening the ideological rationale for their poetry.[51] In fact, in those terms, the lord's absence in 'Ionmholta malairt bhisigh' may well be construed as much symbolically as physically – it is somewhat unusual in a bardic composition for the lord not to be apostrophised, yet this is what happens here. This might remind us in the present context, of the prince's 'absence', or withdrawal, from the social and recreational world of the court in Castiglione's *Cortegiano*. This absence opens a 'play space' for the courtiers of Urbino where they can discuss issues more freely than in the presence of a despot.[52] As Daniel Javitch points out, however, this leads to its own 'tension' in creating the illusion that ultimately they are the arbiters of their own fate.[53]

I suggest, then, that such tension underlies our poem as well. In the *Cortegiano*, grace has a horizontal as well as a vertical dimension – it can also be sought from one's peers. This is alluded to at various points in the book, where it is called 'universal favour', otherwise referred to as 'praise'.[54] In our poem, Ó hEodhasa hints that he could exploit this horizontal dimension of favour should the vertical be found lacking, although he is tactful enough in the final stanza to refer to this eventuality as a hypothetical. In fact, he has already been availing of this, *but only in his lord's absence*. The question of what happens on his return is left hanging, but the poet implies that it depends on which of Rory's political personae shows up – the *'flaith'* or the 'earl'. Ultimately, it is in the poet's positioning of himself relative to the vertical and horizontal sources of preferment that he achieves his own particular 'grace', holding these forces in a delicate though precarious equilibrium.

---

[51] As Caball has pointed out in *Poets and politics*. p. 94.
[52] Robert W. Hanning and David Rosand, 'Preface', in Hanning and Rosand (eds.), *Castiglione: the ideal*, p. xii.
[53] Javitch, '*Il Cortegiano*'.
[54] Saccone, '*Grazia*', pp. 48–9. See also Baldessare Castiglione, *The Book of the Courtier*, Charles S. Singleton (trans.) (New York, 1959), p. 109.

But in the idealised court of Urbino, how is this grace to be attained? Castiglione advises the courtier to cultivate 'a certain nonchalance, so as to conceal all art and make whatever is said and done appear to be without effort and almost without any thought about it'.[55] For this nonchalance, Castiglione coins the Italian term *sprezzatura* (from *sprezzo* 'disdain, scorn'), which signifies an apparent disdain for 'sweat', for effort. Defined negatively, it is the avoidance of a conscious striving for effect, of 'affectation' (*affettazione*). The ideal courtier cultivates the favour of the powerful by appearing to be indifferent as to its attainment. *Sprezzatura*, therefore, can be seen as the application of aesthetic appeal for pragmatic or 'political' ends, an exercise in oblique self-aggrandisement in a potentially hostile world.[56] In my reading of this poem, this is what Ó hEodhasa achieves here. Although he ostensibly addresses issues of changing aesthetic taste, the poem's subtext, as I have tried to argue, is more fundamentally cultural and political. The poet is nowhere crass enough to say as much, but his juxtaposition of Gaelic and English nomenclature deftly adduces parallels between the poet's own position and his lord's predicament – 'my' oxymoron (*suarrach sona*) is maybe also 'his' (as *iarla Chlann gConaill*).

The question of course arises as to the nature of the poet's putative audience for a poem like this. Was the patron ever meant to see or hear it, given his absence from Ireland? Was it supposed to be a kind of in-joke between the poet and 'the many' he keeps evoking in his own support throughout the poem? The audience presents another variable in the interpretation of the phrase '*suarrach sona*' which represents the poet's dilemma. The poem pits 'the many' (whoever exactly they are) against the lord, and the poet jostles for his own advantage between them. It could also be, of course, that the poem is composed precisely for Rory's eyes and ears, as if to say, 'we all should think carefully about the choices we make': Castiglione's courtier as counsellor to his prince. One of the key points about *sprezzatura* is that not everyone, even among the more elite members of society, 'gets' it: only the initiated, the blue bloods, the true aristocrats, understand what this surface ease and nonchalance really occlude. Thus, while many will appreciate the aesthetically pleasing effects of the courtier, they will not understand the concealment of art and effort that is involved; it is a surface appreciation only. These qualities serve therefore as modes of self-definition for the nobility, including the blue bloods (who know) but excluding *arriviste* and *nouveau riche* elements (who do not). As Javitch points out, however, this dissimulation cannot be *too* opaque but must ultimately reveal itself for the delight of the audience, or

---

[55] Castiglione, *Book of the Courtier*, Singleton (trans.), p. 43.
[56] For a discussion of these Italian terms, see especially Saccone, '*Grazia*'.

at least to those members of the audience whom its impact is intended to reach.[57]

So I imagine it to have been with O hEodhasa's audience. Among the many, a substantial number will, no doubt, have heard or read the poem at a (relatively) superficial level. The poet has abandoned the recondite ways of eulogy behind his patron's back and the latter, absent in England, will be suitably aghast (in his guise as *'flaith ó gConaill'*, the heroic Gaelic archetype of a chief, this is what is *'suarrach'* about the transformation). Others (more 'in the know' perhaps) will have understood Rory's laughter in stanza eight as appreciation for the new poetry of courtly love (in his new-fangled guise of *'an t-iarla'*, the aspiring Jacobean courtier, this is what is *'sona'*). But yet others may have pondered the irreconcilable in the condensed incongruity of the hybrid *'iarla Chlann gConaill'* and wondered 'whose advantage?' in the game between poet and patron. The final stanza suggests that perhaps the poet has thought it through. Has his lord, remembering the turbulent political situation at home in Tyrconnell?

The poet's coolness, his studied indifference, is such that he apparently manages to detach himself in the last stanza of the poem: arbitration in this matter of aesthetic taste will be between his absent lord and his fellow courtiers at home. Herein, perhaps, lies the real sting in the tail of this poem, for the lord especially, a consummation of what it is that the poet refuses to expressly articulate. The poet, in other words, can retreat from the political into the aesthetic where he appears to find favour (of the many). This is a refuge, however, that he insidiously denies his lord for whom aesthetic pleasure, his choice of 'foreign' poetry albeit produced by his own poet, implicates his political dilemma. This in itself is paradoxical on a grand scale – one of the last of the great hereditary professional caste of poets, whose central function in the validation of Gaelic lordship was intrinsically political, abdicates his political responsibility and will now enjoy being a 'mere' poet, currying the favour of his fellow aristocrats. Rory, meanwhile, can sweat it out in London. Like a famous champion fighter of not too distant memory, the poet floats like a butterfly among his fellow courtiers, but he stings his absent chief like a bee.[58] That is *'sprezzatura'*: the poet strikes a particular public pose thereby implying something quite different; in other words, the nature of *sprezzatura* itself mirrors the irony of the situation in which poet and patron find themselves. It is itself oxymoronic in structure, being 'the rehearsed spontaneity, studied carelessness, and well-practiced naturalness that underlies persuasive discourse'.[59]

---

[57] Daniel Javitch, *Poetry and courtliness in Renaissance England* (Princeton, 1978), p. 57.
[58] See grammar.about.com/od/rs/g/sprezzatura.htm.   [59] *Ibid.*

However, if *sprezzatura* itself reflects the irony and paradox of the situation it attempts to negotiate, then poetry is the ideal literary medium for its expression. In this poem Ó hEodhasa puts into practice a theory of the relationship between poetry and rhetoric advanced in Elizabethan England. The rise of the English court and its emphasis on courtliness in the sixteenth century had important consequences for the status of poetry in England. As we have seen, Castiglione's courtier best represents this European ideal of courtliness, a courtliness with a hard-nosed pragmatic edge to it. In *The Arte of English Poesy*, published anonymously in 1589 but now accepted as the work of George Puttenham, poetry is presented as the discursive form that most closely mimics the grace, the studied nonchalance, of the ideal courtier. This is because, as Puttenham recognises, poetry relies for its effectiveness on the multi-valence of language more so than the more 'direct' oratorical or epistolary discursive modes. To this extent, Puttenham's treatise is an innovative one for the Elizabethan era in establishing a relationship between poetry and rhetoric that is based more on the obliquity than the perspicuity of language.

Thus, the author consistently stresses the efficacy for the poet of figures that 'mean' something rather different that what they appear to 'say' – irony, overstatement, understatement.[60] For the poet, this has the crucial effect of 'delaying' or deferring meaning and is the equivalent of the graceful effect of the courtier's poses which, as Javitch suggests, 'often rests in their implication of something contrary'.[61] I myself would suggest that such a deferral of meaning is germane to Ó hEodhasa's purpose, the epitome of the 'indirection' so espoused by Puttenham. We have seen how paradox informs the poem, and also how the poet juxtaposes understatement (meiosis) and overstatement (hyperbole) in the cause of irony and to disable criticism of his position.[62] We might also feel that the poet is employing an element of insincere flattery when ostensibly he praises O'Donnell's erudition, the figure of paradiastole.[63] In addition, we recall that final stanza where the poet shifts the onus of adjudication on to his audience, washing his hands of it, as it were, the figure of epitropis.[64] We might also view the poet's use of Gaelic and English nomenclature, so central to his strategy as we have seen, as a type of synecdoche, Rory being

---

[60] See George Puttenham, *The art of English poesy by George Puttenham: a critical edition*, Frank Whigham and Wayne A. Rebhorn (eds.) (Ithaca, NY, 2007); for an excellent discussion of the relationship between Puttenham and Castiglione, see Javitch, *Poetry and courtliness*, p. 50ff.

[61] Javitch, *Poetry and courtliness*, p. 60.

[62] Puttenham glosses the figure of meiosis as 'the disabler' or 'the figure of extenuation'. See Puttenham, *The art*, p. 304.

[63] What Puttenham calls the 'curry favell': *ibid.*, pp. 269 and 305.

[64] Puttenham's 'figure of reference': *ibid.*, p. 311.

'split' into two differing and ultimately irreconcilable political realities.[65]
Also relevant here is the figure of periphrasis where a descriptive word or
phrase substitutes for a proper name.[66]

The cumulative effect of these figures in Ó hEodhasa's poem is to
illustrate Puttenham's ideal of poetic speech, its indirection. As Javitch
again points out, however, the latter's discussion is essentially confined
to a presentation of the local effects produced by these figures whereas
their implications actually extend from this micro-level to the macro-level
of an entire poem.[67] In other words, the same rhetorical principles that
underlie individual tropes (e.g. metaphor) can also inform a poem in its
entirety (e.g. allegory). In this way, our own poem might be regarded
as an extended paradox, the tone of which is set by the opening oxymoronic *suarrach sona*, as well as by the contradiction in terms expressed
by the phrase *iarla Chlann gConaill*.[68] It might also be regarded as an
extended synecdoche, in that a component 'part' of society (aesthetic
taste) ultimately stands for a greater 'whole', the more far-reaching issue
of political governance itself.

In Puttenham's world, therefore, the ideal poet is the ideal courtier:
both rely on the manipulation of an audience through a surface appearance of ease, which, however, both conceals and implies a deeper and
perhaps contradictory reality which only the 'initiated' will understand.
In this poem, Ó hEodhasa moves deftly from literary and aesthetic to
political concerns, showing that for him, as a poet, the two are inextrica-
ble, except that he suggests the possibility of extricating *himself* but not
his patron. He is thus anything but a disinterested observer, and yet he
ends up suggesting that such is precisely what he is, leaving it between
O'Donnell and 'the many' to arbitrate. He fully exploits the possibilities
that the medium of poetry offers for dissimulation and beneath his urbane
exterior is every bit the hard-nosed pragmatist of Castiglione's *Courtier*.
To this extent, I would concur with O Riordan's view that the poem is a
'European' one in a cultural sense;[69] nonetheless, its immediate focus is
urgently and specifically political.

---

[65] Puttenam's 'figure of quick conceite': *ibid.*, p. 279.
[66] For Puttenham, 'the figure of ambage' (roundabout speech): *ibid.*, p. 279.
[67] Javitch, *Poetry and courtliness*, 76ff.
[68] In O Riordan's phrase this 'secures the tone of the poem': *Irish bardic poetry*, p. 252.
[69] *Ibid.*, p. 251.

Recognising Elizabeth I: grafting,
sovereignty, and the logic of icons in an
instance of Irish bardic poetry

B. R. Siegfried

Genealogies have long been used to establish authoritative claims to
sovereignty. The more ancient the lineal traces of recognised rule, the
stronger the foundation of legal precedence. In sixteenth-century Europe,
Ireland could and did lay claim to an oral and manuscript tradition that
documented in great detail several ancient lines of elective kingship in
the tanist tradition.

The histories documenting these branching genealogies were as popular among the Old English in Ireland as they were among the Gaelic
lords – an unsurprising turn, given several generations of intermarriage
between families of Old Irish origin and those of Norman lineage. The
following discussion traces a curious moment in Elizabethan attempts in
the reconquest of Ireland, a moment bracketed by a young queen's need
to lean on the very precedence that her government would later attempt to
erase. In turn, Old English families such as the Burkes found themselves
in the curious position of having to recognise Elizabeth's monarchical
claims even as they worked to establish local sovereignty in Ireland by
reference to a Gaelic–Catholic tradition.

On 4 December 1559, shortly after her accession to the English throne,
Elizabeth I received a formal missive from five of England's Catholic bishops. Nicolas Heath, James Turberville, Edmond Bonner, David Poole,
and Gilbert Bourne each signed his name to a letter admonishing the
young queen to reject the Protestant cause and return England to its
traditional place within a unified 'ancient catholic faith'. Stressing the
venerable pedigree of the church, they warned her not to let her 'subjects
be led astray through the inventions of those evil counsellors, who are
persuading your ladyship to embrace schisms and heresies in lieu of the
ancient catholic faith, which hath been long since planted within this
realm, by the motherly care of the church of Rome'. Her sovereignty
as empress over England, Wales, and Ireland, they insisted, was the
fruit of a family tree whose branches took nourishment from the roots
of the church that 'your ancestors duly and reverently observed and

confessed'.[1] That is, her claim to authority, they asserted, was primarily
a function of a *de jure* (or legal) right to rule granted by the institution of
the Universal Church, and only secondarily a *de facto* (or actual) mode
of power exercised via military enforcement, control of resources, and
the love and submission of her people. As these bishops would have it,
without the recognition of the church, the latter form of rule was literally
lawless, and therefore must be construed as tyranny.

Her humanist education might have prompted the young queen to
engage in a reasoned debate had not the bishops' letter taken a rhetorical misstep. Praising her sister Mary's strong Catholic rule (and thereby
implying that Elizabeth's difficulties under Mary were self-inflicted), the
bishops went on to describe Elizabeth's father and brother as dupes of
English preceptors, 'until by heretical and schismatical advisers your
father was withdrawn; and after him your brother prince Edward'. If the
high-handed tone was already an overt breach of decorum, the subsequent analogy – comparing Elizabeth to Athanasius – only deepened the
implied insult. Athanasius was a second-century patriarch of Alexandria
whose ordination to head the church in Egypt had been challenged as
failing to conform to canonical tradition. The resistance to his fitness was
two-fold: first, he was suspected of being too young (and therefore lacking in wisdom and experience) and, second, his views on the trinity were
declared heretical by the first council of Nicea in 325 AD (his emphasis
on Christ as the Word Incarnate, yet uncreated, was one of the doctrinal sticking points). Athanasius spent seventeen of his forty-five years of
church service in exile, his status as heretic or saint in constant flux.

The comparison of Elizabeth to Athanasius was both warning and
invitation. 'We further entreat your ladyship to consider the supremacy of
the church of Rome', the bishops wrote, 'And histories yet make mention,
that Athanasius was expulsed by her [the church] . . . the emperor also
speaking against him for withstanding the head of the church.'[2] The
implication is that Elizabeth, like Athanasius, is taking up an office for
which she is unfit; and, though she has the potential to do great things,
her influence will be felt only when the church exonerates her from the
implications of heresy. On this note, the bishops return to the central
theme of their epistle, that the annals of the church on the one hand,
and her own family history on the other, jointly testify to the force of

---

[1] Cited *Queen Elizabeth's Reply to an Address from Five Catholic Bishops*, 6 Dec. 1559, in
John Strype, *The Annals of the Reformation . . . during . . . Queen Elizabeth's Happy Reign*,
4 vols. (London, 1709), vol. I, pp. 217–18.

[2] *Ibid.*, p. 218.

Catholic precedent as the foundation of her status as sovereign: 'These ancient things we lay before your majesty, hoping God will turn your heart; and, in fine, make your majesty's evil advisers ashamed; and to repent their heresies.'[3]

Two days later, a furious Elizabeth dictated her reply in the presence of her council. 'As to your entreaty for us to listen to you', she began, 'we have it yet, do return you this our answer.' What follows is a not only a defence of her Protestant faith and the legitimacy of her claim to full sovereignty; it is also an assertion of a peculiarly English Christian tradition, one that trumps Rome's canonical purview:

Our realm and subjects have been long wanderers, walking astray whilst they were under the tuition of Romish Pastors, who advised them to own a Wolf for their head (in lieu of a careful Shepherd) whose inventions, heresies, and schisms be so numerous, that the flock of Christ have fed on poisonous shrubs for want of wholesome pastures. And whereas, you [hit] us and our subjects in the teeth, that the Romish Church first planted the Catholic faith within our realms, the records and chronicles of our realms testify to the contrary, and your own Romish idolatry maketh you liars; witness the ancient monument of Gildas, unto which both foreign and domestic have gone in pilgrimage, there to offer. This author testifieth *Joseph of Arimathea* to be the first preacher of the word of God within our realms. Long after that period when Austin [Augustine] came from Rome, this our realm had Bishops and Priests therein, as is well known to the wise and learned of our realm, by woeful experience, how your Church entered therein by blood, they being martyrs for Christ, and put to death because they denied Rome's usurped authority.[4]

In short, if her people of Britannia had been momentarily led astray, it was not by Protestants, but by pagan-influenced interlopers from Rome's empire. Note that Elizabeth is punning on 'Wolf', here simultaneously alluding to the symbol of succour offered to the orphaned twins Romulus and Remus in the founding myth of Rome, and to the figure of the false pastor in Christ's parables of straying and endangered sheep. More importantly, she is formally taking up England's own myth of origins, one which claimed a purer and more robust draft of early Christianity than that brought later by Rome at sword's point.

Of special interest here is Elizabeth's curious choice of anchor for her legal claim to sovereignty in the midst of religious and political tides of turmoil. The reference to Gildas is, after all, both clever and troublesome. Gildas the Wise, as he was referred to by medieval and Renaissance writers, was best known for his *De Exicidio et Conquestu Britanniae* (*On the Ruin and Conquest of Britain*) written sometime before

---

[3] *Ibid.*, pp. 218–19.   [4] *Elizabeth's Reply*, pp. 217–19.

540 AD. Cited by both the Venerable Bede and Geoffrey of Monmouth in their later histories of Britain, Gildas's treatise singles out five kings for castigation; he compares them to five of the beasts associated with Antichrist in the biblical book of Revelation, elaborating on the ways in which they have strayed from the virtues of their greater British ancestors who had received the gospel in purity at the feet of Joseph of Arimathea. The most constant refrain throughout Gildas's piece – and for which the darkest language is consistently invoked – is that of a corrupt clergy in turn corrupting Britannia's kings: 'Britain has priests, but they are fools; numerous ministers, but they are shameless; clerics, but they are wily plunderers.'[5] By referring to Gildas, the Protestant queen conflates her five Catholic bishops with Gildas's infamous five apocalyptic beasts ruining Britain, and with the clerics who had lead England's early kings astray.

In case they missed the insult she has thrown back at them, Elizabeth makes explicit her point and adds a threat:

As for our Father being drawn away from the Supremacy of Rome by schismatical and heretical counsels and advisers, who, we pray advised him more or flattered him than you, good Mr Father, when you were Bishop of Rochester? And then, you Mr Bonner, when you were Archdeacon? And you Mr Turberville? Nay, further . . . who was more an adviser to our Father than your great Stephen Gardiner, when he lived? . . . Was it not you and such like advisers that . . . stirred up our Sister against us and other of her subjects? Whereas you would frighten us by telling how Emperors . . . have owned the Bishop of Rome's authority. It was contrary in the beginning, for our Saviour Christ paid His *tribute* unto Cæsar, as the chief superior; which shows your Romish supremacy is usurped . . . We give you, therefore, warning, that for the future, we hear no more of this kind, lest you provoke us to execute those penalties enacted for the punishing of our resisters, which out of our clemency we have foreborne.[6]

As Elizabeth saw it, if her father had strayed from the truth, it was thanks to these very advisers whose nature was thrown into revealing silhouette by the light of Gildas's ancient English monument. Though effecting a clever rhetorical move, the new monarch has essentially linked the ancient authority from which she derives her especially Anglican sovereignty to a source famously dependent upon Irish chronicles for its legitimacy. The ogham stone to which Elizabeth refers was thought to have the name of Vortiporious inscribed upon it, one of the early kings singled out for Gildas's attention. Pilgrims treated it as a monument to England's early Christian church, and it continued to be venerated as such precisely because Vortiporius's genealogy and kingship

---

[5] Gildas, *De Excidio Britanniae*, M. Winterbottom (trans.) (Totowa, NJ, 1978). The edition Elizabeth read was that of Polydore Vergil (London, 1524).

[6] *Elizabeth's Reply*, pp. 218–19.

were authoritatively documented – in Irish and Welsh sources. In fact, an eighth-century work, 'The Expulsion of the Déssi', claimed to be a compendium of those antique sources which lent credence to Protestant avowals regarding a pre-Roman Christian church in England. As Kuno Meyer explains, in these records Vortiporius's genealogy is given in the early Irish form: 'Tualodor mac Rigin maic Catacuind maic Caittienn maic Clotenn maic Naee maic Artuir maic Retheoir maic Congair maic Gartbuirmaic maic Alchoil maic Trestin maic Aeda Brosc maic Corath maic Echach Almuir maic Arttchuirp'. Meyer renders this as 'Teudor son of Regin, son of Catgocaun, son of Cathen, son of Cloten, son of Nougoy, son of Arthur, son of Petr, son of Cincar, son of Guortepir, son of Aircol, son of Triphun, son of Áed Brosc, son of Corath, son of Eochaid Allmuir, son of Artchorp'.[7] Eochaid Allmuir, or 'Eochaid from overseas', was an Irish noble who purportedly colonised a portion of Wales and whose kingship was never dependent upon Rome when he established himself in Pembrokeshire.

Elizabeth's ancestor, Owain Tewdr, was said to be of this descent, and English documents seemingly confirmed the link between the Welsh Tewdr and the Irish Teudor. In short, when Elizabeth referred to the Gildas monument in her response to the Catholic bishops, she was linking her own genealogy to the Welsh myth of a Christian church established by Joseph of Arimathea and quite distinct from the later institution developed by Roman missionaries. Or, to put it another way, one of Elizabeth's first public defences of her sovereignty as a Protestant monarch involved Irish genealogies and Irish–Welsh ancestry, ancient lineal claims to legal precedent that antedated those of the Catholic Church.

In an interesting historical twist, that same Irish heritage which gave her a trump card in response to the bishops in England became a thorn in her side as she advanced her Protestant claims in Ireland. Marc Caball notes that 'Elizabeth's reign witnesses the emergence of the idea of an alliance of interests between Irishmen of Gaelic and Old English stock. Racial détente was further developed by the interlinking of Roman Catholicism and Gaelic culture, mainly by Counter-Reformation priests immersed in the bardic tradition.'[8] Evidence of this is easily seen within the first two decades of the Elizabethan government's attempts to reanimate the English colonial process in Ireland. In 1577, for instance, Corc Ó Cadhla heatedly wrote of Elizabeth,

---

[7] Kuno Meyer, 'The expulsion of the Déssi', Y Cymmrodor 14 (1902), 113.

[8] Marc Caball, Review of Michelle O Riordan's The Gaelic mind and the collapse of the Gaelic world (Cork, 1990), Cambridge Medieval Celtic Studies 25 (1993), 91.

And the sovereign of England and Ireland is Queen Elizabeth . . . the English say that she is invested also with the supremacy of religion, but in that they assert an untruth. For we are convinced that the head of the Holy Catholic Church is the Pope. In a sense what the English say is correct, for the Queen is the head of the false faith entirely, in so far as it is under her jurisdiction . . . It is a matter of surprise to me that God tolerates them so long in authority except that he beareth patiently and that his vengeance cometh slow and direct.[9]

The sarcasm with which Ó Cadhla begins and ends his critique is not uncommon, and the fact that he goes on to suggest that the English have remained in power because 'the Irish themselves are bad', only serves to emphasise the disdain in which he holds the English – they and their monarch are of consequence not as an irrepressible wave of royal conquest, but as the temporary means of 'castigation' from 'heaven'. Here, the language of both *de jure* and *de facto* political authority gives way to a broader notion of sovereignty as a question of moral standing.

With this in mind, I turn to a poem notable for its status as both a political document and a work of poetic craft. As a political piece, *The History of the Burkes* explicitly addresses questions of both local and national sovereignty.[10] As a book carefully layered with genealogy and praise poems, the manuscript reminds us that, while a patron's aim in securing such a document may be politically uncomplicated, the poet's craft in developing insights around that purpose may be philosophically sophisticated, structurally elegant, and purposefully advanced.[11]

The book is explicitly Catholic in orientation, and placing it in the context of Counter-Reformation polemics underscores several of its more immediate ideological affiliations. Of special interest here is the braiding together of ancient Gaelic symbols with allusions to specific Catholic doctrines and practices. A thorough analysis of such combinations is not possible here, but even a brief glance at how one of the most common metaphors in Gaelic genealogy and praise poems orchestrates both continuity and change (in this case, the hazel) reminds us that the traditional

---

[9] Cited in Bernadette Cunningham, 'Native culture and political change in Ireland, 1580–1640', in Ciaran Brady and Raymond Gillespie (eds.), *Natives and newcomers: essays on the making of Irish colonial society, 1534–1641*, (Dublin, 1986), p. 169. See also Paul Walsh, *Gleanings from Irish manuscripts*, 2nd edn (Dublin, 1933), pp. 160–1.

[10] For diametrically opposed views, see T. J. Dunne, 'The Gaelic response to conquest and colonisation: the evidence of the poetry', *Studia Hibernica* 20 (1980), 11, and Brendan Bradshaw, 'Nationalism and historical scholarship in modern Ireland', *Irish Historical Studies* 26 (1989), 329–51.

[11] The *duanairí* or poem anthologies still extant were often compiled for poets, as encyclopedias of aesthetic possibility. See Brian Ó Cuív, *The Irish bardic* duanaire *or 'poem book'* (Dublin, 1973), pp. 19–23.

forms themselves – complex alliterative structures, ancient tropes and symbols, familiar themes and figures – enjoyed meaningful metamorphoses from generation to generation.[12]

The following discussion places *The History of the Burkes* in the immediate contemporary context of Reformation and Counter-Reformation debates of the 1570s and traces how particular literary allusions and figurative language within the poem would have been thoroughly interlaced with recognisable threads from such debates – despite the antiquity of the poetic tradition from which some of that language was drawn. Equally visible in context are the philosophical implications of the poem's stance on recognition, justice, and sovereignty as functions of sacred time. Ultimately, the same rationale advanced for recognising the local sovereignty of the MacWilliam Burkes undermines Elizabeth's broader claim to the kingdom of Ireland. The end result is a work that explicitly publicises and enhances the particular patron's local power and status while mounting a general paradigm of sovereignty by which Queen Elizabeth's authority in Ireland could be implicitly parsed and critiqued.

The History of the Burkes

The *Seanchas Búrcach*, or *Historia et genealogia familiae de Burgo*, is written in two languages, partly in Irish and partly in Latin.[13] Internal evidence establishes its date of composition to be in the late 1570s, while legal documents appended to the end of the piece are dated 1584. It was commissioned by Seaán MacOliverus, also known as John Burke, who claimed lordship of the MacWilliam Burkes of Mayo from 1571 to 1580, the year of his death. His long-time rival for the lordship was the *tánaiste* Richard in Iarainn, husband of the famous Gráinne Ní Mháille. The English lord deputy, Henry Sidney, mentioned all three in his memoirs and remembered accepting submission from the first two 'with overmuch clemency'.[14] Despite the fact that Sidney later recollected Gráinne and her husband with more interest than he remembered Seaán, it was the latter who had in fact initially won the lord deputy's trust. By the mid

[12] H. J. C. Tristram (ed.), *Text und Zeittiefe* (Tübingen, 1994). See especially pp. 15–28.

[13] For an English translation of the manuscript, see *Seanchus Búrcach*, T. Ó Raghallaigh [Thomas O' Reilly] (ed. and trans.), *Journal of the Galway Archaeological and Historical Society* 13 (1926–7), 50–60 and 101–37; and 14 (1928–9), 30–51 and 142–67. There was a page numbering error in volume 13, and the index to the *Journal* gives both the original and corrected page numbers. I have followed the original pagination. In keeping with current practice, this work will be referred to as *The History* in all subsequent references.

[14] Sir Henry Sidney, *A viceroy's vindication? Sir Henry Sidney's memoir of service in Ireland, 1556–1578*, Ciaran Brady (ed.) (Cork, 2002), p. 87.

1570s, Sidney confidently wrote of Seaán that he was 'the only man of power that hath showed himself loyal'.[15]

Sidney's support was essential for establishing Seaán MacOliverus's claims to the MacWilliam lordship with the English government, but a more substantial argument would have to be made to convince an Irish population unimpressed by a 'foreign' assertion of authority (especially as it essentially side-stepped the Gaelic *tánaiste* tradition). Hence, Seaán had two audiences in mind when he contracted the poetry meant to establish his entitlement, and each required careful rhetorical attention: the English government was meant to believe that he understood his local sovereignty as an extension of Elizabeth's prerogative as empress, while local Catholic Old English lords and Gaelic princes were meant to construe his authority as harking back to prerogatives that antedated the current monarch's Protestant 'heretical' appropriations of power. For one audience, he had to be seen as submitting to Elizabeth; for the other, he needed a form of recognition independent of, and well beyond, her claims to sovereignty. *The History* develops genealogy as a means of accomplishing both.

The first section of the manuscript is in Irish and develops the lineage and international status of the MacWilliam Burkes, tracing ancestral exploits throughout the Middle East in the Crusades, across Europe, and into Ireland. While on the one hand pointing out shared ancestry with Queen Elizabeth, on the other, it places the MacWilliam Burkes within Ireland's mythic history, describing them as 'those foreigners prophesied of the house of Tara'.[16] The second section is in the hand of a different scribe, who added genealogical and historical material in Latin, an augmentation that seems, as Bernadette Cunningham points out, 'designed to present the history of the MacWilliam Burkes to a wider audience than those who spoke only Irish'.[17] As Brian Ó Cuív adds, '[it] is most unusual among Irish manuscripts in that it has a series of fourteen illuminated pictures'.[18] These are at the centre of the volume, surrounded on either side by several blank leaves (Figure 1). Four religious images of Christ precede the secular depictions of famous figures from the Burke family tree, thus visually placing the sacred history of Catholic Christianity at the heart of the family's lineal legends (Figure 2). Located well after these illustrations are two lengthy praise poems in the hand of the first scribe, and at the very end of the manuscript are attached the two legal

---

[15] *CSPI*, III, p. 99.   [16] *The History*, 39.

[17] Bernadette Cunningham, 'Politics and power in sixteenth-century Connaught', *Irish Arts Review* 21 (2004), 117.

[18] Ó Cuív, *Irish bardic* duanaire, p. 35.

Figure 1 Christ before Pilate, from the *Seanchas Búrcach* manuscript, MS 1440, fol. 17r, Trinity College, Dublin. By kind permission of Trinity College Library, Dublin.

Figure 2 Militant Seaán MacOliverus Burke, from the *Seanchas Búrcach* manuscript, MS 1440, fol. 24r, Trinity College, Dublin. By kind permission of Trinity College Library, Dublin.

documents mentioned above. The carefully spaced blank pages, the wealth of illustrations, and the final legal records suggest that the manuscript was not finished according to plan. Even so, the volume as a whole displays a significant level of thematic continuity.[19]

Before moving directly to a close analysis of the poems in the volume, the poets' history of patronage and the early scholarly response to the manuscript are worth considering. Ó Cuív identifies two poems with distinct authors, 'one by Ruaidhrí Ó hUiginn and the other by Tadhg Dall Ó hUiginn'.[20] Tadhg Dall was an especially popular bard who was based in north-west Connaught and Donegal, and had a succession of patrons, some more fully Gaelic (such as the O'Donnells and O'Rourkes) and some self-identified as Old English (such as the Burkes).[21] In the introduction to her edition of his poems (1921), Eleanor Knott wrote of the bard, 'He shows in most of his poems a calm acceptance of contemporary strife . . . We may take him as a typical figure, utterly unaware of the imminent dawn of a new world.'[22] T. J. Dunne seconds Knott's position and claims that, since this Gaelic poet is perfectly happy to substantiate an Old English family's claim to sovereignty in Ireland, there is no sense in which the bard can be thought to be motivated by a Gaelic nationalist awareness. As Dunne further insists, for this poet – as for most bardic poets – 'the *profession* was the thing'.[23] What marks the poetry's apolitical stance, according to Dunne, is the bardic convention of stressing that all in Ireland are essentially sojourners in the land. That convention, after all, had made it possible much earlier in Ireland's history to develop a special mode of cultural resiliency, including assimilative strategies that folded the Norman invaders back into the established Gaelic social order. In short, both Knott and Dunne suggest that, though highly skilled and deeply proud of their craft, sixteenth-century Irish bards were politically naive and unaware of the fundamental transformations taking place in the world around them.

Dunne is right to emphasise the assimilative strategy in bardic poetry as worthy of close attention, but his conclusion about its function simply does not take into account the manner and context in which that

---

[19] See Bernadette Cunningham, 'Illustrations of the Passion of Christ in the Seanchas Búrcach manuscript', in Rachel Moss, Colman Ó Clabaigh, and Salvador Ryan (eds.), *Art and devotion in late medieval Ireland* (Dublin, 2006), pp. 16–32.

[20] Ó Cuív, *Irish bardic* duanaire, p. 35.

[21] See Pádraig Ó Macháin, 'In search of Tadhg Dall Ó hUiginn', Lecture for summer conference of the Sligo Field Club, 9 May 2009.

[22] Eleanor Knott (ed. and trans.), *The bardic poems of Tadhg Dall Ó hUiginn (1550–1591)*, 2 vols. (London, 1922–6), vol. I, pp. i and xiv.

[23] Dunne, 'The Gaelic response', 14.

strategy is developed. In fact, when set in relation to popular Reformation and Counter-Reformation debates and their attendant implications for claims to sovereignty, the volume's most gifted poet demonstrates a keen awareness of the complexities of thought and belief that necessarily would have to make up his patron's claim to local sovereignty, especially as a Catholic, Gaelic-identified, Old English lord. Indeed, with considerable skill Ó hUiginn is able to put new wine in old bottles, so to speak – many of the most antique conventions of genealogy and praise poems could be used to invoke contemporary themes, allude to famous philosophical works by Aristotle and Augustine (works which figured large in Counter-Reformation polemics), and elaborate on cultural practices valued by Gaelic princes and Old English lords alike.

Sovereignty in Irish genealogy and praise poems

Constituting some of the most popular literary and musical modes held in esteem throughout the local culture (including Dublin), Irish genealogy and praise poems had over the course of several hundred years developed a clear formula for asserting sovereign status on behalf of ruling families. Such works were intended for public performance.[24] Indeed, 'bards were expected to celebrate their patrons' illustrious genealogies', explains Richard McCabe, 'just as assiduously as English poets were expected to celebrate that of Elizabeth Tudor'.[25] By the sixteenth century, typically five elements were asserted as the signs for recognising legitimate sovereignty and were developed either as a unified synthesis in longer poems, or separately as an expanded focus in shorter pieces. These included, first, elaborate accounts of a leader's martial prowess and ability to hold and defend land, goods, and people; second, a detailed and anecdotally laced lineage – that is, a genealogy of heroic ancestors demonstrative of familial traits corresponding to an ideal of good leadership (and which additionally roots that family's past to a particular place in the present); third, references to written legal claims (formal documented inscriptions such as treaties, chronicles, church leases, inscribed monuments, etc.) that additionally stress the importance of legal antiquity and formal justice in establishing sovereignty; fourth, suasion or the proffering of a more convincing model of the just society in the person of

---

[24] In fact, Gaelic lineage poems and histories were 'public and part of the structure of their society', as Eiléan Ní Chuilleanáin points out, not 'produced for a restricted readership'. See Ní Chuilleanáin, 'Forged and fabulous chronicles: reading Spenser as an Irish writer', *Irish University Review* 26 (1996), 242.

[25] R. A. McCabe, *Spenser's monstrous regiment: Elizabethan Ireland and the poetics of difference* (Oxford, 2002), p. 50.

a particular lord or familial line;[26] and, fifth, 'God's pleasure'. This last was frequently asserted as trumping even the most deserving formulation of the previous elements.

All five attributes are readily visible in the long Burke genealogy poem, illustrating how the distinctive threads that make up sovereignty could be woven together and to what effect. Not surprisingly, the reference to divine providence opens the piece. 'From God is shaped every perfect work', we are told at the outset, and 'Each perfect work formed from God / Must belong to the Son of Mary; / May He put the perfect work in readiness – / The Tutor of every science.'[27] The intentional pun on 'work' suggests that God's will embraces the family's deeds (about to be recounted) as well as the poem in which their remembrance will take its public form. Next, a long line of admirably bellicose ancestors comparable to 'Hector' and 'the Royal Roman Caesar'[28] parade across the stage of history to demonstrate the family's heritable martial qualities.[29] The various accounts of ancestral exploits in the Crusades – from 'Jerusalem' to 'Damascus' to 'Egypt', and eventually culminating in a victory over 'the King of Persia of the satin palls' from whom Baldwin de Burgo 'took the kingship by force'[30] – establish a history of successful conquest strictly aligned with Christian intent. Another family branch succeeds in metamorphosing similar modes of force into sovereignty over the English when Edward, a 'brave, truthful King / By force of right, over fair London',[31] came to rule.

After the accounts of the family's conquest over infidels and the English (not an accidental alignment) have been established, the poem turns the focus of the historical drama to the shores of Ireland: Richard Mor – whose immediate family is described as 'Those foreigners prophesied of the house of Tara' – craves further worthy challenges and 'directed . . . The prows of his quick-moving, stately ships, / To the yew-green land of Erin'.[32] The clash with Gaelic princes is immediate, and 'face to face they strike' until the Galls rout the Gaels.[33] Intermarriage with Gaelic nobility and further conquests are traced so that a peculiarly Gaelic inheritance begins to emerge: on the one hand, this is the 'branch by whom was fought the battle, / In which the pillars of Tara were broken', while on the other hand, 'Dalaigh blood is in the soft Burke blood; / The

---

[26] See Standish O'Grady, *Early bardic literature* (New York, 1970, reprint).
[27] *The History*, p. 31.   [28] *Ibid.*, p. 155.
[29] Giovanni Boccaccio's *Genealogia Deorum Gentilium* – by 1520 published in various vernacular versions (including English: *On the Genealogy of the Gods of the Gentiles*) – is an important influence.
[30] *The History*, p. 155.   [31] *Ibid.*, p. 39.   [32] *Ibid.*   [33] *Ibid.*, p. 41.

double ore of gold in thee.'[34] In a keen inversion of what had become a hackneyed metaphor – in which inter-ethnic marriage was imagined as a brittle, mixed-metal alloy – these Gallic–Gaelic marriages continually enhance the family line, alchemically yielding gold's malleability, refinement, and excellence. This, in turn, makes it not only possible but desirable for the 'Gaels of Connacht's plain' to accept the scion of the line as their MacWilliam: 'The trees are bowing... In honor of thee.'[35]

After a quick review of twenty-one battle victories within Ireland, the poet proffers the testimony of the land itself as a further form of persuasion. That is, not only are the MacWilliam Burkes capable of military conquest, but the literal fruits of subsequent wise rule – including 'salmon', 'juicy berries', and groves of fruitful trees – argue for the divine providence behind the initial feats of arms. Moreover, just as the bounty of the land manifests the rightness of Burke sovereignty, so the allusion to Caesar underscores an ideal in which arms are used justly, to right uncivil wrongs by rule of law: 'Against their evil deeds good his hand – / A prince like the royal Roman Caesar.'[36] In a curious twist, providential sovereignty transforms the Burke conquest into a rampart against 'foreign' oppression: 'No cause for which a woman might be startled, / Of oppression of the Foreigner upon the Gael; / No spoil of the Gael with the Gall; / No man suffering injustice.'[37]

When the legal status of records is invoked, the poet acknowledges that such chronicles do make up a strand of sovereignty to which the 'saxon queen',[38] sharing Burke ancestry, also has claim:

> The present woman Elizabeth is
> An odorous branch of the wood of Charles;
> As is each scion of her race,
> Though the half is from Lionel.[39]

Of note is the fact that the prose portion of the book makes the connection even more explicit. Addressed to a broader audience very probably meant to include Elizabeth's envoys, it is not especially modest about the roots of royalty in Seaán's own line:

Be it known to all who read the chronicles of England and of France and of Ireland, that Mac William Burk and his race after him, is the most illustrious royal blood that ever came into Ireland with the invasion, for he was the son of the King of France, who first came to England.[40]

---

[34] *Ibid.*, p. 47.   [35] *Ibid.*, p. 49.
[36] For a contrasting view, see Joep Leerssen, 'For a post-Foucaldian literary history: a test case from the Gaelic tradition', *Configurations* 7 (1999), 227–45.
[37] *The History*, p. 157.   [38] *Ibid.*, p. 165.   [39] *Ibid.*, p. 39.   [40] *Ibid.*, p. 117.

Here, the poem's claims are further bolstered by the explicit invocation of antique chronicles, whose attestation provides a further form of recognition. The record then briefly traces the genealogy to the 'daughter of the King of Scotland' who 'was the mother of Edmond Albanagh':

And of the descendants of Elizabeth, daughter of the Brown Earl, is the queen of England, i.e., Elizabeth that now is, 1578, *so that it is through the blood of the children of William Burk she came to the Crown.* And Mac William's own mother is the noblest of these in direct line upwards, as the daughter of O'Donnell. But what need to say more?[41]

The final twist on inheritance is a nice rhetorical flourish, for as this chronicler would have it, Elizabethan sovereignty derived from Ireland's status as a kingdom under the rule of that shared ancestor, paired with the royal line of the O'Donnells. The coy 'But what need to say more?' suggests that Elizabeth's royal status is really only half as good as the MacWilliam claim to sovereignty in Ireland. To put it another way, in a not particularly subtle move, *The History of the Burkes* construes Elizabeth's sovereignty in Ireland as tenable due to a shared ancestor from the Burke line. Thanks to her Burke relatives who had the good sense to be grafted into the Gaelic line, the queen could lay claim to a birthright that was historically independent of Roman sovereignty and more ancient than Norman assertions of authority.

In short, the manuscript does include the traditional bardic elements meant to mark and enable the recognition of sovereignty. Military prowess and successful conquest are matched with genealogical assertions of power and place. References to antique chronicles are aligned with allusions to Caesar to underscore a historical thematics of law and ethical order. The evidence of the land's bounty is taken as the sign of divine providence and – in combination with the grafting of Gael and Gall, and a familial fruitfulness which parallels that of the land – the history of Burke sovereignty is artfully set forth as antecedent to Tudor claims to authority, even as that same history provides Queen Elizabeth the possibility of a similarly rooted sovereignty. But does it offer anything more than these medieval tropes?

The hazel, the virgin, and the ideal of synthesis

When genealogy is developed as a myth of origins (which in turn establishes the grounds for sovereignty), what is important is not that the myth is repeated, but that each time it is repeated its meaning is added to and

[41] *Ibid.*, p. 119 (emphasis mine).

thus transformed.[42] What was generally apt in the original is no longer true of subsequent versions, unless the bard carefully reorients the old tropes towards contemporary concerns and intentions. For this reason, such myths are not only archaeological, but teleological; their meaning is not only of origins, but also about futures. In other words, genealogy poems posit the recognition of sovereignty as both a chronological and a thematic ordering of time and identity. In order to illustrate this thematic ordering more fully, three elements of the Gaelic literary culture will suffice for our purposes here: the long symbolic association of the hazel branch with Gaelic sovereignty in bardic genealogy poems; the biblical tradition of associating the hazel with the emergence of Israel as a nation; and the further iconic status of the hazel branch in poems venerating Mary as queen of heaven.[43] Taken together, these three factors in *The History of the Burkes* posit an ideal of sovereignty peculiar to its Counter-Reformation context, even as the book continues the medieval tradition of stressing Ireland's pre-Christian heritage at the root of the family tree.

As E. Q. Quiggin explains, '[In] the Brehon Laws the hazel is reckoned a "chieftain-tree".'[44] Examples of Gaelic poems that hark back to pre-Christian traditions are numerous. As late as 1729, Aogán Ó Rathaile would describe his patron as one 'whose forefathers were served by my forefathers before the birth of Christ'.[45] No surprise that hazel branches, clusters (nuts), and blossoms lace *The History* with the ancient symbols of Gaelic sovereignty. In fact, the Burke manuscript seems to echo Gilbride Macnamee's long-admired poem, a thirteenth-century work that was originally addressed to Cathal Redhand, the king of Connaught (*c.* 1220). There we learn that Redhand's leadership has 'rendered fruitful the green woods', and the particular fecundity of the 'white hazel' becomes an assurance that 'His rule has . . . made blossoms to sprout through the tips of the branches.' From the roots of the past, through the main body of the present, and branching into futures emerging from the 'tips of the branches', Redhand's sovereignty is not merely derived from the past, it makes the past flourish in new ways. 'Ireland has recognized her ruler', we are told before the final vision of hazelnuts is developed as a synecdoche for political order, economic bounty, and spiritual renewal: 'A ruddy

---

[42] See Joep Leerssen, *Mere Irish and fíor-Ghael: studies in the idea of Irish nationality, its development and literary expression prior to the nineteenth century* (Notre Dame, 1997).

[43] See P. Mannaerts, 'Creations: medieval rituals, the arts, and the concept of creation', *Music and Letters* 90 (2009), 480–3.

[44] E. C. Quiggin, *Prolegomena to the study of the later Irish bards, 1200–1500* (Oxford, 1911), p. 26.

[45] Seán Ó Tuama and Thomas Kinsella (eds. and trans.), *An duanaire 1600–1900: poems of the dispossessed* (Dublin, 1981), pp. 164–7.

cluster on dark leaves amid green woods with soft grass' becomes a multiplicity of possible desirable futures as 'in plentiful store the nuts fall down with their brown shells'.[46]

Similarly, *The History of the Burkes* describes especially important members of the family line as hazel 'blossoms', 'branches', and 'nuts'. However, in contrast to Macnamee's model poem – which outlines the signs of sovereignty for an audience united in the Catholic faith – Ó hUiginn's poem is aimed at an audience embroiled in highly polemical Counter-Reformation debates. Images such as 'A shovve of the Protestants Petigrevv as ye haue it before at large deducted' (Figure 3) formed a substantial part of the context of reception for the poem's various English and Gaelic audiences.[47] In the tempestuous rhetorical landscape of sixteenth-century religious debates, genealogical trees were understood to be about more than family history; individuals could also be placed in genealogies of orthodoxy or heresy. One's inheritance and offspring could thus include properly devotional amplifications of orthodox theology, or monstrously conceived heretical ideas and the 'disorderliness' or 'zealotry' of schismatic new doctrines. In this representative example, Martin Luther is depicted as 'a wicked deuiser of damnable doctrine' and 'father of all the sectes of the protestants: the Archeheretike of our time'. Luther's family crest is emblazoned with a 'Monster to geue thee a warning', and we are further advised – with considerable sarcasm – that 'faire figures' may conceal 'foule rootes':

> Such faire figures, such like truthes, such foule rootes, such offspring,
> Such holy fathers, such good sonnes, such ghospell, such blessing,
> Yet thou which maiest read, vpon this monster do not muse.
> But to haue more deformities, his broode in this booke peruse.

The other major figures are described as the offspring of Luther's written works – each Protestant theorist emerging from the schismatic tree as a result of reading – a process emphasised with the visual pun on the proliferation of leaves (pages) from each of the three main branches. Genealogies were, in the Reformation context, literary lineages of belief as well as familial histories of conquest (a point the Burke manuscript emphasises, remember, by placing the religious illustrations alongside depictions of famous military ancestors at the centre of the book). This peculiarly literary genealogy deserves close attention.

---

[46] Cited in Quiggin, *Prologomena*, p. 26.

[47] The illustration is found in *The apologie of Fridericus Staphylus counseller to the late Emperour Ferdindandus . . . Of disagreement in doctrine amonge the protestants . . .* , Thomas Stapleton (trans.) (Antwerp, 1565), Gg4–Hh1.

Figure 3 'A Shovve of the Protestants Petigrevv as ye haue it before at large deducted', in Thomas Stapleton (trans.), *The Apologie of Fredericus Staphylus* (Antwerp, 1565). Reproduced by kind permission of the Burke Library at Union Theological Seminary, Columbia University Libraries.

The Christian book most famous for its poetics of genealogy as an elaboration of divine approbation was the Bible – the same book at the centre of Reformation theological debates. Indeed, the parallels between the Old Testament and the bardic *duanaire* are instructive. Though not comparing the Bible to bardic books, Robert Alter and Frank Kermode are nevertheless helpful in this regard: 'The Hebrew Bible', they write, 'quite frequently incorporates as integral elements of its literary structures kinds of writing that, according to most modern preconceptions, have nothing to do with "literature".' Rather, they often include 'genealogies, etiological tales, laws . . . lists of tribal borders, detailed historical itineraries'.[48] All purport to mark temporal truths in relation to potential futures. The Burke manuscript similarly stitches together materials that modern readers have had trouble appreciating in literary terms – yet the literary possibilities for these seemingly reductive documentary modes become clear in relation to more complex theological ideas out of which new thoughts on sovereignty were emerging.

To appreciate how this might be, we return to our sample symbol, the hazel. While on the one hand it was a well-worn sign of sovereignty passed on from the earliest Gaelic literary sources, on the other, it was also the biblical emblem of Israel's status as God's chosen people. Given that sixteenth-century religious debates often took the form of competing for the title of Israel, the place of the hazel in the Bible is especially significant: for Catholic-identified families in Ireland, the hazel was not only associated with genealogies that now had to reflect a Counter-Reformation sensibility, it was also an emblem of Ireland's Catholic status as the true Israel.[49] In fact, the hazel appears in the Old Testament – and crucially it is the *only* place in the entire Bible where it figures – at a key moment when the tribe of Hebrew shepherds is proclaimed a nation by divine fiat, and the patriarch Jacob receives the new name of Israel on behalf of an entire people. A popular focus of sermons, visual representation in the arts, and source for poetry and drama throughout Europe, the story was well known and was the basis for the hazel being associated with Israel in medieval iconography.[50] Indeed, the hazel's symbolic prominence in the Bible's account of Israel's founding myth was fortuitously reflected

---

[48] Robert Alter and Frank Kermode (eds.), *The literary guide to the Bible* (Cambridge, MA, 1990), p. 16.

[49] For a more detailed discussion of this phenomenon in relation to the propaganda of writers affiliated with the English Pale, see B. R. Siegfried, 'Wrestling with the angel: the typology of Israel in John Derricke's *The image of Ireland*', in Michael Potterton and Thomas Herron (eds.), *Dublin and the Pale in the Renaissance, c. 1540–1660* (Dublin, 2011), pp. 319–51.

[50] See also Genesis 27–33.

in the Irish literary tradition where it had always been associated with sovereignty.[51] In effect, genealogy poems rife with the symbols of blossoms, branches, and clusters symbolically gave prominent Gaelic and Old English families Jacob's (and thus Israel's) hazel-trick birthright.

The Gaelic tradition also associated the hazel branch of Israel with the Catholic veneration of Mary as mediator, and with the idea that Christ was the only 'true-judging King of the goodly ambrosial clan', doctrines anathema to English Protestant sensibilities in the Pale.[52] In fact, Irish genealogy poems symbolically grafted the ancestral 'hazel branches' of Ireland to the tree of Christ's church, and the ancient token of Irish sovereignty became evidence for kinship in the typological history of King David's Israel – hence the significance of Jerusalem in the Burke manuscript, where the early ancestral rescue of that city (which signified Israel's rise as a nation of power and providence) is explicitly linked to the Burke conquest of Ireland.

The popular 'A Prayer to the Virgin' models a further link between divine sovereignty and the hazel: 'Queen of queens, pure holy maiden... Pray for us that our wretched transgression be / forgiven for Thy sake... Branch of Jesse's tree in the beauteous hazel-wood / Pray for me until I obtain forgiveness of my foul sins.'[53] Jesse, of course, was King David's father, and both Mary's and Jesus's predecessor. As this poem suggests, it is through Mary's lineage from the hazel-bearing Jacob, through Jesse and David, that her first-born son, Jesus, would inherit the temporal birthright to kingship in Israel. Moreover, in visual representations, the figure of Mary united the hazel of Israel with Christian conquest. As Clodagh Tait explains, the Irish landscape was laden with images of Mary, some of which depicted 'her foot crushing the serpent on a sickle moon, a reference to a passage in the book of Revelation: "and there appeared a great wonder in heaven; a woman clothed with the sun, and the moon under her feet, and upon her head a crown of twelve stars"'.[54] The cultural practice of pilgrimage – whereby

---

[51] Also worth noting are the long-established overlaps between the heroes of Irish epic and the biblical protagonists of Israel. See *The Táin: translated from the Irish epic, Táin Bó Cuailnge*, Thomas Kinsella (ed. and trans.) (Oxford, 2002), p. ix.

[52] Even among Catholics, there was debate concerning how and when the veneration of Mary was appropriate. See Salvador Ryan, '"New wine in old bottles": implementing Trent in early modern Ireland', in Thomas Herron and Michael Potterton (eds.), *Ireland in the Renaissance, c. 1540–1660* (Dublin, 2007), pp. 122–37.

[53] 'A Prayer to the Virgin', in *Ancient Irish poetry*, Kuno Meyer (trans.) (London, 1994, reprint), p. 32. See also Revelation 12:1.

[54] Clodagh Tait, 'Art and the cult of the Virgin Mary in Ireland', in Rachel Moss, Colmán Ó Clabaigh, and Salvador Ryan (eds.), *Art and devotion in late medieval Ireland* (Dublin, 2006), p. 171.

the viewing and veneration of Mary's image were undertaken as part of a passage through the local landscape – re-enacted Israel's journey in pursuit of God's promise. Interestingly, then, the Gaelic grafting of the pre-Christian symbol of Irish sovereignty to the proto-Christian sign of Israel's divine preferment – the hazel – culminates in the figure of Mary.

In other words, when the Burke poem invokes Mary, it does so not as an abstract invitation to meditation, but with the assumption that pilgrimages are regularly taking place (during which sovereignty is regularly recast in terms of Catholic devotion), thus providing a concrete backdrop of recollection and experience for the poetic language. Catholics in Ireland – much like the crusaders of the Burke family history who sought the Holy Land – travelled vast distances in order to be close to something transcendent and sacred, knowing that they would feel differently for the rest of time for having been briefly in its presence. The Marian context of the hazel reminded worshippers that, though texts are necessary, they do not have the same necessity as wonder, praise, and reverence. Placing Mary as the opening frame for a family's genealogy suggests that some dimension of the divine opens forth from human intimacy, including its various avatars of love, familial propagation, and united devotion. These are all things supported by the scriptural texts of the Bible, but which exceed that text. Mary, in short, stood for holy things beyond words, things embracing of *scriptura*, but never reduced to *sola scriptura*. No surprise, then, that both the veneration of icons and the thematics of pilgrimage become crucial threads in Ó hUiginn's poem on sovereignty. Before taking up those threads, though, I turn to another literary strand in the poem's tapestry of recognition.

Sovereignty as the reconciliation of time and potential

In addition to signifying a tripartite literary synthesis – of Ireland's pre-Christian bardic tradition, the biblical account of Israel's emergence as a blessed nation, and the Marian ideal of a pre-schismatic Catholic unity echoed in contemporary catechisms and religious praise poems – the symbol of the hazel now functioned in a social context where the 'clusters' of nuts could be fully affiliated with sophisticated Augustinian ideas about time and potential.[55] Thanks to the work of preservation and dissemination by the Augustinian order in Ireland, the philosophical and

---

[55] For further discussion of bardic sophistication, see Salvador Ryan, 'Creation and recreation in Irish bardic poetry', in Sven R. Havsteen, Nils H. Petersen, Heinrich W. Schwab, and Eyolf Østrem (eds.), *Creations, medieval rituals, the arts, and the concept of creation* (Brepols, 2001), pp. 65–85.

theological writings of Augustine were familiar to the Gaelic intelligentsia.[56] Augustine's writings, in turn, provided an ample introduction
to the ideas of Aristotle. Indeed, Aristotle had been particularly popular in the Middle Ages when the growing scholastic movement fused
his philosophy with Christian theology. By the time of the Reformation,
Aristotelian ideas were used to further link reformed doctrines to political
ideologies.

The works of both Aristotle and Augustine are useful for understanding
what Ó hUiginn accomplishes with his hazel-inflected elaborations of
genealogical time in relation to questions of sovereignty. Although Irish
and English discourses on sovereignty share the language of genealogical
recognition, a fundamentally different conception of *time* and language
drives their respective beliefs about how authority must be enacted in
history. For Protestant England, Aristotle's rationalist notion of time
seems to have dominated ideas about history. This model sees time as
a series of 'nows', each point passing away to give rise to a new point
in a succession.[57] Similarly, sovereigns, while incorporating an ideal that
stands outside time, nevertheless figure as distinct points in a linear series,
separate from the past (with distinctly progressive implications) and apart
from, though looking towards, the future (and thus still anchored to a
sense of tradition). For this reason, establishing lineage in the English
tradition is simply a matter of tracing points in a line of power.

In contrast, *The History of the Burkes* figures time in Augustinian terms.
In his meditation on time in Book XI of *The Confessions*, Augustine
pointed out the gaps in the understanding of time inherent in the Aristotelian theory: if time is a series of 'nows', then whenever one says 'now',
the time of that now has already gone. Trying to isolate the present is
impossible since it is always already in the past. The problem for the
English model of sovereignty-through-time is obvious: of time's three
modes for establishing sovereignty – permanence, simultaneity, and succession – only succession is truly sustained. Permanence could be argued
by a new elaboration of the theory of the king's two bodies, but even on
this model, the grounds for simultaneity are unstable. Interestingly, it is
a loyal Catholic, Edmund Plowden, who nevertheless attempts to make

---

[56] See Michael Benedict, *A presence in the age of turmoil: English, Irish and Scottish Augustinians in the Reformation and Counter-Reformation* (Villanova, PA, 2002); F. X. Martin, 'The
Irish Augustinian friaries in pre-Reformation Ireland', *Augustiniana* 6 (1956), 346–84;
and David Kelly, 'Medieval Augustinian foundations in Britain and Ireland', *Institutum
Historicum* 70 (2007), 187–204.

[57] For a good discussion of further complications inherent in Aristotle's model, see David
Bostock, 'Aristotle, Zeno, and the potential infinite', *Proceedings of the Aristotelian Society*,
new series, 73 (1972–3), 37–51.

this case, concluding his treatise with a prayer for Queen Elizabeth's 'long life and many children and that she and they . . . by lineal descent may inherit and continue this kingdom'. As Plowden explains, each monarch has, by the nature of the office, two bodies, 'to wit, the body natural and the body politic'. The former is mortal, frail, 'more base', and even 'disabled in law by causes criminal'. The body politic, in contrast, is 'the more precious', superior, deathless, and incorruptible. Indeed, even the most crippled natural body, 'by the access of the body politic', can provide the means by which the 'body natural is purged and discharged of all criminal offences'.[58] It is the body politic that comes through succession, with individual inheritors being points in a sequence.

However, as Augustine noted, the attempt to iterate time – or more particularly, *present* time – always lags behind the actual present, the 'now'. This poses a problem for substantiating succession in terms of simultaneity. To say that the present is always present is contradicted by the fact that the moment one attempts to isolate it *as* present (to say *now*), that *now* is gone and in the past. In strict lineal terms, the problem is more complicated yet, for the same is true of the future. Augustine explains the paradox this way: the future does not exist because it has not happened yet; the past does not exist because it is not happening *now*; and *now* does not exist because insofar as iteration constitutes our perception of time, it is never *now*. Despite Plowden's carefully argued theory of the king's two bodies, Augustine's considerations would seem to leave permanence, simultaneity, and succession without a unifying means of emerging from the ideal into the real.

However, as the Burke-supported monastics knew very well, Augustine's proposed solution to this paradox was a notion of a 'threefold present' derived from Trinitarian doctrine. The past and the future exist in the mind, according to Augustine, through memory on the one hand and expectation on the other. To conceive of the past and of the future, the mind must be stretched – distended – and Augustine's tidy formula is that the lack of *extension* of the present (which constitutes our inability to say *now* in the moment) is overcome by the *distension* of the mind. Heidegger would later helpfully explain this as a kind of continuous stretching of the present mediated by memory of the past and expectation of the future. This *continuous present* contains the past and the future within it, so long as the mind is distended in this way. This is precisely what the craft of the bards was meant to accomplish.

---

[58] Edmund Plowden, 'Treatise on Mary, queen of Scots' (1566), in Robert S. Miola (ed.), *Early modern Catholicism: an anthology of primary sources* (Oxford, 2007), pp. 55–7.

To this end, the repeated references to 'trees', 'roots', 'branches', 'blossoms', and 'clusters' in *The History of the Burkes* are more than simply the oldest metaphors for ancestry on record. When especially important figures in the family line are referred to as 'hazel blossoms' and 'hazel nuts', these medieval poetic commonplaces bring with them the newly popular classical debates surrounding the nature of reality, and the role of potentiality versus actuality. Because language is experienced linearly, but must somehow capture the threefold present described above, some kind of synthesis would need to take place. In this, the Irish bards ingeniously reconcile Augustine to Aristotle by way of Aristotle's notion of reality. In Aristotle's work, a nut represents two aspects of reality since it is simultaneously actual and potential. It exists in the present as a seed that has dropped (so its existence refers to its own past) even as it pulls the future to the present, for it is the form out of which a tree will grow (its potential).

Moreover, medieval Christian writing influenced by Aristotle's notion that reality is always made up of two parts (actual and potential) often epitomised Mary as the nexus for both aspects of reality. Irish poetry embraced that conception of Mary, thematising it in both genealogical and devotional poems. In 'A Poem Addressed to the Blessed Virgin', for example, one poet writes, 'Woe to him who has insulted your bright head – a hard thing, since you have not sinned; if your womb is not chaste, Woman, there is no nut on a fair branch in a wood.'[59] That is, if Mary is not indeed the mother of God – the security that Christ was God-made-human, a fullness of reality in which the actual and potential are reconciled in the present – then the very fabric of reality is rent. No surprise that, in Counter-Reformation rhetoric, devotion to Mary was advanced as a sign for the recognition of true sovereignty. Providential authority, that is, must be manifest as a threefold present, and Mary was its matrix. Ultimately, political sovereignty must give way to that which makes its full emergence into reality possible: the Mother of God.

Recognising the sojourner and the foreigner

Though not rising to the same fullness of completion found in Mary or Jesus, the bards insisted that the greatness of certain ancestors was embedded in a similar power of unification across time. The philosophical position that reality is a synthesis of actual and potential is mirrored in bardic poetry stressing assimilation in relation to sovereignty. Indeed,

[59] Osborn Bergin, *Irish bardic poetry: texts and translations* (Dublin, 1970), pp. 254–7.

the long-term success of assimilation in Ireland brackets the fact that, for the Gaelic poets, lineage is a two-pronged strategy for substantiating sovereignty. As we have seen, the bard who traces the royal claims of the MacWilliam Burkes also recognises the affiliated claim of Elizabeth. This prong is meant to *narrow* the pool of candidates based on lineal order and the presumption of inherited qualities fitting one to rule.[60]

The parallel prong does the opposite work, stressing instead the foreignness at the root of all sojourners in Ireland. The term 'Gael' is proffered as a category of genealogical affiliation, branching out and extending in unexpected directions:

> Whoever should say that strangers are
> The Burkes of the lion feats;
> Let there be found one of the blood of Gael or Gall
> Who is not a sojourner amongst us.
>
> Whoever says that it is not lawful for them
> To get their own share of Ireland
> Who in the soft dewy field
> Are more than visitors in Ireland?
>
> Though the race of Gaedhal Glas
> Were wont to call the sons of Charles strangers ...
> Strangers are the race who say it.[61]

As the treatment in this poem of MacWilliam and Elizabeth demonstrates, the Gaelic ideal of sovereignty hinges on a further point of recognition – a distinction between the mere stranger and the outlandish foreigner. But if the MacWilliam Burkes could be embraced by Gaelic Ireland on the basis of an admirable lineage and a shared sense of the Christian sojourner tradition, what, exactly, makes Elizabeth irreducibly foreign, forever inhabiting the diminutive status of 'that saxon queen'?[62]

The veneration of icons

The bardic reconciliation of Augustinian time with Aristotelean reality meant that while Elizabeth's claim of *exclusive* lineage might be recognised (she belonged to a narrow pool of candidates), she nevertheless would always remain foreign because she rejected the very doctrine that

---

[60] For an excellent discussion of this narrowing strategy expressed as hereditary hierarchies, see Brendan Kane, 'A dynastic nation? Rethinking national consciousness in early seventeenth-century Ireland', in David Finnegan, Marie-Claire Harrigan, and Eamonn Ó Ciardha (eds.), Imeacht na n-Iarlaí: the flight of the earls (Derry, 2010), pp. 124–31.
[61] *The History*, p. 147.   [62] *Ibid.*, p. 165.

ratified an *inclusive* genealogy. Simply put, there was a profound philo-sophical difference of opinion between the Protestant English and the Catholic Irish regarding the very fabric of relations at all levels of soci-ety. For the Irish poets, steeped in early Catholic practices and theology, sovereignty was bound up with an idea of relation best exemplified by the very icons that were anathema to the English Reformists. Icons embody a form of recognition not dependent on language, and more akin to the time-unifying function of poetic genealogies than to the creed of *sola scriptura*. In devotional practice, icons are extra-linguistic. And though some people used them superstitiously (as magical tokens), Augustine, Origin, Abelard, and others had forcefully rejected a pagan-oriented stance of superstition, as they saw it.

Rather, icons were to serve as reminders that physical reality is imbued with transcendent potential, just as those who embraced Jesus were touching humanity and divinity simultaneously. Moreover, as Nicholas Sander so carefully explained in *A Treatise on the Images of Christ and of His Saints* (1566), religious icons were not meant to reduce God to mere visibility – to do so would indeed reduce icons to what Protestants feared they were: idols. Rather, venerable icons were about proximity and intimacy, and were understood to stand independent of the mediation of Scripture. An example accessible to modern readers might be the instant when a mother shows a picture of her child to a friend, then impul-sively kisses the picture and presses it to her heart. No one believes that the mother is confused about the reality of representation. She neither believes that the picture is somehow really her child, nor that somewhere her child has just been kissed and held. Rather, the picture allows for a spontaneous gesture that literally embodies the truth of her relationship to that child, in this case a love that is fully present even when her child is not.[63] On this view, her gesture is more than representation – it is manifestation.

The Burke poem similarly pushes genealogical potential beyond lan-guage. Like an icon which wraps temporal relations in spatial terms, an individual situated in a genealogical tree (as a hazelnut of potential and actual reality) literally embodies elements of the familial past, present, and future. Indeed, this notion of genealogy derives directly from the peculiarly Gaelic assimilative twist on a Catholic doctrine of how tem-poral relations may be gathered up in a material figure. In this poem, at least, what made Elizabeth both a sojourner and a *foreigner* was her own

---

[63] I am indebted to Paul Moyeart of the University of Louvaine for this excellent example taken from his lecture, 'Icons as relics: touching God in his image', Brigham Young University, 3 Nov. 2009.

Protestant rejection of the iconic model of genealogy that would have made her sovereignty fully recognisable in the broadly branching terms that allowed for perpetual grafting. The MacWilliam Burkes, in contrast, could be recognised as sojourning strangers and yet be embraced as intrinsically *Gaelic* precisely because they understood sovereignty in the transcendent terms paradoxically embedded in the image of the hazelnut and the veneration of Mary and her icons.

The kinds of grafting made possible (theoretically) by this trope seem to have spurred a special level of fury in New English administrators such as Henry Sidney. As Deanna Rankin explains, 'it is precisely along bloodlines and national inheritance that the battlelines are drawn against the . . . native Irish'.[64] Indeed, Sidney seems especially determined to reject the Gaelic theory of grafting strangers into the family tree, insisting that the Old English lords reject such assimilation and see themselves as *foreign* to the native princes:

> You must not think we love you so evill, nay rather think truely wee tender your quietnesse and preservation, as a nation derived from our ancestours, ingraffed and incorporate into one body with us, disturbed with a sort of barbarous people, odious to God and man, that lappe your bloud as greedily as ours.[65]

Although in many ways exclusive, *The History of the Burkes* espouses a starkly contrasting ideal of grafting. For the Irish bards, true sovereignty exceeds the limits of such narrow definitions in the way that God exceeds – yet extends meaningfully through – material forms of devotion.

Though Elizabeth began her reign by invoking the monument of Gildas – and the legal weight of ancient, Irish-oriented genealogies – the bards who composed the poems of the *Seanchas Búrcach* turned those genealogies back upon the Protestant monarch with wit and philosophical sophistication. We have no pugnacious letter suggesting that Elizabeth was aware of this particular instance. What we do know is that she remained firm in her conviction that her 'Teudor' ancestry confirmed the logic of her claims to sovereignty over all of Ireland.

---

[64] Deana Rankin, *Between Spenser and Swift: English writing in seventeenth-century Ireland* (Cambridge, 2005), p. 88.
[65] Cited *ibid.*

6   Coming into the weigh-house: Elizabeth I and the government of Ireland

Ciaran Brady

> If I had not espied, though very late, leger de main used in these cases, I had never played my part. Nor if I did not see the balances held awry, I had never myself come into the weigh-house.
>
> Elizabeth I to Sir Henry Sidney, 6 January 1566[1]

> We have perceived by many letters both by yourself and other officers in that kingdom in what disordered state it standeth, which we have resolved to have reformed by all convenient means which with the sword to the obstinate and with justice to the oppressed. And therefore ... we command you (without faction or partiality among you) to commit yourselves in counsell and with circumspection, to provide for the cure of these diseases.
>
> Elizabeth I to Lord Deputy Russell and council, 25 May 1596[2]

Sometime in the spring of 1595 an extraordinary meeting took place at Whitehall between two remarkable women, both queens, both dominant personalities in their own right, and both commanders of victorious naval forces. But extraordinary as it may have been, this meeting between Elizabeth I and Grace O'Malley (or Granuaile) was not unprecedented. Two years earlier Grace had also visited court to seek redress for the depredations visited upon her family and her country by Elizabeth's provincial commander in Connaught, Sir Richard Bingham. Elizabeth, at first suspicious of this 'pirate queen', at length made an order in Grace's favour. But it had been ignored. More despoliation by Bingham and his agents followed. And now Grace O'Malley was back demanding the monarch's intervention. It was then that the extraordinary meeting took place in which the two powerful women so similar in their personalities and so different in their circumstances talked for hours in private on an equal basis. And Elizabeth, issuing forth from the interview, commanded

---

[1] *Letters and memorials*, vol. I, pp. 7–8; Elizabeth also warned Sidney explicitly of her personal involvement at this time: 'Seem not to have had but Secretary's letters from me'.

[2] SP 63/187/43.

that Grace and her family be restored to all the lands and goods seized from them and left alone to enjoy their lives in peace and prosperity.

If this sounds like the script of a Hollywood movie or a Broadway show, it is because it is in fact a summary of the plot of the second act of *The Pirate Queen*, a show staged on Broadway (to mixed reviews) in 2007.[3] Like many such productions it is, of course, a fiction, a deliberate and elaborate spinning of mythical tropes for the purposes of artistic creativity or popular entertainment. Though Grace O'Malley was by contemporary accounts a formidable woman, she was not a queen, but a rather lesser and considerably disadvantaged figure in the tense and often ruthless arena of local and provincial Gaelic dynastic politics.[4] There were no substantive grounds on which she could have been perceived by contemporaries, whether Irish or English, of enjoying anything like the status of the queen of England. There is in fact no sound evidence that such a private interview ever took place. The story – whose all too obvious stereotypical features should alert the wary reader – derives from eighteenth-century ballads and antiquarian accounts based upon highly questionable folk memories and supplemented a little later by high Romantic poetic imaginings.[5] On the face of it, moreover, the meeting seems highly improbable: Elizabeth, being acutely aware of the dignity of her royal person, and no less conscious of the dangers spawned by closet meetings, rarely allowed such occasions to arise, especially in her later years; and, if she did, it is unlikely that she would have permitted any intimacy with persons perceived, as was poor Grace, as being of inferior social, cultural, and probably ethnic status. It is not even clear that O'Malley visited the English court on two occasions. There can be little doubt that she was there for a brief period in 1593, but the evidence

---

[3] *The Pirate Queen*, a musical written by Claude-Michel Schönberg and Alain Boublil, ran on Broadway from March to June 2007; details of the plot, script, characters, and cast are available at www.thepiratequeen.com.

[4] Anne Chambers, *Granuaile: the life and times of Grace O'Malley*, 2nd edn (Dublin, 1998); and for more critical commentary the entries under Grace O'Malley by Mary O'Dowd in *ODNB* and by Emmett O'Byrne in *DIB*.

[5] Anon., 'An account of Gran Uile's Castle – with an engraving', *Anthologia Hibernica* 2 (Jul.–Dec. 1793), 2–3, which makes reference to the appearance of ballads concerning Granuaile in the mid 1780s; see also D. F. Mac Carthy, *The book of Irish ballads* (Dublin, 1846), pp. 122–6, and John O'Hart, *Irish pedigrees*, 2 vols. (Dublin, 1892), vol. II, pp. 275–7. A very full account of 'Grainne O'Malley: she pirate' appeared in the *Dublin University Magazine* 50 (1870), 385–400, which in critically juxtaposing the folklore with some original documents from the state papers relates the appearance of ballads to the controversy over the viceroyalty of the duke of Dorset in the 1750s though suggesting an earlier provenance; interestingly, only passing mention is made of Grace O'Malley (with no reference to a meeting with Queen Elizabeth) in Roderick O'Flaherty's *A chorographical description of West –Connaught or Iar –Connacht, 1684*, James Hardiman (ed.) (Dublin, 1846), p. 402.

relating to her second claim for justice in 1595 indicates strongly that it was made at greater distance.[6] And if the meeting ever took place at all it was on the first rather than the second putative occasion.

Yet, improbable though it may have been, the story of the pirate queen's meeting with the virgin queen is illustrative of Elizabeth I's relationship with her Irish dominion in a number of contrasting ways.[7] It indicates in the first place the degree to which, in the absence of substantial evidence, the life of Elizabeth and the history of sixteenth-century Ireland have both been subject to unverifiable anecdote and folklore which, though frequently entertaining, require continuous critical scepticism. In this light it is the story's very exceptionalism that underlines the far more general aloofness and distance of Elizabeth's court. Elizabeth (as the show properly recognised) was jealous of her privacy and deeply suspicious of her male courtiers. It is through her remarkable qualities as a woman that Grace managed to gain entrance where so many powerful Irish nobles failed, sometimes with disastrous consequences. Elizabeth was likewise insufficiently attentive to her Irish kingdom with similarly dire results. She gave orders for redress, but they were often ignored by her agents in the island: it took a second petition for the queen's will to be enforced. But finally it illustrates the manner in which, her distance and her neglect notwithstanding, Elizabeth did on occasion try to see justice done, and law upheld. However they were presented, Grace O'Malley did at length succeed in getting her complaints and her petitions heard by the queen. The queen's agents were instructed firmly to act upon her orders; and Grace O'Malley's family was left relatively unmolested by the officers of the crown for the rest of her life. The encounter displays, furthermore, Elizabeth's profound reverence for English law. In her first petition, Grace as a subject of the Irish kingdom had claimed that her rights as a widow under the (English) law of that kingdom were being abrogated by members of her own family in appealing to the precepts of the Brehon code.[8] Her claims were carefully examined and upheld. But finally, even in this clear and decisive action, the ambivalence of Elizabeth's relationship with her Irish subjects was revealed; in upholding the rights of a woman and a widow, the queen was also asserting that the traditional legal principles and cultural folkways of the Gaelic world had no place in the kingdom of Ireland.

[6] *CSPI*, V, pp. 132–6 and 312, 315; SP 63/179/35.
[7] For a recent highly critical exploration, see Hiram Morgan, '"Never any realm worse governed": Queen Elizabeth and Ireland', *Transactions of the Royal Historical Society*, 6th series, 14 (2004), 295–308.
[8] *CSPI*, V, pp. 132–6.

I

This challenge of assimilating a very different, complex, and sometimes directly conflicting political culture within the framework of the English rule established by the Act of Supremacy and the Act for the Kingly Title passed in the Irish parliaments in 1536 and 1541 lay at the heart of the problem of Tudor government and English policy in Ireland for two-thirds of the sixteenth century. It was, from the beginning, a project faced with massive external obstacles, formidable administrative, financial, and military demands, and no less daunting internal contradictions. Its chances of succeeding without terrible conflict were always slim; and the difficulties it confronted were made immeasurably greater by those quite independent ones also being faced by the woman charged with the realisation of the great experiment in reconstruction for the last forty-five years of the dynasty.[9]

The peculiar set of problems attendant upon Elizabeth Tudor as an unmarried female sovereign have been examined with particular care by scholars over the past few decades and need only brief rehearsal here.[10] The fact that Elizabeth was unmarried – and unbetrothed – at the time of her accession may be adduced indeed as the single most important issue of the reign. At the outset, the question of the queen's marriage plans and thereafter her plans for nominating a successor were at the centre of English national politics, shaping the way in which a whole range of other policy considerations, diplomatic, religious, and constitutional, developed as well as the character and dynamic of Elizabethan court and national politics.

Competition for influence over the young queen's choice of marriage partner became the chief organising force of court politics in the first decade of her reign, as the leading representatives of the traditional aristocracy pressed for a continental and Catholic match and the self-appointed defenders of the Tudor state favoured delay or the discovery of a suitable Protestant alternative. And as these subtly opposing forces manoeuvred for a position of advantage with the queen, a third force emerged in the person of a favourite (Lord Robert Dudley) and his following, encouraged by Elizabeth herself as a means of providing some

[9] This theme is elaborated in Ciaran Brady, 'The decline of the Irish kingdom', in Mark Greengrass (ed.), *Conquest and coalescence: the shaping of the state in early modern Europe* (London, 1991), pp. 94–115.

[10] See *inter alios* Carole Levin, *The heart and stomach of a king: Elizabeth I and the politics of sex and power* (Philadelphia, 1994); A. N. McLaren, *Political culture in the reign of Elizabeth I: queen and commonwealth, 1558–1585* (Cambridge, 1999); Natalie Mears, *Queenship and political discourse in the Elizabethan realms* (Cambridge, 2005); Judith M. Richards, '"To promote a woman to beare rule": talking of queens in mid-Tudor England', *Sixteenth Century Journal* 28 (1997), 101–21.

relief from the two major opposing forces.[11] Elizabeth's acute awareness of the precariousness of her position as a marriageable monarch and of the risks entailed in either decision or delay was reinforced over the 1560s first by the fate of Mary Stuart, whose own mismanagement of her marital affairs had such calamitous consequences, and then by the crisis of 1569–70 (in part provoked by Mary Stuart) when frustration with her indecision led to the treason of the duke of Norfolk and was partially responsible for the Northern Rising.[12]

In the decade immediately following, it was this experience that underlay Elizabeth's extreme sensitivity regarding the questions of marriage and succession, and her apparent inconsistency – especially in regard to a possible link with the house of Valois. By then, moreover, the dangers of political instability which uncertainty over the Tudor dynasty's future had invoked had been supplemented by deeper challenges of a constitutional nature. As early as the mid 1560s, Elizabeth's assertion of her autonomous right to determine such matters had been openly challenged in Parliament, and the controversy this provoked had soon extended beyond immediate matters of political management and financial support, which were the normal context of disputes between crown and Parliament, towards broader questions concerning the nature of the royal prerogative and the relationship of the monarchy to the country as a whole; and increasingly radical statements concerning this exceedingly delicate matter were being explicitly stated on both sides of the case.[13]

Inextricably linked with this troubling constitutional question was the even more pressing one of the religious settlement. The maintenance of the distinctly Protestant character of the early Elizabethan religious settlement as represented in the legislation of 1559 and the convocation of 1563 was a central concern of those opposing a Catholic marriage on any terms. But as Elizabeth's lack of enthusiasm for a Protestant match

---

[11] Susan Doran, *Monarchy and matrimony: the courtships of Elizabeth I* (London, 1995); Derek Wilson, *Sweet Robin: a biography of Robert Dudley earl of Leicester 1533–1588* (London, 1981); Simon Adams, *Leicester and the court: essays in Elizabethan politics* (Manchester, 2002).

[12] Wallace MacCaffrey, *The shaping of the Elizabethan regime* (London, 1969); Stephen Alford, *The early Elizabethan polity: William Cecil and the British succession crisis, 1558–1569* (Cambridge, 2002); for a recent analysis of the complexities of the Northern Rebellion, see K. J. Kesselring, *The Northern Rebellion of 1569: faith, politics, and protest in Elizabethan England* (Basingstoke, 2007).

[13] Having been once subjected to severe criticism by G. R. Elton in *The parliament of England: 1559–1581* (Cambridge, 1989), the classic view of Elizabeth's testy relationship with her parliaments as delineated in J. E. Neale, *Elizabeth I and her parliaments, 1559–1581*, 2 vols. (London, 1953–7), is restated in modified terms in Penry Williams, *The later Tudors* (Oxford, 1995); Michael A. R. Graves, *Elizabethan parliaments 1559–1601* (London, 1996); and David M. Dean, *Law-making and society in late Elizabethan England: the parliament of England, 1584–1601* (Cambridge, 1996).

combined with her even greater lack of commitment to the evangelical mission of the Church of England, so Elizabeth's status as supreme governor of that church gave rise at once to increasing expressions of discontent from within the church and to outright denunciations from Catholic dissidents in exile.[14]

Finally, the cumulative effect of chronic uncertainty over England's dynastic, constitutional, and religious issues was to disrupt and intensify the nature of routine political and administrative engagement between the queen and her most influential subjects both at court and in the regions. On a broader front, the persistence of policy uncertainty enabled (or compelled) the pre-existing associations of family lineage and clientage to reinforce their internal coherence by aligning themselves with one or other side on the broad range of political questions thrown up in constitutional, religious, and foreign policy debate. But also, in a less noticeable but no less significant manner, the persistence of such unresolved debates profoundly altered the way in which the perquisites of royal favour – office, nomination to royal commissions, military and logistical contracts, and the award of ecclesiastical livings and preferments – were sought, held, and exploited by those who had attained them.[15]

Such pressures, generated by the uncertain rule of an unmarried female monarch, operated throughout the Tudor realms, exercising a greater or lesser influence at different times and in different places. But they were never entirely absent; and their impact was to be most sustained and most distinctive in that most unstable and inchoate of the regime's possessions: the kingdom of Ireland.

II

The most obvious way in which the Elizabethan regime's instability affected its presence in Ireland was also, for most of the half-century, the least important. This was the fear of foreign invasion. Though anxiety

---

[14] Norman Jones, *The birth of the Elizabethan age: England in the 1560s* (London, 1995); Christopher Haigh, *English reformations: religion, politics and society under the Tudors* (Oxford, 1993); Eamon Duffy, 'William, Cardinal Allen, 1532–1594', *Recusant History* 22 (3) (1995), 265–90; Garret Mattingly, 'William Allen and Catholic propaganda in England', *Travaux d'Humanisme et Renaissance* 28 (1957), 325–39; Michael Questier, *Catholicism and community in early modern England: politics, aristocratic patronage and religion, c. 1550–1640*, (Cambridge, 2006); A. Hassell Smith, *County and court: government and politics in Norfolk, 1558–1603* (Oxford, 1974); Peter Clark, *English provincial society from the Reformation to the Revolution* (Hassocks, 1977).

[15] Wallace MacCaffrey, 'Place and patronage in Elizabethan politics', in S. T. Bindoff *et al.* (eds.), *Elizabethan government and society: essays presented to Sir John Neale* (London, 1961), pp. 95–126; G. R. Elton, 'Tudor government: the points of contact, III: the court', *Transactions of the Royal Historical Society*, 5th series, 26 (1976), 211–28; Adams, *Leicester and the court*.

concerning the lordship of Ireland's vulnerability to invasion from the continent was expressed long before the accession of Elizabeth – neatly encapsulated in the doggerel of *The libelle of Englysh policie*: 'he that would England win, must in Ireland begin' – the realistic nature of such a possibility began to feature in English strategic thinking only in the aftermath of England's breach with Rome.[16] The appeal to the pope by the Geraldine rebels in the 1530s, the reported intrigues of the house of Desmond with Francis I in the early 1550s, the supposed secret negotiations of the earl of Kildare with the Spanish ambassador at Elizabeth's court in the early 1560s, and the seized correspondence of Shane O'Neill with the cardinal of Lorraine in 1566: each was sufficient to provoke temporary alarm at Whitehall.[17] But in reality they amounted to little. The first indication that an intervention was being seriously contemplated by a European power came only in 1579 when the exiled rebel of the house of Desmond, James Fitzmaurice Fitzgerald, returned to Ireland with a small force of papal troops – in reality it was no more than a bodyguard – and in 1580 when the pope sent a small expeditionary force of about 600 to aid the Desmond rebels. In neither case did such initiatives pose any significant danger: the former was destroyed when Fitzmaurice himself was ambushed and killed, the latter notoriously slaughtered on their surrender. Thereafter Philip II, despite sharply deteriorating relations with England, refused to contemplate any serious action in Ireland. It was only after his death that his successor, Philip III, finally gave permission for the larger expeditionary force which landed at Kinsale in September 1601, and was seen off less than four months later.[18]

If the notion that Ireland might be used as a pawn by England's continental enemies to influence its foreign policy was never strategically realistic, it nevertheless influenced the character of English rule in Ireland in two separate ways. First, whatever the reality of threat, the fear that Ireland might indeed be invaded had the unfortunate effect of frequently misshaping and diverting English policy and administration in the island, distracting the crown's agents from the priorities of constitutional and ecclesiastical reform as required by the great statutes of the early Tudor period, and compelling them to undertake disruptive, expensive, and occasionally violent defensive measures which seriously compromised their credibility with the Irish lords who had

---

[16] For an overview, see William Palmer, *The problem of Ireland in Tudor foreign policy, 1485–1603* (Woodbridge, 1994).

[17] On the alarm caused by French intrigues, see Mary Ann Lyons, *Franco-Irish relations, 1500–1610: politics, migration and trade* (Woodbridge, 2003), esp. chs. 1, 4, and 5. On rumours of Kildare's continental intrigues, see SP 63/2/8, 9.

[18] John J. Silke, *Kinsale: the Spanish intervention in Ireland at the end of the Elizabethan wars* (Liverpool, 1970; Dublin, 2000, reprint).

initially responded positively to their policies. Sometimes, as in the case of Lord Deputy Sir William Fitzwilliam, such substitutions of considerations of defence for those of reform were deliberately engineered by the viceroys themselves – it proffered an opportunity for profit. But more commonly, as in the cases of Lord Justice Arnold, Sir Henry Sidney and most notably Sir John Perrot, the suspension of reform programmes in favour of immediate defensive imperatives took place against the will of the viceroys through the express command of Elizabeth and her privy council.[19]

The second manner in which the Elizabethan régime's perceived international isolation affected England's position in Ireland arose in Ireland itself, and was closely related to the far more serious unresolved problem. This was the uncertain state of the regime's religious settlement. Though it was no more realistic than the fear which it provoked in England, the expectation of foreign intervention within Ireland itself was a powerful influence in reinforcing and extending indigenous resistance to the Protestant Reformation. Though first expressed in the 1530s in the Kildare rebels' appeal to the pope, this transformation of rebellion into a form of Counter-Reformation war was pioneered by James Fitzmaurice Fitzgerald in 1579 in a series of well-broadcast proclamations in justification of his rebellion.[20] But, while Fitzmaurice's particular appeal went largely unanswered, his central message that the character of the religious settlement which the crown was seeking to impose in Ireland was sufficient in itself to justify withdrawal of allegiance, and rebellion was taken up by James Eustace, the Viscount Baltinglass, William Nugent, and their fellow conspirators in the Pale in 1580, and thereafter by a number of religious missionaries and Catholic bishops such as James Archer and Edmund Magauran.[21] And by the later 1590s their defence of the Catholic faith was to be among the principal arguments advanced by the

---

[19] Ciaran Brady, 'England's defence and Ireland's reform: the dilemma of the Irish viceroys, 1541–1641', in Brendan Bradshaw and John Morrill (eds.), *The British problem, c. 1534–1707: state formation in the Atlantic archipelago* (Cambridge, 1996), pp. 89–117.

[20] SP 63/67/32, 33; *Cal. Carew*, 1515–74, pp. 397–400; John O'Donovan (ed.), 'The Irish correspondence of James fitz Maurice of Desmond', *Journal of the Royal Society of Antiquaries of Ireland* 5 (1859), 354–69.

[21] Elizabeth Ann O'Connor, 'The rebellion of James Eustace, Viscount Baltinglass III, 1580–1581' (MA thesis, National University of Ireland, Maynooth, 1989); Christopher Maginn, 'The Baltinglass Rebellion, 1580: English dissent or a Gaelic uprising?', *Historical Journal* 47 (2004), 205–32; Helen Coburn Walshe, 'The rebellion of William Nugent, 1581', in R. V. Comerford, Mary Cullen, Jacqueline R. Hill, and Colm Lennon (eds.), *Religion, conflict and co-existence in Ireland: essays presented to Monsignor Patrick J. Corish* (Dublin, 1990), pp. 26–52; Thomas J. Morrissey, *James Archer of Kilkenny, an Elizabethan Jesuit* (Kilkenny, 1979); John J. Silke, 'The Irish appeal of 1593 to Spain: some light on the genesis of the Nine Years' War', *Irish Ecclesiastical Record*, 5th series,

leaders of the great rebellion in Gaelic Ulster in their appeal to Philip III. Though the linking of 'faith and fatherland' was thus to become an important ideological force in Gaelic Ireland in the closing years of Elizabeth's reign, its appeal was to prove far more limited to the group to whom it had originally been addressed by Fitzmaurice: the English of Irish birth.[22]

Unwilling for the most part to commit themselves to treason, the English of Irish birth in the Pale, in the corporate and port towns, and in scattered settlements throughout Leinster, Munster, and Connaught, had nevertheless been deeply uneasy about the implications of religious reformation long before the accession of Elizabeth. Unlike the political elite of Gaelic Ireland who had regarded the religious and ecclesiastical changes of the 1530s and 1540s with indifference and showed no hesitation in taking the oath of supremacy, the Reformation presented the English of Ireland with a set of historical and cultural challenges that could not easily be ignored.[23] In the first place, King Henry's denial of papal authority seemed to undermine the very legitimacy of the English community's presence in Ireland, which was founded, after all, in the twelfth-century papal bull, Laudabiliter. This was at the very least embarrassing, but what added greater and more palpable point to such a constitutional dilemma was that it was accompanied by a series of ecclesiastical and liturgical reforms which seemed to assert that conventional English religious practices had been wrong all along. Among the many defects of the pre-conquest Celtic church symbolising its deviation from Rome and justifying intervention from abroad, three were notable. These were the persistence of the provision of communion in both kinds (bread and wine) against the Roman rite, the saying of mass in the vernacular (Gaeilge) rather than in Latin, and the common toleration of clerical marriage (concubinage). It had been the object of the church of the English conquerors to suppress such decadent practices and to enforce Sarum rite, the Latin liturgy, and above all clerical celibacy. Even on the eve of the Reformation, the pious and reforming archbishop of Armagh, George Dowdall, was railing against concubinage and threatening dire punishment for those found in breach. Yet these were the very practical changes

---

92 (1959), 279–90; Micheline Kerney Walsh, 'Archbishop Magauran and his return to Ireland, October 1592', *Seanchas Ardmhacha* 14 (1990), 68–79.

[22] Hiram Morgan, 'Faith and fatherland in sixteenth-century Ireland', *History Ireland* 3 (1995), 13–20; Morgan, 'Faith and fatherland or queen and country? An unpublished exchange between O'Neill and the state at the height of the Nine Years' War', *Dúiche Néill: Journal of the O'Neill Country Historical Society* 9 (1994), 9–65.

[23] James Murray, *Enforcing the English Reformation in Ireland: clerical resistance and political conflict in the diocese of Dublin, 1534–1590* (Cambridge, 2009), chs. 2–3.

which the Reformation – long before its doctrinal teachings came into play – aimed to introduce.[24]

The implications of such innovations (or renovations) were most acutely felt by the ecclesiastics within the English community in Ireland, not least Dowdall himself. And it was no accident that it was from this quarter, rather than from Gaelic Ireland or the laity of English Ireland, that the first signs of resistance to the Reformation emerged.[25] For the laity of English Ireland, the potential dangers of this historical, constitutional, and cultural dilemma were softened by a variety of measures, chief among which was the programme of sustained Anglicisation inaugurated in the 1540s under the aegis of the Act for the Kingly Title. As long as the English crown was committed to making Ireland English, and allotting to the English-Irish a leading role in bringing this about under the leadership of an energetic English king, then the embarrassments of recent changes could be obscured by the opportunities of a renewed English conquest of Ireland.

Yet it was this necessary condition for the continuance of the old colonial community's loyalty to the crown that began steadily to fade during the reign of Elizabeth under the pressure of a variety of developments. One was the emergence of the reality of doctrinal change as part of the English Reformation. Never attempted under King Henry, and only briefly essayed in the reign of Edward VI in a manner that was easily and thoroughly expunged under Mary I, the first doctrinal innovations concerning the mass, communion, and the primacy of justification by faith began to be asserted by the crown's political and ecclesiastical representatives in Ireland as the official teaching of the Church of Ireland. The pace at which such innovations were made was, to be sure, slow and the manner of their enforcement lax. But that they were a permanent and irreversible part of the Reformation could no longer be ignored. This realisation now completed clerical alienation from the established church. As in England, the bulk of the Marian episcopal bench refused to take the oath of supremacy and resigned, and the lower clergy expressed their resistance through withdrawal or non-performance of duties. But the doctrinal and liturgical scruples which affected this vocational alienation now began to spread among the laity.[26]

---

[24] *Ibid.*, ch. 6; Henry A. Jefferies, *Priests and prelates of Armagh in the age of reformations, 1518–1558* (Dublin,1997).

[25] Murray, *Enforcing the Reformation*, chs. 3, 7.

[26] Henry A. Jefferies, *The Irish church and the Tudor reformations* (Dublin, 2010), and Jefferies, 'The early Tudor reformations in the Irish Pale', *Journal of Ecclesiastical History* 52 (2001), 34–62.

In part this was, no doubt, a purely intellectual development: a conscientious rejection of the teachings of English Protestantism can be discerned in the attitude of such figures as Richard Stanihurst and William Nugent.[27] But such refined reservations were supplemented and given greater purchase among the less speculative laity by one acute, concrete, and very personal argument which had been raised by the avant-garde of English Catholics in the later 1560s and which centred on Elizabeth herself.

The principal justification advanced for England's break with Rome and the (re-)establishment of an independent Church of England under the authority of a reforming king was, these polemicists had argued, that it was only by these means that the failings and corruptions of the English church could be addressed.[28] Always dubious, this claim was now, they insisted, thoroughly discredited by the accession to the throne and to the office of supreme governor of the church of a woman. Traditionally, the authority of the rule of a female monarch was regarded as legitimate, if unfortunate, a sign, some said of God's displeasure with the people over whom she was set.[29] But the notion that, in addition, a woman could have been granted divine responsibility for the carrying out of a great spiritual renewal was absurd. Though ostensibly directed at Elizabeth, the real intent of this polemic was to undermine the authority of the leaders of the Church of England who had meekly accepted the queen's supremacy and so to assert the right of England's Catholics to continue in their allegiance to Rome. Ultimately, it was to exert little enough influence over the silent majority of England's recusants, and it is arguable even that the bitterness of the attack on the queen actually persuaded doubters to commit to queen and church.[30]

But in Ireland this attack had more complex reverberations. For the English-Irish there the accession of a female supreme governor presaged not merely the improbability of a great renewal, but the reality of a serious

---

[27] Colm Lennon, *Richard Stanihurst, the Dubliner, 1547–1618* (Dublin, 1981); Gerard Murphy (ed.), 'Poems of exile of Uilliam Nuinseann, mac Barúin Dealbhna', *Éigse* 6 (1948–52, pt 1), 8–13.

[28] Diarmaid MacCulloch, *Thomas Cranmer: a life* (New Haven, 1996), esp. chs. 5–7; Virginia Murphy, 'The literature and propaganda of Henry's divorce', in Diarmaid MacCulloch (ed.), *The reign of Henry VIII: politics, policy and piety* (Basingstoke, 1995), pp. 135–58.

[29] Sharon L. Jansen, *The monstrous regiment of women: female rulers in early modern Europe* (London, 2002); Constance Jordan, 'Women's rule in sixteenth-century British political thought', *Renaissance Quarterly* 40 (1987), 421–51; Richards, '"To promote a woman to beare rule"'.

[30] Arnold Pritchard, *Catholic loyalism in Elizabethan England* (London, 1979); Alexandra Walsham, *Church papists: Catholicism, conformity, and confessional polemic in early modern England* (Woodbridge, 1993).

challenge to their status as representatives of a superior religious culture. Following upon the constitutional problems raised by the rejection of Laudabiliter, the seemingly regressive liturgical changes, with the new doctrinal orthodoxies came the realisation that, unlike King Henry, the congenitally weak and inconstant woman who had succeeded him could never possibly lead the great cultural conquest which they had looked forward to in the 1540s. Such disappointed expectations were, moreover, sharpened by what was their direct and inevitable consequence. As the English-Irish, as clerics, as office-holders, or as political leaders in their regions, expressed their disquiet first by prevarication and subversion in the 1560s and later by withdrawal from office, they found themselves displaced by or coming into increasing conflict with those who were fully committed to the new regime.[31] And, given the extent and the depth of English-Irish reservations over the Reformation, it was inevitable that these newly emerging conformist forces should not be drawn from their own ranks, but would be newcomers, in some cases sincere devotees, but more commonly careerists and adventurers come over from England in the hope of bettering themselves in the neighbouring island.

Again it was Fitzmaurice who was among the first to conceptualise this development. As early as 1569 while laying siege to the city of Cork in the midst of his first rebellion, he called on the inhabitants to expel from their town a group whom he described as the 'Huggnetts'.[32] In this demand he was not referring to French Protestants, but to the family and following of Sir Warham St Leger, the English soldier-adventurer who had been acting as the viceroy's unofficial agent in Munster. And in describing them as such, he was not referring to their religious allegiance, but characterising them in a manner in which the followers of Admiral Coligny were being viewed by their rivals and enemies within the court of Henry III: Huguenots – that is, fifth columnists – ruthlessly exploiting the weaknesses of a current regime in order to advance their own interests.[33] Fitzmaurice, as usual, was ahead of his time; and it would be some twenty years before the divisions within the English community in Ireland which he perceived found concrete expression in the nomenclature of 'Old' and 'New' English.[34]

---

[31] The gradual withdrawal of the old colonial community from high office is traceable through the catalogue of office-holders supplied in F. E. Ball, *The judges in Ireland*, 2 vols. (London, 1926), vol. I, pp. 163–228.

[32] SP 63/29/8.

[33] See *inter alios* N. M. Sutherland, *The Huguenot struggle for recognition* (New Haven, 1980); Megan C. Armstrong, *The politics of piety: Franciscan preachers during the wars of religion* (New York, 2004).

[34] Nicholas Canny, *The formation of the Old English elite in Ireland* (Dublin, 1975); Ciaran Brady, 'Conservative subversives: the community of the Pale and the Dublin

The delay was due in no small part to the efforts of several leading figures to resolve and overcome the tensions emerging within the Elizabethan Irish kingdom. Several viceroys, notably Sidney and Perrot, strove to keep alive the idea of a united but Anglicised Irish kingdom, and in this, like their predecessor in the 1540s, Sir Anthony St Leger, they received the support of the most far-seeing members of the English-Irish political elite, figures such as Sir Thomas Cusacke, Sir Nicholas White, and Luke Dillon.[35] But their efforts were to be frustrated and finally thwarted by a variety of obstacles which emerged from the peculiar character of the Elizabethan court and were both deliberately and inadvertently presented by Elizabeth herself.

III

Amidst the febrile marketplace of office- and favour-seeking in the court of Elizabeth, the unfinished kingdom of Ireland occupied a special niche. In contrast to ecclesiastical livings and appointments to office in central, regional, and local government, which were limited because their occupancy was usually for life, commissions in the Irish service were characterised by abnormally frequent turnover. Between the beginning of the 1550s and 1603, the office of Irish chief governor was occupied by more than twenty nominees. The changes of administration were only infrequently the result of great political upheavals, as when St Leger was replaced by Sussex in 1556, or Sussex by Sidney ten years later, or when Sir John Perrot was recalled in disgrace, but when they occurred changes throughout the Irish administrative structures were extensive.[36] But even when they were the consequence of more routine processes, they were normally accompanied by extensive turnover of personnel in the viceregal household and in the military establishment. In the years after 1560, moreover, the Irish administration began a steady process of expansion through the creation of new offices of central government, the revival of local government, the setting up of institutions of regional administration, and above all the expansion of the garrison.[37] As the opportunities for gain through royal service grew scarcer in England itself, the attractions of

administration, 1556–1586', in Patrick J. Corish (ed.), *Radicals, rebels and establishments* (Belfast, 1985), pp. 11–32.

[35] See the entries under each name in *ODNB* and *DIB*.

[36] Ciaran Brady, *The chief governors: the rise and fall of reform government in Tudor Ireland, 1536–1588* (Cambridge, 1994), chs. 2–3; Hiram Morgan, 'The fall of Sir John Perrot', in John Guy (ed.), *The reign of Elizabeth I: court and culture in the last decade* (Cambridge, 1995), pp. 109–25.

[37] Jon Crawford, *Anglicizing the government of Ireland: the Irish privy council and the expansion of Tudor rule, 1556–1578* (Dublin, 1993).

a career in Ireland, whether permanent or temporary, grew increasingly stronger.

The availability of career advancement in Irish service supplied a relatively painless way of gaining relief from the constant demand for reward which was an essential component of the early modern court. Yet, however useful they may have been domestically, the operations of court patronage and clientage produced effects which were far from salutary in Ireland. First there was cost. Funding for many of the offices had to be met by the Irish revenues which were altogether swallowed up in the maintenance of the administration. Unseen (and immeasurable) costs were worse, as Irish office-holders sought to extend their official incomes through the exploitation of the unofficial fees required from those who used their services, or more brutally in the case of the military servitors through the commandeering of goods, cattle, and cash.[38] There were political implications also. As more Irish offices came into the possession of newly arrived English careerists, the less influence the local English community could exert within the administration as a whole. And as most of the new arrivals owed their appointment to some great figure at the English court, their allegiance lay primarily with their English patrons, rather than with the community in which they found themselves. And thus a dual process of fateful significance for the English presence in Ireland began to accelerate, as a sharp divergence in the cultural and political identity of the English community initiated by the break with Rome was furthered by the disappearance of the traditional integration of new arrivals into the English-Irish community through intermarriage.[39]

To all of this Elizabeth was for the most part personally indifferent. Though the Irish state papers of her reign are peppered with royal letters confirming appointments to office, and certifying grants and leases, the formal character of such documents indicates that Elizabeth herself was rarely directly concerned, but was merely adding a royal seal to a routine decision made at the privy council. Already compelled by the

---

[38] Some indication of the size, cost, and turnover within the lower ranks in the civil and military establishment can be derived from the accounts of Vice-Treasurer Sidney (Historical Manuscripts Comission, *Report on the manuscripts of Lord de l'Isle and Dudley preserved at Penshurst Place*, 6 vols. (London, 1925–66), vol. I, and Vice-Treasurer Fitzwilliam, *Fitzwilliam accounts, 1560–1565*, A. K. Longfield (ed.) (Dublin 1965); the parlous state of the crown's Irish revenues at the beginning of the reign is revealed in SP 63/11/71; an equally revealing summary of revenues and expenditures at the close of the reign can be found in Vice-Treasurer Carey's account at SP 63/209/212; on the cost of the unofficial exactions of the cess, see Brady, *Chief governors*, pp. 219–30.

[39] Donald Jackson, *Intermarriage in Ireland, 1550–1650* (Montreal, 1970). For particular case studies, see P. H. Bagenal, *Vicissitudes of an Anglo-Irish family, 1530–1800* (London, 1925), and Hubert Galwey, *The Wall family in Ireland, 1170–1970* (Cork, 2009).

disadvantages of her sex to maintain an austere and distant attitude among her courtiers, Elizabeth was even more remote from her Irish subjects.[40] And, while the prospect of a royal visit to the Irish kingdom had sometimes been contemplated in the past, it was now considered quite unthinkable. Moreover, the absence of a royal consort or a royal male heir who might have supplied an alternative focus of allegiance for the political elite of the Irish kingdom further extended the distance between the monarch and her Irish subjects.[41] Thus, because she had no direct dynastic interest in the development of an Irish interest, and because most of the offices and commissions that arose were too minor and too temporary directly to engage a monarch's attention, Elizabeth was content to leave the emerging Irish patronage system in the gift of competing or co-operating courtly political interests.[42] As her letters quoted in the epigraph to this chapter suggest, Elizabeth was for the most part equally removed from the initiation of a development of specific Irish policies, preferring to leave such matters in the hands of her secretaries, Cecil and later Walsingham, the privy council, and the appointed viceroys, and characterising her role as that of the ultimate source of authority, justice, and mercy.[43]

Occasionally, amidst this largely formal correspondence, the true voice of Elizabeth can be discerned, as in her letter to Sidney, quoted at the outset, in her terrifying injunction to Lord Deputy Fitzwilliam to rebuke the earl of Kildare for his abuse of his countess, the Lady Frances Howard, her former lady-in-waiting, and her compassionate intervention on behalf of the widow of Lord Deputy Burgh who had been left in dire circumstances on her husband's death.[44] Elizabeth's letter to Lord Grey de Wilton congratulating him on the massacre of the expeditionary force at Smerwick reveals an uncharacteristically vicious streak, while her sympathetic and engaged private conversation about Ireland amidst a hunt and under a chestnut tree as reported by Sir Edward Fitton shows a rather different side.[45] These, however, were unusual instances, occasioned by

[40] Pam Wright, 'A change of direction: the ramifications of a female household', in David Starkey et al. (eds.), *The English court from the wars of the roses to the civil war* (London, 1987), pp. 147–72; Jane Stevenson, 'The court culture of England under Elizabeth I', in Martin Gosman et al. (eds.), *Princes and princely culture, 1450–1650*, 2 vols. (Leiden, 2005), vol. II, pp. 191–212.

[41] Ciaran Brady, 'Court, castle and country: the framework of government in Tudor Ireland', in Ciaran Brady and Raymond Gillespie (eds.) *Natives and newcomers: essays on the making of Irish colonial society, 1534–1641* (Dublin, 1986), pp. 22–49.

[42] Elizabeth took a very different attitude towards senior appointments in the English military establishment; see Rowland Whyte to Sir Robert Sidney, 5 Aug 1599, Historical Manuscripts Commission, *De l'Isle and Dudley MSS*, vol. II, p. 381.

[43] See nn. 1 and 2 above.   [44] SP 63/174/66; *CSPI*, VII, p. 285.

[45] SP 63/79/13; SP 63/53/59.

specific connections and accident. There is no further evidence of confidential conversations between the queen and individual Irish administrators.

Yet, ironically, if Elizabeth's general indifference towards the government of Ireland was in the long term to be a source of a deep destabilisation of the English presence in the island, the few occasions in which she deliberately intervened in matters of policy formulation produced consequences that were even more acutely disruptive. At the time of her accession, Elizabeth's attitude towards the government of Ireland was, as with so much else, to maintain the greatest level of continuity possible. Unlike Mary I, who had made a clean sweep of the senior Irish administration in 1556, Elizabeth retained Sussex as her viceroy, even elevating him to the title of lord lieutenant in order to encourage him to stay in office.[46] As Sussex's administration foundered in the mid 1560s under the combined weight of military defeat and allegations of incompetence and corruption, Elizabeth began to take heed of rising criticism at court spearheaded by his greatest rival, the earl of Leicester. But she did so reluctantly. Recognising that Leicester's attack on Sussex was merely part of his more general campaign to undermine the authority of his enemies among the older nobility, within the circle of the duke of Norfolk, she was unwilling to give Leicester the satisfaction of complete victory. Thus she refused to sanction the appointment of Leicester's first nominee for the Irish office, Sir Nicholas Arnold, and instructed that the commission of enquiry into Sussex's conduct in office which Arnold had been chairing be brought to an early and inconclusive end.[47] More seriously, she remained deeply suspicious of Leicester's second candidate, Sir Henry Sidney, whose extensive experience in Ireland and whose service under Sussex made his appointment impossible to refuse. On accepting office, Sidney, to his great frustration, found many of the preconditions he had set down ignored. His demand to inherit the title of lord lieutenant was refused, and several of his nominations for senior positions in the civil and ecclesiastical establishment rejected.[48] Among the most serious of these was Elizabeth's refusal to appoint Sir Warham St Leger to the position of lord president of the projected council of Munster. The introduction of a regional council in Munster (along with another in Connaught) had been a central component of Sidney's programme for government. It had been strongly and repeatedly advocated by Sussex, and had secured the support of the earl of Desmond as early as the 1550s. There was,

---

[46] SP 63/1/3; SP 63/2/24, 25, 30.   [47] SP 63/13/69; SP 63/18/46.

[48] Brady, *Chief governors*, pp. 120–1; for the change of title, compare Sidney's draft Instructions (SP 63/14/2) with the final version (SP 63/15/4).

therefore, nothing controversial in the proposal itself. Rather it was Sidney's (and Leicester's) nominee for the post that aroused Elizabeth's suspicions. Like Arnold and Sidney, St Leger was known to be a client of Leicester, as his father Sir Anthony had been a client of Leicester's father, the duke of Northumberland.[49] But in St Leger's case there was another factor underlying Elizabeth's suspicion, additional to a concern to balance court rivalries, which was derived from the one direct contact which she had with her Irish kingdom in the person of Thomas Butler, 10th earl of Ormond.

Elizabeth's connection with Ormond was in small part genealogical and in a far larger part personal. As the daughter of Anne Boleyn, her paternal great-grandmother was Lady Margaret Butler (d. 1539), daughter of the 7th earl of Ormond, who married Anne's grandfather, Sir William Boleyn, around 1475.[50] There was therefore a relatively close family connection. But in the intervening years relations between the Boleyns and the Butlers, and within the Butler dynasty itself, had been so turbulent as to dilute whatever ties of allegiance may have existed.[51] But Princess Elizabeth had first met young Lord Butler while both were wards of the Edwardian court and both under heavy suspicion. The friendship begun then survived the reign of Mary when Thomas (well liked by the queen) may have been a source of some succour to the embattled princess. At any rate, upon her accession he was immediately accorded signs of the highest favour. He was given a central place of honour in the coronation ceremony; at court he was given special access to the queen, who conferred on him the affectionate pet name of 'Tom Duff' and promoted to the honorary but prestigious position of lord treasurer of Ireland, a position which in the protocols of the Irish council gave him a status above all the other Irish nobility.[52] Elizabeth's favour continued to be shown to Ormond in the following years, mediated through the enthusiastic good offices of the earl of Sussex. Ormond's legal suits were sympathetically heard, his arrears and outstanding fines tolerated, the breaches of peace and cattle raids perpetrated by his relations and followers frequently overlooked.[53]

---

[49] Elizabeth I to Sidney, 31 Mar., 14 May, 15 Aug. 1566, 24 Mar. 1567, *Sidney SP*, nos. 13, 15, 23, 34; also SP 63/18/80, 94.

[50] For details, see George E. Cokayne, *The complete peerage of England, Scotland, Ireland, Great Britain, and the United Kingdom*, 8 vols. (London, 1887–98), sv. Ormond.

[51] Thomas Butler was the grandson of Piers Butler, whose claim to the earldom had been vigorously and (for a while) successfully opposed by Elizabeth's grandfather, Sir Thomas Boleyn, the earl of Wiltshire.

[52] See the entry on Thomas Butler by David Edwards in *DIB*.

[53] SP 63/7/47; SP 63/15/71, 72; SP 63/16/5, 6, 7, 8.

The degree of favour shown to him by Elizabeth had the effect of establishing Ormond into the most influential of the English-Irish nobility, far more powerful than the recently restored house of Kildare and the aspiring house of Desmond. In particular, Ormond's sustained success in his territorial and seigniorial disputes with the house of Desmond had the effect of further disaffecting the young and personally unstable 15th earl, compelling him to have resort to increasingly violent methods of retaliation. To Elizabeth, Desmond's violence, culminating in a full-scale battle which he provoked with Ormond in 1565, was merely a confirmation of Ormond's righteousness, and she determined to support him. To her agents in Ireland, however, not merely Dudley adherents like Sidney and St Leger, but older English-Irish counsellors such as Sir Thomas Cusacke, the matter was more complex. The unqualified favour of one of the great Irish feudal alliances over all others was, to them, a highly dangerous development which threatened to alienate many locally powerful figures and destabilise the delicate balance of Irish politics. It was imperative, therefore, that the effects of Ormond's advance should be conditioned by lesser forms of favour to his rivals, Desmond and Kildare, and that the most serious threats to their position presented by Elizabeth's pro-Ormond directives be alleviated by deflection and delay. This was the thinking behind Arnold's mild defence of Desmond's actions in his feud with Ormond, and Sidney's desire to have St Leger, a long acquaintance of the house of Desmond, as his president in Munster.[54]

But Elizabeth was not to be persuaded. She demanded St Leger's withdrawal (though the evidence shows that he continued to serve Sidney in the province in an unofficial capacity) and Desmond's dispatch to face trial at court; she even demanded that Sidney's appointment of Desmond's brother, Sir John Fitzgerald, as temporary governor of the lordship be rescinded and that Sir John be sent over to court also. And, when Sidney procrastinated, she threatened him with dismissal.[55] The immediate effect of these actions was, as anyone could have predicted, rebellion in Desmond and the fateful emergence of James Fitzmaurice Fitzgerald. But there were further consequences more directly bearing on the authority of English government in Ireland. Sidney's embarrassment in Munster was temporarily compensated by his unexpected success against Shane O'Neill in the following year. But the fact that he had been worsted by Ormond could not be overlooked. Thus, on his

---

[54] Ciaran Brady, 'Faction and the origins of the Desmond rebellion of 1579', *Irish Historical Studies* 22 (1981), 289–312.

[55] Elizabeth I to Sidney, 15 Jan., 23 Apr., 24 May 1567, *Sidney SP*, nos. 32, 34, 37; SP 63/20/66.

reappointment as governor in 1568, he returned to Ireland with a second reform programme, several components of which were designed both indirectly and (as in the case of the grant of the barony of Idrone to Sir Peter Carew) directly to challenge Butler influence. The Butlers reacted, as the Desmond Fitzgeralds had done, by revolt, even aligning temporarily with the hated Fitzmaurice. It is possible that Sidney welcomed the opportunity of outing the Butlers, but to his astonishment Elizabeth allowed Ormond to return from court to take charge himself of suppressing the rebellion of his followers, a feat which he accomplished with ease. The viceroy scored some points: Ormond's brothers were attainted in the very parliament that rescinded the attainder of the house of Desmond, and though they were pardoned the attainder remained in place, and with it their loss of any right to succeed the heirless earl on his death. But Ormond's own standing in Elizabeth's eyes remained untarnished, if anything enhanced by the efficient and economical way in which he brought the rebellion to an end.[56]

Thereafter, no English viceroy could challenge Ormond with impunity. Sidney's successor, Sir William Fitzwilliam, was deeply respectful, pursuing anti-Geraldine policies against both Kildare and the restored earl of Desmond in a manner which the earl thought satisfactory; and, when Sidney returned in 1575 with a third reform programme, Ormond was among the most powerful forces behind his final recall in 1578.[57] Ormond's reputation as the most dependable and efficient defender of the crown was consolidated during the second Desmond Rebellion (1579–83) when it appeared that he alone, rather than any of Elizabeth's English-born commanders, had the ability to crush the rebels.

But it was in the immediate aftermath of that rebellion that Elizabeth's personal relationship with Ormond began to open up a second major breach within the English community in Ireland, which arose from the second most important form of preferment which Ireland offered to the Elizabethan patronage system: the opportunity to acquire Irish land.

Before the mid 1580s the speculative possibilities of investment in plantation were limited and hazardous. The number of permanent settlers in the mid-Tudor plantation of Laois-Offaly was small, and those who invested in colonial enterprise in Munster and in Ulster in the 1560s and 1570s tended not to fare well: but the efforts were sustained nonetheless.[58] In relation to this feverish activity Elizabeth herself was, for the most part, little involved. She made, for example, no intervention

---

[56] David Edwards, 'The Butler revolt of 1569', *Irish Historical Studies* 28 (1993), 228–55.

[57] Edwards, 'Thomas Butler, 10th earl of Ormond', *DIB*.

[58] For an overview, see Brady, *Chief governors*, pp. 247–65.

in the midlands plantation which had been initiated in the reign of her sister Mary and which under Elizabeth continued its development as a local enterprise dominated by a few powerful figures in the military estab-lishment and the English-Irish nobility. She was little involved also in the private colonial projects which emerged in the later 1560s in relation to pockets of land in Ulster and Munster, and her lack of support may have been a cause of their generally abortive nature. She appears even to have been indifferent to the pet scheme of her own secretary of state, Sir Thomas Smith, in the Ards peninsula, which perished because of lack of support at Dublin and at court.[59]

There was, however, one significant exception to this general lack of interest in colonial enterprise on the part of Elizabeth. This was her sustained enthusiasm for the ambitious, under-planned, and ultimately disastrous 'enterprise of Ulster' devised and developed by Walter Dev-ereux, 1st earl of Essex, in the years between 1572 and 1575.[60] The attractions of Essex's enterprise to Elizabeth were several. It was cheap: in return for a grant of feudal autonomy Essex promised to undertake the establishment of English rule in Ulster east of the Bann entirely at his own charge (and that of his fellow investors). In contrast to the novel, uncer-tain, and potentially costly alternative policy of tenurial reform being proposed contemporaneously by Sir Henry Sidney, it was a far more attractive way of re-establishing an English presence in Gaelic Ulster. It was strategically important in another way. In concentrating on east Ulster, Essex envisaged that his principal targets of attack would not be the queen's Irish subjects, but the Scottish interlopers – the Clan Donald and their adherents – who had been settling in increased numbers across the region over the previous century. In the 1570s, as fears of possible threat from Scotland re-emerged, the sealing off of this exposed frontier seemed a prudent move. Finally, as the territory was supposedly part of the house of Tudor's particular dynastic inheritance, by line of descent from Hugh de Lacey, of the ancient earldom of Ulster, this revival of a dynastic interest in Ireland by indirect, though perfectly traditional, methods seemed to offer an appealing means of reaffirming Elizabeth's direct involvement in her Irish kingdom.[61]

---

[59] Hiram Morgan, 'The colonial venture of Sir Thomas Smith', *Historical Journal* 28 (1985), 261–78.

[60] The best source for the project remains W. B. Devereux (ed.) *Lives and letters of the Devereux earls of Essex*, 2 vols. (London, 1853), vol. I.

[61] SP 63/40/59, 62; SP 63/50/68 (v); SP 63/43/36. Elizabeth's intense interest in the project can be traced in her surviving correspondence with the earl, 30 Mar., 27 Apr., 13 Jul., 9 Nov. 1574, printed in *Cal. Carew*, 1515–74, pp. 460–1, 471, 477, 485; and 24 Feb., 18 Apr., 5 May, 22 May 1575, in *Cal. Carew*, 1575–88, pp. 2–3, 7, 9–10, 11.

All of these expectations were confounded in a relatively brief space of time. Essex failed to expel the Scots. Despite his expressions of good will, his treachery and his violence towards the native Irish lords provoked widespread rebellion in the region, and he went broke, unable to repay the royal loans advanced to him. Yet, for all that, Elizabeth remained loyal to Essex and his project, rebuking those who criticised him, excusing even his atrocities against women and children, and insisting, even while being forced to conceded to Sidney's alternate way, that Essex be made president of Ulster.[62]

The damage done by the enterprise of Ulster cannot easily be over-stated. It not only deepened mistrust among the native Irish of the province as to the real intentions of the English government, it also raised doubts about the coherence and stability of English government in Ireland as a whole. In the short term, however, such doubts were qualified by the advantage which several provincial powers were able to make of the affair – Hugh O'Neill was a supporter of the enterprise, while Turlough Luineach O'Neill used the debacle to strengthen his claims as the protector of native interest in the east – and by the ascendancy of the alternative strategy of tenurial reform.

Elizabeth was never again to become as directly or as enthusiastically engaged with colonising enterprise in Ireland. But in the wake of the lengthy and costly Munster rebellion many pressures began to act simultaneously on the crown as to the best means of compensating for the expenditure and benefiting from the confiscation of Desmond's very substantial estate. At court there was increasing interest among leading courtiers and their allies in the prospects of investment and development in some of the richest land in Ireland. Overlapping but also competing with this group were the 'servitors', the English soldier-adventurers who had served during the rebellion in the expectation of reward in land. And then there were Elizabeth's loyal Irish subjects, English-Irish and Gaelic Irish who had actively served or who had been persuaded to serve by her beloved Ormond. At first Elizabeth tried to do well by all. Courtiers such as Sir Christopher Hatton, Sir Edward Denny, Sir Walter Raleigh, and their dependants among the servitors, were encouraged. Ormond too was reassured. But before long, as the impossibility of reconciling such competing claims became obvious, Elizabeth withdrew and decisions were held in abeyance.[63]

---

[62] SP 12/45, fol. 901; SP 63/55/34.

[63] *CSPI*, III, pp. 84–9; Michael MacCarthy-Morrogh, *The Munster plantation: English migration to southern Ireland 1583–1641* (Oxford, 1986), pp. 41, 55.

At first Elizabeth's procrastination was personal – a desire to do right by those who she considered loyal and useful subjects. But as the arguments about various competing claims continued, a larger issue which had never been far from the centre of the queen's thoughts came into view. This was her concern to see that, whatever was done in regard to the settlement of current legal disputes, the authority of the crown as the defender of English law and the ultimate provider of justice within that law should never be compromised. Ironically, in the case of the Munster plantation, this sincere and profound concern with justice and equity under the law was to lead to many delays, reversals of legal judgement, the disappointment of expectations, and the encouragement of false hopes which were to contribute to the destabilisation of the scheme in the later 1590s.[64] But there were three further – and larger – areas of Tudor policy in Ireland in which the monarch's insistence that consistency and authority of English law be upheld at all costs was to issue in even more grave and entirely unintended consequences.

IV

The most specific and therefore the least calamitous of these was Elizabeth's insistence that the terms of any of the formal agreements sealed between the lords of Ireland and her royal predecessors should be honoured, and not abandoned for short-term exigencies. Though it was to embroil the English government in Ireland in chronic and irresolvable conflict among the O'Briens of Thomond, and even more seriously in a war with Shane O'Neill, the principle underlying this attitude was from the monarch's perspective entirely proper. It was not simply a matter of asserting the monarch's power and glory, or of warning miscreants of the consequences of their actions, it was of central importance in maintaining the claim that the authority of the monarchy was derived not from force, but from its role in providing justice and equity through the fair and balanced execution of the time-honoured principles and procedures of English law.[65]

The sincerity of Elizabeth's conviction on this issue is most clearly seen in her responses to such disputes as took place between her political and administrative agents in Ireland and her English-Irish subjects.

---

[64] A. J. Sheehan, 'Official reaction to native land claims in the plantation of Munster', *Irish Historical Studies* 23 (1983), 297–318; Ciaran Brady, 'Spenser, plantation and government policy' in Richard A. McCabe, *The Oxford handbook of Edmund Spenser* (Oxford, 2011), pp. 86–105.

[65] See, for example, SP 63/2/25, 30; SP 63/3/83; SP 63/4/45; SP 63/45/1; and *CSPI*, V, p. 139.

On two separate occasions in the 1560s and 1570s, as serious conflict arose between the viceroys and the community of the English Pale over demands which were being made by the governors for the maintenance of the military establishment, representatives of the Pale travelled to court without licence of the governor to lay their grievances before the queen. At first, in both cases, Elizabeth reacted with grave displeasure. The plaintiffs were refused admission and imprisoned. They were forced to submit and to recognise the power of the royal prerogative. But their disobedience thus purged, the essence of their case, that as English subjects they were not to be forced indefinitely to pay a tax without their consent being registered in their own parliament, was heard and accepted. And in both cases Elizabeth ordered her viceroys to desist from enforcing the exactions known collectively as the cess.[66]

The queen's concern for the rights of her English subjects in Ireland arose from exactly the same principle as underpinned her determination to uphold the 'surrender and regrant' agreements of the 1540s. But despite its integrity and consistency, this unquestioned conviction rested on an assumption of a very dubious nature. This was the supposition that, through careful, consistent, and equitable action on the part of the royal administration in Ireland, English law and English culture might be extended throughout the whole island with the peaceful assent of the majority of its inhabitants. On the surface this was an optimistic, reasonable view, rather different from the bloody-minded and overtly exploitative attitudes sometimes attributed (erroneously) to the Elizabethan regime as a whole and (more accurately) to a section of its Irish executives. It was sustained by its practical advantages: it promised a more economical, less strategically dangerous, and, since it was the principal justification for the English presence in Ireland in the first place, more morally acceptable approach. But increasingly it began to become clear that such comfortable assumptions were being subjected to a formidable challenge in Ireland which few Elizabethans, including Elizabeth herself, were prepared to confront.

In the 1560s the source of the conflict over the military cess between Lord Lieutenant Sussex and the community of the Pale was largely perceived to be a practical matter. Sussex's exactions were too high, the wars in which he had engaged (and which the Palesmen had once enthusiastically endorsed) were too protracted and unsuccessful, and the unpunished depredations of his soldiers intolerable. But all of this could be –

---

[66] SP 63/6/12, 13, 44, 49; 'Report on the protest against the cess', 1578, BL Cotton MSS, Vespasian, F IX, no. 22; Brady, *Chief governors*, pp. 238–44; SP 63/60/23, 24.

and was – remedied by relief.[67] When it re-emerged under Sidney in the later 1570s, however, the implications of the viceroys' demands for cess went altogether further. Sidney's request that the Pale should yield a cess arose not from any immediate emergency or war: it was simply one element of his broader political initiative which he termed 'composition'. Primarily directed towards the lordships of Ireland outside the Pale, composition aimed at giving practical reality to the earlier surrender and regrant settlements by identifying and measuring the true political and social standing of the lords and of powerful figures within the lordships through their ability to yield an agreed tax. Payment of the tax, referred to with deliberately constructive ambiguity by Sidney as a 'rent', would form the basis for the legal recognition of the payer as a freeholding subject of the crown and the tax itself (usually to be paid in cattle) used to fund regional administration.[68]

In so far as it appeared to copy the existing modes by which power and wealth were measured within the Irish lordships, 'composition' seemed to be a sensible means of initiating their integration within the kingdom of Ireland.[69] Though it encountered opposition in several quarters as the terms of the deal were being worked out, it is remarkable how many of the major powers in the Irish provinces – Ulster included – responded positively to the initiative. But when Sidney attempted to negotiate a similar deal in Leinster, including the shires of the Pale, he encountered major opposition. It was then that the leaders of the English-Irish, many of them already deeply disturbed by the cultural implications of the Reformation noted earlier, were driven to make their unambiguous claim on their queen. They were English, entitled to the same rights as her subjects in England. They should not be subject to any form of taxation without their consent given in Parliament. To this Elizabeth assented. But in doing so she inadvertently undermined the only practical means by which the kingdom of Ireland could be realised.[70] Ten years on, even in the wake of the Desmond rebellion, the realisation that some form of interim tenurial recognition along the lines first mooted in Sidney's policy of composition was again asserted during the viceroyalty of Sir John Perrot. But again, while Perrot avoided direct conflict with the Pale, his insistence that the continuation of negotiations with the

---

[67] Relief came in the form of the despatch of a commission of enquiry to investigate the allegations of abuse by the English garrison in Ireland: SP 63/9/45.

[68] Sidney's 'Discourse on coign and livery', Mar. 1578, LPL, MS 607, fols. 136–9; SP 63/57/13(i); SP 63/64/23.

[69] The development of Sidney's thought along these lines is traced in the editorial introduction to Sir Henry Sidney, *A viceroy's vindication? Sir Henry Sidney's memoir of service in Ireland, 1556–1578*, Ciaran Brady (ed.) (Cork, 2002), pp. 1–37.

[70] 'Submission of the gentlemen of the Pale', Jun. 1577, LPL, MS 628/128; also SP 63/58/42.

provincial lords over some form of agreed 'rental' provoked resistance among the recently settled planters and speculators in Munster. Their pressure, combined with Elizabeth's own concern in the mid 1580s that the defence of the realm should take precedence over any such controversial policies, undermined Elizabeth's confidence in him and determined his recall.[71] Ironically, therefore, in terms both of her determination to uphold the original treaties of surrender and regrant and of her deep mistrust of the constitutional implications of 'composition', Elizabeth's conscientious conservatism thus contributed substantially to the failure of efforts to make the aspiration of an Irish kingdom a reality.

But there remained a third manner in which this reflex, perfectly understandable, in the case of the government of England, but increasingly inappropriate in the circumstances of Ireland, contributed further to the Tudor experiment in cultural assimilation, if in an entirely different way. Even as they began to realise that the central forms of English land law concerning title, inheritance, and sub-infeudation could not readily be applied to Ireland without some realistic and intricate adaptations to the existing system of the Irish lordships, so the English governors in Ireland began to see that a similarly subtle approach was required in regard to the equally important imperative of establishing the Reformation.

Yet, whereas the principal obstacle to success in the former lay in the challenge which compliance with English law – especially land law – presented to the Gaelic Irish lords, the main source of resistance to religious change arose, as we have seen, from within the English-Irish themselves. As their appreciation of the dilemma deepened, Elizabeth's viceroys resorted to a variety of strategies to address it, the most important of which was delay. In the early years of the reign Sussex's preferred strategy was inaction. The principal constitutional elements of the English Reformation having been re-established perfunctorily by a parliament which he summoned for few weeks in 1560, Sussex resolved to do little more. Conformity with the Reformation changes among the English in Ireland, he appeared to believe, would eventually be won after the secular authority of English government had been asserted through the vigorous suppression of political dissent. In this he had the support of the archbishop of Dublin, Hugh Curwen, a Marian appointment whose allegiance to the Reformation was generally recognised as superficial and who did little while in office (he held the post until 1565) to enforce conformity.[72]

---

[71] SP 63/118/55; *CSPI*, III, pp. 32, 255.

[72] The lack of progress in the enforcement of ecclesiastical and liturgical change under Sussex is detailed in the section on religion in SP 63/10/35; some of this is extracted in Evelyn Philip Shirley (ed.), *Original letters and papers in illustration of the history of the*

While initially Elizabeth was prepared to indulge Sussex's caution, no such licence was granted to his successor; and Sidney took office in 1565 with an extensive list of instructions specifically related to the enforcement of the Reformation.[73] There is no reason to doubt that Sidney concurred in this programme – it is likely that he drafted the instructions himself. But once in office he found himself frustrated in several ways by Elizabeth's personal interventions, which worked in practice to disrupt a policy she had so strongly supported in principle. At the outset Elizabeth intervened to spoil Sidney's key nominations to the sees of Armagh and Dublin. Sidney had proposed Terence Donnelly, an influential figure in the politics of Gaelic Ulster for the former, and even more importantly he sought to have Hugh Brady, a Palesman who was at once well respected in the country and fully committed to the Reformation, installed as archbishop of Dublin.[74] Later Elizabeth listened sympathetically to complaints made against another of Sidney's further nominees to ecclesiastical office, George Acworth, the aggressive civil lawyer whom Sidney had imposed upon an unwilling Archbishop Adam Loftus as official principal and vicar-general of the see of Dublin, and had him dismissed.[75]

Similarly, Elizabeth offered no support for initiatives which Sidney regarded as essential to the successful introduction of the reformation in Ireland, such as the establishment of grammar schools and the foundation of a university. Central to the package of reform bills which Sidney brought to the parliament of 1569, these proposals had been presented to Elizabeth well in advance and had received royal approval. But when they encountered serious opposition in that parliament Sidney was given no support from Whitehall. No royal letters were forthcoming declaring the queen's desire to have such measures passed or her displeasure with those who opposed them, which would have aided Sidney in his struggle against the opposition, and he was forced to abandon them.[76]

Most serious of all, however, was Elizabeth's opposition to Sidney's ambitious initiative in religious policy in his establishment in 1577 of a new Court of Faculties and a new ecclesiastical High Commission for all of Ireland. Designed to place responsibility for the enforcement of religious change firmly under the secular administration, these initiatives were derived from Sidney's frustration with the efforts of the ecclesiastical

---

church in Ireland, during the reigns of Edward VI, Mary, and Elizabeth (London, 1851), pp. 139–41.
[73] SP 63/13/51; SP 63/15/85.   [74] SP 63/15/51.   [75] SP 63/66/7.
[76] Victor Treadwell, 'The Irish parliament of 1569–1571', *Proceedings of the Royal Irish Academy* 65 C (1966–7), 55–89.

leadership of the Church of Ireland and were aimed at initiating a thorough reform of the personnel of the church as a preliminary to a sustained address to the laity.[77]

Based on sad experience, and increasing frustration with the gradualist measures of Archbishop Loftus and the bulk of the English-born Irish episcopacy, Sidney's new strategy was at once bold and shrewd. The intervention of the secular agents of the crown into the affairs of the church would have had the coercive effect of indicating to the country as a whole that this time the crown was serious about Reformation. But the use of distinctively English institutions of governance would have allowed the opportunity for those leading figures within the English-Irish community who remained loyal to the idea of an Irish kingdom under English forms to regain an initiative which had been steadily draining from them since the 1540s, and to reassert the Reformation, for all its embarrassing complexities, as a distinctively English movement and part of the continuing conquest of Ireland through cultural rather than military means. In practice, however, it was a strategy that directly invited confrontation with the official leadership of the Church of Ireland: and it was at this that Elizabeth baulked.[78]

As in the case of her attitude towards his secular political initiatives, Elizabeth's resistance to Sidney's Reformation policies arose from several considerations. Suspicion of his involvement in the machinations of patronage and clientage was no doubt partly behind her rejection and dismissal of his nominees to office. The belief that Sidney was being unnecessarily provocative in his dealings with the community of the Pale and the house of Ormond also underlay her reluctance to lend overt support to his legislative proposals in 1569 and his establishment of a court of High Commission in 1577. But more important than any such factors was Elizabeth's conviction that the institutional structures and procedures which were normative in regard to the governance of England should be applied without alteration in Ireland. In terms of Sidney's attempts at tenurial reform this conservatism led, as we have seen, to Elizabeth's rejection of 'composition' on firm constitutional grounds. And, in regard to religious affairs, Elizabeth's objection to Sidney's actions lay in her deep concern that under her supreme governorship of the Churches of England and Ireland the authority of the episcopacy should never be usurped by her lay servants.

---

[77] Ciaran Brady and James Murray, 'Sir Henry Sidney and the Reformation in Ireland', in Elizabethanne Boran and Crawford Gibben (eds.), *Enforcing Reformation in Ireland and Scotland, 1550–1700* (Aldershot, 2006), pp. 14–39.

[78] *Ibid.*, pp. 36–9.

Elizabeth's sense that the maintenance of the authority of the bishops was inextricably linked with the preservation of the authority of the monarchy was extremely acute in terms of England, and the alliance which she forged with John Whitgift as archbishop of Canterbury in the years after 1580 was to be of no small aid in curbing religious and ideological dissent in the final decades of her reign.[79] But in Ireland, where the ideological implications of Reformation were immensely complex and where the practical relations between the episcopacy and the lower clergy, as well as between the clergy as a whole and the laity, were altogether different, the consequences of Elizabeth's admirable consistency were particularly unfortunate. In defending her archbishop of Dublin against Sidney's plan for clerical reform through political and legal pressure, Elizabeth ensured that Adam Loftus and his supporters on the episcopal bench might persist in their gradualist strategy of piecemeal progress with minimal interference without fear of pressure from the organs of the state. And as a consequence she did nothing to halt the drift of both the lower clergy and the laity away from their bishops which Sidney and his advisers had seen as the central challenge of the Irish Reformation. But Elizabeth remained convinced of the propriety of her actions. And when Sir John Perrot, Sidney's successor as governor, attempted to revive Sidney's strategy in regard to the enforcement of Reformation just as he had sought to implement an adapted form of 'composition', Elizabeth again intervened on behalf of her archbishop. Perrot's complaints against the laxity of clerical discipline and the failure to enforce the Reformation statutes were ignored, his own attempts at imposing pressure on the clergy discouraged; and, when he sought to implement a plan to establish a public university on the revenues of St Patrick's Cathedral he was ordered to desist.[80] Perrot's confrontation with the archbishop of Dublin contributed substantially to his recall in 1588. Thus Loftus triumphed once again; and when, four years later, a university scheme through private contributions was at length initiated under Loftus's chancellorship, Trinity College Dublin, the institution that finally emerged at the close of Elizabeth's reign, turned out to be far less than the powerhouse of religious evangelisation for which both Sidney and Perrot had hoped.[81]

---

[79] Claire Cross, *The royal supremacy and the Elizabethan church* (London, 1969); Peter Lake, *Anglicans and Puritans? Presbyterianism and English conformist thought from Whitgift to Hooker* (London, 1988).

[80] Perrot to Burghley, 24 Sep. 1585, printed in *State papers concerning the Church of Ireland in the time of Queen Elizabeth*, W. M. Brady (ed.) (London, 1868), pp. 100–2; SP 63/121/50.

[81] Perrot to Walsingham, 21 Aug., 20 Oct. 1584; *State papers concerning the Church of Ireland in the time of Queen Elizabeth*, Brady (ed.), pp. 90–3; James Murray, 'St Patrick's Cathedral and the university question in Ireland, *c.* 1547–1585', in Helga

There is therefore an irony of considerable depth underlying all of Elizabeth I's dealings with her Irish subjects. Generally and perhaps necessarily distant, and ignorant of the conditions prevailing in her Irish kingdom, she intervened only occasionally in the affairs of its government, and did so in the firm conviction that she was acting justly and for the good.[82] Unwilling to immerse herself in the historical and cultural complexities which had rendered Ireland so different from England, she persisted, like Spenser's Eudoxus, the ignorant but well-meaning foil of his *View of the Present State of Ireland*, in the innocent belief that with sufficient persistence, firmness, and justice the norms of English public culture could be developed in Ireland. As such, she remained uncomprehending of and resistant to the alternative strategies of securing political and cultural control in Ireland as advanced by the most perceptive of her officers there. And, in rejecting their unorthodox but essentially assimilative proposals, she inadvertently made it inevitable that the far more radical alternative advanced by Spenser's terrifying Irenius should steadily come into play.

Robinson-Hammerstein (ed.), *European universities in the age of Reformation and Counter-Reformation* (Dublin, 1998), pp. 1–21.

[82] As in the letters quoted in the epigraph at the beginning of the chapter.

7   An Irish perspective on Elizabeth's religion: Reformation thought and Henry Sidney's Irish lord deputyship, *c.* 1560 to 1580

Mark A. Hutchinson

The question of Elizabeth's religion has been widely discussed by historians of England, and scholars tend to agree that she held to a conservative line in church policy. It is even argued that Elizabeth's reformed Protestant councillors in England, in response to her conservatism, sought to bypass the queen as much as possible in the policy-making process.[1] The English evidence, nevertheless, remains ambiguous.[2] In particular, historians of England have found it difficult to add theological detail to the respective policy positions taken by Elizabeth and her Protestant councillors. This is despite the fact that reformed theology did have important implications for early modern notions of good government, in that it posed serious questions about man's ability to govern himself. For example, Calvin's *Institutes* argued that because man was born in sin man lacked free will and, furthermore, that it would only be through the action of God's grace that man would be brought to know God and therefore to act for the wider good.[3] In particular, from a reformed Protestant perspective, it was through God's word that man would come to know grace and, as a result, for reformed Protestants the dissemination of God's

---

This essay was made possible by an Irish Research Council Postdoctoral Fellowship in the Humanities and Social Sciences held at University College Cork as well as funding from the Royal Historical Society.

[1] See Patrick Collinson, 'The monarchical republic of Queen Elizabeth I', in Collinson, *Elizabethan essays* (London, 1994), pp. 31–58; and Stephen Alford, *The early Elizabeth polity: William Cecil and the British succession crisis, 1558–1569* (Cambridge, 2002).

[2] For the various views on Elizabeth's religion, see Christopher Haigh, *Elizabeth I* (London, 1988; 2nd edn, 1998), pp. 38–41; William P. Haugaard, 'Elizabeth Tudor's book of devotions: a neglected clue to the queen's life and character', *Sixteenth Century Journal* 12 (1981), 79–106; Patrick Collinson, 'Windows in a woman's soul: questions about the religion of Queen Elizabeth', in Collinson, *Elizabethan essays*, pp. 87–118; and Susan Doran, 'Elizabeth I's religion: the evidence from Elizabeth's letters', *Journal of Ecclesiastical History* 51 (2000), 699–720.

[3] See John Calvin, *Institutes of the Christian religion*, Henry Beveridge (trans.) (Peabody, MA, 2008), book second, ch. 2, 'Man now deprived of freedom of will, and miserably enslaved'.

word was thought to be essential in a healthy and functional political community.[4]

Ireland provides an important window on to this theological dimension of civil government and in turn on to Elizabeth's view of church and societal reform. This is especially true of Irish government under Henry Sidney, a reformed Protestant associate of the earl of Leicester and Elizabeth's Irish lord deputy from 1565 to 1571 and from 1575 to 1578. This chapter will argue that it was the nature of Irish policy discussion to draw the various theological assumptions behind church and civil policy into open political debate.[5] Irish government, after all, was tasked with reforming Ireland to a level of long-term civil obedience, and the Irish church, unlike its counterpart in England, was in a general state of disrepair, since it lacked even the bare minimum of qualified clergy to allow it to function. As a consequence, Sidney and his associates felt the need to explain exactly why God's word and grace were thought so important. Here it was argued, first, that Ireland remained in a state of civil disobedience because man lacked free will and, second, that the island would be reformed to obedience if provision was made for the dissemination of God's word and so the operation of God's grace. In response, Elizabeth was to clarify her own position, in that she was to reject the view set out by Sidney's government.

It should be noted, therefore, that a very different picture of Sidney's time in Irish office will be presented here from that found in secondary studies of the period. This chapter will argue that Sidney's 'extreme' Protestantism did not lead straight to a policy of conquest, as Nicholas Canny suggests, but that the lord deputy also looked to offer the Irish redemption.[6] It will further demonstrate, in contrast to Ciaran Brady's view, that an English system of land tenure and law was not the primary reform model, since reformed theology raised fundamental questions about man's ability to govern himself and as a result about the efficacy of such an approach.[7] This chapter also moves beyond the recent

---

[4] See *ibid.*, book first, ch. 6, 'The need of scripture, as a guide and teacher, in coming to God a creator'; and Martin Luther, *The bondage of the will*, Henry Cole (trans.) (Peabody, MA, 2008).

[5] See Simon Adams, *Leicester and the court: essays on Elizabethan politics* (Manchester, 2002).

[6] Nicholas P. Canny, *The Elizabethan conquest of Ireland: a pattern established, 1565–1576* (Hassocks, 1976), pp. 119–36; and Brendan Bradshaw, 'Sword, word and strategy in the Reformation in Ireland', *Historical Journal* 21 (1978), 475–502.

[7] Ciaran Brady, *The chief governors: the rise and fall of reform government in Tudor Ireland, 1536–1588* (Cambridge, 1994), pp. 113–58. This chapter, however, does not call in to question Brady's examination of English attempts to establish common law practice in Ireland or his suggestion that the violence of Irish government was often unintended and usually the byproduct of the failure of an overambitious reform programme. This chapter

reassessment offered by Ciaran Brady and James Murray in 'Sir Henry Sidney and the Reformation in Ireland' (2006), by directly examining the efforts Sidney made to provide for the dissemination of God's word.[8]

I will, however, veer away from discussing the specific Irish implications of this reassessment of Sidney's time in Irish office. Instead, the chapter will concern itself with the way in which political conditions in Ireland – the question of Irish civil disobedience – drew out the various assumptions that underlay policy, and it will attempt to relate this to a more muted discussion about England. With this in mind, I will also touch upon a well-known exchange of correspondence between Elizabeth and the reformed Protestant archbishop of Canterbury, Edmund Grindal, which took place in the late 1570s around the end of Sidney's second appointment as Irish lord deputy. The exchange between Elizabeth and Grindal specifically concerned religious Reformation in England but, similar to discussions in Ireland, questions were raised concerning grace and the common good. This suggests that what informed policy debate in Ireland also underlay policy discussion in England, and I will argue on this basis that a more general reassessment of the relationship between religious reformation and civil government in England, as well as in Ireland, may be in order.

I

Historians of England have found it difficult to add theological or intellectual detail to the respective policy positions taken by Elizabeth and her Protestant councillors because the evidence is far from obvious. England was after all, in contrast to Ireland, perceived to be a fully functional state or civil society, and so there was little reason for Elizabethan policy-makers to debate or discuss the assumptions behind policy, since they tended to work from a common body of ideas. We do not find, for instance, ready explanations of why English law was thought important in English or Irish government correspondence. That it would regulate the behaviour of man was accepted and understood. In the same way, it was accepted that provision should be made for the dissemination of God's

---

simply suggests that there was another dimension to Sidney's approach to Irish reform policy which needs to be considered, i.e. religious reformation/reformed theology.

[8] Ciaran Brady and James Murray, 'Sir Henry Sidney and the Reformation in Ireland', in Elizabethanne Boran and Crawford Gribben (eds.), *Enforcing the Reformation in Ireland and Scotland, 1550–1700* (Aldershot, 2006), pp. 14–18. For a wider discussion of the Irish historiography and a revised account of the place of religious reformation in the programme of government in Ireland, see Mark A. Hutchinson, 'Reformed Protestantism and the government of Ireland, *c.* 1565 to 1580: the lord deputyships of Henry Sidney and Arthur Grey', *Sidney Journal* 29 (2011), 71–104.

word without the matter being debated and discussed. In other words, the various ideas concerning man, God's grace, and the common good tended to lie at the level of unspoken assumptions. In Ireland, however, the condition of the Irish church and the general political condition of the island drew these ideas into open political debate, and this is especially true of Henry Sidney's two periods in Irish office.

Sidney's government perceived Ireland to be in a state of civil disobedience because Irish society was highly militarised. The prevalence of bastard feudal practices known as coign and livery, whereby Old English and Gaelic Irish lords collected rents in kind, i.e. as meat and drink, meant that Irish lords employed military retainers as a way of enforcing their rights to these charges, and as a consequence Ireland's lords were often engaged in armed conflict with one another. The major lords, such as the Old English earls of Ormond, Desmond, and Kildare, as well as O'Neill in Ulster, were even able to act to a degree independently of government in Dublin, although the crown was by far the largest military player.[9] Government in Ireland, therefore, relied on the sword as a way of maintaining a basic level of civil order/external obedience, but more importantly Irish government also sought to bring about a more long-term change in the behaviour and habits of Ireland's lords.

Prior to Sidney's appointment, Irish government had looked to Renaissance political philosophies in its formulation of policy, which rested on the assumption that man could and should better himself. It was argued that the introduction of an English system of land tenure and law would effect a more long-term civil obedience – that the shiring of land would allow agriculture to flourish, while the operation of circuit courts in the provinces would allow the crown to act as chief arbitrator in disputes and so foster political stability. This, it was suggested, would persuade Irish lords to dispense with coign and livery as they came to realise the benefits of an English model of government, and that in turn Irish government would be able to dispense with its reliance on the sword. (Such a policy will be referred to throughout this chapter as standard reform practice.) There had, however, been little change in the behaviour and habits of the various lords. This raised serious questions about such an approach, as well as man's ability to effect his own reform, and this was to resonate with Reformation-era views of man born in sin and without free will.[10]

---

[9] Brady, *Chief governors*, pp. 72–8; also see K. W. Nicholls, *Gaelic and Gaelicized Ireland in the Middle Ages* (Dublin, 2003).

[10] See Brendan Bradshaw, *The Irish constitutional revolution of the sixteenth century* (Cambridge, 1979), pp. 32–57, which describes the influence of Renaissance political philosophies on Irish reform policy. Brady, *Chief governors*, pp. 11–158, describes the continued failure of such a policy. Sidney, however, was not to reject standard reform practice in its

Reformed theology, however, not only explained why standard reform practice had been ineffective, it also offered a solution to Irish civil disobedience. Sidney and his reformed Protestant associates would argue that, while man on his own could not further his own reform, man would be brought to know what was good through the operation of God's grace. In particular, it was through the dissemination of God's word, it was argued, that man could come to know grace and so be reformed. Elizabeth, however, was reluctant to support Sidney's programme of religious reformation, and in response Sidney and his associates would begin to explain in urgent terms why the dissemination of God's word, i.e. evangelism, was so important to the island's longer-term reform. In doing so, they outlined the various reformed Protestant assumptions about man and God's grace in open political debate, and it is the initial build-up of tension between queen and deputy on the subject of Irish church reform that we now turn to examine.

Signs of tension between how Elizabeth and Sidney thought of the church can be identified from the outset of Sidney's appointment. The lord deputy was issued with instructions for government in October 1565, which arose out of a number of drafts involving Elizabeth, the English privy council, and Sidney. The first draft possessed little evangelical intent and directed Irish government simply to enforce Reformation statute. The lord deputy was 'faithfully and earnestly to regard the due and reverent observation of all good laws and ordinances made and established for the maintenance of the Christian faith and religion among her people'.[11] Sidney, however, tried to alter the tone of his instructions. The draft asked 'the said lieutenant by the advice of the clergy of that realm, in what parts the same [the church and clergy] is defective, and by what means it may be repaired and amended', and Sidney, in his 'opinion upon the minute', which was written in reply, responded that 'the only way' to correct the defects of the church was 'by finding learned pastors from home and by giving them competent living there'.[12] In short, the lord deputy looked to make provision for preachers, although Sidney's comment would not make its way into the final October version as Elizabeth was to ignore her lord deputy.

Sidney also took steps to distance himself from Elizabeth's known conservatism in church policy. By the time of his appointment as lord deputy, the vestment controversy in England was in full swing. Those Marian

---

entirety, as it was accepted that the behaviour of Ireland's lords needed to be regulated. The lord deputy and his associates simply made the argument that without a level of internal reform brought about by God's grace little would/could be achieved.

[11] SP 63/14/2.   [12] SP 63/14/3.

exiles who had returned to take up positions in the English church after Elizabeth's accession looked to a reformed church model, which drew on the example of the primitive church in Scripture, and as a result they opposed the wearing of the surplice and square cap as required by the Church of England. Elizabeth, however, insisted that the surplice and square cap stay.[13] Sidney's decision to appoint the Marian exile Christopher Goodman as his chaplain sometime in 1566 was, therefore, a pointed gesture on his behalf. Goodman was author of the controversial resistance pamphlet, *How superior powers oght to be obeyd* (1558), which argued that individuals could actively disobey an ungodly ruler. Goodman categorised such acts of disobedience as 'true obedience', because they were consonant with God's will. For the cleric, man would know how to act correctly in a political setting through knowledge of God's word and the action of God's grace on conscience, a position very close to the way in which Sidney's administration would define long-term civil obedience in Ireland.[14]

Furthermore, there are indications that Ireland, with its distance from Elizabeth, may have been viewed as a sort of reformed Protestant experiment. For example, Goodman had ministered in St Andrews between 1560 and 1565 and had turned Scotland's ecclesiastical capital into a model reformed burgh.[15] He possessed the skills, then, to move the Irish church beyond the 'act of uniformity', i.e. the church established by statute. He even asked John Knox, the leading Scottish reformer with whom he had ministered in Geneva, to join him in Ireland. Knox, however, declined, as he was frightened 'that your politic bishops within England should storm at our conjunction and so travail to dissever us'.[16] The twelve Irish Articles of Religion published in Dublin on 20 January

---

[13] See Patrick Collinson, *The Elizabethan Puritan movement* (Oxford, 1967).

[14] See Christopher Goodman, *How superior powers oght to be obeyd of their subjects* (Geneva, 1558), in particular pp. 153–4. It could be argued that Ireland in this respect inverts resistance theory, where in Europe and England resistance writers asked how they could disobey an ungodly ruler, while in Ireland reformed Protestants asked how they could bring the island to obey a godly ruler. Ireland, therefore, draws out the broader position upon which resistance theory rests, something my current research is examining. My thanks to Brendan Kane and Hiram Morgan for discussion on this topic.

[15] See Jane E. A. Dawson, 'Goodman, Christopher (1521/2–1603)', *ODNB*.

[16] John Knox to Christopher Goodman, 27 Oct. 1566, in Jane E. A. Dawson and L. K. Glassey, 'Some unpublished letters from John Knox to Christopher Goodman', *Scottish Historical Review* 84 (2005), 183–5. The reference was kindly provided by Jane Dawson. See also Jane E. A. Dawson, 'John Knox, Goodman and the example of Geneva', in Polly Ha and Patrick Collinson (eds.), *The reception of the continental reformation in Britain* (Oxford, 2010), pp. 107–35, which explores some of the aspects of Goodman's and Knox's links to Ireland.

1566, at Sidney's behest, also left room for an Irish reformed church to be established.

Brady and Murray have drawn attention to the conservative tone of the Irish articles which, unlike the Thirty-Nine Articles agreed on in England in 1562, did not mention justification by faith and did not define the sacraments.[17] But it is also important to note that the Irish articles did not include the prohibition found in the Thirty-Nine which made it clear that bishops, surplices, and other ceremonies, which were to be found in the English church but not in the biblical church or in Geneva, should continue.[18] The Irish articles even hinted at the model of the 'primitive church' found in Scripture, which reformed Protestants held up as evidence that the English church needed further reform. Article 6 described the authority of the bishop of Rome as 'contrary to the scriptures and the word of God, and contrary to the example of the primitive church'.[19] This could easily have been said of the position of bishop in general – an argument English Presbyterians would soon come to make.

It seems then that Elizabeth's physical distance from Ireland had led some reformed Protestants to look to carry through the sort of church reform not allowed in England. This, however, came to very little. Elizabeth would make clear her dislike of innovation, and she would also refuse Sidney's requests for preachers to be appointed to the Irish church. Elizabeth would also hold to the view that standard reform practice, i.e. negotiated agreements and English law, could, on its own, effect Ireland's longer-term reform, and in response Sidney and his reformed Protestant associates began to make clear their position on the question of free will, grace, and man's reform.

II

There was a degree of consensus between Elizabeth and Sidney on more basic questions of law and order. It was agreed, for example, that Shane O'Neill's intransigence in Ulster was a significant block to the progress of political reform there.[20] This was because O'Neill, despite agreements

---

[17] Brady and Murray, 'Sidney and the Reformation in Ireland', p. 19.

[18] Article 34 – 'It is not necessary that traditions and ceremonies be in all places one, or utterly like; for at all times they have been divers . . . Whosoever through his private judgement doth openly break the traditions and ceremonies of the church . . . offendeth against the common order of the church.'

[19] Elizabeth to Sidney, 12 Nov. 1565, no. 3, pp. 4–6; 11 Dec. 1565, no. 4, pp. 6–7; 7 Jan. 1566, no. 8, pp. 11–12; and 12 Jan. 1566, no. 10, pp. 14–15, all in *Sidney SP*.

[20] SP 63/17/8.

made with the crown, continued to exert his authority over minor Ulster lords, and to bring armed men over from Scotland in order to bolster his military strength.[21] The difference in Elizabeth's and Sidney's respective views of standard reform practice quickly emerged, however, in an exchange of correspondence which took place over the first two years of Sidney's appointment.

The lord deputy, for example, on assuming office, began to question whether the earl of Sussex, his predecessor in Ireland, had in reality begun to bring Ireland to a more sustainable level of order. He explained to the earl of Leicester that 'my lord of Sussex left and evil I found it [the condition of the island] no[ne] the better for [being] denied. It cannot be but that no horrible murders, as [well as] great stealths as contemptuous disobedience hath been committed within the xii months before mine arrival'. Sidney observed that on Sussex's departure from office Irish civil disobedience was still a pressing concern. He noted that order had broken down even where an English system of land tenure and law had begun to take hold and described how disorder had occurred 'all in shire ground and among civil people as hath been in memory of men'.[22]

This view, however, Elizabeth rejected, and she informed Sidney that his opinion of the 'evil estate' of Ireland at Sussex's departure was contradicted by 'the contrary advertisements given to us before found that our realm both generally and particularly' was in good order.[23] Elizabeth made clear that she thought Sussex had managed to establish a degree of political reform that was not reliant on force of arms and, unsurprisingly, in his reply, Sidney made the doubts he had about standard reform practice somewhat clearer. He reminded Elizabeth of the difficulties encountered by Sussex when he had attempted to draw the Irish into an English system of land tenure and law. In 1562 Sussex had proposed to plant English colonies in the midlands in Ireland and then portion out the remaining land to Gaelic Irish clans. Sussex argued that in doing so he would be able to gradually extend English land holding practice among the Irish. The revolt of the O'Connors and O'Mores, however, quickly put an end to such a proposal.[24] Sidney explained that 'the conquest of Laois and Offaly is to be remembered, which I am assured hath cost the queen and this country more than would purchase so much rent no times told in England'.[25] In response, Elizabeth only hardened her position, and she sent a set of interrogatory questions to be answered by the Irish council concerning the earl of Sussex's service in Ireland, in which

[21] Brady, *Chief governors*, pp. 99–101, 122–4.   [22] SP 63/16/35.
[23] Elizabeth to Sidney, 28 Mar. 1566, *Sidney SP*, no. 12, pp. 16–20.
[24] Brady, *Chief governors*, pp. 94–5.   [25] SP 63/17/14.

she made clear, for a second time, her belief that Sussex had brought Ireland to a longer-term civil obedience. The first of the questions asked 'Whether the earl of Sussex of his departure out of Ireland did not leave the Byrnes in good obedience', the next 'whether the O'Connors had not so submitted themselves at the coming repair of the said earl as they received and possessed lands of the queen', and whether 'the lord[s] of Upper Ossery, O'Carroll, O'Maugher, O'Molloy, O'Doyne, McCoughlin, Mageoghegan, O'Molaughin, O'Madden, O'Kelly, the O'Ferrall, and O'Rayle', and 'the earls of Clanricard and Thomond' had not been in similar 'obedience'?[26] The queen made clear, once again, that she thought of reform in simplified terms, as arising quite easily from nothing more than political agreements made with the crown.

A year into Sidney's deputyship, then, there were clear indications that Elizabeth held to a more optimistic view of man's capacities, in that she continued to look to a set of policies which assumed man capable of effecting his own reform. Such an observation sits comfortably beside Susan Doran's reading of Elizabeth's English letters, wherein she comments that Elizabeth 'seems to have been frozen into the religion of her youth which was heavily dependent on Erasmian, evangelical and Lutheran (of the Melanchthon ilk) influences'.[27] It was, after all, Erasmus and then Melanchthon who moved away from the particularly dark view of man found in both Luther's and Calvin's theology.[28]

On the other hand, Sidney's assessment of standard reform practice – that it would not bring about a sustainable change in the behaviour of Ireland's lords – tallies with the darker view of man present in reformed theology. David Edwards's observation that 'during the five and a half years of his first deputyship . . . Sidney issued at least eighty nine martial law commissions' which allowed crown officers 'arbitrary authority over life and death in most areas of the island', reinforces the impression that Sidney doubted the efficacy of standard reform practice, since the lord deputy sought to give legal sanction to coercive practice at the expense of the normal operation of English law.[29] Crucially, however, it was religious reformation that Sidney's government thought key in the island's long-term reform and, at the same time as Sidney wrote on the subject of standard reform practice, it also emerged that Elizabeth was reluctant to

---

[26] SP 63/17/23.   [27] Doran, 'Elizabeth I's religion', 720.

[28] See Ernest F. Winter (trans. and ed.), *Discourse on free will: Erasmus and Luther* (London, 2005), p. 17; Mark A. Hutchinson, 'Sir Henry Sidney and his legacy: reformed Protestantism and the government of Ireland and England, *c.* 1558–1580' (PhD thesis, University of Kent, 2010), pp. 14–19.

[29] David Edwards, 'Ideology and experience: Spenser's *View* and martial law in Ireland', in Hiram Morgan (ed.), *Political ideology in Ireland, 1541–1641* (Dublin, 1999), p. 129.

support church reform in Ireland. It was this that would lead the lord deputy and his associates in government to outline in more detail what I will term the reformed Protestant critique of standard reform practice, as they sought to explain why evangelism was so important.

III

Sidney in April 1566 raised the question of church reform by commending Adam Loftus, the archbishop of Armagh, Hugh Brady, the bishop of Meath, an Irish-born Protestant and associate of Elizabeth's chief secretary William Cecil, and Hugh Curwen, the archbishop of Dublin, for their diligence in preaching and 'also in the earnest calling on and looking to the other pastors and ministers within their provinces and dioceses to do the like [preach]'. Hugh Curwen had been appointed archbishop of Dublin in Mary's reign, and it had been noted earlier that year that the archbishop had filled St Patrick's Cathedral in Dublin with 'papist' incumbents. It seems, therefore, that Sidney praised Curwen, who continued to sit on the Irish council, because etiquette required it.

Nevertheless, it was from this position that Sidney then addressed Elizabeth's personal failure to make available God's word.[30] He asked why, if the three clerics preached, so little progress had been made in terms of religious reformation, writing 'howbeit that for all this, it goeth slowly forward'. There is a sense here of Sidney's assumption that God's word should have made obvious and rapid progress, and he looked to Elizabeth and her responsibilities for an answer. He wrote that there was 'want of living sufficient for fit entertainment of well chosen and learned curates amongst them, for that those livings . . . being most part appropriated benefices in the queen's majesty's possession, are letten by leases unto farmers with allowance or reservation of very small stipends or entertainments for vicars or curates'.[31] He explained that no progress had been made because God's word had not been preached and this was because the finances of the church needed reforming and the benefices concerned were in Elizabeth's possession. Elizabeth, however, did not respond to the lord deputy's request, even though the Irish church was in an obvious state of disrepair and the land which should have been used to support the church was 'in the queen's majesty's possession'.[32]

---

[30] See James Murray, 'St Patrick's Cathedral and the university question in Ireland c. 1547–1585', in Helga Robinson-Hammerstein (ed.), *European universities in the age of Reformation and Counter-Reformation* (Dublin, 1998), pp. 11–21.
[31] SP 63/17/8.   [32] *Ibid.*

Significantly, it was in the midst of this uncertainty over the queen's commitment to religious reformation in Ireland, and the growing distance between monarch and deputy on the subject of standard reform practice, that Adam Loftus explained for the first time why religious reformation was so critical to the island's longer-term reform. Here he hinted at the broader position taken by Goodman in *Superior powers* on the question of obedience. He told Cecil, no doubt in frustration, that 'your honour knoweth right well that the queen's highness shall never have just obedience unless the cause of the gospel be first promoted and alas how then can that be except such sit in the chief place ecclesiastical as are of approved zeal and knowledge in god his holy law'.[33] He implied that there was a distinction between the type of civil obedience gained through standard reform practice, which Elizabeth continued to adhere to, and the type of civil obedience that was to be gained through the dissemination of God's word, which Sidney's government sought, i.e. 'just obedience'. The distance between Elizabeth and her lord deputy, moreover, only increased as Sidney continued to push forward into 1567 with his preferred agenda.

He was successful in convincing the queen to agree to requests that an Irish parliament be called. This would mean Irish government would not have to wait for Elizabeth's final agreement on policy, which seldom came, and Sidney could simply gain Parliament's consent and move on.[34] The lord deputy, therefore, returned to England to discuss parliamentary legislation in late 1567, and at the end of that year William Cecil had drawn up a 'Memorial touching Ireland for the parliament matters'. The 'Memorial' placed church reform and the dissemination of God's word at the top of the agenda and began with '1. Edifying of parish churches' and '2. Erection of free schools'.[35] Cecil's involvement in this particular aspect of Sidney's programme of government gives some initial indication that what was being discussed in Ireland resonated within reformed Protestant circles in England.[36] Also around the same time another reformed

---

[33] SP 63/18/12.

[34] There are parallels here with what Patrick Collinson termed 'the monarchical republic', in which Elizabeth's councillors, frustrated with her lukewarm Protestantism, sought to bypass her in the policy-making process. See Collinson, 'The monarchical republic of Queen Elizabeth I'; and Collinson, 'Puritans, men of business and Elizabethan parliaments', in Collinson, *Elizabethan essays*, pp. 59–86. The idea of the 'monarchical republic' is further explored in Alford's *The early Elizabethan polity*.

[35] 'Memorandum' by William Cecil, SP 63/21/99.

[36] Sidney's government would continue to write to Cecil, no doubt because he was Elizabeth's chief secretary. The bold tone and content of the letters suggest, however, that Sidney and his associates assumed Cecil understood and agreed with their position. See section V of this chapter, p. 159.

Protestant, Dr Robert Weston, was appointed Irish chancellor.[37] Weston had served as vicar-general of Exeter in the early 1550s, when Miles Coverdale was bishop of Exeter, and later as dean of arches, under the reformed Protestant archbishop of Canterbury Matthew Parker.[38]

The lord deputy, however, had also proposed that Christopher Goodman be appointed archbishop of Dublin, and later on in 1567 he suggested that Goodman be appointed dean of St Patrick's instead.[39] This no doubt was a response to Elizabeth's failure to replace Hugh Curwen as archbishop of Dublin, since Sidney had written asking for Curwen's removal throughout 1566.[40] Unsurprisingly, however, the queen would not agree to Goodman's appointment to either position, and Adam Loftus was translated to the archbishopric in Goodman's place; this increased distance between queen and deputy sat beside another breakdown in existing political arrangements.[41]

The queen stuck rigidly to an English model of lordship governed by primogeniture. So while Sidney had sought to recognise the position of Turlough Luineach O'Neill in Ulster, after the death of Shane O'Neill, who had been killed by the Scots in June 1567, Elizabeth contravened her deputy's instructions. The queen ordered that Turlough be sidelined in favour of the baron of Dungannon, Hugh O'Neill, whom she had previously recognised as the legitimate heir to the earldom of Tyrone. In response, Turlough began to rally armed support to secure his position within Ulster, thus exposing the inadequacies of the strict application of an English model of lordship.[42] Munster also descended into violent conflict because the earl of Desmond had been called over to England, along with the earl of Ormond, after breaking the queen's peace. Sidney had hoped to maintain a level of political stability in Desmond's absence by extending the powers given to Sir John, the earl's brother, who was a commissioner in the province. Elizabeth, however, because she distrusted the Fitzgeralds, sent instructions that Sir John should be arrested, and James Fitzmaurice Fitzgerald, one of Desmond's armed retainers, went into revolt in an attempt to defend Fitzgerald interests.[43]

---

[37] SP 63/21/6.

[38] Andrew Lyall, 'Weston, Robert (b. in or before 1522, d. 1573)', *ODNB*.

[39] SP 63/20/12, 36.

[40] SP 63/18/54; SP 63/19/11, 51, 71. Sidney in many letters wrote ostensibly for the removal of the Irish chancellor, a position Hugh Curwen held along with the archbishopric of Dublin.

[41] SP 63/20/52, 52(i).   [42] Brady, *Chief governors*, pp. 127–9.

[43] *Ibid.*, pp. 123–9, argues that Elizabeth distrusted the Fitzgeralds partly because she listened to the counsel of her Irish favourite, the earl of Ormond, who was head of the rival Butler faction in Ireland. Brady also argues that Sidney's predecessor as lord deputy, the earl of Sussex, who had identified the Fitzgeralds as one of the main blocks to the

The collapse of these agreements drew out further the detail of the reformed Protestant position. The Irish government reported that the people would not permit Fitzmaurice to appear before the commissioners and that all of Ulster was in revolt; and the new Irish chancellor Robert Weston turned to Protestant theology to explain the Irish situation. He argued, in line with Calvin's *Institutes*, that man was by his very nature inclined towards civil disobedience, that the Irish 'are all universally blind through corruption of nature . . . void of all knowledge of God . . . with disobedience to God and their prince'. He also suggested that it would be through knowledge of God's word that the island would be reformed – that it would be the Irish church and the gospel that would effect a more sustainable level of civil obedience in Ireland. For Weston, if the Irish were 'taught Christ, and the will of God . . . [in his] opinion it would work a willing and a more perfect obedience in all subjects, than any fear of the sword or punishment can do', and he pointed out that so far Irish government had only been able to maintain a level of external obedience which was reliant on recourse to the sword.[44]

IV

On Sidney's return to office at the end of 1568, political conditions only worsened. The lord deputy did have Elizabeth's agreement to parliamentary legislation which addressed the shiring of the island and the wider introduction of English law, as well as legislation aimed at furthering religious reformation.[45] The relationship between Elizabeth and Sidney, however, remained strained. The queen's new instructions to her deputy informed him that he was not to allow the clergy to deviate from the liturgy and orders of the English church as established by law. She could not 'allow that any persons of any sort or quality, should by their doctrine, example, or other innovation alter the form and order in the matters ecclesiastical contrary or disruptant from the order limited by our laws'.[46]

This no doubt was a pointed comment on Sidney's relationship with Goodman. But Elizabeth's instruction may also have been a direct reference to Loftus's behaviour in Sidney's absence. The new archbishop of

---

progress of political reform in Ireland, on his return to the English court continued to lobby against the Fitzgeralds. See also Anthony McCormack, *The earldom of Desmond 1463–1583: the decline and crisis of a feudal lordship* (Dublin, 2005).

[44] SP 63/24/2.

[45] See Victor Treadwell, 'The Irish parliament of 1569–1571', *Proceedings of the Royal Irish Academy* 65 C (1966–7), 84.

[46] SP 63/24/29.

Dublin had moved the communion table into the centre of St Patrick's Cathedral, which followed practice in Geneva, and he explained his behaviour with the dubious explanation that he had acted thus because the cathedral church had been too crowded. The archbishop even let it be known that Lady Sidney had taken communion at the service – a slightly impolitic move given the difficulties the lord deputy faced in winning Elizabeth's support for Irish church reform.[47] This also gives another indication of the freedom allowed reformed Protestant clergy in Ireland because of Elizabeth's physical distance from the island.

On top of this an Irish parliament was summoned in January 1569, but crucial legislation aimed at both political and religious reform failed to pass. Here Weston outlined in greater detail the reformed Protestant critique of standard reform practice as he sought to explain once again why furthering religious reformation was so crucial and why Ireland continued to remain in a state of civil disobedience. He wrote of those bills aimed at church reform and the dissemination of God's word, the bills 'for building schools [and] for repairing of churches and chapels (which are so universally down and decayed as though there were no god nor religion)', and bills 'to call churchmen to their cures, whose non-residence, is a great cause of this great desolation and waste... [and a] motion also... made for the founding of a university', which all struggled.[48] It was hoped a university would train Irish preachers and that schools would help disseminate God's word to the population at large, but the Commons opposed the bills 'for repairing churches' and to curb 'non-residence' because lay impropriators did not want to have to meet the cost of these reforms, and the university bill had problems because the Pale was unwilling to fund such a project, as was the crown. A schools act, however, would eventually be passed.[49]

Moreover, the legislation that aimed at the abolition of bastard feudalism also faced opposition, once again pointing to the inadequacies of standard reform practice and Irish opposition to an English system of land tenure and law. In particular, a new arrival in Ireland, Sir Peter Carew, had begun to pursue ancient claims to the barony of Idrone, which the house of Ormond had recently purchased, and these claims were upheld by Sidney's government. As a consequence Sir Edmund Butler, the earl of Ormond's brother, who had a significant portion of land in Idrone, went into revolt, and he was quickly joined by another brother, Edward. It was further understood that the broad thrust of

---

[47] SP 63/23/18. [48] SP 63/30/29.

[49] See Hutchinson, 'Sidney and his legacy', p. 85; and Treadwell, 'The Irish parliament of 1569–1571', 74–7.

Sidney's tenurial legislation, which would have seen the abolition of coign and livery, would have significantly reduced the status of Ormond's brothers within the earldom, because a system of fixed rents meant military retainers would no longer be required as a means of extracting/enforcing a mixture of feudal obligations.[50]

As before, Weston raised questions about whether or not standard reform practice would further a sustained change in the behaviour of Ireland's lords. It was, however, the failure to achieve consensus on Irish church reform that was to be his primary concern. Once again, he explained Ireland's civil disobedience – i.e., the outbreak of rebellion in Ulster, Munster, and now Connaught – in terms set by Protestant theology, and argued that Ireland had remained in civil disobedience because God's word had not been made available. He argued that it was 'the ignorance or neglect [of God's word] whereof is the cause (in my opinion) that this cursed people continue so still in their great disobedience, ever stirring, conspiring and rebelling against her majesty as oft as they dare'.[51] Weston further pointed out that Irish government had been able to maintain a level of outward obedience only through recourse to the sword and explained that 'only the fear of the sword . . . can contain them in their office no longer than it hangeth over their head'. He even made note of Elizabeth's failure to meet her godly responsibilities and pointed to the queen's Irish subjects 'committed by god to her highness to be preserved and kept'. On this basis Weston then turned to the operation of God's grace. He described how 'contrary wise learning and understanding and the knowledge of god grounded and in their hearts would breed in them good liking and love of honesty, civility, and true obedience'.[52] He explained that God's word would act upon man's heart, i.e. grace, and that it was this that would effect a sufficient degree of internal reform in man and so bring the island to the level of long-term obedience which the government sought. He echoed Loftus, who had written in June 1566 of 'just obedience' and Goodman's definition of 'true obedience' as set out in *Superior powers*.[53]

---

[50] The earl of Ormond had also insisted on a series of exemptions from any legislation that dealt with the outright abolition of coign and livery, which as Elizabeth's Irish favourite he gained. The Pale representatives therefore barred the passage of any bill, as they were concerned that any shortfall in government finances, arising because of a reduction in Ormond's own obligations to the crown, would end up being met by the Pale in general. See Brady, *Chief governors*, pp. 133–4; Treadwell, 'The Irish parliament of 1569–1571'; and David Edwards, *The Ormond lordship in County Kilkenny, 1515–1642: the rise and fall of Butler feudal power* (Dublin, 2003), pp. 194–6. 'An act for taking away captainships', along with 'an act for turning of countries . . . into shire grounds', was approved by Parliament, but an agreement on more comprehensive measures could not be reached.

[51] SP 63/30/29.   [52] *Ibid.*   [53] SP 63/18/12.

V

It was thus against the backdrop of Ireland's continued civil disobedience, Parliament's failure to co-operate, and the Irish government's inability to gain Elizabeth's support for Irish church reform that Weston came to outline the assumptions upon which Sidney's government's view of political and religious reform rested. Elizabeth as usual did not respond to Weston's commentary, and in the wake of Parliament's failure to pass crucial parts of Sidney's religious and political reform programme the lord deputy left office in March 1571 to be replaced by Sir William Fitzwilliam.[54] Such a critique, however, was reinforced only in the lord deputy's absence due to the continued level of civil disorder; and on resuming office at the end of 1575 Sidney made note of the disorders in Drogheda, Dundalk, and Newry, the spoiling of King's and Queen's counties (Laois and Offaly), the showcase of plantation policy in Ireland, and unrest in Connaught. He also restated the case for religious reformation.[55]

Sidney outlined three 'heads for reformation' and, while the second and third dealt with the legal and financial reform of the kingdom, the first addressed 'the church now so spoiled, as well by ruin of the temples, as the dissipation and embezzling of the patrimony, and most of all for want of sufficient ministers, as so deformed and overthrown a church, there is not I am sure in any region where Christ is professed, and preposterous it seemeth to me, to begin the reformation of the politic part and to neglect the religious'.[56] The lord deputy clearly identified the furthering of religious reform as key in the Irish kingdom's broader reform. Moreover, this sat beside an ever widening distance between the queen and her Irish deputy. For example, the surveyor of the queen's majesty's inheritance in Ireland, Michael Fitzwilliam, had repeated Sidney's assessment of the financial condition of the Irish church in the mid 1570s. He had pointed to 'the lamentable estate and ignorance of many of the inhabitants . . . [because] there is not a preacher nor two fit ministers', and he argued that Elizabeth was directly responsible for the

[54] The reformed Protestant critique remained strong, no doubt because the experience of Irish government under Fitzwilliam's deputyship from 1571 to 1575 only came to confirm what Weston had argued. Fitzwilliam made little effort to further Irish church reform and at the same time Irish government became increasingly reliant on the sword in an attempt to maintain a basic level of civil order. For a more detailed discussion of Fitzwilliam's deputyship, see Hutchinson, 'Sidney and his legacy', pp. 104–32.

[55] Sidney to English privy council, 15 Oct. 1575, BL Cotton MSS Titus BX fol. 6r; Sidney to English privy council, 16 Dec. 1575, BL Cotton MSS Titus BX fols. 14r–19v; and Sidney to English privy council, 28 Apr. 1576, BL Cotton MSS Titus BX fols. 34r–45v.

[56] Sidney to English privy council, 28 Apr. 1576, BL Cotton MSS Titus BX, fol. 43v.

poor condition of the church in Ireland, because it was 'many [of] her highness farmers' of appropriated benefices who failed to provide sufficient stipends for clergy.[57] The queen's response, just before Sidney's reappointment to the deputyship, however, was that 'the late surveyor by his unwise surveys did rather hinder the crown revenues than further them'.[58]

The earl of Essex, Walter Devereux, who had arrived in Ireland in July 1573 intent on founding a colony in Ulster, had even told Lord Burghley that Elizabeth had informed him he 'should not seek too hastily to bring people that have been trained in another religion, from that which they have been brought up in', and it was on the basis of such advice that Essex took the opposite view from Sidney and his associates. The earl argued that civil obedience was a precondition of right religion, not right religion the precondition for civil obedience. He continued, 'to this I answered, that for present I thought it was best to learn them to know their allegiance to her majesty, and yield their due obedience, and after they had learned that, they would be easily brought to be of good religion'.[59]

Sidney therefore repeated the criticisms of his April 1566 letter, in which he had pointed out that the farmers of 'appropriate benefices in the queen's majesty's possession' made little provision for clerical stipends.[60] He drew the queen's attention to a report by the bishop of Meath, Hugh Brady, who had 'found that there are within his diocese 224 parish churches of which number 105 are impropriated to sundry now of your highness . . . [and] no parson or vicar [was] resident upon any of them'.[61] He also made sure Elizabeth knew she was directly culpable for the present condition of the Irish church, and he asked the queen to 'write earnestly to me – and to whom else it may please you – to examine in whom the fault is that the churches are so ruinous'; he added that 'if the fault, for the churches of your highness' inheritance, be not in the farmers, nor they bound to repair them (and most ruined be them are such as are of your possession)', then clearly it was her responsibility.[62] He also restated the link between God's word and the island's reform, and he explained in a letter to Francis Walsingham, Elizabeth's new privy secretary, that 'by good preaching and doctrine the people are drawn first to know their duty to god, and next their obedience to their prince, and civil order'.[63]

---

[57] SP 63/33/17.   [58] SP 63/50/3.

[59] Essex to Burghley, 20 Jul. 1573, in Walter Bouchier Devereux (ed.), *Lives and letters of the Devereux earls of Essex*, 2 vols. (London, 1853), vol. I, pp. 31–2.

[60] SP 63/17/8.

[61] Sidney to Elizabeth, 28 Apr. 1576, BL Cotton MSS Titus BX fols. 47v–50r.

[62] *Ibid.*   [63] SP 63/55/57.

The particular importance of Sidney's second deputyship, however, is not simply that it allows us to see the positions taken by Elizabeth and Sidney on Irish policy in increasingly clearer terms; his reappointment also allows us to link the policy discussion in Ireland, concerning God's word and man's reform, into a wider English debate. As mentioned at the opening of this chapter, the detail of such a reformed Protestant view has tended to go unnoticed by historians of England. This is because such a view tended to rest at the level of an unspoken assumption and so there was no wider context to give it significance. By the beginning of 1577, however, Sidney, notwithstanding his initial bold statements, all but dropped the subject of Irish church reform, and this directs our attention to a parallel English discussion concerning the role of God's word and grace in societal reform. In particular, the lord deputy's decision to draw back from religious reformation coincides with a letter he received from Lord Burghley in which the lord treasurer withdrew his support despite his own involvement with Sidney's first deputyship in the 1560s. He informed Sidney that, while he accepted the rationale behind his programme of government, he thought the lord deputy should pause and take advice. Burghley referred to

the conclusion of your letter of 27th April [meaning 28th], you gather certain principal heads requisite for the reformation and establish[ment] of good government in that realm . . . those points collected be indeed the very foundation of all good govern[ment] . . . Yet, considering all circumstances, it hath been thought more meet by her majesty and by us also even for the furtherance of the cause that you should first consulteth upon those matters.[64]

The lord deputy was told in clear terms to leave the subject of Irish church reform alone. This coincides with a change of atmosphere in England, where within a year of Sidney's reappointment the question of church reform had become very controversial. Crucially, Burghley wrote to Sidney around the same time as the archbishop of Canterbury, Edmund Grindal, had become involved in a dispute with Elizabeth which went to the root of the reformed Protestant view of civil government and the church. Elizabeth had asked Grindal to put an end to prophesying – the combined lay and clerical gatherings where Scripture was discussed – but the archbishop told her it was not his responsibility. What Grindal really meant was that he disagreed with the queen and thought prophesying beneficial and warranted by Scripture.[65] Nevertheless, it emerges in an exchange of letters which took place the next year, at the end of 1577,

<hr />

[64] SP 63/56/7.
[65] Patrick Collinson, *Archbishop Grindal, 1519–1583; the struggle for a reformed church* (London, 1979), p. 222.

that similar to government in Ireland a difference in respective views of man and his reform underlay the disagreement between the queen and her archbishop.

Elizabeth responded to Grindal in May 1577, and in line with the advice the earl of Essex claimed he had received, she argued that prophesying would lead to 'inconveniences to the disturbance of our peaceable government', that it was a 'breach of common order, and to the offence of all our other quiet subjects'.[66] She told Grindal that the free discussion of Scripture, i.e. the free dissemination of God's word, would lead to civil disobedience. This was the reverse of Sidney's position, and Grindal's lengthy response to the queen set out a view similar to that taken by the Irish lord deputy and his associates, as well as Goodman's 'true obedience' more broadly defined. He told Elizabeth that it was actually through God's word and grace that a level of internal reform would be brought about in her subjects, that 'by preaching also due obedience proceedeth of conscience, conscience is grounded upon the word of god, the word of god worketh this effect by preaching, so as generally where preaching wanteth, obedience faileth'.[67]

This is not to suggest that Grindal, or Sidney for that matter, did not think preaching was important first and foremost because God willed it. As Patrick Collinson noted in his biography of the archbishop, this was a central theme of Grindal's letter. There has also been some discussion by scholars of the way in which sermons were used in England to communicate why obedience to the crown was important.[68] What Grindal described, however, was not simply how a set of arguments might persuade man of a certain course of action. He described an internal transformation that would be brought about by God's word and grace; and like Weston and Sidney, who had used the political condition of Ireland to make their case, Grindal drew on the contemporary political condition of England to make his own. In particular, he showed how in places where God's word was preached there was civil obedience and in places where God's word was not preached there was civil disobedience. He explained that

If your majesty come to your city of London never so oft, what gratulation [*sic*] . . . and other manifest significations of inward and unfeigned love, joined with most humble and hearty obedience are there to be heard. Whereof cometh

---

[66] Elizabeth to Grindal, May 1577, LPL, MS 2003, fols. 40–1.

[67] Grindal to Elizabeth, endorsed Dec. 1577, BL Lansdowne MSS 23, no. 4.

[68] See Arnold Hunt, 'Tuning the pulpits: the religious context of the Essex revolt', in Lori Ann Ferrell and Peter McCullough (eds.), *The English sermon revised: religion, literature and history 1600–1750* (Manchester, 2000), pp. 86–114.

this Madam? But of the continual preaching of God's word in the city . . . On the contrary what bred the rebellion in the North? Was it not papistry and ignorance of God's word, through want of often preaching [?][69]

Grindal pointed out that in London, where many reformed Protestant preachers were resident and where prophesying was more common, the citizens were loyal. He also made reference to the Northern Rebellion in England of 1569, which had been led by the earls of Northumberland and Westmorland ostensibly in defence of the old religion, and he argued that it was because God's word had not been preached that the two earls had been able to lead the population into revolt.[70] Importantly, Grindal's letter led to his sequestration from office. Not only was it the case that he had openly admonished the prince, he had also set out a view of civil society and the church which she clearly did not share. In line with such a division, Sidney left Ireland in 1578, where once again he had failed to further Irish church reform.

VI

This chapter has argued that it is the nature of the Irish policy debate which provides us with the evidence for a more general reassessment of Elizabeth's relationship with her reformed Protestant councillors, something which we can identify in the exchange between the queen and the archbishop of Canterbury, Edmund Grindal. In particular, this chapter has attempted to demonstrate that underlying the division between Elizabeth and her more godly councillors in both kingdoms was a difference in theology that manifested itself in very different views on the nature of man and the role of the church in societal reform. On the one hand, Elizabeth remained confident in the ability of an English model of government, on its own, to bring her subjects to act for the wider good. On the other hand, her reformed Protestant councillors took the position that man, born in sin and without free will, could not be brought to act for the common good without the action of God's grace. In particular, for reformed Protestants, such as Sidney, Weston, and Goodman, it was only through the dissemination of God's word that man would be brought to know grace, and so for the queen's Protestant councillors the

---

[69] Grindal to Elizabeth, endorsed Dec. 1577, BL Lansdowne MSS 23, no. 4.
[70] For a more detailed discussion of the Northern Rebellion of 1569, see Mervyn James, 'The concept of order and the Northern rising 1569', *Past & Present* 60 (1973), 49–83. See also Hutchinson, 'Sidney and his legacy', pp. 89–94, which discusses how reformed Protestants in England also drew on Reformation thought, i.e. ideas about free will and God's grace, in an attempt to understand why the rebellion had occurred.

construction of a functional Reformation church was deemed critical to societal reform.

Such views, however, are difficult to identify in England, because with a basic level of political stability these assumptions about man, free will, and grace did not need to be examined with the same urgency as in Ireland, where the lack of a functional church and the pressing question of perceived Irish civil disobedience meant the role of God's word and grace in reforming a community to obedience came to be directly examined. To conclude, however, there was an inherent problem in such a reformed Protestant position, as it posed the question, to differing degrees, as to how exactly civil obedience could be maintained in Ireland and England if provision was not made for the dissemination of God's word. Elizabeth's conservatism in church policy would by the late 1570s make this a particularly pressing issue. The question that was to be asked, then, was how could either the Irish or the English kingdom be governed in the absence of a functioning church? This was to be instrumental in a more coercive style of government in both kingdoms, as Elizabeth's councillors looked to bridle a population deemed redeemable, though as yet unredeemed. For instance, it was in light of a failure to provide for the dissemination of God's word, the very thing which was thought to effect a level of internal reform in man, that in 1581 Parliament in England moved to legislate directly on a question of conscience, i.e. conversion to Catholicism, and John Perrot as Irish lord deputy was to attempt to follow suit in Ireland in 1585–6.[71] In this respect, the division over the question of free will, grace, and man's reform, as highlighted here, was to continue to inform policy in both kingdoms for the remainder of Elizabeth's reign.

[71] See J. E. Neale, *Elizabeth I and her parliaments, 1559–1581*, 2 vols. (London, 1953–7), vol. I, pp. 384–92; Victor Treadwell, 'Sir John Perrot and the Irish parliament of 1585–1586', *Proceedings of the Royal Irish Academy* 85 C (1985), 259–308; Hutchinson, 'Sidney and his legacy', pp. 192–209; and Hutchinson, 'Reformed Protestantism', 96–103.

8 Elizabeth I, the Old English, and the rhetoric of counsel

Valerie McGowan-Doyle

On taking up his appointment as viceroy of Ireland in July 1580, Lord Grey de Wilton was instructed by Elizabeth that 'as our subjects of that country birth have conceived that we have a determination to root them out, and place there our subjects born in this realm, seek to remove that false impression'.[1] It is not surprising if those Elizabeth considered her subjects in Ireland, Gaelic or Old English, had this impression. By 1580, loss of land in Laois and Offaly, the suppression and massacre of the O'Mores, and the violence associated with attempted plantation schemes in Ulster, to cite but a few examples, could hardly have assured the Gaelic Irish that English control would ensure their security.[2] The security of the Old English colonial community had also been challenged by the time Grey took office, though of a very different nature. Loss of key offices such as viceroy and lord chancellor, repeated requests to replace Old English judges with English-born appointees, failure to obtain posts such as provincial presidencies, or the imprisonment of Old English nobles during the cess controversy in 1577 and again 1578 undermined their traditional role as administrators of conquest and failed to reassure the Old English, also 'our subjects of that country birth', that they were not in the midst of displacement by the New English, 'our subjects born in this realm'.[3] Reduction in Old English status was a function of intensified Tudor conquest, and their struggle to reverse their declining position was an essential thread in the evolution of English control during Elizabeth's reign. Their declining position was in fact not merely an

---

[1] *Cal. Carew*, 1575–88, p. 277.

[2] On the O'Mores, see Vincent Carey, 'John Derricke's *Image of Irelande*, Sir Henry Sidney, and the massacre at Mullaghmast, 1578', *Irish Historical Studies* 31 (1999), 305–27.

[3] *Cal. Carew*, 1575–88, p. 277. For general studies of the Old English in this period, see Nicholas Canny, *The formation of the Old English elite in Ireland* (Dublin, 1975), and Ciaran Brady, 'Conservative subversives: the community of the Pale and the Dublin administration, 1556–1586', in Patrick J. Corish (ed.), *Radicals, rebels and establishments* (Belfast, 1985), pp. 11–32. For a study of the Old English in the early Tudor period, see Gerald Power, *A European elite: the nobility of the English Pale in Ireland, 1450–1566* (Hanover, 2011).

Elizabethan development, but a process in which Elizabeth played a direct part.

Historians have debated the degree of Old English displacement, particularly in the early decades of Elizabeth's reign, its causes, and its impact, and Nicholas Canny has cautioned against exaggerating Old English decline.[4] However, the Old English impression that displacement was underway, as described in Elizabeth's instructions to Grey, was hardly a false one. Sidney had used the term 'displacement' several years earlier when writing to Elizabeth in self-defence against Old English cess complaints, attributing the lawyer Barnaby Scurlocke's opposition to the cess to resentment harboured ever since 'he was displaced' from office 'in the tyme of my lord of Sussex government'.[5] The year prior to Grey's instructions, the Old English noble, Christopher St Lawrence, 7th baron of Howth, completed *The Book of Howth*, a compilation generated by fears of displacement and devoted to a defence of his community.[6] Helen Coburn Walshe's study of the Nugent rebellion emphasised the critical impact of Old English displacement, arguing that it was a substantial factor in William Nugent's activities.[7] Though often portrayed by New English writers as homogeneous, the Old English community represented a range of economic, social, and political positions, and the effects of and responses to intensified Tudor conquest consequently varied within the group. Thomas Butler, 10th earl of Ormond, fared exceptionally well, principally as a function of his close relationship with Elizabeth.[8] Another magnate, the 11th earl of Kildare, was far less successful.[9] Families such as the Dillons worked co-operatively with the Dublin administration over

---

[4] Canny, *Formation of the Old English elite*, p. 32. See also Brady, 'Conservative subversives', and Brady, *The chief governors: the rise and fall of reform government in Tudor Ireland, 1536–1588* (Cambridge, 1994), p. 213.

[5] SP 63/58/29.

[6] Valerie McGowan-Doyle, *The Book of Howth: Elizabethan conquest and the Old English* (Cork, 2011).

[7] Helen Coburn Walshe, 'The rebellion of William Nugent, 1581', in R. V. Comerford, Mary Cullen, Jacqueline R. Hill, and Colm Lennon (eds.), *Religion, conflict and coexistence in Ireland: essays presented to Monsignor Patrick J. Corish* (Dublin, 1990), pp. 26–52.

[8] See David Edwards, *The Ormond lordship in County Kilkenny, 1515–1642: the rise and fall of Butler feudal power* (Dublin, 2003). Ormond increased his Irish and English land holdings, became lord general of the Irish army, served as Irish privy councillor, was made knight of the garter (1588), and received even the unusual position of deputy lord deputy as well as permission to bury his son at Westminster Abbey in 1590 (*ibid.*, p. 99). Ormond would suffer displacement only after Elizabeth's death. He is unique as an example from Ireland of Elizabeth's 'social conservatism' in permitting those who had already established a relationship with her prior to her accession to remain influential; see John Guy, 'The 1590s: the second reign of Elizabeth I?', in John Guy (ed.), *The reign of Elizabeth I: court and culture in the last decade* (Cambridge, 1995), pp. 4–5, and Simon Adams, *Leicester and the court: essays on Elizabethan politics* (Manchester, 2002), pp. 31–2.

[9] See Vincent Carey, *Surviving the Tudors: The 'wizard' earl of Kildare and English rule in Ireland, 1537–1586* (Dublin, 2002).

the Elizabethan period, retaining existing offices as well as obtaining new ones. Others had greater difficulty accommodating themselves to new policies and resisted their declining position, some in rebellion, occasionally capitalising on Counter-Reformation zeal as in the Baltinglass Rebellion.[10]

The focus here is on those members of the Old English, principally members of the nobility such as Viscount Gormanston and the barons of Howth, Louth, and Slane, who maintained their loyalty to crown government but nonetheless resisted their deteriorating status. Because their resistance often registered itself in opposition to viceroys, frequently through constitutional means, their displacement has been viewed to date as a function of viceroys' policies or within the context of New English polemical denigration of them. Jon Crawford argued in fact that 'the prevailing view of an estrangement between Anglo-Irish office-seekers and the government rests on a narrowly focused analysis of the rhetoric of Elizabethan policy-makers'.[11] However, this element within the Old English community often registered their opposition by petitioning Elizabeth directly. Their appeals to Elizabeth as a strategy of opposition to viceroys are necessarily referenced in studies of the period, but they have not yet been studied systematically. Attention to their petitions reveals their employment of the rhetoric of counsel in response to their displacement.

Reconsidering this avenue of direct interaction with Elizabeth offers multiple new frameworks of interpretation. It reopens, first, reassessment of Old English displacement and importantly Elizabeth's role in it. Second, consideration of Elizabeth's response to their petitions, in which she often called on royal prerogative in rejection of their claims to counsel, offers a new perspective from which to assess the nature of her personal rule in Ireland as well as in England. Attention to her exercise of personal rule within this critical colonial context exposes her role in the Tudor reconquest of Ireland. Finally, the Old English have not yet been contextualised within studies of the Elizabethan nobility or more broadly within studies of Tudor political culture. Consideration of their place within Elizabeth's body politic indicates the incomplete nature of debates central to such studies when Ireland and its colonial context are not taken into account.[12]

---

[10] Christopher Maginn, 'The Baltinglass Rebellion, 1580: English dissent or a Gaelic uprising?', *Historical Journal* 47 (2004), 205–32.

[11] Jon Crawford, *Anglicizing the government of Ireland: the Irish privy council and the expansion of Tudor rule, 1556–1578* (Dublin, 1993), p. 99.

[12] See, for example, Dale Hoak (ed.), *Tudor political culture* (Cambridge, 1995); Guy (ed.), *The reign of Elizabeth I*. For an overview of the recent historiography of Tudor political culture, see Natalie Mears, 'Courts, courtiers, and culture in Tudor England', *Historical*

Old English displacement

Though the term 'Old English' was not coined until 1596 by Edmund
Spenser, this colonial grouping, primarily descended of the Anglo-
Norman conquest, was emerging by early in Elizabeth's reign as a community distinct from newly arriving servitors, who came to be known as
the New English. Prior to Spenser's use of the label, individuals in this
community were described variously, often as 'English of Irish birth' or
'of that country birth' as in Grey's instructions.[13] Identity was central
to distinction of this group, and thus identity-formation constitutes an
important component of their experience.[14] Accusations of degeneration,
or Gaelicisation, suggesting questionable loyalty, often served as rationale for their displacement. Edmund Campion, for instance, devoted the
second chapter of his 1571 work, *Two Bokes of the Histories of Irelande*, to a
list of Old English families and the degree to which they had succumbed
to Gaelicisation.[15] These depictions were challenged by the Old English,
notably the 7th baron of Howth, who asserted that Old English displacement was a function of New English misrepresentation of them.[16] Failure
to have completed the Anglo-Norman conquest after four centuries, as
the 1569 Act for the Attainder of Shane O'Neill asserted, constituted

---

Journal 46 (2003), 703–22. Exceptions that do include consideration of Ireland within
Tudor political culture have come principally from historians of Ireland; see for example
David Edwards's work on the 10th earl of Ormond, such as *The Ormond lordship in
County Kilkenny*. See also Steven G. Ellis, *Tudor frontiers and noble power: the making
of the British state* (Oxford, 1995), and Christopher Maginn, 'The Gaelic peers, the
Tudor sovereigns, and English multiple monarchy', *Journal of British Studies* 50 (2011),
566–86.

[13] For examples of this usage, see SP 63/19/25; SP 63/95/26; SP 63/131/50; SP 63/202/pt
4, 81.

[14] See Colm Lennon, *Richard Stanihurst, the Dubliner, 1547–1618* (Dublin, 1981), and
Lennon, 'Richard Stanihurst (1547–1618) and Old English identity', *Irish Historical
Studies* 21 (1978), 121–43; Vincent Carey, '"Neither good English nor good Irish":
bi-lingualism and identity formation in sixteenth-century Ireland', in Hiram Morgan
(ed.), *Political ideology in Ireland, 1541–1641* (Dublin, 1999), pp. 45–61, and Carey, 'A
"dubious loyalty": Richard Stanihurst, the "wizard" earl of Kildare, and English-Irish
identity', in Vincent Carey and Ute Lotz-Heumann (eds.), *Taking sides? Colonial and
confessional mentalités in early modern Ireland* (Dublin, 2003), pp. 61–77.

[15] Edmund Campion, *Two Bokes of the Histories of Ireland (1571)*, A. F. Vossen (ed.) (Assen,
1963), pp. 10–14. For studies of the Old English in Campion's text, see Colm Lennon,
'Edmund Campion's *Histories of Ireland* and reform in Tudor Ireland', in Thomas M.
McCoog, SJ (ed.), *The reckoned expense: Edmund Campion and the early English Jesuits*
(Woodbridge, 1996), pp. 67–83, and Valerie McGowan-Doyle, '"Ancient English gen-
tlemen"? The Old English communities of Tudor Ireland in Edmund Campion's *Two
Bokes of the Histories of Ireland* (1571)' (unpublished MA thesis, John Carroll University,
1999). For debate on Gaelicisation, see Steven G. Ellis, 'More Irish than the Irish them-
selves? The "Anglo-Irish" in Tudor Ireland', *History Ireland* 7 (1) (1999), 22–6, and
Kenneth W. Nicholls, 'Worlds apart? The Ellis two-nation theory on late medieval
Ireland', *History Ireland* 7 (2) (1999), 22–6.

[16] McGowan-Doyle, *The Book of Howth*, esp. pp. 94–7.

another charge against the Old English, a powerful rationalisation for their displacement.[17] Concern about Old English attachments to Catholicism provided yet another New English challenge to their security, a concern that surfaced early in Elizabeth's reign, rose – along with the rise of Counter-Reformation attachments in Ireland – especially after 1580, and reached its height during the Nine Years' War, when it was feared that religion would provide a source of alliance between Hugh O'Neill and the Old English.[18]

The following overview outlines briefly the key areas in which the Old English were confronted with displacement and offers initial comparison with studies of their peers in England. Importantly, although they were able to maintain a number of offices and responsibilities at the local level – for example, in commissions as justices of the peace, thus fulfilling some of the traditional functions of the nobility – their position did not expand to keep pace with the expansion of English control at the national level.[19] Two of the principal areas in which offices were increasingly filled by the New English were in the military and administrative positions, judicial appointments in particular. More critically, the Old English nobility were also confronted with a declining ability to offer counsel, an issue in its own right as well as a function of their declining roles in the military and administration.[20] Land served as a lesser source of concern, though a concern nonetheless. In perhaps the most notorious case, Sir Peter Carew successfully pursued claims to land held by the Butlers and Sir Christopher Cheevers in 1569.[21] More problematic was the declining

---

[17] *Statutes at large, passed in the parliaments held in Ireland, 1310–1800*, 20 vols. (Dublin, 1786–1801), vol. I, pp. 322–38. On O'Neill's attainder, see Ciaran Brady, 'The attainder of Shane O'Neill, Sir Henry Sidney and the problems of Tudor state-building in Ireland', in Ciaran Brady and Jane Ohlmeyer (eds.), *British interventions in early modern Ireland* (Cambridge, 2005), pp. 28–48. For assessment of its denigration of Old English failures in completing the conquest, see McGowan-Doyle, *The Book of Howth*, p. 92.

[18] On concerns about Old English Catholicism during the Nine Years' War, see for example, SP 63/207/pt 3, 63, 109; SP 63/202/pt 4, 81. See also Hiram Morgan, 'Hugh O'Neill and the Nine Years War in Tudor Ireland', *Historical Journal* 36 (1993), 24, and Morgan, 'Faith and fatherland or queen and country? An unpublished exchange between O'Neill and the state at the height of the Nine Years' War', *Dúiche Néill: Journal of the O'Neill Country Historical Society* 9 (1994), 9–30; Valerie McGowan-Doyle, '"Spent blood": Christopher St Lawrence and Pale loyalism', in Hiram Morgan (ed.), *The Battle of Kinsale* (Bray, 2004), pp. 179–91.

[19] For a selection of commissions obtained, see *The Irish fiants of the Tudor sovereigns during the reigns of Henry VIII, Edward VI, Philip & Mary, and Elizabeth I*, 4 vols. (Dublin, 1994, reprint), vol. II, pp. 42, 325, 435, 499, 505–6.

[20] Linda Levy Peck notes the nobility in England faced similar challenges; see Levy Peck, 'Peers, patronage and the politics of history', in Guy (ed.), *The reign of Elizabeth I*, pp. 87–108.

[21] Brady, *Chief governors*, p. 214. Carew's land claims served as one of the factors catalysing the Butler revolt; see David Edwards, 'The Butler revolt of 1569', *Irish Historical Studies* 28 (1993), 228–55.

Old English ability to acquire new land as plantation schemes got under-way. Although some had acquired lands after the dissolution of the monasteries, they failed to obtain land as hoped in the Laois– Offaly plantation in the early 1560s, and struggled to retain land on the Munster plantation only through lengthy legal suits.[22] It had been recommended in fact that only those of English birth inhabit land in Munster.[23]

The nobles' traditional military role was threatened substantially by England's increasing military presence in Ireland over the Elizabethan period. With a standing army came ever larger numbers of soldiers and English officers. Complaints about the abuse committed by the soldiers were frequent, and complaints about loss of military appointments to New English officers were repeated even throughout the Nine Years' War, though a few Old Englishmen, notably Ormond and Christopher St Lawrence, obtained appointments, Ormond as lord general of the Irish army. New English appointments to office had begun, however, in the 1550s under Sussex, who allotted key offices to a close circle of family and friends. Many of his appointments would become influential figures in the Elizabethan period, including Sir Henry Sidney and Sir William Fitzwilliam, both later to serve extended periods as viceroy. In spite of an increasing military presence, the Dublin administration remained depen-dent on Old English military services, particularly through hostings, but their function fell increasingly to Pale defence from Sussex's period as viceroy thereafter. Comparison with the military role of nobles in England in the Tudor period underscores Old English displacement in this arena. Declining military influence is in fact at the heart of debates over the position of the Tudor nobility, a debate that emerged in the 1960s with Lawrence Stone's thesis regarding a 'crisis of the aristocracy'. G. W. Bernard challenged Stone's conclusions regarding lost military roles, arguing that this could only have occurred had a 'standing army staffed by professional officers' been in place in England.[24] While this did not happen in England, it did in Ireland, where many of the professional officers were New English.

Many Old English were also confronted with a declining ability to obtain administrative and judicial appointments, a subject that has

---

[22] Brendan Bradshaw, *The dissolution of the religious orders in Ireland under Henry VIII* (Cambridge, 1974). For the Munster plantation, see Michael MacCarthy-Morrogh, *The Munster plantation: English migration to southern Ireland, 1583–1641* (Oxford, 1986).

[23] *Cal. Carew*, 1575–88, p. 42.

[24] Lawrence Stone, *The crisis of the aristocracy 1558–1641* (Oxford, 1965); G. W. Bernard, *Power and politics in Tudor England* (Aldershot, 2000), p. 35. Neither Stone nor Bernard included the nobility in Ireland, Gaelic or Old English, in their studies of the Tudor nobility. See also Levy Peck, 'Peers', p. 92. For application of this debate to Ireland, see McGowan-Doyle, *The Book of Howth*, pp. 129–30.

received more attention from historians of Ireland, although as Ciaran Brady has noted this happened gradually over several decades. After the Kildare Rebellion of 1534, the office of viceroy was held only by New English. After 1556, the offices of lord justice, lord chancellor, and vice-treasurer were similarly lost to the Old English. Whereas in 1541, at the time of the Act for Kingly Title, the Old English held 75% of government posts, this was reduced to 66% by 1556 and 50% by 1580.[25] Complaints about prejudicial and incompetent Old English judges were rife over the Elizabethan period, leading to repeated requests for their replacement, a particular concern given efforts to extend English law over the entire island. Here again the loss of office was gradual, and families such as the Dillons were able to maintain appointments and receive new ones, but from the 1570s on New English acquisition of judicial posts increased. Furthermore, it was not only lost appointments, but lost access to potential income, as Canny has pointed out, for with the extension of the English legal system over the island came an increased need for lawyers.[26] However, as Canny also notes importantly, lawyers unable to obtain official posts quickly found their services needed elsewhere, defending Old English and Gaelic clients alike against New English land claims. This may have had the consequent impact of alienating the Old English yet further from government and New English interests. The cost in lost income due to displacement should not be underestimated; both Walshe and Canny have emphasised Old English frustration over the economic impact of displacement as a factor in the Nugent Rebellion, for instance.[27]

Seats on the Irish council remained relatively evenly divided over the Elizabethan period, as Crawford's study of the council demonstrates.[28] However, as with other offices, consideration needs to be given to more than raw numbers, taking into account the outlook of the Old English who obtained seats on the council. The Old English were a large and diverse community and, as noted above, families and individuals such as the Dillons remained in power because they worked co-operatively with new administrators and evolving policies. Sir Lucas Dillon, chief justice of the common pleas, for example, was praised highly by Sir Nicholas Malby to both Walsingham and Burghley. Malby described Dillon as the 'only

---

[25] Brady, *Chief governors*, p. 213. For comparison with noble acquisition of posts in England, see Levy Peck, 'Peers', pp. 92–4.

[26] Canny, *Formation of the Old English elite*, pp. 32–3.

[27] Walshe, 'Rebellion', pp. 33–4. Brady also identified economics as a key factor in Old English opposition, though with emphasis on the economic burden of the cess rather than lost income: *Chief governors*, p. 214.

[28] Crawford, *Anglicizing*, pp. 90–106.

true affected gentleman that ever I have found of this country byrthe', implying of course that the others were not.[29] Those who disagreed with new policies and did not hold government posts, i.e. those members of the nobility of concern here, became increasingly frustrated with their inability to influence government policy or even to offer counsel.

Lost offices, compounded by the decline of the Great Council and the rarity of parliamentary sessions in Ireland – it met only three times during Elizabeth's reign, in 1560, 1569–71, and 1585–6 – also undermined Old English ability to influence policy.[30] The subject of lost counsel had certainly arisen as an Old English concern by the early 1570s.[31] Taxes and war were two areas of particular concern. During the cess controversy of 1577–8, Sidney's opponents, including Lords Baltinglass, Delvin, and Howth, insisted that cess could only be levied with the consent of a great council or parliament.[32] Although those Old English who opposed viceroys were on some occasions successful, this came at the cost of considerable struggle which included terms of imprisonment, as during the 1577–8 cess controversy or during their attempts to thwart Sir John Perrot's parliamentary programme of 1585–6.[33] On some occasions, there was more ready collaboration between the Dublin administration and the Old English, as when the barons of Slane and Delvin and members of the Barnewall, Plunkett, Cusack, and Bermingham families advised on affairs concerning Turlough Luineach O'Neill in 1579.[34] The Old English would maintain a firm insistence on their right to be consulted on matters of state such as war. In 1584 the baron of Delvin asserted that the Dublin administration could not 'make war or peace with the Irish without consent of the nobility and counsel'.[35] This assertion was repeated early in the Nine Years' War when the lords of

---

[29] SP 63/95/25. Dillon's amicable relationship with New English officials was enhanced by his role in revealing the Nugent conspiracy: Brady, *Chief governors*, p. 214.

[30] See D. B. Quinn, 'Parliaments and great councils in Ireland, 1461–1586', *Irish Historical Studies* 3 (1943), 60–77. Quinn identified no meeting of a great council after 1493 though the Old English continued to insist upon their right to advise on policy in such a body. They were in fact called to a number of council sessions over the course of Elizabeth's reign.

[31] It served, for instance, as one of the overriding themes of *The Book of Howth*; see McGowan-Doyle, *Book of Howth*, esp. pp. 100–02.

[32] SP 63/58/29. See also SP 63/58/23, 24; SP 63/60/16, 17. Their complaint was as much about the extortionate cess rates and its economic impact as about the source of its imposition.

[33] For negotiation at the end of the cess controversy, see SP 63/61/37. On Old English problems with Perrot, see SP 63/122/42, 63. See also Brady, *Chief governors*, p. 294 and Victor Treadwell, 'Sir John Perrot and the Irish parliament of 1585–1586', *Proceedings of the Royal Irish Academy* 85 C (1985), 259–308.

[34] *Cal. Carew*, 1575–88, p. 156.   [35] SP 63/108/58.

Gormanston, Howth, and Trimleston and the earl of Kildare attended an Irish council session in 1596. Speaking for the group, Gormanston insisted not only that the lord deputy was unauthorised to make war without their consent, but that the council had failed in its obligation to consult them before even declaring Hugh O'Neill a traitor.[36] Their declining ability to offer counsel is again underscored by comparison to the nobility's experience in England under Elizabeth. As with his interpretation of lost military roles in England, Bernard challenged Stone's contention that lost counsel constituted a transformation in the position of the English nobility. And again, as with the military, the Old English nobility in Ireland were confronted with this very situation. Lost counsel would prove a fundamental source of discontent for the Old English. Claiming their rights as 'English and free subjects', they were led to petition Elizabeth for redress.[37]

Elizabeth and Old English displacement

It is difficult, if not impossible, to ascertain Elizabeth's perception of the Old English as she came to the throne. She would already have known Thomas Butler, later to become 10th earl of Ormond, who spent time at court as an adolescent in the company of the future Edward VI, though precisely how much interaction Elizabeth had with other members of the Old English prior to her ascension is unknown.[38] Nonetheless, she would have become familiar with other members of the Old English community relatively quickly once queen. Over the first few years of her reign, Elizabeth received numerous petitions from the Old English, most relatively innocuous dealing with lands, or from towns such as Knockfergus requesting to have their city walled, or from Waterford for the transport of grain.[39] She responded positively to these, initiating what stood to be an amicable relationship with the Old English, even intervening on behalf of Thomas Bathe in 1560 for the restoration of

---

[36] SP 63/196/13(i). The privy council referred their request back to William Russell, the lord deputy, and the Irish council; see SP 63/196/27. Russell rejected their claims. My thanks to Ruth Canning for these references.

[37] For this self-identification, see SP 63/58/29.

[38] Edwards, *The Ormond lordship in County Kilkenny*, p. 92; see also Keith Sidwell and David Edwards, 'The Tipperary hero: Dermot O'Meara's *Ormonius* (1615)', in Jason Harris and Keith Sidwell (eds.), *Making Ireland Roman: Irish neo-Latin writers and the republic of letters* (Cork, 2009), pp. 60–8.

[39] For a selection of these early petitions, see SP 63/1/22; SP 63/1/51, 52, 63. For a study of Old English petitions to Elizabeth during the Nine Years' War, see Ruth Canning, 'War, identity, and the Pale: the Old English and the 1590s crisis' (PhD thesis, University College Cork, 2012).

family lands attainted after the Kildare Rebellion.[40] She also initially appeared to display a concern to preserve the Old English nobility's role in advising on policy. Writing to both the nobility and the Irish council in January 1561, for instance, Elizabeth requested that they advise Sir William Fitzwilliam while Sussex was away, and wrote then to Sussex in May instructing him to seek the counsel of the nobility regarding Shane O'Neill.[41] In addition to correspondence, over her first few years as monarch Elizabeth had direct contact with members of the Old English visiting court, as the 7th baron of Howth and John Plunkett, Chief Justice of the King's Bench, did in 1562.[42] As noted in the Introduction to this volume, it was during this visit to court that Elizabeth asked Howth whether or not he spoke English, a remark that certainly raises questions about her perception of the Old English.[43] It is possible that Elizabeth was already aware of concerns regarding their Gaelicisation, a concern that dated to the medieval period and resurfaced early in the sixteenth century. More immediately, in the same year that Howth and Plunkett attended court Sussex reported that 'the strongest of the nobility . . . leave for the most part the use of the laws of the realm and oppress the people . . . with all kinds of Irish exactions and extortions'.[44]

Elizabeth was also aware by this date of conflict that had arisen the previous year between the Old English and Sussex. As Old English opposition to Sussex mounted, those involved relied on their strategy of petitioning Elizabeth as they had done for private suits. In July 1561 the barons of Slane, Baltinglass, and Dunsany and Viscount Gormanston wrote to Elizabeth requesting that she appoint a commission to 'examine howe the pore people and other your majesty's subjects of the Englishe pale are used'.[45] The following year several Old Englishmen, including Thomas Barnewall, Patrick Hussey, and Patrick Nangle, wrote to advise Elizabeth again of the poor conditions in the Pale.[46] Soon thereafter Elizabeth began to receive complaints from Sussex about the Old English, their recalcitrance in complying with the cess or in hostings against Shane O'Neill, for instance.[47] Thus, while some such as Howth and Plunkett worked co-operatively with Sussex, others began to complain to Elizabeth and were complained of to her.

---

[40] SP 63/2/37, 43; SP 63/4/83.   [41] SP 63/3/8.
[42] SP 63/7/51; SP 63/8/12, 20.   [43] LPL, MS 623 (The Book of Howth), fol. 124v.
[44] *Cal. Carew*, 1515–74, p. 335. Concerns about Gaelicisation resurfaced early in the Tudor period, most notably in Patrick Finglas, 'Breviate of the getting of Ireland and the decay of the same', in Walter Harris (ed.), *Hibernica, or some ancient pieces relating to Ireland*, 2 vols. (Dublin, 1770), vol. I, pp. 79–103. On the periodic reapplication of Finglas's text as English conquest intensified, see McGowan-Doyle, *The Book of Howth*, pp. 5–6.
[45] SP 63/4/17.   [46] SP 63/7/31.   [47] SP 63/8/12, 20.

The early rapport Elizabeth established with some members of the Old English community was quickly altered just two years into her reign. Her January 1561 letter instructing the nobility and council to advise Fitzwilliam would seem to suggest that she intended the full participation of the Old English nobility in a great council, a forum in which they could offer counsel on Shane O'Neill. However, her May 1561 letter reveals otherwise, for there Sussex was instructed to seek only the counsel of those he chose. And her simultaneous letter to the nobility instructed them only to follow Sussex's orders – not advise as in her earlier letter – on the suppression of O'Neill.[48] Any specific concerns she may already have developed about the Old English by that date, such as Gaelicisation, are not evident in her letter. However, a clearly identifiable concern soon surfaced: Old English conformability in religion. Elizabeth's 1563 instructions for the commission of investigation against Sussex to be led by Sir Thomas Wrothe and Sir Nicholas Arnold included a lengthy list of Old English who were to assist them, including among others, Roland Eustace, Viscount Baltinglass, James Bathe, Chief Baron of the Exchequer, and Robert Cusacke, Second Baron of the Exchequer, again suggesting her concern for their inclusion in an important matter of state.[49] However, a second set of instructions was given to Arnold and Wrothe which they were expressly forbidden from sharing with the Old English listed in the commission of investigation. This second, secret communication instructed them to ascertain who among the Old English was conformable in religion and who was not.[50] Clearly Elizabeth, possibly already aware of concerns about the Old English given her query as to Howth's ability to speak English less than a year earlier, had by now become aware of concerns regarding their Catholicism. In spite of Elizabeth's expressed reservations, Arnold soon earned a degree of support from the Old English unusual for Irish viceroys in the Elizabethan period, and they anticipated the extension of this co-operative relationship when Sidney became lord deputy in 1565.[51] However, their hope for the reversal of declining influence that had begun under Sussex was soon dashed. Much of this was due certainly to Sidney, but Elizabeth also played a role. Old English counsel, to become such a pre-eminent

---

[48] SP 63/3/68.
[49] *Cal. Carew*, 1515–74, pp. 354–9. On the inquiry into allegations against Sussex, see Brady, *Chief governors*, pp. 103–5.
[50] *Cal. Carew*, 1515–74, p. 359. Levy Peck outlines a similar situation in which Elizabeth requested a list of the nobility in England who had contributed to fortifications in Plymouth and those who had not; Levy Peck, 'Peers', p. 89.
[51] SP 63/15/14.

concern for them over Elizabeth's reign, was raised immediately. Elizabeth wrote to Sidney in 1566 warning him against taking the counsel of the Old English which, she wrote, 'we neither can allow nor ever could hear good reason to allow'.[52]

Sidney's policies did not entail a restoration of the Old English as they had hoped; rather, he advanced policies such as the abolition of coign and livery and implementation of the cess that brought him into conflict with them. Displacement from office, as well as their exclusion from new offices such as provincial presidencies, saw the position of the Old English further eroded. This was a development of which Elizabeth was not only aware, but in which she played a role despite reports she received praising the Old English.[53] In addition to advising Sidney in 1565 against taking their counsel, she also notified him that same year that if any further complaints were heard about Old English judges she would replace them with new appointments from England.[54] The same year she also raised concerns about the office of lord chancellor.[55] In 1566 she instructed Sidney to overturn Arnold's appointment of the baron of Dunboyne to a captainship in Tipperary.[56] And in 1567 Elizabeth again raised the issue of replacing judges with English-born appointments, noting specifically the justices of the Common Pleas and the Queen's Bench as well as officials in the Irish Exchequer's office.[57] Ten years later Elizabeth would continue to be involved in requests to replace Old English judges on grounds of incompetence and Gaelicisation. In 1577 the Irish council wrote to her:

And like as we must confesse unto your Majesty, that the people within the Pale are over much blemished with the spots of the Irishry; and that the sundry good lawes from age to age devised to wipe out those stains, have rather been hid and now known than duly executed; so are we to beseech your Highness of the continuance of that your gratious care, to send justices to put those and other needful laws fit to pass at this next parliament.[58]

The renewed challenge to the Old English that occurred when Sidney returned for another term as lord deputy in 1575 saw the Old English renew their strategy of petitioning Elizabeth directly for redress. The

[52] SP 63/19/25.

[53] Sidney wrote to Elizabeth in 1566, for instance, praising the barons of Delvin, Howth, Louth, and Trimleston for their assistance against Shane O'Neill: SP 63/19/55.

[54] SP 63/15/4.   [55] SP 63/14/8.

[56] *Sidney SP*, p. 23, Queen to Sir Henry Sidney, 14 May 1566.

[57] *Sidney SP*, p. 64, Queen to Sir Henry Sidney, 11 Jun. 1567.

[58] *Letters and memorials*, pp. 216–17, Lords of the Council in Ireland to Queen Elizabeth, 12 Sep. 1577.

conflict over Sidney's cess is of particular concern here.[59] Sidney's Old English opponents, including the barons of Baltinglass, Delvin, and Howth and sixteen others, wrote simultaneously in January 1577 to Sidney and the Irish council, the privy council, and Elizabeth outlining their opposition, as well as sending three lawyers to present their case at court.[60] The lawyers, Barnaby Scurlocke, Richard Netterville, and Henry Burnell, were examined and imprisoned in the Fleet. The cess opponents' initial complaint centred on two issues: the extortionate rates of the cess, and thus its economic impact on the Pale; and the origin of its imposition. Their insistence that cess could be levied only with the consent of either parliament or a great council underscores their declining ability to influence policy through counsel. Following consideration of the matter by Elizabeth and the privy council, Elizabeth reported to Sidney that cess was not 'a matter against law and the ancient customs of that our realm', but rather that the opposition 'tendeth manifestly to the overthrow of our prerogative'.[61] The question of royal prerogative would remain central to the events that unfolded.

Elizabeth guarded royal prerogative intensely and used it carefully, though in this case a prerogative delegated to her viceroy. Sidney was reprimanded for permitting this challenge to prerogative as well as for failing to imprison the opposition leaders on a matter of such importance.[62] The opponents were imprisoned for two months in spite of their protestations of loyalty and insistence that they intended no challenge to royal prerogative. Following their release, the conflict continued, escalating again in January 1578. The opponents were then imprisoned a second time, on this occasion for five months, events of which Elizabeth was again well aware.[63] The cess opponents' claims to counsel and their employment of the rhetoric of counsel in this episode brought them into conflict with the

---

[59] Sidney also aggravated problems in other areas, particularly in the midlands; see Carey, 'John Derricke's *Image of Irelande*'.

[60] SP 63/57/1, 1 (i), (iv).

[61] SP 63/58/20. For Sidney's self-defence in this matter, see SP 63/58/49. In this case, Elizabeth's prerogative regarding the cess had been delegated to Sidney. She similarly delegated extraordinary powers to her viceroys in Ireland, including the prerogative right to raise individuals to the peerage; Maginn, 'The Gaelic peers', 575, 578. Sidney was also reprimanded by Elizabeth for imposing such a heavy cess: *Cal. Carew*, 1575–88, p. 105. For the privy council's instructions to reach some compromise with the cess opponents, see *Cal. Carew*, 1575–88, p. 106.

[62] SP 63/58/20.

[63] SP 63/60/12, 47. On the cess controversy, see McGowan-Doyle, *The Book of Howth*, pp. 22–8; and Brady, *Chief governors*, pp. 215–42. Canny interprets Elizabeth's involvement differently, suggesting that without her intervention the Old English might have gone into rebellion against Sidney: *Elizabethan conquest*, p. 152. Neither archival evidence nor *The Book of Howth* indicates such an option was considered, though officials feared the possibility that the Old English might enter into rebellion.

very core of Elizabeth's definition of monarchy manifest in her protection of royal prerogative.[64]

The rhetoric of counsel

The rhetoric of counsel was fundamental to Tudor political thought and practice, as John Guy emphasised, noting that it 'underpinned not only the assumptions, but also some of the most important practices and political structures of the Tudor and early-Stuart polity'.[65] Occurring in a variety of genres, it afforded 'the politics of access' as Jacqueline Rose described it, between Elizabeth and members of her body politic.[66] It was a system in which Elizabeth was as well versed as her subjects, as Mary Crane demonstrated, responding to and employing it to her advantage.[67] The rhetoric of counsel was as familiar to the Old English as it was to those in England. They were increasingly barred from positions of influence, afforded limited access to institutional counsel through Parliament, and lacked the personal ties to Elizabeth through which to influence her, so employing the rhetoric of counsel was a vital avenue of access to the queen, to whom they turned when problems with viceroys arose.[68]

The cess controversy of 1577–8, along with the episode of conflict over the cess that arose under Sussex in 1561, affords the opportunity to reconsider such appeals to Elizabeth not only as an oppositional strategy but importantly within the rhetoric of counsel. Opponents of the cess have been characterised on the one hand as 'inflexible', 'ignorant

---

[64] See, for instance, her response to the monopolies issue in 1601; David Harris Sacks, 'The countervailing of benefits: monopoly, liberty, and benevolence in Elizabethan England', in Hoak (ed.), *Tudor political culture*, pp. 272–91.

[65] John Guy, 'The rhetoric of counsel in early modern England', in Hoak (ed.), *Tudor political culture*, p. 292. On rhetoric, see also F. W. Conrad, 'The problem of counsel reconsidered: the case of Sir Thomas Elyot', in Paul A. Fideler and T. F. Mayer (eds.), *Political thought and the Tudor commonwealth* (London, 1992), pp. 75–107; A. N. McLaren, 'Delineating the Elizabethan body politic: Knox, Aylmer and the definition of counsel 1558–1588', *History of Political Thought* 17 (1996), 224–52. These studies, however, do not take Ireland into account. For one study of the rhetoric of counsel as applied in Ireland, see McGowan-Doyle, *The Book of Howth*, pp. 100–1.

[66] Jacqueline Rose, 'Kingship and counsel in early modern England', *Historical Journal* 54 (2011), 70. Rose speculates that the 'disparate nature' of the many genres in which the rhetoric of counsel can be found accounts for its failure to receive greater attention from scholars (p. 48).

[67] Mary Crane, '"*Video et taceo*": Elizabeth I and the rhetoric of counsel', *Studies in English Literature* 28 (1988), 1–15.

[68] Ormond's close relationship with Elizabeth is an exception here again. On the role of personal ties to Elizabeth, see Adams, *Leicester and the court*, pp. 31–2.

of economic forces', and 'unable to keep pace with the ideological shift occurring in England', and on the other hand as constituting a movement grounded in nothing more than 'fundamental economic resentment'.[69] These approaches effectively reject any political acumen on the part of the Old English, and they do not give critical attention to the chosen method of opposition. There are multiple advantages to considering that opposition to the cess reflects more than backward obstinance or self-serving legal ruse to overturn policy economically detrimental to the Old English.[70] If we consider oppositional appeals to Elizabeth as a function of lost counsel and within the rhetoric of counsel, a more complex framework within which to consider Old English opposition emerges that ultimately contributes to reassessment of Elizabeth's personal rule as displayed in her relationship to the Old English. It contributes, moreover, to the nature of her rule within a colonial context and thereby her role in the Tudor conquest of Ireland.

The cess opponents held to a basic dictum of counsel: the subject's duty to inform the monarch as problems arose. Their adherence to this premise appears in a number of locations as they theorised, debated, and employed it. When writing to Elizabeth at the outset of the cess controversy in January 1577, for instance, the cess opponents declared that, 'after long tolerance', they were 'driven by necessity to complain being no longer able to endure the same'.[71] This was more than defiance, though, as Nicholas White pointed out to Burghley when he urged Burghley to 'make some difference between complaining and disobedience. The gentlemen who now feel themselves aggrieved with the greatness of cess imagined that *to complain was the very gate of obedience through which they must enter with humble petition.*'[72] Alerting Elizabeth to the economic destabilisation of her kingdom as a result of the cess thus was grounded in their claim of one's duty to inform the monarch. In a similar and earlier application of their duty to inform, the Old English wrote to Elizabeth in 1565, alerting her to declining conditions in the Pale as a result of Sussex's government.[73] The duty to counsel included not only the obligation to alert the monarch to problems, but extended as well to proffering solutions. Rowland White, for instance, employed the dictum

---

[69] Canny, *Formation of the Old English elite*, pp. 14, 21, 28; Brady, *Chief governors*, p. 214.

[70] See Brady, *Chief governors*, p. 215.

[71] SP 63/57/1. Their initial complaint was not over the cess *per se*, but over its excessiveness, which aggravated poor conditions in the Pale, a charge Sidney denied.

[72] White to Burghley, 13 Jun. 1577, Cecil MSS 60/130–2, as cited in Brady, 'Conservative subversives', p. 23 (italics mine).

[73] SP 63/15/14.

of one's duty to counsel as the principle introducing his proposals for reform outlined in 'Discors touching Ireland':

Consideringe honorable sir the dutie of everie true christen subject is not onelie dischardged in usinge outwarde obedience towardes his soveraigne but also in covetinge, sekinge, shewinge, and faithfullie fulfillinge to his uttermost power whatsoever mighte sounde to the open settinge forthe of gods glorie, the honor and welthe of his prince and the common proffet of his people whereof his enformacion mighte any wise geve lighte or his care and studie understandinge.[74]

In yet another application of the rhetoric of counsel, Howth utilised its language to assess Old English displacement and the failure of policies such as the cess and the abolition of coign and livery in *The Book of Howth*. There he employed the language of counsel but went beyond merely the premise that one was obligated to offer counsel to blame failed conquest on evil councillors, another of the precepts standard to Tudor discourse on this subject. Employing the rhetoric of counsel yet further, Howth also incorporated debate over what constituted the wisdom that validated counsel, another of this subject's key considerations. By his definition it was the 'old experienced learned with bloody hands', the Old English, whose counsel should take precedence over that of 'new' men with little experience in Ireland.[75]

The cess opponents held not only to the principles of counsel that dictated their obligation and their legitimacy in offering it, but moreover to the monarch's obligation to receive it. During the 1562 cess opposition, for instance, when Elizabeth failed to respond as anticipated to the legal students' initial petition, she received a letter from Sir Oliver Plunkett, Sir Christopher Cheevers, and others expressing surprise that she 'gaveth no credite to such declarations'.[76] In the 1577–8 cess controversy, the opponents expected not only that Elizabeth would receive their counsel: they were also confident she would act upon it. Even as Baltinglass, Delvin, Howth, and the others were threatened by Sidney with imprisonment, they asserted confidently that they expected remedy from Elizabeth.[77] This echoed their complaint to Elizabeth several months earlier wherein they stated that their intent was 'to disclose our griefs to you our gracious sovereign from whom only after God we expect relief'.[78]

---

[74] SP 63/31/32. For a partial transcription of this document, see Rowland White, 'Rowland White's "Discors touching Ireland, *c.* 1569"', Nicholas Canny (ed.), *Irish Historical Studies* 20 (1977), 446.

[75] McGowan-Doyle, *The Book of Howth*, pp. 101–2. For Howth's use of this language, see LPL, MS 623, fols. 129v–130r.

[76] SP 63/6/12. See also Brady, *Chief governors*, pp. 102–3.

[77] HMC, *Salisbury*, II, pp. 154–5, Nicholas White to Burghley, 13 Jun. 1577.

[78] SP 63/57/1.

The Old English definition of counsel – key to their assumptions about their place in the body politic and thus their relationship to Elizabeth – reflects assumptions about the role of the aristocracy, but it was a position reinforced by education at the Inns of Court. This background underscores the corporate nature of the cess opposition as members of the aristocracy, gentry, and legal community co-ordinated their efforts. Models of the rhetoric of counsel traditionally identify two basic schools of counsel, defined as the 'feudal-baronial' and the 'humanist-classical' by Guy. Both schools agreed that the fundamental purpose of counsel was the preservation of the commonwealth; however, the models were at odds in defining wisdom and therefore which group was best suited to offer counsel, placing the aristocracy, or 'natural-born councillors' in competition with a university- or legally trained community.[79] There was no such division as the rhetoric of counsel was employed by the Old English cess opposition under Sussex or again under Sidney. Rather, as the aristocracy, gentry and legal community co-ordinated their efforts in utilising counsel, they elided what would otherwise have represented different positions within interpretations of the rhetoric of counsel. Such an alignment across the boundaries of status is not surprising in the case of the Old English, given their pattern of attendance at the Inns of Court, essential background that further advances our appreciation of the cess opponents' position, their appeals to Elizabeth, and the contribution this episode makes to a more comprehensive assessment of Tudor political culture, one that takes Ireland into account.

The Old English nobility was just as likely to send their sons to the Inns of Court as were gentry families. Inns of Court class lists for the 1550s and 1560s include the legal students and lawyers involved in both episodes of the cess controversy as well as other participants from aristocratic families such as the Nugents (barons of Delvin) and St Lawrences (barons of Howth), including even the 7th baron of Howth who, as already noted, played a leading role in the 1577–8 cess opposition.[80] Howth's definition of those best suited to counsel as 'the old experienced learned with bloody hands' included the Old English nobility, but it included those beneath the nobility as well. This group thus represented

---

[79] Guy, 'The rhetoric of counsel in early modern England', p. 292. On the nobility and rhetoric, see also Markku Peltonen, 'Rhetoric and citizenship in the monarchical republic of Queen Elizabeth I', in John F. McDiarmid (ed.), *The monarchical republic of early modern England: essays in response to Patrick Collinson* (Aldershot, 2007), pp. 111–12, 118–21.

[80] *The Records of the Honorable Society of Lincoln's Inn. The Black Books. Volume 1 from AD 1422 to AD 1586* (London, 1897); see p. 55 for instance. On the 7th baron of Howth's time at Lincoln's Inn, see McGowan-Doyle, *The Book of Howth*, pp. 16–18.

a new political network based on shared colonial experiences and shared grievances rather than shared aristocratic status.[81] The specific nature of this new political network's shared education is of critical importance, for they were all students at Lincoln's Inn precisely when the subject of the relationship between counsel and royal prerogative became a particular concern there. During their tenure at Lincoln's Inn, William Staunford both lectured on and composed a treatise on royal prerogative. Staunford stressed one's duty to offer counsel and moreover to do so even when it was in conflict with the monarch.[82] Howth specifically cited Staunford, as well as John Fortescue and Henry of Bracton, on whom Staunford had relied as precedents for his position, as rationale for the cess opposition in 1577–8.[83] The cess opponents who appealed to Elizabeth were thus all educated in a definition of counsel at the Inns of Court that insisted on one's duty to counsel under any circumstance. Of equally critical importance, as Margaret McGlynn demonstrated, the definition of counsel espoused by the Inns of Court in this period also asserted the fundamental obligation of the monarch to receive counsel, a lesson not lost on its Old English students.[84]

Elizabeth's response to the cess opponents reveals a different definition of counsel, or more specifically of her obligation to receive it. She was as experienced in the rhetoric of counsel as those who sought to use it to their own advantage, deftly turning it to her advantage to assert her authority.[85] And, as Wallace MacCaffrey has noted regarding her attitude to counsel in England, Elizabeth made it clear that 'councillors were her servants, not her tutors'.[86] The same held true for Ireland, and its bearing on colonial developments exposed her role in the Tudor conquest. In holding to royal prerogative in the cess controversy of 1577–8, as she did on a number of occasions in England, Elizabeth effectively rejected the Old English right to counsel. Natalie Mears argued that Elizabeth rejected the counsel of John Stubbs against her marriage, for which he lost his right hand, because Stubbs had not been 'specifically chosen by Elizabeth to act in an advisory capacity'.[87] In other words, he had not been sanctioned by Elizabeth to offer this advice, and neither

---

[81] On political networks and political structures, see Steven Gunn, 'The structures of politics in early Tudor England', *Transactions of the Royal Historical Society*, 6th series, 5 (1995), 59–90.

[82] Margaret McGlynn, *The royal prerogative and the learning of the Inns of Court* (Cambridge, 2003), p. 15.

[83] LPL, MS 623 (The Book of Howth), fol. 134v.

[84] McGlynn, *The royal prerogative*, p. 25.   [85] Crane, '"Video et taceo"', 2, 4.

[86] Wallace MacCaffrey, *Elizabeth I* (London, 1993), p. 81.

[87] Natalie Mears, 'Counsel, public debate, and queenship: John Stubbs's "The Discoverie of a Gaping Gulf", 1579', *Historical Journal* 44 (2001), 648.

were the Old English whose displacement precluded their acquisition of institutional positions from which they could advise on policy.

The Old English were not deterred in their attempts to petition Elizabeth for redress. The lords of Gormanston, Howth, Louth, and Slane petitioned her again in 1585 when Sir John Perrot attempted to introduce policies with which they disagreed.[88] Perrot's Old English opponents were successful in preventing his attempt to enforce the oath of supremacy or the repeal of Poynings's Law, for instance, but only with great difficulty, as before. Louth was imprisoned, a fate Slane and Howth escaped by relenting in their position after being threatened with arrest.[89] By this point, even long-time and loyal appointees who had managed to retain seats on the Irish council began to fear their displacement and inability to counsel. Even Lucas Dillon expressed concern that instructions had been sent to Dublin that 'those of this country birth which were of the council should be secluded from consultation in matters of weight and secrecy'.[90]

As Elizabeth entered the last decade of her reign she continued to thwart Old English attempts to reverse their decline. The long-standing complaint about the incompetence of Old English judges and officials took their toll in 1594 when Elizabeth's instructions to Sir William Russell upon taking office as viceroy noted that English-born men were being sent to hold the offices of the Master of the Rolls, Chief Baron of the Exchequer, and Chief Justice of the Queen's Bench, offices formerly held by 'men native of that country'.[91] Following Gormanston's failure in insisting on the right of the nobility to be called to council in 1596 to advise on the course of the Nine Years' War, the Old English attempted to place one of their number on the Irish council. In 1600 a group of Old Englishmen wrote Elizabeth requesting the appointment of Nicholas St Lawrence, 8th baron of Howth, to the Irish council.[92] Howth was highly regarded by Old and New English alike, several of whom endorsed his appointment, including Sir Geoffrey Fenton.[93] Fenton's endorsement of Howth in particular conveys the esteem Howth commanded, for Fenton was far more regularly opposed to Old English advancement. He routinely expressed concerns about their loyalty, had advised Burghley against appointing an Old Englishman to the office of Chief Baron of the Exchequer, and even complained to Walsingham about the

---

[88] SP 63/121/35.

[89] SP 63/122/62, 63. See also Brady, 'Conservative subversives', p. 29, and Treadwell, 'Sir John Perrot and the Irish parliament of 1585–1586'.

[90] SP 63/127/21.   [91] Cal. Carew, 1589–1600, pp. 90–1.

[92] SP 63/207/pt 3, 148.   [93] SP 63/207/pt 5, 26.

appointment of Sir Nicholas White to a constableship.[94] Yet, in spite of this, he encouraged Sir Robert Cecil to use his influence with Elizabeth to obtain her consent to Howth's appointment.[95] But Elizabeth, as is well known, was not always pliable to the advice of her counsellors, even rejecting proposals from advisers as powerful as Burghley and later, his son, Cecil.[96] Howth's appointment would have been a strategic move to ensure the loyalty of the Old English in the midst of the Nine Years' War and fears of Old English defections to Hugh O'Neill. However, on this occasion, when this increasingly alienated element of her Old English nobility was poised to reverse their declining status, Elizabeth neither vacillated nor procrastinated, but again rejected her subjects' right to counsel her. The Dublin administration received a terse response denying the request because it 'is not meet Her Majesty be prescribed in so royal a point by her subjects'. They were instructed additionally to cease all such requests immediately, leaving 'to Her Majesty's princely mind to call to that junction whom she will and when she will'.[97]

Elizabeth was not universally opposed to the Old English. Two years after refusing to consider Howth's appointment to the Irish council she praised the earl of Clanricard as 'one of our principal councillors in that state' and 'an honour to the nobility of that kingdom'.[98] She even continued to support Howth's son, Christopher St Lawrence, in the aftermath of his bellicose support of Essex at court.[99] Elizabeth certainly had not created the displacement of the Old English; its first glimmerings under Sussex were inherited by her as with so much else in the Tudor conquest of Ireland, but neither did she work aggressively to sustain their traditional role as administrators of conquest.[100] At a pivotal moment during the Nine Years' War, when it was in her hands to reverse the declining status of the Old English, against the advice of virtually all her advisers and administrators, Elizabeth invoked royal prerogative to reject out of hand the request for an Old English appointment to the Irish council, thus personally exacerbating their decline. She could not blame this on her

---

[94] *CSPI*, XI, p. 471; SP 63/207 pt 5/26; SP 63/163/52; SP 63/132/27. For a complaint about Fenton's prejudice against those born in Ireland, see SP 63/132/37.

[95] SP 63/207 pt 5/26.

[96] On Burghley's frequent complaint that Elizabeth did not follow his advice, see Crane, "'Video et taceo'", 7; on Cecil, see John Guy, *Tudor England* (Oxford, 1988), p. 392.

[97] SP 63/207 pt 6/123.   [98] *Cal. Carew*, 1601–3, p. 392.

[99] McGowan-Doyle, "'Spent blood'", p. 185.

[100] On Elizabeth's conservatism regarding office and rank, see Adams, *Leicester and the court*, p. 28. It should be stressed that Elizabeth did not interfere with noble rank in Ireland; the nobility retained titles but lost effective power.

viceroy or anyone else.[101] Christopher Maginn's observation that 'local elites could be a powerful tool for a monarch in the governance of his kingdoms' was not a policy that had been employed by Elizabeth in Ireland, where the benefits of the increasing bureaucratisation of government and growing military as a function of expanding conquest went instead to the New English.[102] In Ireland, the Old English nobility's opportunity to exercise authority was diminished substantially. Their difficulty obtaining offices, military appointment, and the rewards they believed they merited was shared by many of their peers in England.[103] But in Ireland this was complicated by the Tudor reconquest. It was a process in which the rhetoric of New English policy-makers, office-seekers, and those seeking new land may well have played a role in influencing Elizabeth, but it was a process in which she played the final hand by rejecting Old English noble claims to traditional rights and power through counsel.

[101] See Hiram Morgan, '"Never any realm worse governed": Queen Elizabeth and Ireland', *Transactions of the Royal Historical Society*, 6th series, 14 (2004), 295–308.
[102] Maginn, 'The Gaelic peers', 567.
[103] On similarities with the English nobility, see Levy Peck, 'Peers', pp. 88–93.

9 'Base rogues' and 'gentlemen of quality': the earl of Essex's Irish knights and royal displeasure in 1599

Paul E. J. Hammer

Robert Devereux, 2nd earl of Essex, has been almost universally derided by scholars for the number of knights he dubbed during his expedition to Ireland in 1599. This derision takes its cue from well-known sources of the period. In one of his famous series of letters to Dudley Carleton, John Chamberlain mockingly reported that 'the earle of Essex hath made many new knights, but I cannot yet come by the beadrolle'. Chamberlain was shocked that Essex had so far made fifty-nine new knights in Ireland: 'yt is much marvayled that this humor shold so possess him that, not content with his first dosens and scores, he shold thus fall to huddle them up by halfe hundreds ... yf he continue this course, he will shortly bring in tag and rag, cut and longe tayle, and so draw the order into contempt'.[1] Another oft-quoted source is the spy William Udall, who claimed that Essex had made 'so many unworthy knights, which is jested at in Ireland, and sayed that he made more knights then he killed rebells'.[2] More significantly, this tone of scorn for Essex's creation of new knights was echoed in furious letters and orders emanating from the queen herself.

After Essex's unexpected return from Ireland at the end of September and subsequent arrest, Elizabeth's anger remained unabated. In October, she ordered that a statement of the earl's 'contempts' be drawn up, including 'that he had knighted many, contrary to her pleasure'.[3] Although Essex's ill health and uncertainty about how to deal with him delayed affairs for months, these 'contempts' finally featured as charges against him in an informal trial in early June 1600. However, the queen remained 'very vehement' to undo his actions. On 25 June, she even signed a

---

[1] SP 12/272/68, fol. 111v. This letter is printed in John Chamberlain, *The letters of John Chamberlain*, N. E. McLure (ed.), 2 vols., (Philadelphia, 1939), vol. I, p. 84.

[2] Cecil Papers, Salisbury House, Hertfordshire (hereafter in this chapter CP), 186/159 (fol. 159v). I am grateful for permission to cite from the papers of the Marquess of Salisbury. A very abbreviated description of this document is calendared in HMC, *Salisbury*, IX, p. 385.

[3] *Letters and memorials*, II, p. 135.

proclamation stripping thirty-eight named gentlemen of the knighthoods which Essex had given them in August and September 1599.[4] Although the queen's initiative was supported by legal advice from Francis Bacon, it was soon clear that she was entering a legal and political minefield.[5] One of those who stood to lose his distinction, Sir John Harington, likened knighthood to 'babtisme... [as] a marke of Christianitye' and argued that it was equally impossible to revoke: 'soche vertue hath water and the word in the sacrament of owr sowles, soch forse hath the royall sword and the word for the sacred dignitye of knighthood'. In a less lofty but no less pointed tone, Harington also noted the proclamation would occasion 'the secreat and most bitter curses of dyvers, and some very fayr, ladyes, who are not yet so good philosophers as to neglect honor and embrace paciens'.[6] Despite the queen's insistence, Sir Robert Cecil, the principal secretary of state, also felt this was a step too far. He protested that the proclamation 'shold wrestle with the Great Seale of England and bringe the authoritie therof in question'.[7] In the end, this argument proved decisive and the order was never enforced.[8] Nevertheless, the radical nature of Elizabeth's plan shows the depth of her fury with Essex's dubbings.

---

[4] SP 12/275/21; Chamberlain, *Letters*, vol. I, p. 104. John Chamberlain noted that the proclamation would have stripped knighthoods from thirty-nine men, but the actual document lists only thirty-eight names: SP 63/205/241. The missing name (for which a space is left on the proclamation) seems to be that of Edward Essex. This document bears the sign manual. Chamberlain's report that it 'was signed on Wensday last' fixes the date on which the queen authorised the proclamation as 25 June 1600.

[5] *Letters and memorials*, II, p. 204.

[6] CP 80/62; HMC, *Salisbury*, X, p. 199. The letter is printed in Sir John Harington, *The letters and epigrams of Sir John Harington, together with The prayse of private life*, N. E. McLure (ed.) (Philadelphia, 1930), pp. 81–3.

[7] SP 12/275/21; Chamberlain, *Letters*, vol. I, p. 104. Cecil's point – which directly contradicted Bacon's advice – was that Essex had formally been granted the power to make knights as part of his commission as lord lieutenant of Ireland, which had been confirmed under the Great Seal. Essex's commission, dated at Westminster on 12 March 1599, is printed from the patent rolls in Thomas Rymer, *Foedera, conventiones, literae, et cujuscunque generis acta publica inter reges Angliae et alios quosvis imperatores, reges, pontifices, principes vel communitates*, 20 vols. (London, 1704–35), vol. XVI, pp. 366–73. The modern reference for the Essex's commission in the patent rolls is TNA, C 66/1497, m. 41d. Essex's own copy is Devereux Papers, Longleat, Box 6, no. 90. Essex's commission was also enrolled in the Irish patent rolls: *Calendar of the patent and close rolls of chancery in Ireland in the reigns of Henry VIII, Edward VI, Mary and Elizabeth*, James Morrin (ed.), 2 vols. (Dublin and London, 1861–2), vol. II, pp. 520–2.

[8] On 3 July 1600, Harington thanked Cecil for having 'very honorably... dellt with us all in that matter'. However, feelings about the Irish knighthoods and their potential revocation still ran hot at court. As Harington informed Cecil in the same letter, 'I was very lately charged, by a noble parson, before as noble a person, and from a great lady, to have been the informer to her Majestie of the names and number of those knightes that wear made after the 4th of Awgust, as thowgh I had' (Harington, *Letters and epigrams*, p. 83).

Essex's profligate dubbing of knights was, in fact, only one of several issues which provoked the queen's ire over his conduct in Ireland in 1599. Other problems included Essex's appointment of Sir Christopher Blount as marshal of the army, the appointment of the earl of Southampton as general of the horse, the arrival in Ireland of the earl of Rutland and others without her approval, and the ultimate failure of Essex to confront the 'arch traitor', Hugh O'Neill, earl of Tyrone, in open battle. However, the dubbing of knights became the chief lightning rod for the queen's anger towards Essex.

For Elizabeth, the knighthoods of August and September 1599, in particular, were a matter of wilful disobedience. According to the abortive proclamation, the queen sent Essex a letter before August 'all writen with her owne hand', giving him 'an absolute commandement that he should not confer knighthod upon any one man more, but leave that rewarde to herself'.[9] In effect, she responded to what she perceived as Essex's misuse of a power granted to him by his commission as lord lieutenant of Ireland by demanding he stop using that legal power. Elizabeth took the same approach over Essex's right to return to court at his own discretion, sending him another private letter countermanding this right, even though it had been deliberately separated from his commission and passed independently under the Great Seal.[10] She also took a similarly restrictive view of Essex's actions on campaign, finally ordering him to advance on Ulster regardless of the arguments which he and other officers made against this decision.[11]

---

[9] SP 63/205/241. Elizabeth's holograph letter to Essex does not seem to have survived. Essex's surviving letters from Ireland during the summer of 1599 also make no obvious reference to this letter.

[10] An undated draft of this separate commission, signed by the attorney-general, Edward Coke, is SP 63/203/74. The final version of this right of return to England, dated 27 March 1599, is printed from Bodleian Library, Oxford, Tanner MS 76, fol. 53, in E. M. Tenison, *Elizabethan England: being the history of this country 'in relation to all foreign princes'*, 14 vols.) (Leamington Spa, 1933–61), vol. XI, pp. 118–19. As with Essex's main commission, this document was also formally enrolled in the Irish patent rolls: *Calendar of the patent and close rolls of Chancery in Ireland*, Morrin (ed.), pp. 531–2, where it is printed *in extenso*. A copy of Elizabeth's private letter to Essex of 30 July 1599, made by Thomas Windebank, clerk of the Signet, is SP 63/205/121. In this letter, the queen describes Essex's commission as merely 'our former lycence provisionally given', and she requires him to forego its use 'as you tender our pleasure'.

[11] SP 205/114, 121, 132, 170. Note that the latter letter did not reach Essex in Ireland before his return to England. Most modern commentators have uncritically accepted Elizabeth's view. However, her determination to press ahead with the plan without delay, regardless of the conditions Essex had found in Ireland after his arrival, was militarily reckless, and potentially disastrous: John McCavitt, *The flight of the earls* (Dublin, 2002), pp. 26–7.

In each of these instances, the real issue for Elizabeth was obedience to her royal wishes. Understandably, the queen was determined
to exert political control over what was, by far, the largest army in the
British Isles and to prevent Essex from treating it as his own personal
possession.[12] Events during 1598 had given her good cause to be wary
of Essex, despite his deep personal loyalty to Elizabeth herself. During
the summer of 1598, Elizabeth and Essex had engaged in a 'great quarrel' sparked by disagreement about who should command in Ireland.
Perhaps more importantly, the queen knew Essex had also argued so
profoundly with other councillors about the prospect of peace talks with
Spain that he responded to their attacks by circulating a manuscript
'Apologie' which made a public case for a very different kind of war
policy than the queen herself wanted.[13] Elizabeth's missives to Essex in
Ireland in 1599, therefore, were informed by a determination to prevent the earl from unilaterally trying to change royal policy by fighting a different campaign from that which had been agreed before his
departure – as he had actually tried to do with the Cadiz expedition of
1596.[14] However, Elizabeth's efforts to assert her political control also
undermined the conduct of a campaign which she very clearly did not
understand. Her hectoring letters to Essex expressing amazement that
he was having difficulty defeating mere 'bushe kerne' and 'base roagues'
which have been quoted with approval by so many historians over the
centuries are, in fact, demonstrations of Elizabeth's profound lack of
understanding of the challenges of fighting in Ireland.[15] Essex himself
had seriously underestimated these same difficulties before he arrived
in Ireland and learned them for himself by painful experience. Essex's
successor, Charles Blount, Lord Mountjoy, would require three years of
sustained effort to force O'Neill into a peace – and even that would only
be possible because the landing of a Spanish army in southern Ireland in

---

[12] For the king-making potential of the military command in Ireland during the early
modern period, see Hiram Morgan, 'Overmighty officers: the Irish lord deputyship in
the early modern British state', *History Ireland* 7 (1999), 17–21.

[13] For the events of spring and summer 1598, see, for example, G. B. Harrison, *The life and
death of Robert Devereux earl of Essex* (London, 1937; Bath, 1970, reprint), pp. 192–210.
Essex's 'Apologie' was later printed as *An apologie of the earle of Essex against those which
jealously and maliciously tax him to be the onely hinderer of the peace and quiet of his countrey.
Penned by himselfe in anno 1598* (London, 1603). For the ferocious debate about war
and peace in 1598, see A. Gajda, 'Debating war and peace in late Elizabethan England',
Historical Journal 52 (2009), 851–78.

[14] P. E. J. Hammer, *The polarisation of Elizabethan politics: the political career of Robert Devereux, 2nd earl of Essex, 1585–1597* (Cambridge, 1999), pp. 250–7 and 367–9; Hammer,
'Myth-making: politics, propaganda and the capture of Cadiz in 1596', *Historical Journal*
40 (1997), 621–42.

[15] For example, SP 63/205/114.

188   *Paul E. J. Hammer*

late 1601 transformed the strategic situation and finally gave the English a single clear target for their military resources.[16]

The point here is not that Essex was in the right, but that there were serious problems with the actions of *both* Essex *and* Elizabeth in 1599. Essex's desperation to succeed in circumstances which proved far more difficult than he had anticipated and his fear that his rivals at home would take advantage of his absence to undermine him drove him to surround himself with subordinates whom he could trust implicitly. To Elizabeth, this seemed like Essex was again seeking to hijack a major military expedition for his own political purposes, and she responded accordingly. Unfortunately, these actions created a vicious circle in which Essex's conduct provoked growing fury from Elizabeth, which merely reinforced Essex's sense that she was not listening to him and that therefore he could not trust in any support at court and must look out for himself – which further infuriated Elizabeth. Something of the nature of the problem can be seen in Elizabeth's response to an attempt by the Irish council to support Essex's arguments against an unrealistic order, which began: 'the lettre which we have reade this day from you of that Counsell concerninge your opinions for the northern accion dooth rather deserve reproof then much answeare'.[17]

This comment says much about Elizabeth. Whatever the specific failings of Essex and the Irish council, Elizabeth's instinctive reaction to attack her servants in Ireland for wilful disobedience was characteristic of her behaviour on countless occasions during her reign and is suggestive of a profound insecurity which manifested itself, for example, in her notoriously frequent allusions to her father, Henry VIII. In the past, when Elizabethan history was dominated by scholars in awe of Gloriana, this characterisation might perhaps have seemed insufficiently respectful towards Elizabeth, but modern scholarship is now much less dazzled by the queen.[18] Indeed, the combination of her frankly often capricious behaviour and her deep ignorance of the realities of Ireland, in particular, help to explain why there was 'never any realm worse governed'.[19]

---

[16] M. C. Fissel, *English warfare, 1511–1642* (London and New York, 2001), p. 225.
[17] SP 63/205/132.
[18] For example, Christopher Haigh, *Elizabeth I* (London, 1988; 2nd edn, 1998); P. E. J. Hammer, *Elizabeth's wars: war, government and society in Tudor England, 1544–1604* (Basingstoke, 2003); and the recent series of Ford Lectures delivered at the University of Oxford by Prof. Peter Lake, Mar.–Apr. 2011, 'Bad Queen Bess? Libelous politics and secret histories in an age of confessional conflict'.
[19] Hiram Morgan, '"Never any realm worse governed": Queen Elizabeth and Ireland', *Transactions of the Royal Historical Society*, 6th series, 14 (2004), 295–308. For Elizabeth's often difficult and emotional behaviour, see, for example, her words and actions when Essex led an army to Normandy in 1591: P. E. J. Hammer, 'Letters from Sir Robert

Elizabeth's increasingly angry replies to dispatches from Ireland in 1599 also reflect the fact that she and Essex were effectively arguing at cross-purposes. While the queen focused on the broader political perspective from the court, almost regardless of the implications on the ground in Ireland, Essex focused on the demands of the situation in Ireland and his own tactical and strategic needs there. This made it hard for each to find much satisfaction in the other's responses. It also created a particular problem for Essex because he recognised that *only* military success in Ireland could salvage his political career after the problems of 1598 – failure in Ireland would undo all that he had achieved over the past decade and threaten him with political oblivion at a time when the peace talks with Spain which he had opposed so bitterly still seemed possible. Although he could not express it openly, he also knew that Elizabeth's advanced age and lack of an accepted heir meant the great question of the royal succession was also looming. Unless he could secure some kind of military victory in Ireland, Essex knew he would be denied a voice in these urgent political issues and at the mercy of their outcome.

Even so, why did Essex act like such a 'fool' (as various writers have described him)[20] in failing to obey his queen's prohibition on new knighthoods? The argument here is that Essex did so as a rational, calculated response to the challenges posed by what had become an emergency situation in Ireland. In essence, Essex dubbed so many knights because it enabled him to hold together his army when it began to crumble.

Essex's commission as lord lieutenant of Ireland gave him 'full power and authority' ('plenam potestatem & auctoritatem') to create new knights at his own discretion, according to the merits of those who had performed exemplary actions in battle, or would do so. Bestowing the rank and insignia of knighthood on men would be recognition of their 'virtue' and committed service to the state.[21] Essex was also expected to follow a lengthy set of instructions which accompanied his commission as lord lieutenant. These instructions (dated 25 March) made it very clear that Elizabeth believed too many knighthoods had been granted in recent years and enjoined Essex 'to conferre that title uppon none that shall not deserve it by some notorious servyce or have not in possession or

Cecil to Sir Christopher Hatton, 1590–1591', in Ian Archer (ed.), *Religion, politics and society in sixteenth-century England* (Cambridge, 2003), esp. pp. 214–17.

[20] For example, C. Jowitt, 'Political allegory in late Elizabethan and early Jacobean "Turk" plays: *Lust's dominion* and *The Turke*', *Comparative Drama* 36 (2003), 421.

[21] Rymer, *Foedera*, p. 372. The concept of virtue specified here ('virtus') includes bravery, but is also laden with other implications, including living up to one's elevated social rank. The service to be rewarded is also explicitly stated as being to the state, not to the queen: 'strenueque navatam Reipublicae operam'.

reversion sufficient lyvinge to mayntaine that degree and callinge'.[22] The criteria for knighthood, therefore, included not only actions of notable worth, but also the personal wealth to support this distinction. Essex also knew that this was a matter of real sensitivity for the queen.

Despite this, Essex made at least eighty-two new knights in Ireland between 5 May and 24 September (Appendix I). If one plots these dubbings out against events in the campaign (Appendix II), it is clear that these were at first only a small trickle (only nine knights in the first two months), reflecting the careful 'moderation' envisaged in his instructions. Essex resorted to mass dubbings of new knights – twelve on 12 July and seven more over the following ten days – only after the trial and execution on 3 July of soldiers blamed for cowardice in the defeat suffered by Sir Henry Harrington's troops on 29 May. This shocking rout at Wicklow had drowned out the news of Essex's own dramatic success in capturing Cahir Castle and prompted him to take the drastic step of ordering the decimation of survivors from the companies which had broken and run. The creation of new knights was intended to reward boldness in action and boost the army's severely bruised morale. The next burst of dubbings came on 24 July, when Essex met up with Sir Conyers Clifford's force at Meath, and on 30 July, three days after the army was informed that the queen commanded the removal of the earl of Southampton as general of the horse and shortly after a major skirmish. On this latter date, no fewer than nine new knights were made. The following week saw a further twenty knights dubbed. This orgy of honourable ceremonial was intended to galvanise the relatively small force of less than 4,800 foot and 400 horse which Essex could take north to confront O'Neill's defences in Ulster.[23]

These preparations were rudely interrupted by the shocking news that Clifford and his command had been virtually wiped out in an ambush in the Curlew mountains on 5 August.[24] This defeat was personally and strategically disastrous for Essex – far worse than the humiliation suffered by Sir Henry Harrington's troops at Wicklow in May. Not only was Clifford an experienced commander and a relative of the earl, but his small army had been essential for stretching the Irish defences of Ulster and giving Essex's main army any chance of penetrating northward into O'Neill's home territory. Clifford's defeat meant that the frontal assault on Ulster which Elizabeth was insisting upon was now most likely to result in the same sort of military catastrophe which Sir Nicholas

[22] LPL, MS 601, fol. 170r.   [23] SP 63/205/128.

[24] Cyril M. Mattimoe, 'The Battle of the Curlieus, 15th August, 1599', *Journal of the Roscommon Historical and Archaeological Society* 1 (1986), 47–51.

Bagenal had suffered at the Yellow Ford in August 1598 – the very defeat which had almost cost Elizabeth control of Ireland and forced her to pour unprecedented resources into recovering it under Essex in 1599. Although the earl of Ormond and a few subordinate officers had managed to stave off disaster in the months following Yellow Ford, it was far from certain that Elizabeth's hold on Ireland could survive another defeat of similar magnitude, despite Essex's own recent efforts in Leinster and Munster.[25] Essex dutifully marched north on 28 August, but refused to risk another Yellow Ford and instead agreed a truce with O'Neill that protected the gains he had made in the south over the previous months. He dubbed another ten knights on this rather dispiriting journey. Essex's final decision was to head back to court and explain the truce and his own actions to Elizabeth in person. On 24 September, the day he set sail for England, he dubbed six more knights, four of them on the Dublin Sands.

This chronology suggests two key points. First, it highlights Essex's dramatic change of practice in dubbing knights in mid July. Essex's decision to revive the ancient Roman punishment of decimation was 'much descanted of' in England, but it demonstrated that he was willing to take drastic action to hold his army together.[26] When he had arrived in Ireland in April, Essex had been confronted with a situation verging on the chaotic. The outgoing treasurer for the military establishment in Ireland 'yelded up the ghost' on the very day he reached Dublin.[27] The drowning of the earl of Kildare and 'eighteen of the chiefs of Meath and Fingall', who had sailed for Ireland at the same time as Essex, was another unexpected blow.[28] The unprecedented size of the new army being assembled

---

[25] Ormond's role in saving Munster is emphasised in A. J. Sheehan, 'The overthrow of the Plantation of Munster in October 1598', *Irish Sword* 15 (1982), 11–22, and David Edwards, *The Ormond lordship in County Kilkenny, 1515–1642: the rise and fall of Butler feudal power* (Dublin, 2003), pp. 253–4. Edwards argues that Essex effectively built upon Ormond's efforts in the south, but did not stay in Ireland long enough to reinforce these successes adequately (*ibid.*, pp. 254–6).

[26] Chamberlain, *Letters*, vol. I, p. 79. Essex's decision was highly unusual, but considered to be within the accepted laws of war. The Roman practice of decimation had been described (with detailed references) in Henry Savile's *The ende of Nero and beginning of Galba. Fower bookes of the Histories of Cornelius Tacitus. The life of Agricola.* (London, 1591), pp. 29–30 and on p. 18 of the 'Annotations upon first book of Tacitus' at the end of this volume. Decimation was also mentioned in Matthew Sutcliffe's *The practice, proceedings and lawes of armes* (London, 1593), p. 324. Savile was a client of Essex, as was Sutcliffe. Sutcliffe was also the judge marshal for Essex's army in Ireland in 1599 (TNA, E 351/238, m. 24d).

[27] C. L. Falkiner, 'William Farmer's Chronicles of Ireland from 1594 to 1613', *English Historical Review* 22 (1907), 112.

[28] John O'Donovan (ed.), *Annals of the kingdom of Ireland by the Four Masters, from the earliest period to the year 1616*, 7 vols. (Dublin, 1851), vol. VI, p. 2093. The fate of

also created all kinds of logistical and command problems.[29] Essex, therefore, had both to bring order to this organisational chaos and publicly demonstrate his viceregal power and authority. Perhaps the most conspicuous way in which he sought to achieve the latter objective was the highly elaborate commemoration of St George's Day on 23 April, which celebrated his status as a knight of Order of the Garter in truly magnificent fashion: 'there was not greater state, plentie and attendance used at that time in the Court of England on the Queene and all hir knightes of the Order'.[30] Indeed, the event in Dublin was a massive display of knightly prestige involving many of the army's officers and soldiers. The defeat at Wicklow, when raw English troops panicked and an Irish company ran away instead of covering the retreat, threatened to undo all this hard work.[31] Crucially, it also raised the spectre of deadly mistrust between English and Irish troops. Essex's shocking decision to court martial and decimate the Irish survivors of the disaster showed the extreme lengths to which he would go to deter such incidents in the future. On the other hand, once the point had been made by the executions, Essex consciously sought to revive the spirit of the St George's Day celebration by dubbing a whole batch of new English knights, headed by a group of aristocrats.[32] These new knights were expected to provide the positive role models which would erase the disastrous example of Wicklow. Their high-profile mass dubbing also created a pattern for multiple knightings by Essex thereafter.

The second point which emerges from the chronology of Essex's dubbings is that it actually fits well with the explanation which he gave for creating so many knights in Ireland at his informal trial in June 1600:

Kildare's bark was still uncertain as late as 27 April: CP 179/4 (HMC, *Salisbury*, IX, p. 144).

[29] As Sir Robert Cecil observed in a letter of 23 May 1599, Essex 'must have wrought miracles to have setled and distributed an army of 16000 foote and 1300 horse, and to have accommodated them with all necessaries in a countrey full of misery and disorder, in a shorter tyme then he did': *Memorials of affairs of state in the reigns of Q. Elizabeth and K. James I. Collected (chiefly) from the original papers of . . . Sir Ralph Winwood*, E. Sawyer (ed.), 3 vols. (London, 1725), vol. I, p. 40.

[30] Sir James Perrot, *The chronicle of Ireland 1584–1608*, Herbert Wood (ed.) (Dublin, 1933), p. 162. See also 'A new ballade of the tryumpes kept in Ireland uppon Saint Georg's day last, by the noble earle of Essex . . . ', in *The Shirburn ballads, 1585–1616*, A. Clark (ed.) (Oxford, 1907), pp. 322–6, and CP 179/4 (HMC, *Salisbury*, IX, p. 144).

[31] Cyril Falls, *Elizabeth's Irish wars* (London, 1950; 1970, reprint), pp. 235–6.

[32] The mass dubbing on 12 July included Lord Grey of Wilton, Lord Cromwell, Lord Mounteagle (although this title remained legally unconfirmed until 1604), Thomas West, the son and heir of Baron De La Warr and a first cousin of Essex, Robert Vernon, another first cousin of Essex, and Henry Carey, a slightly more distant cousin of Essex whose father was a groom of the Bedchamber and Master of the Jewels to the queen. Another new knight, William Constable, was a servant to Essex, but also a kinsman of the earl of Rutland, who had recently married Essex's step-daughter. George Manners was a younger brother of Rutland.

having many gallant gentlemen voluntaries who had spent themselves very farre in following him this weriesome journey, havinge noe other imployement for them and having bestowed amonge them all that he was able to make, and fearing theire discontentment and shrinking awaie, having (as hee said) noe ymployement for them, no other treasere or guifes to bestowe uppon them, he rewarded manie of them for theire valure and forwardness in divers enterprises that he passed with the honour of knighthoode, thereby to hold the rest on with the like hope of the same rewarde thereafter.[33]

While scholars have endlessly quoted Elizabeth's letters condemning Essex, this response by Essex himself seems to have been almost entirely neglected.

The main point which Essex makes here is the critical importance of 'gentlemen voluntaries' for the military effectiveness of his army and the need to keep them in action. This reflects basic facts about the nature of Elizabethan armies sent abroad. Since the best men in the county militias were reserved for home defence as members of the trained bands, expeditionary forces had to be created largely from conscripts who (by definition) were deemed to be men not worth drafting into the trained bands. Such poor-quality soldiers put a premium on the ability of captains and their under-officers to drill and lead them effectively.[34] These often unwilling levies were supplemented by a leavening of volunteers – the most important of whom were young gentlemen who attached themselves to senior officers in the army as self-funding 'voluntaries', many of them bringing a small retinue of their own with them. Experience of the battlefield had long ago convinced Essex that 'those gentlemen and adventurers thatt serve withowt pay shall do more service in any fight then the whole trowpes besides, for where good men leade they will all follow', even those who 'weare peasawnts 2 monethes agoe'.[35] The gentlemen voluntaries, in effect, gave the army its cutting edge because they were well equipped and highly motivated to prove themselves in combat. Many of them also helped to supplement the all-important cavalry, which the crown consistently under-resourced for reasons of cost.[36] The impact of this became starkly apparent after Essex was replaced as commander in Ireland, and the Irish council was forced to report that

[33] Historical Manuscripts Commission, *The manuscripts of the Marquess of Bath preserved at Longleat, Wiltshire*, ed. G. Dynfault Owen, 5 vols. (London, 1904–80), vol. V, *Talbot, Dudley and Devereux Papers, 1533–1659*, p. 274.

[34] Hammer, *Elizabeth's wars*, pp. 176, 257.

[35] SP 78/25, fol. 366r. This holograph letter by Essex is dated 27 September [1591]. The words 'gentlemen and adventurers' have been underlined by its addressee, Lord Burghley, who also added the marginal annotation 'Adventurers withowt paye'. Almost certainly, these (and other) annotations on the letter reflect Burghley's preparation for briefing the queen on its contents.

[36] For example, Hammer, *Elizabeth's wars*, pp. 125, 193.

'when the late lord liuetenaunt of the kingdom departed for England, a greate manye which served on horsebacke as voluntaries departed also at that tyme, with their horsses'.[37] The return home of so many gentlemen volunteers with their servants and precious horses severely weakened the one military arm in which the English enjoyed a major advantage over the Irish.

Remarkably, Elizabeth does not seem to have understood the nature of these 'voluntaries'. When Essex requested reinforcements to fill out his depleted foot companies, the privy council responded by passing along the queen's suggestion that he simply use the 'voluntaries' to make up the shortfall.[38] Essex had to explain that these were 'either some fewe men of quallitie that serve on horsback and will never supplie the places of ordinarie men or [e]ls such of our attendants as cannot be anywhere enrolled'.[39] It is not clear that Elizabeth ever comprehended this basic characteristic of her armies. On the other hand, several members of the council board – including the lord admiral – were extremely familiar with how expeditionary forces functioned and should obviously have advised the queen about the unrealistic nature of her suggestion as soon as it was raised.[40] The fact that they failed to do so and instead endorsed this impossible advice could only have heightened Essex's doubts about the ability, or willingness, of his fellow councillors to represent his position accurately to the queen. Even if Elizabeth herself failed to understand the nature of 'voluntaries', members of the council certainly knew better and should have advised her accordingly.

Being a gentleman volunteer was expensive. Sir John Harington, the famed wit and godson of Elizabeth, claimed he spent no less than £300 to join the action in Ireland in 1599.[41] John Bargar complained in 1601 that he had 'served hyr Majestie as a voluntarye in fouer actyons under hyme [Essex], which hath coste me vearye nye a brace of thowsande

---

[37] SP 63/207(i)/87. A preliminary list of 'all such gentlemen as hath subscribed to follow me in this journey' includes only sixteen names, not all of whom actually went to Ireland in person. Nevertheless, these gentlemen pledged to provide some 228 foot and no fewer than 212 horsemen. The document also notes that 'there are ffiftie other gentlemen that have faithfull[y] promised their assistance and to follow me in this journey which are in the country preparing themselfs but because they have not subscribed I forbeare to name them': SP 63/203/118, fol. 280r.

[38] SP 63/205/52.   [39] SP 63/205/54.

[40] In 1596, the lord admiral had shared with Essex command of the Cadiz expedition, which had been accompanied by large number of gentlemen volunteers. In August 1599, he wrote to Sir Robert Cecil about the defensive mobilisation around London that 'it is the horse must dow the pryncypall did [deed] and the voluntarys be the best. They that come out of the shers [the cavalry units of the trained bands] are very wek and nothyng neere the nomber that is expected' (CP 72/57; HMC, *Salisbury*, IX, p. 289).

[41] Harington, *Letters and epigrams*, p. 74.

poundes'.[42] Quite apart from the costs associated with food, weapons, horses, and servants, gentleman volunteers were expected to live and dress like gentlemen. This often involved expensive clothes and extravagant display.[43] Wearing large plumes of feathers on their helmets seems to have been especially popular, which drew a mixture of wonderment and disdain from the Irish.[44]

Although Bargar complained that he received no more than 'smyles' for his troubles, Essex consistently attracted very large numbers of gentlemen volunteers for each of his expeditions. In Ireland, the numbers were 'soe great' and many of them were 'of soe extraordinary qualitie' that

> the principall places he had to bestow were not sufficient to satisfie the principall persons whoe followed hym with great charge (for the most part on theyr own purses); soe that the multitude of them made many more burdensom to hym and themselves then they should have byn, and rather left some of them unsatisfied or discontented then did further the service. But greate commanders in the warres generally followed and beloved must runne this hazard, or else want followers of worth.[45]

Whenever possible, Essex sought to reward such commitment from his own resources, but these were soon strained to breaking point, especially given the large numbers of volunteers. His entourage in Ireland was about 400 strong, while another 40 or 50 gentlemen (many of them probably voluntaries) dined at his table each day. Meat and drink alone cost about £40 a day, with about the same again for stable costs, liveries, and servants' wages: the money was indeed flying 'daly out off my lord's pursse'.[46]

---

[42] CP 82/94; HMC, *Salisbury*, XI, p. 30.

[43] John Sammes, for example, rejected the claim that he had worn plain attire during his time in Ireland, claiming that he had been 'richly and expensively furnished with [a] great variety of suits of apparel of very great price': A. Thrush and J. P. Ferris (eds.), *The history of Parliament: the House of Commons, 1604–1629*, 6 vols. (Cambridge, 2010), vol. VI, p. 159.

[44] The Irish writer Philip O'Sullivan Beare later used this predilection of English gentlemen for wearing plumes to claim a major victory by the O'Mores over Essex's troops on 17 May which he called the Pass of Plumes to commemorate all the English helmets that had been lost in the battle: Philip O'Sullivan Beare, *Ireland under Elizabeth: chapters towards a history of Ireland in the reign of Elizabeth . . . by Don Philip O'Sullivan Bear*, Matthew J. Byrne (ed. and trans.) (Dublin, 1903), p. 124. English sources report a very different story, with only two men 'of note' (one of them a voluntary) and three or four common soldiers being lost in a skirmish which killed many of the Irish and resulted in an uncontested passage through Cashel pass the next day: *CSPI*, VIII, pp. 39–40. Despite this, a monument to the supposed Irish victory was erected in 1999 to commemorate the 400th anniversary of the event.

[45] Perrot, *Chronicle of Ireland*, p. 161.

[46] CP 72/24; HMC, *Salisbury*, IX, p. 271. This would put the cost of Essex's household for his five months or so in Ireland at more than £11,000. Essex received substantial

Many of these supernumeraries who attached themselves to Essex's army also did not join the expedition solely for Essex's sake, but were kinsmen, clients, and servants of friends of Essex, especially the earls of Southampton and Rutland.[47] As a result, Elizabeth's insistence that both of these earls return to England (in late May and late July, respectively) not only sparked a general demoralisation in the army, but raised the prospect that they would be followed by many of the 'voluntaries' associated with them – unlike captains, 'voluntaries' were not tied to the army by the responsibilities of command. Even before Southampton's recall was confirmed, Essex warned the privy council that 'I doubte not but our Englishe voluntaries and persons of quality will aske passporte of me (who am utterly unable to advance them or defende them)' to go home.[48] Elizabeth tartly responded that she was sure 'the love of our servyce and the duty which they owe us have been as strong motyves to these their travaylls and hazards as any affeccion to the erle of Southampton, or any other'.[49] Nevertheless, this is precisely what began to happen by August.[50] Essex's use of knighthoods during this period was therefore

---

[47] Southampton was the general of the cavalry, while Rutland was considered to be general of the foot companies. Southampton was married to Essex's first cousin, Elizabeth Vernon. Rutland was newly married to Essex's step-daughter, Elizabeth Sidney, the daughter of the famous Sir Philip Sidney. The queen insisted that she had not given permission for either earl to join Essex's army and recalled them home. Essex's army also included a contingent of followers of the earl of Derby, who had originally planned to join the expedition himself: *Calendar of letters and state papers, relating to English affairs, preserved principally in the archives of Simancas, Elizabeth*, M. A. S. Hume (ed.), 4 vols. (London, 1896–1947); vol. IV, p. 650. At the end of November 1598, the expectation in London was that Derby would take over no fewer than 3,000 men to Ireland: anon., 'The earl of Essex (1598–1601)', *Notes & Queries for Somerset and Devon*, 24 (221) (Jun. 1944), 110–11. Among the knights created by Essex in Ireland, Cuthbert Halsall, Edward Warren, and perhaps also John Radcliffe can be seen as Stanley men: Thrush and Ferris (eds.), *The House of Commons, 1604–1629*, vol. IV, pp. 521–2; vol. VI, p. 7; P. W. Hasler (ed.), *The history of Parliament: the House of Commons, 1558–1603*, 3 vols. (London, 1981), vol. III, p. 585.

[48] SP 63/205/111. In his previous letter to the Council, on 11 July 1599, Essex had warned that, 'in obeyinge this commandement, I must discourage all my freinds, whoe, nowe seeinge the dayes of my sufferinge drawe neere, followe me afarr of and are, some of them, tempted to renownce me; when I must dismay the Armye, which allready lookes sadly upon me, as pittyinge bothe me and it selfe in this comfortles action; when I must encourage the Rebelles, whoe doubtles will thinke it tyme to hewe upon a wytheringe tree, whose leaves they see beaten downe and branches in parte cut of; when forever I must disable my selfe in the course of this service': LPL, MS 621, fol. 142r.

[49] SP 63/204, fol. 179v. The queen's letter pointedly concluded that, 'yf it prove otherwyse . . . we shall have the lesse cause ether to acknowledge or reward' the service of such voluntaries.

[50] CP 72/77; HMC, *Salisbury*, IX, pp. 300–1. After the death of Sir Conyers Clifford on 5 August, Essex was also desperate to assure 'those Irishe lords of cuntreyes, captaines, gentlemen, and others that depend uppon Sir Conniers Clifford's favoure' that he would

forms of income from the crown (£100 per month as lieutenant general in Ireland, for a start), but nothing close to matching this sort of expenditure.

intended to stem this outflow of 'gentlemen of quality' and to overlay the other personal loyalties of these new knights with a direct personal connection to Essex himself. This was not only vital for maintaining his army's fighting power in Ireland in 1599, but also would have been important if Essex had needed to raise more troops for future campaigns – perhaps for a fresh campaign in Ireland in 1600.

The significance of the gentlemen volunteers can be seen by drilling down into the details of the men whom Essex knighted. Obviously, a chapter of this length cannot examine all of the knights in detail. Nevertheless, a few interesting patterns are worth highlighting. First, some sixty of the eighty-two knights were not officers in the queen's pay at the time when they were dubbed.[51] Overwhelmingly, therefore, they were gentlemen voluntaries, just as Essex explained. However, the nature of Essex's knights also reveals some other challenges which he sought to resolve in Ireland.

A second group of interest are the fifteen captains, headed by Sir Henry Docwra and Sir Charles Percy, who accompanied some veteran troops withdrawn from the English forces in the Low Countries. Such veterans constituted the other elite component of Elizabethan expeditionary forces, along with the gentlemen voluntaries.[52] Six of these captains had been knighted by Essex in previous campaigns.[53] In Ireland, six more of them were dubbed as knights by Essex.[54] This leaves only three of the captains of veteran troops who missed out on a knighthood from Essex. Of these three men, one was replaced in July and may perhaps have been killed. If so, it makes one wonder why Captains Tyrwhitt and Lloyd missed out on a knighthood from Essex.[55]

---

personally 'suppley theire losse of him': LPL, MS 632, fol. 176r. Essex also urged Sir Tybott (i.e. Theobald) Dillon to reassure 'the Irishrye that depended uppon Sir Con. Cliffords purse or favoure (of what quallitie soever)' that he would 'suppley that losse they have of him [Clifford] in all respects' (*ibid.*, fol. 175r).

[51] Calculated using the dates for which captains and other officers were paid, as specified in TNA, E 351/238.

[52] Hammer, *Elizabeth's wars*, pp. 257–8. The captains assigned to these veteran troops are listed in TNA, E 351/238, m. 47. Note that not all of these captains had commanded these men in the Low Countries. Sir Charles Percy, for example, had arrived there only in late 1598 and had not secured a command there. He had previously commanded troops temporarily stationed in south-west England between 31 October 1597 and 10 September 1598: TNA, E 351/250. This period of service is omitted in Mark Nicholls, 'Sir Charles Percy', *Recusant History* 18 (1986–7), 237–50.

[53] Sir Charles Percy (knighted in 1591), Sir Henry Docwra (1596), Sir Robert Drury (1591), Sir Garrett Harvey (1596), Sir John Shelton (1596), and Sir Oliver Lambert (1596).

[54] Henry Carew, John Chamberlain, Henry Masterson, Edward Michelborne, Edmund Morgan, and Richard Morison.

[55] Edward Turner (or Turnour) was replaced as captain with effect from 20 July 1599. William Tyrwhitt and Walter Lloyd both retained their captaincies into 1600. Tyrwhitt

The broader context for the dubbing of so many of the captains commanding veteran troops transferred from the Low Countries was Essex's growing struggle with Sir Francis Vere and his allies at court over patronage in the English forces in the Low Countries. Vere, who commanded the main body of English troops in the Netherlands, had been a loyal partisan of Essex until the summer of 1597, when he turned against the earl for appointing Lord Mountjoy (instead of Vere himself) as commander of the land forces on what became the Azores expedition.[56] Thereafter, relations between them became embittered, and Vere looked to Sir Robert Cecil and other patrons on the privy council to help him resist and roll back Essex's influence over English military patronage in the Netherlands.[57] By 1598, Essex's clients were struggling to win captaincies there, and those who already held them were being bullied by Vere. Arguably, this intense pressure on a crucial area of patronage was one of the key factors which impelled Essex to pursue the Irish command during the winter of 1598–9. Although he was deeply aware of the political and military risks involved in going to Ireland, the desire for fresh martial success and the lure of being able to fill so many new colonelcies and captaincies ultimately proved irresistible. Nevertheless, the bitter quarrels over billets in the Low Countries cast a shadow over Essex's new army. When Essex demanded 2,000 veteran soldiers for Ireland under officers of his choosing, Vere released fewer troops and these from the poorest-quality units.[58] At the same time, a clash between Essex and the lord admiral over filling a vacant colonelcy in the Low Countries sparked 'great unkindness' and 'high words' between them, which delayed and embittered the preparations for Ireland during January and February.[59] By knighting so many of the captains who commanded the troops who

had been a captain in the Low Countries since January 1596. Part of his company had joined Essex's expedition to Cadiz that year but, perhaps significantly, Tyrwhitt himself stayed in the Low Countries to command the remaining men. He may not have been a captain closely associated with Essex so much as an officer who was eager to escape the monopolistic influence of Sir Francis Vere (see below, pp. 198–9). Lloyd is harder to identify, but may have been a captain since 1592.

[56] Hammer, *Polarisation*, pp. 236–7, 258.

[57] D. J. B. Trim, 'Fighting "Jacob's wars". The employment of English and Welsh mercenaries in the European Wars of Religion: France and the Netherlands, 1562–1610 (unpublished PhD thesis, University of London, 2002), esp. pp. 179–85.

[58] Essex used his position on the council to ensure that Vere was sent a furious letter of reprimand for his actions on 25 February: *Acts of the privy council of England, 1532–1631*, new series, J. R. Dasent et al. (eds.), 46 vols. (London, 1890–1964), vol. XXIX, pp. 607–9.

[59] TNA, PRO 31/3/30, fols. 14v–15r, Sieur de Boissise to Henry IV of France, 25 [15] Jan. 1599. The quarrel became even more bitter after Sir William Woodhouse, the lord admiral's candidate, ambushed Sir Robert Drury, a follower of Essex whose suit for a captaincy had been rebuffed a few months earlier. This violent fight in the streets of

were eventually transferred from the Netherlands, Essex can be seen as rewarding these captains for siding with him, rather than with Vere, and choosing to join his army in Ireland.

Such rewards may have been all the more important because of what had happened with the previous force of veteran troops who had been sent to Ireland from the continent. In the spring of 1598, the remnants of an English force serving in Picardy were shipped to Ireland. This force had been in place since 1596 and had been dominated by officers associated with Essex.[60] The removal of these English troops from France ended the earl's ability to find captaincies there for his military dependants and made winning commands in the Low Countries all the more critical. When these troops were transferred to Ireland to serve under the earl of Ormond, several captains saw their companies dissolved and lost their captaincies. Ormond reorganised the force into a regiment of 700 men under the colonelcy of Essex's client, Sir Henry Power.[61] The regiment was soon divided up to conduct a variety of military operations in Ireland, and part of it was destroyed in the great disaster of Yellow Ford in August 1598. On 11 May 1599, shortly after Essex assumed military control in Ireland from Ormond, the remnants of the regiment were effectively dissolved.[62] By then, only two of Power's captains still survived and one of them, Francis Rushe, was among the first officers to be knighted by Essex in Ireland.[63] Almost certainly, Rushe's knighthood was personally recommended by Ormond, who met up with Essex near Athy on 11 or 12 May. Ormond had appointed Rushe as 'governor' of the fort at Maryborough a few months earlier and Essex emphatically

---

London left Drury wounded and one of his companions dead: Chamberlain, *Letters*, vol. I, pp. 62, 67, 69, 72.

[60] A list of the captains in this force in December 1596 is CP 47/24; HMC, *Salisbury*, VI, p. 523.

[61] Captains Bosseville, Poley, Gorges and Annesley lost their companies when the force left France and did not sail to Ireland. Captain Gibbs travelled to Ireland but promptly saw his men folded into the other companies by Ormond, leaving him without a captaincy. This left Sir Henry Power with a company of 200 men (reflecting his status as colonel of the regiment), Captains Wilton and Fortescue with 150 men each, and Captains Rushe and Esmonde with 100 men each: SP 63/202(i)/93. Power (also spelled Poore), had served under Essex in Normandy in 1591–2 and was knighted by the earl there.

[62] Andrew Graham, 'The Picardy companies, 1598–1599: an Elizabethan regiment in Ireland', *Irish Sword* 21 (1998), 43–50.

[63] Two of Colonel Sir Henry Power's four captains seem to have been killed in 1598 (Fortescue and Wilton: the latter had already been badly wounded in France in 1597). Of the other two captains, Rushe was knighted by Essex, while Lawrence Esmonde had to wait until 1603 for a knighthood. Power described Esmonde in March 1598 as 'one Capt. Esmond who was lefftenant to Capt. Bossevile' (SP 63/202(i)/93). This suggests that Lawrence Esmonde was both less well known to Power than the other officers and also junior to them, having only recently been promoted from lieutenant.

reconfirmed this appointment by his knighting of Rushe there on 17 May.[64] Nevertheless, Rushe was very much a client of Essex and, like Power, had ties to the earl going back to at least 1591.[65] Rushe's knighthood was therefore a recognition both of his recent meritorious service under Ormond and of his longer-term association with Essex's military following. As such, his dubbing set a precedent for the officer followers of Essex who arrived with troops from the Low Countries in 1599.

Another conspicuous group among Essex's Irish knights in 1599 were actually Irish, or at least born in Ireland. The dubbing of Sir Terence O'Dempsey on 22 May was one of the first knighthoods bestowed by Essex in Ireland and came after O'Dempsey had personally captured 'two or three . . . famous rebelles (one of them called Captayne Nugent reconned to be one of Tyrone's best captaynes)'. Although Essex was 'offred 2000li sterlinge to have given them theyre lyves', he ordered Sir Francis Rushe to execute the prisoners and set their heads on the gates of the fort at Maryborough.[66] By knighting O'Dempsey, Essex underlined his own refusal to be corrupted by conspicuously honouring the loyal Irish officer who had captured the rebels. This was both a sign that Essex was determined to put an end to the old ways of administering justice in Ireland and an effort to encourage other Irish officers to demonstrate their loyalty. Three other Irish knights – Sir John MacCoghlan, Sir Hugh O'Connor Don, and Sir Mullmore MacSweeney Ne Doe – were dubbed on 24 July, just before Essex sent Sir Conyers Clifford back to Connaught to prepare for their abortive joint attack on Ulster. The Old English gentleman, Sir Theobald Dillon, was knighted at the same time. All four

[64] SP 63/203/101; SP 63/205/67.
[65] Graham ('Picardy companies', 44) suggests that Rushe was a cousin of Essex. In fact, Rushe was a 'kinsman' of Robert Radcliffe, 5th earl of Sussex (CP 28/82; HMC, *Salisbury*, V, p. 4), although Sussex's own kinship to Essex, in turn, gave Rushe a distant personal tie to the latter. Like Sir Henry Power, Rushe served as a captain in Normandy. Both men were among ten captains initially 'apoynted to goe to Normandye & afterwardes stayed'. Power subsequently joined the main body of Essex's army as captain of 100 foot in July 1591, but Rushe had to wait for his captaincy in Normandy until March 1592 – shortly after Essex himself had returned to England (TNA, E 351/244). Rushe subsequently joined Essex's expedition to Cadiz in 1596 (serving as a captain in the earl of Sussex's regiment), before joining the force sent to Picardy. After the transfer of the surviving Picardy troops to Ireland, Rushe wrote to Essex's secretary, Edward Reynoldes, reminding him that 'I rest and relye uppon his [Essex's] favor wholye and by God have ever.' Rushe professed to 'hoope well of my Lord of Ormond as an olde, cold, careless Lord, but my assured trust is from my Lord Essex' (CP 177/118; HMC, *Salisbury*, VIII, p. 387). Rushe's appointment as 'governor' of Maryborough in January 1599 presumably showed Rushe that Ormond was no longer 'careless' (i.e. not actively supportive) of his preferment.
[66] SP 63/205/63(i).

men had come under intense pressure to abandon their loyalty to the crown and had paid a high personal price for resisting these overtures. The knighthoods they received from Essex were an attempt to ensure they remained supportive of Clifford's operations and did not succumb to the pressures from O'Neill and his allies.[67] In the wake of Sir Henry Harrington's defeat at Wicklow at the end of May and the subsequent accusations of cowardice against Irish troops, these knighthoods were perhaps also intended to shore up the prestige of Irish soldiers in Essex's army. This was especially important because Essex was forced to raise at least eight new companies of foot from within Ireland in mid July.[68] Unfortunately, Clifford's defeat and death in the Curlew mountains on 15 August brought a fresh round of recriminations about soldierly cowardice.

Another group of Irish-based knights seems to reflect Essex's relationship with his chief ally in the queen's administration in Ireland, Lord Chancellor Adam Loftus. John Talbot, for example, had been associated with Loftus 'even from his childehode'.[69] Sir William Warren's brother, Sir Henry Warren, was also married to one of Loftus's daughters.[70] These dubbings – together with those of two of Loftus's sons as Essex was about to leave Ireland[71] – clearly served to reinforce the political partnership between them, which Essex probably expected to renew if he had returned to Ireland after convincing Elizabeth of the merits of his truce with O'Neill.

Finally, at least one French gentleman was knighted by Essex in Ireland, a Monsieur Pechdoue. Pechdoue figures in none of the lists of knights, but he proudly mentions his knighthood from Essex in a tract dedicated to James VI & I dating from about 1610.[72] At one level,

---

[67] *Ibid.*; SP 63/205/136, 182; SP 206/26, 85. To Essex's acute embarrassment, Mac-Sweeney eventually joined the Irish cause in a dramatic act of treachery in July 1600: Historical Manuscripts Comission, *Report on the manuscripts of Lord de l'Isle and Dudley preserved at Penshurst Place*, 6 vols. (London, 1925–66), vol. II, pp. 480, 484; J. McGurk, *Sir Henry Docwra, 1541–1631: Derry's second founder* (Dublin, 2006), pp. 74–5.

[68] Companies 'raysed in harvest tyme 1599': TNA, E 351/238, m. 45r–v. Five companies (four of 100 men and one of 150 men) were paid beginning on 18 July, while three more companies (one of 100 men and two of 150 men) were paid beginning on 17 July 1599. Further new companies were raised in mid August.

[69] SP63/207(i)/60, fol. 140r.

[70] Note that Sir William Warren fell out in spectacular fashion with Lord Chancellor Loftus after Essex's return to England. Essex also knighted Warren's English kinsman, Sir Edward Warren of Poynton, Cheshire, on 22 July 1599.

[71] Edward and Thomas Loftus, who were both knighted on the Dublin Sands on 24 September as Essex prepared to board a ship for England. Their brother, Adam, had been killed in the rout at Wicklow in May after his lieutenant and soldiers had broken and run away.

[72] BL Royal MS 19.B.VIII, fol. 2r.

Pechdoue's knighting reflects the European-wide phenomenon of bestowing rewards upon foreign gentlemen for military service.[73] More specifically, however, Pechdoue's knighting points to an unappreciated aspect of Essex's Irish expedition, namely the extent to which Henry IV of France directly encouraged Essex to take up the Irish command. The correspondence between Henry IV and his ambassador to England, Boissise, suggests that the French king not only urged Essex to seek 'great glory and benefit' in Ireland, but also urged him to maximise his chances of success by demanding the greatest possible resources from Elizabeth.[74] After Essex informed Boissise of how many men the queen had agreed to let him take to Ireland, the earl 'prayed me [Boissise] to let your Majesty know that, next to the commands of his own sovereign, there was nothing which had so encouraged him to take this command than the opinion which it had pleased your Majesty to make of him'.[75] As the presence of Pechdoue and other French soldiers in Ireland demonstrates, Essex's friendship with Henry IV also drew more concrete support in the form of volunteers who wished to serve under his command.[76] Some French

---

[73] Notoriously, Elizabeth reacted with fury when the French king bestowed the Order of St Michael on two English gentlemen, Sir Nicholas Clifford and Sir Anthony Sherley, in 1594: 'my dogs wear my collars' (Hasler (ed.), *The House of Commons, 1558–1603*, vol. I, p. 617; Philip Gawdy, *Letters of Philip Gawdy of West Harling, Norfolk, and of London to various members of his family, 1579–1616*, I. H. Jeayes (ed.) (London, 1906), p. 82; HMC, *Salisbury*, IV, pp. 519, 523; BL, Harleian MS 6996, fols. 82r, 84r–v, 85r, 136r). However, the Order of St Michael was a prestigious higher order of knighthood (Clifford had already been dubbed an ordinary knight by Essex in 1591) and required the recipient to take a special oath which was problematic for English Protestants. Although much cited, this affair gives an exaggerated slant on Elizabeth's views about international reciprocity in making knights. A more typical case was the French king's entirely uncontroversial knighting of four English gentlemen as a token of his 'love' for Sir Henry Unton, Elizabeth's new ambassador to France, in November 1591: SP 78/26, fol. 166v.

[74] For example: 'je luy dis que Vostre Majesté m'avoit commandé de l'y exciter comme à une occasion qui luy pourroit apporter beaucoup de gloire et d'advancement' (TNA, PRO 31/3/29, fol. 259v, Boissise to Henry IV, 17 [7] Nov. 1598).

[75] 'Sur quoy ledict sieur comte m'a prié de faire entendre à Vostre Majesté qu'auprès les commandemens de sa soveraine il n'y a rien qui l'ait tant encouragé audict voiage que le jugement qu'il a pleu à Vostre Majesté de luy' (TNA, PRO 31/3/30, fol. 3r, Boissise to Henry IV, 6 Jan. 1599). Essex also requested that the king might send 'fréquentes admonitions' to the queen to keep him supplied with necessities for the campaign, which he trusted would remind her of the importance of the matter.

[76] The official journal of Essex's march into Ulster in September mentions that one of those wounded in a cavalry skirmish was 'a French gentleman of the Lord Lieutenant's troupe' (SP 63/205/164, fol. 310r). Among the minor payments listed in the declared accounts for the campaign is an undated entry for 40 shillings paid to 'Lewes la Breete de la Roche, a French gentleman, in rewarde for his service and deserte and to carrie him home into his countrie' (TNA, E 351/238, m. 43d). Several English horsemen received an identical sum for being maimed in the queen's service and returning home, so it is

troops remained in Ireland until at least early 1602.[77] Indeed, it is possible that Pechdoue was not the only gentleman among his French adherents whom Essex sought to reward by making him a 'chevalier d'Angleterre' in 1599.

To sum up, Essex's dubbing of so many new knights in Ireland was not simply a sign of his rashness, as usually claimed, but a calculated, rational gamble intended to preserve the fighting power of his army at a time of acute crisis. In July and August 1599, after Sir Henry Harrington's defeat at Wicklow and the queen's recall of Rutland and Southampton, the vital gentlemen voluntaries were beginning to drift home, weakening his army's military potency when he needed it most. Essex clearly gambled that he could ignore Elizabeth's prohibition on new knighthoods after July by securing a favourable outcome to his campaign and then convincing the queen of the necessity of his actions. Even though he realistically had very little choice but to risk the queen's wrath, Essex's own career probably also convinced him this was a gamble worth taking. In each of his previous campaigns as a general, he had angered Elizabeth by dubbing new knights and had always managed to ride out the resultant political storm. In Normandy in 1591, he had made twenty-nine new knights, most of them at a time when his army was on the point of disintegration because the queen demanded his return home to make a diplomatic point to Henry IV.[78] At Cadiz in 1596, he and the lord admiral had celebrated the most spectacular English victory in Spain itself by jointly dubbing more than sixty knights.[79] In the Azores in 1597, Essex had again been about to try to heal divisions in his fleet and army by dubbing new knights, 'but the wind growinge faire in the night, ancor was wayed and gale grew so stronge as the fleete was severed, and the Generall not seene untill all met in Plimowth Sound, wherby manie lost ther expectation'.[80]

Such mass dubbings by generals were also by no means unique to Essex. The earl of Leicester had dubbed many in the Low Countries – including Essex himself – in 1586, while a look at Holinshed's *Chronicles* would show, for example, the names of fifty-four knights made by Protector Somerset after the Battle of Pinkie in 1547 or the fifty-eight knights made by the same lord (while still merely earl of Hertford) after sacking

---

possible that 'Lewes la Breete de la Roche' was the gentleman in Essex's horse troop who was hurt on 6 September.

[77] SP 63/211(iii).   [78] Hammer, *Polarisation*, pp. 106–7, 115, 223–4.

[79] SP 12/257/103, fol. 163r–v.

[80] BL Add. MS 72407, fol. 21r. This unpublished account of the expedition also claims that 500 volunteers accompanied the voyage, while another '2000 voluntaries had dismissed themselves' after the fleet's initial departure had been shattered by a fierce storm which drove it back to port (*ibid.*, fol. 17v).

Leith in 1544.[81] Henry VIII had been even more lavish in bestowing knighthoods, dubbing no fewer than 160 men during his 1513 campaign in France.[82]

In 1599, however, such extravagant use of his general's sword to dub new knights terminally damaged Essex's military career. In part, this reflects a cultural shift which had occurred during the first half of Elizabeth's reign. Thanks to the queen's policy of eschewing open war between 1563 and 1585, knighthood had been transformed from a military honour into a civilian one, with an increasing proportion of the realm's knights having been dubbed in England at the queen's direction for domestic political reasons.[83] This created a problem after war broke out in 1585, and the queen's generals sought to reclaim their traditional right of dubbing knights for conspicuous bravery on campaign. The tensions became even more acute in the 1590s, when Essex consciously sought to reassert the martial character of knighthood as a counter to what he regarded as the excessive civilianisation of England's landed elite at a time when the realm's religion and 'liberty' seemed to be imperilled by Spanish 'malice'.[84] This had a galvanising effect on the war effort in the mid 1590s, but it also challenged Elizabeth's essentially civilian conception of knighthood and sparked brief outbursts of royal fury against him in 1591 and 1596.

These episodes also highlight another reason why Essex's knightings in Ireland proved so damaging to him. On those earlier occasions, once he returned to court, Essex was able to make his case to Elizabeth in person and quickly regain her trust. After his return from Ireland, however, Essex soon found himself entirely cut off from direct contact with Elizabeth, which made it impossible for him to repair his relationship with her, as he done so often before. Essex's detention after his sudden return to England at the end of September also triggered O'Neill's

---

[81] For Hertford's knights, see Raphael Holinshed, *Holinshed's chronicles: England, Scotland and Ireland*, 6 vols. (London, 1587), *The third volume of chronicles, beginning at Duke William the Norman, commonlie called the Conqueror; and descending by degrees of yeeres to all the kings and queenes of England in their orderlie successions . . .* , pp. 962–3, 991. For Leicester in the Low Countries, see Hammer, *Polarisation*, p. 51. Leicester's 'princely' celebrations of St George's Day at Utrecht in 1586 – in which Essex himself participated and which were clearly the model for his display at Dublin in 1599 – are described in John Nichols (ed.), *The progresses and public processions of Queen Elizabeth*, 3 vols. (London, 1823), vol. II, pp. 455–7.

[82] H. Leonard, 'Knights and knighthood in Tudor England' (unpublished PhD thesis, University of London, 1970), p. 128.

[83] *Ibid.*, pp. 112–13. Beginning in 1570, Elizabeth began to dub an unprecedented number of civil knights (*ibid.*, p. 115). Note that, as a woman, the queen did not dub knights herself, but instead employed a senior male courtier to do so on her behalf in her presence.

[84] Essex, *Apologie*, passim.

abandonment of the truce which he had made with Essex and the publication of new demands which were utterly incompatible with the Tudor state, which convinced Elizabeth (wrongly) that all of the money and effort that had been invested in Essex's campaign had produced absolutely nothing.[85] O'Neill's renewed defiance also probably helped to make Elizabeth more insistent on punishing Essex for failing to bring him to heel, as he had promised to do before he began his expedition. Crucially, however, Essex's dubbing of knights served as a lightning rod for all of Elizabeth's anger at the earl's actions in Ireland and encouraged her to think of them in terms of simple wilful disobedience. Even in late June 1600, when the hearing at York House had apparently cleared the way for Elizabeth to forgive him, she recalled the warrant she had already sent to dismiss the earl's gentleman keeper, 'being somewhat troubled with the remembrance of his making soe many knights'.[86] Because Essex was never able to convince the queen of the reasons for his actions in Ireland, they were all interpreted in the most hostile light possible and Elizabeth continued to personalise events there as a matter of individual betrayal. This delighted his enemies at court, such as Cobham, Raleigh, and Grey, who encouraged such thoughts, but it drove Essex himself into despair and convinced some of his die-hard followers that the only way to open the queen's eyes and ears was to remove by force those who they believed were deliberately poisoning her against the earl. The scene was being set, therefore, for some of those about Essex to suggest that swords should be used for more than merely dubbing new knights.

Appendix I: The names of Essex's knights in 1599, by date

Mostyn, Sir Thomas	5 May, Dublin
Tasburgh, Sir Thomas	9 May, Dublin
Rushe, Sir Francis	17 May, the Fort of Leix at Maryborough
O'Dempsey, Sir Terence	22 May, Kiltanan, Munster
Manners, Roger, Earl of Rutland	30 May, Cahir Castle
Berkeley, Sir Francis	12 June, Askeaton
Thornton, Sir George	19 June, Kilmallock
Devereux, Sir James	20 June, at Sir John Colley's house
Masterson, Sir Richard	30 June, at his own house at Fernes
Carey, Sir Henry	12 July, Dublin
Champernowne, Sir Arthur	12 July, Dublin

(*cont.*)

---

[85] Hiram Morgan, 'Faith and fatherland or queen and country? An unpublished exchange between O'Neill and the state at the height of the Nine Years' War', *Duiche Neill: Journal of the O'Neill Country Historical Society* 9 (1994), 9–65.

[86] Historical Manuscripts Comission, *De l'Isle and Dudley MSS*, vol. II, p. 470.

Appendix I (*cont.*)

Constable, Sir William	12 July, Dublin
Cromwell, Edward, Lord Cromwell	12 July, Dublin
Davies or Davis, Sir John	12 July, Dublin
Grey, Thomas, Lord Grey of Wilton	12 July, Dublin
Manners, Sir George	12 July, Dublin
Parker, William, called Lord Mounteagle	12 July, Dublin
Poley, Sir John	12 July, Dublin
Reynell, Sir Carew	12 July, Dublin
Vernon, Sir Robert	12 July, Dublin
West, Sir Thomas	12 July, Dublin
Courtenay, Sir William	13 July, Dublin
Godolphin, Sir William	13 July, Dublin
Lacon, Sir Francis	13 July, Dublin
Bassett, Sir Robert	15 July, Dublin
Constable, Sir Robert	22 July, Dublin
Halsall, Sir Cuthbert	22 July, Dublin
Warren (or Warham), Sir Edward	22 July, Dublin
Dillon, Sir Theobald	24 July, at meeting with Sir Conyers Clifford
MacCoghlan, Sir John	24 July, at meeting with Sir Conyers Clifford
MacSweeney Ne Doe, Sir Mullmore	24 July, at meeting with Sir Conyers Clifford
O'Connor Don, Sir Hugh	24 July, at meeting with Sir Conyers Clifford
Osborne, Sir Hewett	24 July, Meath
Bourke, Sir Thomas	30 July, Offaly, after skirmish
Finch, Sir Theophilus	30 July, Offaly, after skirmish
Gascoigne, Sir William	30 July, Offaly, after skirmish
Harington, Sir John	30 July, Offaly, after skirmish
Lindley, Sir Henry	30 July, Offaly, after skirmish
Lovelace, Sir William	30 July, Offaly, after skirmish
Percy, Sir Jocelyn	30 July, Offaly, after skirmish
Vaughan, Sir John	30 July, Offaly, after skirmish
Warren (or Warham), Sir William	30 July, Offaly, after skirmish
Blount, Sir Edward	4 August, Dublin
Digby, Sir Robert	4 August, Dublin
Cornwallis, Sir William	am, 5 August, Dublin
Essex, Sir Edward	am, 5 August, Dublin
Goodyer, Sir Henry	am, 5 August, Dublin
Lovelace, Sir Richard	am, 5 August, Dublin
Carew, Sir Henry	pm, 5 August, Dublin
Heydon, Sir John	pm, 5 August, Dublin
Meyrick, Sir Francis	pm, 5 August, Dublin
Michelbourne, Sir Edward	pm, 5 August, Dublin
Morgan, Sir Edmund*	pm, 5 August, Dublin
Morison, Sir Richard	pm, 5 August, Dublin
Read, Sir Edward	pm, 5 August, Dublin
Wilmot, Sir Charles	pm, 5 August, Dublin
Bowstred, Sir William	6 August, Dublin
Crofts, Sir John	6 August, Dublin
Foulkes (or Fowkes), Sir Henry	6 August, Dublin
Leicester, Sir George	6 August, Dublin

Sammes, Sir John	6 August, Dublin
Wallop, Sir Henry	6 August, Dublin
Weston, Sir Simon	Aug. ?, ?
Brocket, Sir John	31 August
Clovell, Sir William	31 August
Draycott, Sir John	31 August
Chamberlain, Sir John	6 September [Dublin]
Conway, Sir Fulke	6 September [Dublin]
Foliot, Sir Henry	6 September [Dublin]
Manners, Sir Charles	6 September, Dublin
Moore, Sir Garret	6 September, Dublin
Talbot, Sir John	6 September, Dublin
Yaxley, Sir Robert	6 September, Dublin
Brooke, Sir Robert	10 September, Dublin
Petto, Sir Jonathan	10 September, Dublin
Osborne, Sir Robert	24 September, Sir Robert Gardiner's house, Dublin
Poley, Sir John [?]**	24 September, Sir Robert Gardiner's house, Dublin
Baynham, Sir Edward	24 September, Dublin Sands
Loftus, Sir Edward	24 September, Dublin Sands
Loftus, Sir Thomas	24 September, Dublin Sands
Ratcliffe, Sir John	24 September, Dublin Sands
+ Mons. Pechdoue	?

Note: Except where there is compelling evidence to the contrary, the dates and locations of dubbings follow the information given in W. Shaw, *The knights of England*, 2 vols. (London, 1906), vol. II, pp. 95–8.

  * Shaw (*ibid.*, p. 97) lists this knight as either Edward or Richard Morgan, but he is noted as Edmund elsewhere: Folger Shakespeare Library, Washington DC, MS V.b.142, fol. 29r. The latter identification seems more convincing because Edmund Morgan is listed as one of the captains assigned to the veteran troops transferred from the Low Countries. Captain Edmund Morgan had served under Essex in Normandy in 1591. He also captained a company on Guernsey for six months in 1593 (again, apparently with Essex's backing) before securing a permanent captaincy in the queen's forces in the Low Countries from 1 June 1594. He surrendered this captaincy to join Essex's army in Ireland in January 1599.

  ** Shaw (*Knights of England*, vol. I, p. 98) lists the knight dubbed on 24 September as 'Sir John Pooley', and this is supported by the list of men whose knighthoods would have been stripped by the proclamation of June 1600 (SP 63/205/241, fol. 459r). However, the knighting of a John Poley suggests that there were two men with the same name who were both knighted by Essex in Ireland. A 'C[aptain] John Pooley' is included in the list of 'foote apointed to go into the feild with the Lord Lieutenant in his journey towardes the North the [c. 29th] of [August] 1599', which was copied by Essex's secretary in England, Edward Reynoldes, from an original list enclosed with a letter to Reynoldes from Essex dated 30 August 1599 (CP 73/43: HMC, *Salisbury*, IX, p. 331). This suggests the captain was not yet knighted. The Sir John Poley who was knighted in July is not included in the list of captains, so he was either not a captain (i.e. he was a gentleman volunteer) or he returned to England before the end of August 1599.

Appendix II: Essex's dubbing of knights in 1599, by date

Number dubbed	Date and place of dubbing
	16 April: Essex takes up the sword
1	5 May, Dublin
	9 May–2 July: march through Leinster & Munster
1	9 May, Dublin
1	17 May, the Fort of Leix
1	22 May, Kiltanan, Munster
	24 May: Essex receives letter ordering recall of Rutland
	25–29 May: siege and capture of Cahir Castle
	29 May: defeat of Sir Henry Harrington's troops near Wicklow
1	30 May, Cahir Castle
1	12 June, Askeaton
1	19 June, Kilmallock
1	20 June, Sir John Colley's house
1	29 June, Fernes
[9 total]	
	3 July: court martial of Wicklow survivors
12	12 July, Dublin
3	13 July, Dublin
1	15 July, Dublin
3	22 July, Dublin
[19 total]	
	23 July–c. 4 Aug: expedition to Leix and Offaly
5	24 July, Meath, at meeting with Sir Conyers Clifford
	27 July: Southampton dismissed as general of the horse
9	30 July, Offaly, after skirmish
[14 total]	
2	4 August, Dublin
4	am, 5 August, Dublin
8	pm, 5 August, Dublin
	5 August: Sir Conyers Clifford's defeat in Connaught
6	6 August, Dublin
1	August ?, Dublin
[21 total]	
	28 August–9 September: march into Ulster
3	31 August
7	6 September, Dublin
[10 total]	
2	10 September, Dublin
6	24 September, Dublin and Dublin Sands
	24 September: Essex sails for England
[8 total]	

+ Mons. Pechdoue [knighted on unknown date]
total: 82 knights

10 'Tempt not God too long, O Queen': Elizabeth and the Irish crisis of the 1590s

Hiram Morgan

We use the term 'Elizabethan Ireland', even though Elizabeth I was never in Ireland. The term remains an apt one because the English queen's reign had a huge impact there. The decisions she made in relation to Ireland, the decisions she omitted to make, and what she simply let happen there had enormous significance in the country's history. Yet until very recently little attempt was made to pass judgement on Elizabeth's relationship with Ireland and her Irish subjects.[1] This is because we had come to see Elizabethan Ireland from the standpoint of Elizabeth's lord deputies – Sussex, Sidney, Fitzwilliam, Grey, Perrot, Russell, Burgh, Essex, and Mountjoy – and, surprisingly, not from the perspective of the monarch who hired and fired them. No doubt this stemmed from the fact that, while there was plenty of contemporary comment on and criticism of Ireland's erstwhile governors, there was never any complaint in public of the queen's own performance of her Irish office. In fact there was only one major exception – a little-known manuscript entitled 'The supplication of the blood of the English most lamentably murdered in Ireland, cryeng out of the yearth for revenge', which at the end of 1598 passed a damning verdict on the queen and her lack of direction in Irish affairs.[2] This chapter, following a detailed analysis of the queen's role in the protracted and deepening crisis, makes the case for the planter-poet Edmund Spenser being the hitherto unidentified author of this superlative piece of prose.

The author wishes to acknowledge support funding made available under the Higher Education Authority's Programme for Research in Third-Level Institutions.

[1] Hiram Morgan, '"Never any realm worse governed": Queen Elizabeth and Ireland', *Transactions of the Royal Historical Society*, 6th series, 14 (2004), 295–308; Wallace Mac-Caffrey, *Elizabeth I* (London, 1993), pp. 430–3.

[2] 'The supplication of the blood of the English most lamentably murdered in Ireland, cryeng out of the yearth for revenge (1598)', Willy Maley (ed.), *Analecta Hibernica* 36 (1995), 3–77. Unfortunately this transcription is faulty in places, largely due to poor copy-editing by the publisher, and needs to be checked against the original source in British Library Additional MS 34313, fols. 85–121.

The abject and long-standing failure to make a judgement about Elizabeth and Ireland is not for want of sources with which to elucidate the queen's opinion of the Irish situation and her subjects there. We have plenty of evidence from officials and courtiers who relayed and reflected on her reactions to developments in Ireland. Furthermore, we have her own letters. Many of these from the Patent and Close Rolls are formulaic grants but they are mostly to individual recipients and can sometimes be highly personalised. For instance, the queen's order for a lease of lands to be given to Piers Hovenden in 1587 states that it was given at the request of his foster-brother, the earl of Tyrone, 'to whom the queen would not willingly deny any favour, knowing his devotion to her'.[3] Letters survive which she had sent to Irish chieftains, including some in Latin. Intended to display power and elicit loyalty, these appear to be more form than substance. More crucially, there are letters from the queen to her lord deputy and the Irish council, and often to the lord deputy alone. These contain her views on Irish policy and show that she was well briefed and at times of crisis fully engaged. These were usually dictated and are possessed of a distinct voice, and on rare occasions they have postils of praise or more often censure in her own hand. Some, of course, may have been composed for her by secretaries but we can be sure that they did reflect her opinion. Furthermore, since these letters relate to key points of policy, there are often letters written simultaneously by the privy council or by Lord Treasurer Burghley or his son Sir Robert Cecil, which also refer to the queen's mood and thinking.

If we look at the queen's letters to Lord Deputies Sir William Fitzwilliam, Sir William Russell, and Thomas Burgh between 1593 and 1597 (and to the stop-gap lords justice who followed in 1598), we see her Irish polity being overtaken by a deepening and widening crisis. Lord deputies were supposed to represent her person sitting under the cloth of state in Dublin Castle, but these men were failures and they ultimately represent her failures and limitations too. Such officials, who had authority through her and who, being on the spot, could take the initiative, were never in reality simple proxies in her absence; yet she nevertheless was responsible for appointing them and resourcing them. In her letters to them there was much talk of 'our honour' as the queen's reputation was termed. But honour, however important to majesty, sovereignty, and authority, is not a bankable commodity unless it is backed by money and might. The Irish War was ultimately to cost £1,924,000, as much as

---

[3] *Acts of privy council of England, 1532–1631*, new series, J. R. Dasent *et al.* (eds.), 46 vols. (London, 1890–1964), vol. XV, pp. 74–5; *Calendar of the patent and close rolls of chancery in Ireland*, James Morrin (ed.) (Dublin and London, 1861–2), vol. II, pp. 125, 129.

fighting Spain at sea and supporting the Netherlands rebels put together.[4] And it might have been avoidable, or at least not so catastrophic, had faction and gender not become mixed up with the demands of honour. Ultimately these letters reveal, as the crisis unfolds, a case of the emperor's new clothes. It is Elizabeth herself who is exposed; in the end the ever increasing torrent of her complaints against officials there leads one to question her political judgement as well.

The background to this situation was the end to programmatic government with the deputyship of Sir John Perrot in the mid 1580s. Perrot's policy – a combination of all the programmes engaged in the previous half-century – was as expansive as his personality; he was independently wealthy as well as independently minded. But war with Spain entailed retrenchment in Ireland and an end to his schemes – in particular for a composition to complete the reform of Ulster. This was made more difficult when Hugh O'Neill went to court in 1587 and persuaded the queen to grant him a very large patent to the earldom of Tyrone. The queen not only seems to have been susceptible to O'Neill's charms but also to have been influenced by Leicester (probably) and Ormond (possibly) in his favour. In the new situation Perrot was forced into a containment policy in the north, most notably by kidnapping and imprisoning O'Neill's son-in law, Red Hugh O'Donnell. Also tensions, which had been latent in the government between Perrot and New English councillors, now broke out into furious and at times violent rows. Nevertheless, when Perrot left in the summer of 1588 and when the Spanish Armada was shipwrecked shortly afterwards, Ireland was under control and relatively quiet.[5]

Fitzwilliam, who was appointed his successor, had no set policy, at least not initially, apart from keeping costs down. Furthermore, it quickly became clear that Perrot continued to exercise influence over Irish policy and may have been angling for a new appointment to finish the job he had started in 1584. Fitzwilliam who had been a stop-gap before in 1572–5, sandwiched between two of Sidney's stints in office, had no wish to suffer a repetition. As a result a conspiracy was launched with the assistance of Fitzwilliam's patron in England, Lord Burghley, to stop Perrot. The main allegation was that Perrot had connived with a priest called Denis O'Roughan to assist a Spanish invasion. The priest produced a letter which Perrot had supposedly written to the king offering his support in return for the grant of Wales. This forgery was completely ridiculous

[4] HMC, *Salisbury*, XV, pp. 1–2; Deeper analysis is available in Paul Hammer, *Elizabeth's wars: war, government and society in Tudor England, 1544–1604* (Basingstoke, 2003), pp. 240–5.

[5] Hiram Morgan, *Tyrone's rebellion: the outbreak of the Nine Years War in Tudor Ireland* (Woodbridge, 1993), ch. 2.

but in the course of the investigations expletive remarks were revealed
in which Perrot had made derisory comments about female government
when he received countermanding orders as lord deputy from the queen.[6]
When these remarks reached the queen, Perrot's career was effectively
over. His show trial in Westminster Hall was preceded by that of Brian
O'Rourke, an Irish chief, whom he had previously supported in a dispute
with the provincial president, Sir Richard Bingham. O'Rourke had been
accused of getting his galloglasses to chop up an image of the queen as
well as assisting Armada survivors. Perrot did not follow O'Rourke to
Tyburn – although he was condemned as a traitor, the queen allowed
Perrot to die a prisoner in the Tower.[7]

As a result, Ireland had nearly six years of the bribe-taking Fitzwilliam
as chief governor. At first he was inclined to pardon O'Neill's misde-
meanours. It was said that he received a large jewel after the earl had
executed a rival, Hugh Gavelach MacShane, and the queen too had
acquiesced in this after O'Neill visited court, even though Perrot and
the Irish judges, who were there, were trying to force a composition on
him and the north. Instead a more makeshift policy came into operation,
with Fitzwilliam working hand in hand with Sir Henry Bagenal, another
rival of O'Neill, based in Newry. In 1591 Fitzwilliam used his power
to grant commissions to make Bagenal, unbeknownst to London, chief
commissioner of Ulster. This might have been a rather innocuous title,
but at the same time Sir Henry succeeded his father as marshal of the
queen's army in Ireland for which he had a reversionary grant. Instead of
having an overall composition *à la* Connaught to support a neutral lord
president, a piecemeal reform began in Monaghan with the execution of
MacMahon and the division of the lordship from which Bagenal bene-
fited with lands, Fitzwilliam by bribes, and the Exchequer by revenue.
The queen had agreed to MacMahon's execution for march offences and
was pleased with the financial outcome but even Sir Richard Bingham,
the notorious governor of Connaught, thought the Monaghan settlement
had been 'painfully effected'. When O'Neill managed the escape of Red
Hugh from Dublin Castle the next year, and when Catholic bishops
returned from Spain, the scene was set for confrontation.[8]

The queen's reaction to the crisis can be seen in letters addressed
to her 'Right Trusty and Well-beloved' instruments in Dublin. In June
1593 the state's hearings in Dundalk had accused O'Neill of assisting

[6] Oxford, Bodleian Library, Willis MS 58, fols. 247–8, 263–305.

[7] Morgan, 'The fall of Sir John Perrot', in John Guy (ed.), *The reign of Elizabeth I: court and
culture in the last decade* (Cambridge, 1995), pp. 109–25. My view of this case has been
somewhat altered in the light of discussions with Professor Wallace MacCaffrey.

[8] Morgan, *Tyrone's rebellion*, ch. 3.

the revolt of Maguire and of engaging in foreign conspiracy with the Catholic bishops, but he was excused, having agreed to suppress Maguire. However, at Dundalk the Irish council, with few troops and little money, had felt threatened by O'Neill's power, and Fitzwilliam was ill and was applying to leave office. The queen told Fitzwilliam and his council: 'we have found many causes of great misliking in the manner of your proceedings both to our dishonour and the comfort of notable offendors'. She had obviously formed conclusions from reading the depositions: 'he aspiring to that Tyrannical government as it seemeth by the depositions he doth, the informers shall for fear of him, have cause to go back on their confessions or hereafter not to adventure to do the like' and went on to condemn Fitzwilliam and the council not only for their failure to charge O'Neill with notable crimes but also for their appointment of him to deal with Maguire, his confederate in those crimes. In the same letter, she also accepted Fitzwilliam's resignation.[9] However, there was an addendum to the letter. She had now received Tyrone's version of events in which he made accusations against Bagenal and Fitzwilliam, and as a result she accepted his suggestion of having his case referred to the perusal of the Irish judges. Clearly the letter O'Neill had written to the earl of Essex – 'mine only best friend'– had done the trick.[10] So the crisis rumbled on with O'Neill covering himself by more and more charges against Fitzwilliam, whom the queen for some reason had not moved to replace.

When Maguire had been defeated with O'Neill bravely but reluctantly serving against him, it was decided that O'Donnell be reduced as well. It was the queen's suggestion that the earl on account of ties of marriage and dependence should deal with O'Donnell on the crown's behalf. Maybe the queen had set the earl a test – at first refusing to comply point blank, he in the end agreed to take O'Donnell to the commissioners at Dundalk. The meeting in Dundalk has been misunderstood as the earl being forced into rebellion by his underlings. It was more like a choreographed charade to confuse the state. However, the commissioners – Adam Loftus, Sir Robert Gardiner, and Sir Anthony St Leger – concluded that the Ulstermen were at the earl's command and that their combination was caused by the Monaghan settlement and the earl's hatred of Bagenal. They advised prompt action: either concessions, in particular the grant of some form of authority to the earl, or a rapid prosecution of O'Neill and his followers.[11] The response of the authorities in London was to ignore

---

[9] SP 63/170/36; *Acts of the privy council*, vol. XXIV, pp. 364–9.
[10] SP 63/170/15, 15(1), 16, 36; *Acts of the privy council*, vol. XXIV, pp. 364–9.
[11] *CSPI*, V, pp. 221–2; SP 63/173/89.

the urgency of the situation and the weight of the commissioners' letter and instead to put their own gloss on the events in Dundalk. The queen found the manner of proceedings with O'Neill, in particular Gardiner's private meetings and special pleadings with him, to be 'derogatory to our honour' and a 'disgrace to us in government'. She ordered a different approach. Since the earl had agreed to restrain his followers, he should be required to appear before the Irish council as soon as possible in the knowledge that Fitzwilliam was being replaced and Bagenal was being warned off. This was in fact another test of loyalty, and in case the earl failed it she was calling up 1,500 troops to be sent to Ireland.[12]

Whilst the Dundalk meeting was in progress, the queen had decided that Sir Richard Bingham and Sir Robert Gardiner should succeed the ailing lord deputy as lords justice. However, when the appointment arrived, Fitzwilliam, who had long been a suitor for revocation, refused to hand over the reins of power. He seized upon the clause in the queen's letter relating to a recovery in his health. Whatever Fitzwilliam's motivations – presumably he feared charges of maladministration – his decision to remain in office was a major blow to the crown's dealings with O'Neill.[13] The earl had been given a pretext to excuse himself from the Irish council and an opportunity to consolidate his position in the north. At the end of April 1594 the queen was in a fury at Fitzwilliam's action. She marvelled at his sudden recuperation after allegedly being at death's door. He had no right to elect governors or upset policies which were predicated upon his recall. She announced that Sir William Russell, the former governor of Flushing, would be his successor as lord deputy.[14]

This was quite an extraordinary choice. Essex's man for the job, Russell had no experience at executive level and his only experience of Ireland was a year as head of a horse troop during the Baltinglass revolt. Since he was given neither extra resources to prosecute O'Neill nor concessions to make to him, the assumption seems to have been that this blue blood – he was second son of the earl of Bedford – would somehow impress the rebellious Irish lords into submission. By the time Russell arrived in August to take the sword from Fitzwilliam, the general instructions he had were out of date, and he was reliant entirely on the experience of the Irish council when O'Neill came to make his submission. Even though Cormac, the earl's brother, had only a few days before defeated government forces attempting to relieve the besieged garrison at Enniskillen, the earl was allowed to return to the north in the expectation that he

---

[12] University Library Cambridge (hereafter in this chapter ULC) MS Kk 1 15 no. 17 fols. 58–9.
[13] SP 63/173/85; SP 63/174/18.   [14] ULC MS Kk 1 15 no.18 fols. 59–60.

would promote peace. He had come to the meeting having first obtained word of safe return and at the meeting itself the intervention of Bagenal enabled him to play the victim. In fact, a good number of the councillors were old friends or in his pay, and the state was virtually defenceless.[15] Although Russell had deferred to the majority view of the Irish council in not detaining O'Neill, it was plain to every other observer that he had called their bluff and would go back to Ulster in triumph. Elizabeth was infuriated when she heard that her council in Ireland had not taken the opportunity to arrest the earl of Tyrone. She attributed the council's decision to 'fear, faction or corruption'; and, applying a double standard in relation to keeping one's word, she continued her lacerating letters on the matter for nearly a year terming it 'as foul an oversight as ever was committed in that kingdom'.[16]

At the time she wrote a separate letter to her new lord deputy. In her opinion 'this slight manner of proceeding both eclipsed the greatness of our estate there and served to glorify him, to the comfort of all his followers and to the amazement of those who have opposed themselves against him'. She knew how status-conscious the Irish were and how that decision would serve to puff up O'Neill. She reminded him that he had been specifically instructed at Theobald's before his departure to beware of the earl's promises and not to dismiss him without adequate answers. That advice must have been given *viva voce* because it is not in his written instructions. Russell was then given a lesson in statecraft that all treasons were necessarily contrived in secret and that it was his duty to uphold the dignity of the sovereign's rule. Nevertheless, the queen was willing to give Russell the benefit of the doubt. She recognised that he had yielded to the experience of others and advised him in the future to be wary of those councillors 'tied by nature or country's bond'. She also added a personal note in her own hand: 'Good Will, let not others neglect what they should make you for company do, what is not fit, and above all things, hold up the dignity of a king's rule which more consists in awe than liberty, which honours more a prince than fears a traitor. God bless you and send you mend what hath been amiss.'[17] One could quote this whole letter; it shows just how knowledgeable the queen was about Irish affairs and what a shrewd politician she was. On the other hand, one

[15] SP 63/175/56; SP 63/176/16, 33, 40; Thomas Lee, 'Brief declaration of the government of Ireland . . . 1594', in *Desiderata Curiosa Hibernica*, John Lodge (ed.), 2 vols. (Dublin, 1772), vol. I, pp. 101–2, 115–16. On bribery, see Paul Walsh (ed. and trans.) *The Life of Aodh Ruadh Ó Domhnaill, transcribed from the Book of Lughaidh Ó Clérigh*, 2 vols. (Dublin, 1948–57), vol. I, p. 27; SP 63/176/60(11).

[16] ULC MS Kk 1 15, no. 31, fols. 87–9; no. 28, fols. 81–2.

[17] ULC MS Kk 1 15, no. 29, fols. 82–3.

must ask why she had sent Russell with no experience, no money, and no soldiers into such a difficult situation. Thus, one must wonder not just about the quality of the decision-making of the lord deputy and the Irish council in this instance but also about the quality of the queen's own decision-making in the appointment of her chief governor there.

The slide to war was now seemingly unstoppable. O'Neill wanted Chief Justice Gardiner to go to England. However, the queen was opposed to 'a person of that quality and place' being absent at such a time and wondered at the earl's interest in his mission. The adventurer Captain Thomas Lee was in England, and he made a case for a compromise settlement.[18] The English government was reluctant to fight a major war in Ireland, with the Cecils favouring a peaceful resolution. Sir Robert referred to 'the unfitness to make war' and his father, Lord Treasurer Burghley, regretted that the queen was unwilling to concede a grant of authority to the earl linked to payment of the revenues due to her in Ulster.[19] A key criterion dictating the queen's decision was the matter of honour. At the end of October, the queen was enraged that a subject such as O'Neill should talk in terms of 'truce and peace', and she now instructed the Irish council to make one final demand for his submission in person or else he would be proclaimed a traitor.[20] The council's subsequent letter made their mistress's disposition plain to the earl of Tyrone: 'Her Majesty finding in her princely wisdom how far her honour is touched in the eye of the world, with these foul disorders of Ulster and your bad course holden therein.'[21] Given that the queen wanted him arrested, there was no way he was going to comply. As a result, she decided to redeploy to Ireland 2,000 of her troops then serving in Brittany.[22] Although the transfer of these troops was subject to countless delays and it was not until 18 March that the first companies arrived in Ireland, the queen's reasoning remained consistent: 'we are constrained (for our honour's sake) to be at the charge of sending over new great forces'.[23] In January she still held out some hopes of achieving the earl's compliance.[24] But when his men attacked the Blackwater fort on 16 February 1595, he had to be proclaimed a traitor.[25]

The queen now made another perplexing appointment. In April 1595 she announced the dispatch of Sir John Norris to act as general in the lord deputy's absence even though there had been disputes between the two men dating back to their time in the Netherlands. Sir Robert

[18] Lee, 'Brief declaration', pp. 89–90, 98–102, 107–8, 115–16, 140–5, 149–50.
[19] ULC MS Kk 1 15 no. 30, fol. 85; Ee 3 56, no. 32.
[20] ULC MS Ee 3 56, no. 32; Kk 1 15 no. 31, fols. 87–8; SP 63/177/30(1).
[21] SP 63/177/30(1).   [22] *CSPD*, III, p. 564.   [23] ULC MS Kk 1 15 no. 38, fols. 97–8.
[24] HMC, *Salisbury*, V, pp. 80–1.   [25] SP 63/178/53(5)68, 84, 100.

Cecil described this appointment as 'a matter of form' to place Norris over the other military men in Ireland.[26] Russell had indeed requested the assistance of a 'martial man' but he and Lord Chancellor Loftus would have preferred Bingham to Norris. In Loftus's view, Bingham was better suited 'for this broken and running service', more easily managed, and not likely to demand a large stipend for himself and an entourage.[27] Neither Russell nor Loftus mentioned the crucial factional alignment: like themselves, Bingham depended on Essex, while Norris had strong connections with the Cecils. Norris received his commission as lord general in June. He was empowered to exercise full martial law, parley with rebels, and grant protections and pardons. Not surprisingly, the drafting of this commission occasioned a quarrel. According to Norris, Russell at first refused to sign claiming that 'it was prejudicial to his patent'. By turns, Russell blamed the row on Norris's discontent with the terms in his commission.[28] Whatever the incidental details, the real fault lay with the original decision of the queen and her privy council in London to divide the command. Even though the queen provided detailed instructions about how the war should be waged, the decision itself was more important in the long run.

The campaign against O'Neill, already slowed down by Norris's reluctance to take up the new post in Ireland, was therefore stymied by a division of crown forces. After an initial joint campaign as far as Armagh, Norris was left to take on Hugh O'Neill while Russell was able to continue a personal obsession with the far less significant Feagh MacHugh O'Byrne. Not surprisingly, the ill-coordinated and inadequate crown war machine soon ground to a halt. With the state forced back to the negotiating table, O'Neill was then able to take full advantage of the divisions between Russell and Norris and the distance from court. At first the English authorities wanted grovelling submissions from the Irish, reductions in their patents, and even reparations. The capture of O'Neill's messenger en route to Spain changed all that. A note of urgency is apparent in the queen's letter of 16 October 1595. Since the traitors wanted Spanish assistance by May 1596, Russell and Norris were to put aside the 'causeless formalities' between them and to proceed with full-scale negotiations as soon as possible.[29] The shift of emphasis is detectable in her instruction to bargain with O'Neill rather than simply force terms upon him. With intelligence reports arriving about Spanish fleets being prepared in the peninsula, London demanded prompt and concerted action by the Irish administration in the matter without any referral back to

---

[26] ULC MS Kk 1 15 no. 40, fols. 99–100.   [27] SP 63/178/82, 98, 130.
[28] SP 63/181/43, 48.   [29] ULC MS Kk 1 15 no. 56, fols. 121–2.

London. With time at a premium, the queen quickly became displeased about the delay in starting negotiations with the Irish confederates. The problems between lord deputy and lord general continued to mount. Norris stormed back to Munster and, even though Russell knew of the queen's willingness to grant pardons by 1 December, he waited until a meeting of the council eighteen days later before notifying O'Neill and O'Donnell. Russell admitted to Burghley that he had not been anxious to deal with Tyrone as he had shown himself completely untrustworthy in the past, and in any case the conduct of Ulster affairs had been handed over to Norris. It was less fair for the queen to blame the delays on the Irish council as a whole. The English privy council backed her up, accusing the members of its counterpart of occupying 'the room of dumb councillors' because they constantly referred matters to London. In fact, it was the queen's criticisms and exceptions which had made the Irish council, as a body and as individuals, so tentative in their dealings with Tyrone.[30]

Elizabeth's criticisms continued. With the fall of Monaghan, the niceties being used with O'Neill and the lack of information, let alone any initiative from Ireland, the queen rounded on her lord deputy and council about 'things too common in foreign service'. 'It is conceived by many that either you are all become so stupid and senseless, as you know not how to order things, or else that there are grown such suspicious jealousies amongst you that one or the other that either you are bent purposely to cross each other in your courses and counsels or careless what be done or committed so as you may pass the blame from one to the other.'[31] For his part, O'Neill simply took advantage of the time-wasting rivalry of Russell and Norris to make military gains and of the queen's own promise of a pardon to make big demands when negotiations began with Gardiner and Henry Wallop, the government's commissioners, in January 1596. Then, when Gardiner went to England to brief the queen and the privy council, she refused to admit him into her presence because of the dishonourable way in which he and Wallop had conducted the negotiations. She frowned upon her councillors taking part in meetings in open country at the behest of rebels and disliked their use of 'your loving friends' and 'your very good lord' in letters to rebels. Most of all, she was displeased that they had condescended to conclude a truce, let alone meet with rebels, after the latter had sent in such insolent demands. In the queen's view, the actions of her commissioners were 'utterly repugnant to all royal considerations'. Yet Gardiner's mission proved successful in spite of the queen's public stance. The Irish chief justice acquitted

[30] Morgan, *Tyrone's rebellion*, pp. 94–7.   [31] ULC MS Kk 1 15, no. 61, fols. 126–7.

himself well before the privy council and as a result his views were relayed to the queen. So the queen received the message but blamed the messenger. Gardiner had also made accusations against Fitzwilliam, and another way out of the honour fix the queen had put herself in was to blame the former governor for causing the situation in the first instance. Because of 'great extremities and most hard courses offered unto them by you', she now ordered Fitzwilliam to supply answers to the complaints being made by the Ulster lords.[32]

With a possibility of Spanish intervention in Ireland and worries about France concluding a separate peace with the enemy, the queen decided at the start of March 1596 to commission Norris along with Fenton 'to proceed with them to some final end'.[33] While the commissioners could use considerable latitude in reaching an agreement, they were to uphold the queen's honour to the utmost. Writing to Norris 'who ought to know what is true honour', she demanded 'that the place and manner may as little derogate from us, as you can devise, considering you and the rest are sent from a Sovereign to a pack of rebels'.[34] In the conditions then being prepared by Cecil, only liberty of conscience 'a matter meet for no subject to require' was off limits. Basically concessions could be made *sotto voce*, so long as the façade of the queen's honour was maintained. Thus in the second half of April agreements between Norris and Fenton on behalf of the crown and O'Neill and O'Donnell on behalf of the Irish confederates were patched up. The queen's honour was maintained this time because the talks were conducted through intermediaries – what today are called proximity talks. And although there were many loose ends, the queen in the middle of May signalled her approval in the hope that the confederates would quickly take their pardons and make their submissions so as to cut them off from Spanish blandishments.[35]

Believing her honour against the rebels and safety against Spain to have been secured, she would now turn to that other aspect of kingship, dispensing justice – in this case to the poor oppressed people not only in Ulster but also in Connaught, where she was willing to put Bingham on trial if necessary. Knowing Russell to be opposed to the settlement, she now urged the Irish government to unite in this work of pacification.[36] However, it was already becoming clear that Spanish agents had met O'Neill and O'Donnell in Donegal with an alternative offer. While Russell could claim he read the situation correctly, Norris and Fenton were left defending a peace process in which they had invested heavily, even

---

[32] Morgan, *Tyrone's rebellion*, pp. 201–2.
[33] LPL, (Carew Papers) MS 612, fol. 67; also ULC Kk 115 no. 64, fol. 177.
[34] SP 63/187/24.   [35] ULC MS Kk 1 15 no. 69, fol. 196.   [36] SP 63/189/43.

after Tyrone failed to make a personal submission, and as details of his meeting with the Spaniards continued to leak out. Norris asserted that it was the opposition of Russell and others which gave the confederates rather 'occasion of jealousy than encouragement to obedience'. He was willing to think the best of O'Neill and reminded the queen how Henry IV had recently won over the Catholic League magnates of France by 'commandments, honours and rewards'.[37] The divisions apparent between Norris and Russell in wartime now became unbridgeable as a result of the peace process. When O'Neill went back on the offensive in the autumn of 1596 in the expectation of a Spanish landing, the queen was left with no option other than to revoke both Russell and Norris from office.

According to the queen, there was 'never any realm worse governed by all our ministers from the highest to the lowest', and as a result she was sending Sir William Burgh, another Essex man and Netherlands veteran, to remedy the situation.[38] With Burgh, the queen at last seems to have got the man she needed in Ireland. Immediately on taking the sword of office on 22 May, Burgh acted with urgency. He was not going to be deflected by any of O'Neill's wiles, which had humiliated the queen and frustrated her service so often in the past. This tough-minded Protestant regarded the Irish as barbarous people who, if they were not treated firmly, were always going to take advantage any way possible. He held that the only means of breaking the Irish rebellion was to attack its source in Ulster by establishing garrisons there to tie down the chief rebel until he was ultimately vanquished. When O'Neill wrote to him requesting implementation of the agreement with Norris which Russell had allegedly frustrated, Burgh told him in no uncertain terms that he had never been held back from returning to his allegiance. Both Russell and – in the end – Norris had realised that O'Neill was waiting for the fulfilment of Spanish promises. No longer would he be allowed to pervert Her Majesty's offers of clemency and to animate and combine with others in irreligious and disloyal actions. She who had defeated the king of Spain in his enterprise against the realm and had attacked him in his own heartland was not going to let an internal rebel like Tyrone go unchastised. He should not presume on the strength of his bogs or bushes but look into his conscience. 'It is high time', he concluded, 'you have remorse in your soul, and prostrate yourself for mercy, lest the heavy stroke of your sacred queen inflict that which no guilty mind can resist nor obdurate avoid. Leaving with yourself how to value that which is best for you, I end these. By me, Her Majesty's subject

---

[37] ULC MS Kk 1 15 fols. 220–5; *CSPI*, VI, pp. 48–59.   [38] SP 63/198/100.

and servant, and Deputy and Governor-General in this her Realm, *T. Burgh.*'[39]

Burgh's exploits thrilled the court in England, and Cecil wrote to him on the queen's behalf. His letters and actions were praised, and the queen was agreeable for him to knight men who had fought alongside him if he sent over their names. 'Believe me, therefore, that this is true; Her Majesty's conceit of you is infinitely raised and by nothing more than you promise as well to look to the reformation of expense as to make war.' The queen, though congratulatory about the forward policy, was worried about his risk-taking: 'You are a deputy, and in you her person represented, to which you must look, not to hazard any more than of necessity, which now she knew you could not avoid.'[40] Burgh did indeed seem to represent the right stuff. O'Neill tried again to make overtures to the lord deputy as he completed the building of a new royal fort on Blackwater, only to receive another verbal lashing from the queen's representative:

To the contents of your letter, you say you seek peace; a proud word to your Sovereign, wherein you are as false as unwise. The conditions of peace are to be propounded between equals; from you, the proposition to be made is to ask forgiveness, which as you dutifully crave not, it argues your meaning to be treacherous; and as the phrase wanteth comeliness, so it signifieth you have as little wit as honesty. To be short, Her Majesty hath committed me to the rule of this kingdom, wherein her princely charge was that I should cherish her good subjects, and chastise those who, by their own pride, would not be conformable to law and obedience ... The capital of these troubles in this common weal you manifestly declare yourself to be; wherefore I must, as I am bound in allegiance, care to reduce Her Majesty's people, whom you have led out of the way; and as there is no other remedy to save them, I must pursue you; from the vengeance whereof all your popish shaven priests shall never absolve you, God destroying the counsels of the wicked taken against his anointed.[41]

Yet for all of Burgh's rhetoric and bravery, he could not win the honour which he and the queen so desired; these stirring attributes could not make up for the fact that he was operating on the edge of his resources. Taking and fortifying the Blackwater was his high point; he was very soon thereafter running short of options. In fact he had achieved all he could with the men and money the queen had afforded him. Frustration with O'Neill and aggravation with his government were already setting in. He rarely consulted his council and had not even shown them his instructions, and he had physically struck Sir William Warren who had

[39] SP 63/199/81(2); *CSPI*, VI, pp. 306–9.   [40] *CSPI*, VI, p. 361.
[41] *Ibid.*, VI, pp. 385–6.

acted as intermediary with Tyrone. In September Cecil wrote to him about his autocratic manner, his rashness, and his demands for men and money.[42] The idea that later emerged – that Burgh was having too much success and O'Neill therefore had some of his friends poison him – can be easily dismissed.[43] He died of a fever at Newry in October 1597 and, indeed, had he not done so at that juncture, he would almost certainly either have been killed in battle or ended up – hoist by his own petard – like Sir John Perrot.

Burgh's sudden death left the queen's Irish policy completely unhinged. It was not until the spring of 1599 – a full eighteen months' gap – that Essex arrived as chief governor. Ireland was being governed in the interim in a completely disjointed fashion, with Loftus and Gardiner as lord justices heading the civil establishment and the earl of Ormond as lord lieutenant general in charge of military affairs. As they attempted intermittently to negotiate with and to fight O'Neill, things drifted from dangerous to downright disastrous. It need not have been thus. In the fraught military and political situation immediately following Burgh's death, the Irish council had appointed Thomas Norris, then on his way to take over as president of Munster, as lord justice. He was elected – contrary to his own wishes, apparently – in accordance with the statute of 34 Henry VIII because he was 'a person in our conceits tempered both for martial affairs and civil government'.[44] However, the queen thought differently – she had already decided on the triumvirate, and so Norris was packed off to his province. Plainly the queen was not going to permit the exercise of sovereignty by any authority other than herself, nor was she going to let one faction – the Cecils – gain the Irish post *faute de mieux*. And even though the English parliament was offering fresh subsidies, having the lords justice and lord lieutenant general was a way of keeping costs down, whereas as a single governorship necessarily entailed men and money whether its holder was waging war or not. The latter was evident to Norris himself when he said either 'some man of sufficiency may be sent over to take this charge, or if the Queen shall be pleased to continue me in it, I may be supplied as is requisite or others have been'.[45]

Instead, the queen sent Ormond and his colleagues instructions for defence and containment as well as various nit-picking minutiae via her privy council about matters in the army.[46] This coincided with Fenton, the Irish secretary, advising that 'it was time to consider whether

---

[42] *Ibid.*, VI, p. 398.
[43] Hiram Morgan, 'Hugh O'Neill – not guilty', *Dúiche Néill: Journal of the O'Neill Country Historical Society* 18 (2010), 29–34.
[44] SP 63/201/38. Under the statute, the appointee had to be an English-born servitor.
[45] SP 63/201/60.   [46] *CSPI*, VI, pp. 450–1.

a milder course were more convenient for a time, to break the knot of these treasons, then to depend further upon prosecution by arms, which you see hath done nothing hitherto to stay the evil, but rather hath increased it, almost to a sensible hazard of the loss of the whole',[47] and with the fact that peace negotiations were in prospect in France, which offered an opportunity of lessening the Spanish threat. Furthermore, the victualling of the Blackwater fort, which Burgh had re-established in O'Neill's territory, necessarily meant harkening to the Irish requests for another round of negotiations, in which case the appointment of Ormond, a former patron of Tyrone, seemed at last to identify a man who might be trusted by both the O'Neill and the queen of England. If the crown was hoping that Ormond would perform at a national level the role he had played at the conclusion of the second Desmond war, it was mistaken, because the role he had played then led the Irish to be wary of him.[48]

The peace negotiations – of which we have very good accounts from Bishop Thomas Jones, one of the government commissioners – ended up further undermining the crown's authority. At the outset, O'Neill was able to dictate the terms of his submission and then to argue over the ceasefire conditions as if he were an independent potentate. His demands in relation to the ceasefire, wrote Jones, 'were so crooked and untoward, as we were forced to enter into a particular debating of every article, and of his answer thereunto, and by reasoning we procured him to alter some of his answers in some few points; but notwithstanding such correction, as we procured from him of those answers, they still remain very unseemly and undutiful to proceed from a subject'.[49] When O'Neill refused to give one of his sons as a hostage, the negotiators reminded him of the assistance he had received from the queen as a young man. 'Hereunto he answered most ungratefully, that Her Majesty had given him nothing but what belonged unto him, and he ascribed the things which he had gotten to his own scratching in the world than Her Majesty's goodness.'[50] O'Neill further enraged the government side when in the afternoon of 22 December he submitted a 'humble petition' containing general demands.[51] Fenton said that O'Neill's petition contained things of such arrogance that it was 'neither

[47] *Ibid.*, p. 438.
[48] O'Neill was warned by his secretary, Henry Hovenden, that 'hast thou no body to treat with of the conditions of peace but the earl of Ormond? Who having like commission in the Earl of Desmond's time, to treat with him concerning the peace, did underhand clip his wings, and did draw his followers from him, and when he had so done, did quite overthrow Desmond, his house and posterity' (*ibid.*, VII, p. 120).
[49] SP 63/201/122.   [50] *CSPI*, VI, pp. 483–4.   [51] SP 63/201/114.

meet for a rebel to prefer to his Prince nor fit for any good servitor to receive'.[52]

O'Neill had demanded liberty of conscience. When it was read out as first item on the list in Tyrone's 'humble petition', the lord lieutenant general said, 'My lord, what have you and I to meddle in matters of religion.' Asked why he dared to prefer such articles, O'Neill said that he made the motion not on behalf of himself and O'Donnell 'but for all the Catholics of the land'. Even though Ormond insisted that he would throw the petition into the first fire he came across, O'Neill knew that its airing was a means of applying pressure on the government. Jones concluded that the demand 'showeth his drift to become popular amongst this idolatrous people'.[53] O'Neill also brought up the rights of his confederates to ancestral lands, which in the particular case of the O'Mores and O'Connors, entailed a direct challenge to the plantation of Laois and Offaly. These general demands were backed up by a book of grievances which was a list of abuses and treacherous dealings the Irish elite had suffered as regards lives and lands since the 1550s.[54] The negotiators were taken aback – Secretary Fenton said that O'Neill had dragged up 'these old sores of the kingdom, to draw a popularity to himself and to give him scope to be the head of all dangerous factions in the realm, and to bind and loose at his pleasure'.[55] Jones, for his part, called O'Neill 'a most dangerous, cunning and crafty traitor' and listed nineteen reasons for this opinion 'grounded upon Tyrone's insolent behaviour and carriage in this parley before so honourable a personage as the lord lieutenant is (who used all things with great honour and gravity) and before us being councillors to Her Majesty of this state'.[56]

In spite of Jones's conclusions, the council in Dublin believed that the negotiation route had to be pursued; the army was in a lamentable state and, if Ormond was given plenipotentiary powers, O'Neill might still prove amenable. Indeed, Fenton thought that peace was urgently needed to re-establish government on a proper footing after three years of the disjointing and costly effects of war.[57] In a letter to Ormond on 29 December, then on its way to Ireland, the queen had already signalled her willingness to right the legitimate grievances and expressed her confidence in Ormond's ability to uphold her dignity: 'we are not so alienated from hearkening to such submission as may tend to the sparing of effusion of Christian blood, but that we can be content, in imitation of God Almighty (whose minister we are here on earth, and who forgiveth all

---

[52] *CPSI*, VI, p. 478.   [53] *Ibid.*, VI, pp. 487–90.
[54] Bodleian Library, Laud MS (Miscellaneous) 612, fols. 55–9.   [55] SP 63/201/117.
[56] SP 63/201/122.   [57] *CPSI*, VII, pp. 1–8.

sins) to receive the penitent and humble submission of those traitors that pretend to crave it; wherein we doubt not but you, that are of noble blood and birth, will so carry all things in the manner of your proceedings, as our honour may be specially preserved in all your actions'.[58] When, the following month, the queen was shown all O'Neill's demands, including that for liberty of conscience, she of course spurned the latter as an infringement of her prerogative. However, she was willing to offer some concessions by proposing to inquire into the claims of the O'Mores and O'Connors and to give O'Neill his pardon in the hope of whittling down his demands and of separating him as patron of the rest. 'Her Majesty is moved in compassion of the miseries of that realm to extend her mercy and favour in a larger sort than otherwise the offences of her rebels by any kind of submission can deserve.'[59] This was quite remarkable because O'Neill and his allies were no longer complaining about local grievances and the dealings of specific officials but challenging the whole of English policy towards Ireland since the start of Elizabeth's reign. The queen's apparent flexibility in relation to Ireland may relate to the possibility of a positive outcome to the multi-lateral peace talks then underway in France, but the hopes that she harboured in both directions were to be dashed.

O'Neill used delaying tactics to make the most of the ceasefire in Ireland. While the crown's northern garrisons were low on supplies and near mutiny, a proxy war was proceeding in Leinster as Ormond tried to prevent O'Connor, O'More, and Richard Tyrrell taking advantage of the situation. Eventually talks resumed at Dundalk between 15 and 18 March, with the queen's offers being made to Tyrone, but he would not agree to anything unless his confederates were satisfied. O'Neill made vigorous claims for Onie O'More, whom he brought forward, and others, but the commissioners said they could not do this as it would have meant tearing up the plantation of Laois and Offaly, the division of the O'Reilly lands, and the composition of Connaught. At first, O'Neill was willing to see arbitration on these cases but, when at the end of the second day, he was asked to sign up to an agreement he baulked and refused to sign because O'Donnell was not there.[60] When O'Donnell turned up for the next session of talks a month later, the state was better prepared having just won over Brian Og O'Rourke from the confederate side and having captured correspondence between O'Neill and his Leinster allies.[61] At first the confederate side made much of the alleged internal pressure

[58] *Ibid.*, VI, pp. 490–1.   [59] *Ibid.*, VII, pp. 43–4.   [60] *Ibid.*, VII, pp. 86–96.
[61] *Ibid.*, VII, pp. 54–6, 109; Sir James Perrot, *The Chronicle of Ireland 1548–1608*, Herbert Wood (ed.) (Dublin, 1933), p. 146.

on O'Neill not to settle, but from the government intermediaries going into their camp, the commissioners concluded that 'all this was but a flourish'. In discussions, O'Neill and O'Donnell kept making demands for Tibbot Burke to be MacWilliam and have Mayo, but the government commissioners could not satisfy them in this. Then, suddenly, many of secondary figures in the confederate camp were arrested; it was put out that O'Neill and O'Donnell were collecting hostages for a ratification of the peace. Jones dismissed this as 'deep dissimulation' – it was obvious that they were more in favour of an agreement than their leaders and may even have been tempted by the example of O'Rourke's defection. The talks had in effect broken down with only a six-week truce concluded.

A further meeting on 17 April was very instructive. Jones found O'Neill and O'Donnell united, committed to Spain, and possessed of an escalating list of demands on behalf of their expanding alliance which he described as 'infinite'.[62] This was apparent when four days after the parley at Dundalk, O'Neill had the audacity to send Ormond another petition. He had now extended his demands to South Leinster where he wanted restitution to his confederates of lands which the Irish had not controlled since the Norman conquest. O'Neill was willing to act as guarantor for an agreement which would have included the release of prisoners such as priests and other individuals whom the state had deemed malefactors. According to Sir James Perrot, whose manuscript *Chronicle of Ireland* preserves the only summary of this missing document, the Ulster leader was setting himself up as 'this great arbitrator and (on his own conceit) governor, or rather monarch of the kingdom'.[63] Not surprisingly the Dublin government, holding firm to the articles prescribed by the queen, was against any further meetings with O'Neill.[64] Although the ceasefire was subsequently extended by another month, it was honoured more in the breach, especially in Leinster, with all eagerly awaiting the outcome of the talks in France. There, much to Cecil's chagrin, France and Spain made a separate bargain – what was eventually formalised as the Peace of Vervins. England had to fight on as it could not so readily abandon the Dutch as allies. As a result, it now had to act urgently to close the Irish back door, which O'Neill was holding ajar for the Spaniards, with the Ulster leader himself hoping that if England had to sue for peace on weaker terms his cause might be included too.[65] As a result, London committed itself to the much heralded Lough Foyle expedition to open up a new front behind Irish lines.

[62] *CSPI*, VII, pp. 116–20.   [63] Perrot, *Chronicle*, pp. 146–8.   [64] *CSPI*, VII, p. 141.
[65] HMC, *Salisbury*, VIII, p. 154; *CSPI*, VII, pp. 146, 173–4, 187.

In the midst of these negotiations, the queen was again criticising the Irish council's endeavours in 'this most unhappy government'. Her original letter of 17 March about disorders and divisions in government is missing, but we can divine from replies that these relate to the spending and allocation of the treasure being sent from England and the fears that it was being wasted on a large paper army, now mostly Irish, while the front-line soldiers starved and Ormond, who was doing the fighting, was not seeing the pay that was arriving in the civil authorities' coffers passed on for martial purposes. The lords justice contested 'the untrue informations which have been written or reported from hence' about disagreements between themselves or a division between the two of them and the lord lieutenant 'with whom we have cherished all good correspondency for the advancement of Her Majesty's service and for ourselves we have lived together as brethren'.[66] That said, there was clearly tension about the time that Ormond was spending in the midlands, which seemed to be holding up talks in the north. We have the letter of the full Irish council written on 4 May after Ormond had returned to Dublin to its English counterpart. It expressed thanks for pacifying the queen and obtaining her acceptance that it was the situation confronting her servants in Ireland and not the fault of the servants themselves. It contested vehemently the queen's superscript to her letter relating to alleged internal disagreements claiming that even though 'most parts of the realm stand divided and distracted, yet we have been careful amongst ourselves to hold firm unity and agreement'.[67] The lord lieutenant general, the lords justice, and the rest of the councillors insisted that they stood united, but the following six months would test their unity and performance to the limits.

Of course, there were divisions in Elizabeth's English privy council as well.[68] The return of Cecil from France, still favouring a peace with Spain, occasioned a heated debate with Essex, who remained committed to a full-scale offensive war with Europe's leading power. During Cecil's absence, Essex, encouraged by Francis Bacon,[69] had also begun to take a more active interest in Irish affairs and, when matters turned from Europe to Ireland at a privy council meeting in late June or early July 1598, the situation exploded. Camden's *Annals,* which is the only source for the famous incident, tell us that the queen was proposing Sir William Knollys as lord deputy of Ireland but that Essex favoured Sir George Carew, partly to get rid of him from court as he was an ally of the Cecils. When he failed

---

[66] SP 63/202/pt2, 19(1).   [67] SP 63/202/pt2, 26.
[68] MacCaffrey, *Elizabeth I*, ch. 32, esp. pp. 411–12.
[69] 'Sir Francis Bacon's MSS relating to Ireland', www.ucc.ie/celt/published/E600001–015/, docs. 3 and 4.

to win the argument, he turned his back in contempt. Then she cuffed him on the ear, at which he went for his sword. Fortunately, Howard, the lord admiral, intervened, and Essex hastened from court swearing that such an indignity would never have occurred under Henry VIII.[70] In the event no appointment was made. Certainly Ireland could have done with a single governor at this juncture, though it would in any case have been too late for such an appointee to have taken on the managing of the Lough Foyle venture or the relief of the beleaguered garrison at the Blackwater fort. The latter, of course, proved a complete disaster – Sir Henry Bagenal, the queen's marshal, and a large part of her army were routed at the Battle of Yellow Ford on 14 August 1598 – and as a result the soldiers intended for Lough Foyle had to be diverted to the northern borders of the Pale to shore up its defences. The privy council, hearing of the defeat and heeding the 'haste, haste, haste' importunings of its Dublin counterpart, had changed the orders and redirected the 2,000-strong expeditionary force instead to Carlingford. It also ordered a further additional levy of 2,000 men for Ireland.[71]

We can only imagine the queen's reaction to hearing the news of what was the greatest Irish victory ever over the arms of England. She was scathing in the next communication with her Irish government. 'Our cousin of Ormond' – who was known to have been in favour of abandoning the Blackwater fort rather than mounting a rescue mission[72] – was not spared:

It was strange to us, when almost the whole forces of our kingdom were drawn to head, and a main blow like to be stroken for our honour against the capital rebel, that you, whose person would have better daunted the traitors, and would have carried with it another manner of reputation, and strength of the nobility of the kingdom, should employ yourself in an action of less importance, and leave that to so mean a conduction. And therefore, whosoever of our Council should dissuade you from that course, lacked both judgment and affection to our service and did that which is repugnant to the writings of divers of the best and greatest of them in that kingdom.

The implication here was that Ormond was more concerned with his own lands in Leinster and that the rest of the council were primarily concerned with their own defence in the Pale. Certainly their fear was implicit and the weakness explicit in the letter which they wrote to O'Neill after his victory, begging his mercy for the men he had now trapped.[73]

---

[70] William Camden, *Annales Rerum Gestarum Angliae et Hiberniae Regnante Elizabetha* (London, 1615–25), sub anno 1598, on Dana F. Sutton's online edition, www.philological.bham.ac.uk/camden/.
[71] *CSPI*, VII, pp. 235–9.   [72] *Ibid.*, VII, pp. 212, 214, 225.   [73] *Ibid.*, VII, pp. 228–9.

Though it was in fact left undelivered, 'we may not pass over this foul error to our dishonour, when you of our Council framed such a letter to the traitor, after the defeat, as never was read the like, either in form or substance, for baseness, being such as we persuade ourself, if you shall peruse it again, when you are yourselves, that you will be ashamed of your own absurdities, and grieved that any fear or rashness should ever make you authors of an action so much to your Sovereign's dishonour, and to the increasing of the traitor's insolency'. Overall, the queen saw her Irish administration as completely discredited: 'yet is there no person, be he never of so vulgar judgment, but doth plainly see notorious errors in that Government'.[74]

Criticising and underpinning the Irish government by turns did not necessarily right the situation. It did manage to detect a conspiracy against the city and castle of Dublin and executed its leaders, but was unable to control events elsewhere.[75] In the south, Thomas Norris had long been demanding extra men and money from Dublin; the queen sent an express order to the Irish council via Cecil for the dispatch of reinforcements to Munster as a preventive measure.[76] It was already too late, and Norris himself was considered too slow in reacting as another sharp missive from the queen implied:

We have understood by divers reports, as well of your letters as also from our Council of State in Ireland, how strange a revolt is happened in our Province of Munster, a matter which we cannot deny to have been foreseen by you and written hither; and yet are you not freed by all reporters from this information; that in the beginning, when the first traitor drew to head with a ragged number of rogues and boys, you might better have resisted than you did, especially considering the many defensible houses and castles possessed by the undertakers who, for aught we can hear, were no way comforted nor supported by you; but either for lack of comfort from you, or out of mere cowardice, fled away before the rebels upon the first alarm.[77]

Finally, we have the queen's letter of 1 December 1599. She was fed up with receiving 'naught else but news of new losses and calamities in that state' and suffering affronts 'from a rabble of base kern', and had at last determined to send over a large army (which of course appeared increasingly likely to have Essex as its commander). In the meantime, she recommended reforms: 'to this end specially, that until those things may be sent (wherein no cost nor charge shall be spared, fit for a provident Prince to afford, in care for her loving subjects) such things may be reformed, and such course taken presently, as may serve to prepare a safe

[74] Ibid., VII, pp. 257–9.   [75] Ibid., VII, p. 308.
[76] Ibid., VII, p. 285.   [77] Ibid., VII, p. 379.

foundation for that great work which shall follow'. What remained of the supposed 9,000-strong army had to be properly trained, disciplined, and enumerated; army commanders were to stay in the area of operations. In particular, Ormond was to reside in Dublin. His 'being far remoted, in whose judgement most is reposed' had entailed delays as he was not always available when orders arrived or when consultations were necessary. Having the superintendency of military affairs, he was to ensure that the regional commanders were properly supplied and enabled. For now, the latter were to stand on the defensive, ensuring the security of the towns and vital fortifications, taking good pledges from any suspect lords or gentry, and protecting good subjects who had too long suffered oppression.[78]

The queen was great at heaping the blame on her Irish council, but she must shoulder a good part of it too. She had created the division of civil and military government which attempted to govern Ireland in the eighteen months between the death of Burgh and the arrival of Essex. That triumvirate obviously did not work. Plainly during this period she had one eye on the continent, hoping – vainly as it turned out – that an all-round peace might be established. She also did not want to spend money and knew that the English commons were suffering. Another reason for her indecision was the increasing factionalism that was plaguing her regime. The problem of Irish appointments in this regard is symbolised above all by the incident in the council chamber in which Essex lost his temper. That meant that a chief governor was not appointed until it was too late. Whether or not it would have prevented the defeat at the Yellow Ford and the subsequent overthrow of the Munster plantation is questionable, yet it indicates how faction had gained so great a sway over the queen's decisions about who she sent to Ireland. These were critical appointments and, even when they were made, they were obviously not always made for the right reason.

What do these letters tell us for the 1590s and for the queen's reign more generally? First, they show the queen to have been a very shrewd observer of Irish affairs: not least, she had decided that Tyrone was a traitor long before many of her councillors there. Second, it was her policies that had antagonised and then failed to contain this Irish leader, who was rapidly emerging as one of the most capable politicians and generals in the country's history. She had wanted an inexpensive but nevertheless activist government in Dublin upholding her honour against all challenges. These goals were incompatible – honour could not be maintained on the cheap – and they became completely unstuck when

[78] SP 63/202/pt 4, 1.

she had to fight at the same time on the continent, at sea, and in Ireland. Money, and the military power which flowed from it, was required to maintain and enhance a prince's honour. Henry IV of France, with the most populous and most taxable country in Europe, could afford a few indignities en route to gaining control. Philip II, who had the riches of the Indies, was obsessed with threats to his '*reputación*' but at least he saw the need to resile from this and make compromises in the last years of his reign. Elizabeth, on the other hand, in Ireland and against Spain, wished to maintain her honour to the bitter end. In maintaining 'honour', these monarchs had to choose the right individuals as representatives and actors of their behalf. In Elizabeth's case with Ireland, these appointments were not easy. She wanted men who were not too king-like but who would yet give off just enough authority to show the Irish who was in charge. Furthermore, and critically as regards competence, their appointment was becoming too much subject to faction, which was running out of control as the rival leaders jockeyed for position to back her successor. It was crucial that Ireland, the back door to England, had a governor, but for the pivotal year of 1598 it had none. This reflected on the queen's own competence. In many respects, the virgin queen was by the 1590s in a survivalist mode. One then must wonder about gender, and about the effects an expansive, dynastically inclined male monarch, even an English one, would have had for Ireland.

It was at this nadir in England's fortunes in Ireland that one of the few criticisms of the queen – and almost certainly the severest – was undertaken. Whereas most of the queen's letters have been available in the calendars of state papers for over a century, it is only recently that 'The supplication of the blood' saw the light of day thanks to the enterprise of the literary scholar Willy Maley. This anonymous 30,000-word tract was written by a highly talented and very angry individual in the immediate aftermath of the sudden collapse of the Munster plantation in October 1598. It had been the Elizabethan state's single largest project in Ireland and intended to transform the strategically sited, rebellion-prone southern province of Ireland. Now it had disintegrated in the space of forty-eight hours with the settlers in flight to the ports and over to England. The author, himself a settler, painted a shockingly vivid, almost apocalyptical picture of how the colony had been overwhelmed in an orgy of rape, murder, and destruction. He urged the queen – 'unto whom God hath committed the sword of Justice' – to fulfil her duty to punish the offenders and maintain and defend the innocent. According to the suppliant, the colonists planted 'among that faithless, unmerciful, idolatrous and unbelieving nation of the Irish' had been left undefended and now felt abandoned – 'these dangers we adventured upon the assurance of your princely care and motherly affection towards us, upon the assurance of your royal power and ready will to protect us'.[79] The subtle serpentine Irish were not just plotting the ruin of the colonists: their ultimate aim was 'to thrust Your Majesty from the possession of the throne, that is the mark they aim at'.[80]

The Irish had gained their successes so far because 'they have ever used yourself against yourself; in their dissembled subjection, they secretly undermined you with your own commissions, now in war they do openly assail you with your own weapons'.[81] This dispossessed settler highlighted how the Irish had for their own purposes perverted the English state's own institutions and law. They won any disputes with the English by telling straight lies and by swearing false oaths to commissions of enquiry and in the law courts. When they were unable to prevail 'by means of your own authority, to swear you out of the country... then fell they to open rebellion, then turned they their weapons that yourself had put into their hands, against yourself; they trained soldiers upon your charge, to cut the throats of your true subjects, they strengthened themselves with your cost to weaken you. Who made Tyrone so great a captain, his country beggars so expert soldiers but your bounty, your liberality, your allowance? Who trained the most dangerous rebels? Who made them so ready in matters of war but your own captains that by lived by your own pay?'[82] These Irish insurgent armies were operating everywhere in Ireland and had gained control of the most of it, save the towns, and they were not secure because their Catholic inhabitants could not be trusted. A second English conquest was needed. Delay had already been costly. Had Her Majesty been properly informed of even a fraction of these indignities the crown of England had sustained, 'the blood of your most renowned and magnanimous father remaining in you would have boiled out long ere this a revenge'. The queen's estate in Ireland was in its last hours without hope of restoration unless she used her God-given power, which had already redressed far greater enormities, to revenge and right the situation. He wondered why that honest and honourable governor, Lord Burgh, whose zeal towards God and the queen had promised such hope, had met such an untimely death? Why was it that English arms, which had won victories abroad in Spain, France, and the Low Countries, were unable to master such base traitors at home? He felt that the English were being punished for their sins – for allowing

---

[79] 'The supplication', 12 (BL 34313, fol. 85r).   [80] *Ibid.*, 14 (BL 34313, fol. 86r).
[81] *Ibid.* This quotation has been corrected after checking against the original – BL 34313, fol. 86r.
[82] *Ibid.*, p. 16 (BL 34313, fols. 87r–v).

religion to go unreformed in Ireland, for divisions in government to run unchecked, for pardons and protections to be abused at every turn, for corruptions in the army to reach such a height that it was impeding the conduct of war, and for the bribes of Irish to become determinants of policy.

She should not trust any of the Irish apart from Thomond and Ormond. They were all suspect and would rebel against her authority, spurning her good offices when opportunity offered. Most of all, he greatly suspected the Catholic townsmen, especially any who might have charge of town walls or fortifications, and this when a Spanish intervention was daily predicted. The queen had already tempted God's providence too long.[83] What was needed urgently was a massive royal army, spending if necessary seven times the annual expenditure in one year, persecuting the Irish rebels continuously and without mercy or remorse. Then the English conquerors must proceed to subject the country in a thorough fashion, as all conquerors do, by implanting their own religion, law, and language so as to bring about a systematic reform of the country and its people. 'The supplication' ended in a crescendo intended to shame action from a once great and highly regarded queen:

What your noble progenitors have gotten from strangers, lose not you to your false sworn subjects.

Let not a beggarly brat, basely blown out of a smith's forge,[84] blow you out of a kingdom. It is a dishonour to England, to you, to your crown to suffer so contemptible a wretch to stand up so long against you. He makes viceroys, creates Earls, bestows baronies, sets up, pulls down. He takes from subjects, gives to rebels; yet hath nothing by right, but that which yourself of your mere bounty hath given him, having no foot of land that he could challenge from the anvil, his father's own inheritance.

Can you beard mighty monarchs in their own kingdoms? In the strength of their own countries? Within their walled towns? And shall a base rascal brave you at home in your own dominions? In the open fields? Having no wall to save him, no city to receive him? Shall an Irish bagpipe dare your drums, your trumpets, your ensigns out of the field? Never was there any prince in England that hath had a more glorious reign than yourself; none whose fame hath spred further; whose regard hath been greater, not only amongst Christian Princes, but also beyond the bounds of Europe, from the beginning of your government until this day. And never was any that hath had a greater dishonour done him, then yourself hath, at this day by the traitors of Ireland.

---

[83] *Ibid.*, p. 59 (BL 34313, fol. 112r).

[84] Hugh O'Neill's father was Matthew, Baron of Dungannon. The latter, whose father was the son of a Dundalk blacksmith named Kelly, had been affiliated by Conn O'Neill, first earl of Tyrone, into the O'Neill dynasty.

Many of your subjects they have murdered; many have they ravished, they have spoiled all. They have thrust them out of their lands, and yourself, as much as in them lieth, out of your kingdom. They have despised your officers; they have cooped them up in corners; their rhymers spend their brains daily in deriding them, in mocking them. Wipe away this dishonour. Let it continue no longer to eclipse the glory of your memorable reign. Let your poor subjects whose dismayed hearts make them think, that you have forgotten them, that you have clean cast away the care of them, know that you remember them, that you are careful of them, that you regard them, and tender their safety. And let your enemies that vaunt hourly to their confederates that you are not able to suppress them, feel the force of your arm, feel the force of England, let them feel that as your years increase, so your strength groweth; that as you are not asleep; that you are not dead, as the wicked villain vaunt and report.

You that have been long the defender of many strangers, from the oppression of tyrants, leave not your subjects to the rage of rebels, you that have been the protector of innocency through Christendom, leave not the blood of innocents unrevenged in your own countries. You that from the beginning of your reign have been the professed defence in the world of all the professors of true religion, maintain it, underprop it, keep it up. So shall the poor flock of Christ dispersed in many corners of this crooked world, pray to God incessantly that it will please him to triple the government of Deborah upon you, for the honour of His church, for the wealth of England, and Ireland, and for the good of the faithful subjects of both realms. So be it, good God.[85]

'The supplication of the blood of the English' can only be by one man – Edmund Spenser. The great modern Spenserians, Professor Willy Maley, who himself edited this manuscript and brought it to public attention, and Professor Andrew Hadfield, do not believe Spenser to be its author.[86] Maley, attributing authorship to be an unidentified New Englishman, who was ideologically engaged and most likely a cleric, did not seriously consider Spenser. Hadfield dismisses the contention. He acknowledges that Spenser may have a hand in 'The supplication', discussing it alongside the similarly entitled second part of the 'Brief Note' which he considers to be a collective complaint by aggrieved Munster planters. However, 'The supplication' fits well with Spenser's persona, his intellectual and literary development, and the particular circumstances in which he found himself in 1598. First, this is a most remarkable piece

---

[85] 'The supplication', 75–6 (BL 34313, fols. 121r–v).
[86] See Maley's Introduction to 'The supplication' in *Analecta Hibernica* 36 (1995), 3–11; Andrew Hadfield, *Spenser's Irish experience: wilde fruit and salvage soyl* (Oxford, 1997), pp. 48–50, and more recently in his *Edmund Spenser: a life* (Oxford, 2012) pp. 387–8. In n. 162 to ch. 11, p. 388 (appearing on p. 534), Hadfield suggests that 'The supplication' may have been owned by Lord Deputy Chichester whereas it is patently obvious that it is in a compendium of Irish tracts copied in the 1610s for Sir George Carew, who had been the last Elizabethan Lord President of Munster.

of Late Elizabethan prose. It is a sustained piece of writing done at a single sitting or perhaps dictated to a scribe. It can only be the work of an individual of the highest literary ability. Read aloud, it has unmistakable poetic phrasing and cadences. Besides that, there is internal evidence pointing to Spenser and relational evidence to other Spenserian tracts. It was written in England by a survivor of the Munster revolt – by one, like the author of the *View of the Present State of Ireland,* who 'foresaw many imminent and great dangers'.[87] Although the writer provides plenty of religious imagery and allusions, he was not a cleric, because he refers to preachers as a category separate from himself when he says: 'Let this ring in each pulpit, O ye preachers; bestow your eloquence herein; it is God's cause, and therefore your business to set it forward.'[88] This writer was annoyed at the Irish lobbying and litigating against the Munster land settlement – Spenser regarded himself as having been especially disadvantaged by this in disputes with his neighbours. And furthermore the suppliant describes refugees coming before the presidential council in Munster, something that Spenser, if he managed to take up the post of sheriff of Cork, may have witnessed. Also, most of the individuals and places named in this tract were located in either North Cork, South Limerick, or South Tipperary, in other words near Spenser's castle at Kilcolman[89] and, unsurprisingly, the author has vivid accounts of the actions in that vicinity by people he plainly knew. Hadfield says that 'The supplication' differs in terms of language and register from *A View,* Spenser's prose work but this is because it has the language of his poetry, with which there are obvious links. For instance, the passage about O'Neill making viceroys quoted above is a transposition of Canto II, Verse XLI, of 'The Legend of Artegall' in Book 5 of *The Faerie Queene*:

> He maketh kings to sit in soveraity;
> He maketh subjects to their power obay;
> He pulleth downe, He setteth up on by;
> He gives to this, from that He takes away:
> For all we have is His: what He list doe, He may.[90]

[87] 'The supplication', 12 (BL 34313, fol. 85r).
[88] 'The supplication', 58 (BL 34313, fol. 111v).
[89] When I asked K. W. Nicholls to read this tract because I believed that Spenser was the author, he said he had already done so and reached the same conclusion. He had come to this judgement on the basis that most of the action and characters were from the area close to Spenser's base in North Cork and because the author wrote in a high literary style.
[90] Ironically, this section of the Book 5 of *The Faerie Queene* is quoted on p. 374 of the same chapter of Hadfield's *Spenser* that deals with 'The supplication'!

Some phrases used in Spenser's poetry have equivalents in 'The supplication'[91] and the love of archaisms so strong in *The Faerie Queene* is also evident in it.[92] And while *A View of the Present State of Ireland* may not share the same language as 'The supplication', it does significantly share the following key themes: concerns about native abuse of the common law, the treachery of the Irish and the duplicity of the Old English, the failure of evangelisation, the problem of degeneration, and the need for a large army engaged in a no-mercy-given, famine-inducing conquest.[93] 'The supplication's' use of the '*Bona terra, mala gens*' theme has a more general resonance in Spenser's work. Also tangentially but equally significant, *A View* and 'The supplication' are acknowledged sequentially as a sort of homage in Ralph Byrchensa's anti-Irish Battle of Kinsale poem of 1602.[94] Above all, 'The supplication' stands out as the work of an accomplished writer, one who can handle biblical citations and quote Latin tags, who uses lists, oppositions, and extended metaphors, and who engages in antanaclasis (the repetition of the same word with different meanings and senses). In fine, 'The supplication' is a singular work of linguistic virtuosity, sustained intensity, and direct authorial voice which extends and humanises the work of Spenser on Ireland. By extension, given that the 'Brief Note' has a similar title-paragraph addressed to the queen, more poetic usages of language and overlapping content in common with 'The supplication', it follows logically that it too must be a late piece of Spenser's.[95] Taken together, these two tracts, written in the dramatically altered circumstances of late 1598, show Spenser's

[91] For instance, 'The supplication' has 'Cursed Seed of Esau' (fol. 89v) while the then unpublished *Mutabilitie Canto IV* has 'th'Earths cursed seed'; 'The supplication' has 'Cursed Brood' (fol. 112v) while *Tears of the Muses*, l. 315, has 'Accursed Brood'.

[92] In 'The supplication' the author uses 'housen/howsen' as the plural for house in eleven of the twelve instances where the word appears. Maley's unmodernised transcription of the document employs the regular plural but perusal of the original shows 'housen'.

[93] See Edmund Spenser, *A View of the State of Ireland*, Andrew Hadfield and Willy Maley (eds.) (Oxford, 1997).

[94] See Ralph Byrchensa, *A Discourse Occasioned Vpon The Late Defeat, Giuen To the Arch-Rebels, Tyrone and Odonnell, by the right Honourable the Lord Mountioy* (London, 1602), stanza at bottom of C1v:

> View well their bogs furd all with bloodie hew,
> View well their fastnes of the selfesame stampe,
> View well their hedges sprinkled all with red,
> View well their brookes how bloodie they doe looke:
> The blood that Ireland sheds from day to day,
> For vengeance cries to God without delay.

[95] *CSPI*, VII, pp. 431–3. The attribution of the 'Brief Note' to Spenser was challenged by V. P. Hulbert, 'Spenser's relation to certain documents in Ireland', *Modern Philology* 34 (1937), 345–53; Hadfield, cited above, follows this view to some extent.

impassioned religious views – providentialism, support for evangelism, and fear of Catholicism – and political discontent, in particular annoyance, even anger, at the queen and frustration that earlier pleas and warnings had gone unheeded.

The author of 'The supplication''s analysis of the crisis makes an interesting contrast with the queen's own. He has no wish to conciliate any of the Irish, nor give any space to the practice of Catholicism. He wants to spend money in a timely fashion rather than to scrimp now and pay a heavy price later on. He wants a full conquest under a single governor, such as Lord Burgh appeared to be, rather than a series of divided imperiums of which the Irish were taking complete advantage. And while she targeted her officials in Ireland, crucially, 'The supplication' blamed Elizabeth herself. Its author blamed the war on her permissive policies towards Ireland and felt that its increasingly disastrous and dangerous course was the result of a lack of attention and commitment on her part. And it also, like Essex in the council chamber, touches on the question of gender and of not having a male monarch with accompanying macho *virtù* like Henry VIII. On the other hand, the suppliant shared the queen's concerns over the danger of foreign intrigue and involvement in Ireland and over corruption, though Elizabeth was more worried about the army than the administration. Interestingly, there is a common harping on the question of honour – but with 'The supplication' it is a more demotic honour, more about the honour of England and its Protestant people. As well as harking back to Stubbs's *Gaping Gulf* (1579) at the time of the Anjou marriage negotiations, this type of writing ties in well with what has been called 'the literature of disillusionment' in the 1590s, associated with Greville, Raleigh, and of course Spenser. The queen is no longer such a cult-like figure, an earthly deity or version of the Virgin Mary, but is all too fallible, human, and subject to mutability. With her decline into old age and her foreseeable imminent death, figures such as Spenser were putting their faith in God rather than His English representative on earth.[96]

The compelling climax to this is that perhaps the queen received this shrill and challenging supplication and acted upon it. We know that Spenser carried Norris's dispatch of 9 December 1598 but maybe he carried earlier dispatches as well.[97] Did Spenser meet the queen or have 'The supplication' pressed into her hands? She did at last act urgently – her throne was under threat because Munster was the part of Ireland

---

[96] For example, Helen Hackett, *Virgin mother, maiden queen: Elizabeth I and the cult of the Virgin Mary* (Basingstoke, 1995), ch. 6, esp. pp. 196–7.

[97] *CSPI*, VII, pp. 401, 414.

lying most open to Spain, and Ireland was an obvious strategic stepping stone to England itself. She was at last sending a big army and a single governor; nothing would be spared. She was appointing Essex, who was to pay for Spenser's funeral a month later, with a patent and a puissance not dissimilar to that envisaged in *A View*. The end of the letter, already cited above, to the triumvirate in Dublin on December 1, may indicate that she had indeed engaged with 'The supplication' and its message because it appears to be an answer to its demands in similar though toned-down language – 'we, that have prevailed (under God's favour) against the greatest monarchs or enemies, will never suffer our good subjects any longer to be oppressed, but will graciously consider of all that stand to us and to their duty, and will make them able to revenge themselves upon those vile and wicked rebels, by sending a sufficient force of horse and foot, both out of England, strengthened with the old soldiers of the Low Countries, and provided of all things necessary, whereby we doubt not but to yield them the due reward for their viperous and rebellious crimes against our state and person'.[98]

[98] SP 63/202/pt 4, 1.

11   War poetry and counsel in early modern Ireland

Andrew Hadfield

It is now widely accepted that Elizabeth was a much criticised monarch in the 1590s.[1] There was an understanding that she had been somewhat unlucky in living rather too long and that her failure to produce or name a successor had become a problematic rather than an admirable policy. Furthermore, many felt she had become capricious and unpredictable, so that it was hard enough to be at her court, impossible to follow her orders. Perhaps the most dangerous criticism of Elizabeth was levelled at her treatment of her male courtiers and the ways in which she subjected the military men she depended on to her 'petticoat government'. The female monarch was at odds with the masculine forces on which she depended, a neat inversion of the popular image of Elizabeth as a man's woman, celebrating the daring achievements of her most dashing courtiers, Raleigh, Drake, and Frobisher. Crown and army were probably most divided over Ireland, more so even than the protracted war with Spain in the Low Countries.[2] There, at least, the issue was support for fellow Protestants against a tyrannical enemy; in Ireland, one of the queen's kingdoms, the matter was the survival of the crown itself.

In celebrating the defeat of the forces of Hugh O'Neill and Hugh Roe O'Donnell at the Battle of Kinsale, 24 December 1601, the muster-master and poet, Ralph Byrchensa (Birkenshaw), expresses what was a widespread ambivalence about female rule:

> O famous Queene, who holds this land by right,
> Whose care hath been and is, to cure their sore:
> What louing favours hath her Grace bestowed,
> On mightie men, and subiects of this land?
> Whose wise foresights in time might stop full well,
> The streames from whence these mischiefs so do swell.

---

[1] John Guy, 'The 1590s: The second reign of Elizabeth I', in John Guy (ed.), *The reign of Elizabeth I: court and culture in the last decade* (Cambridge, 1995), pp. 1–19; Julia M. Walker (ed.), *Dissing Elizabeth: negative representations of Gloriana* (Durham, NC, 1998).

[2] R. B. Wernham, *After the Armada: Elizabethan England and the struggle for western Europe, 1588–1595* (Oxford, 1984), ch. 10.

But well her Highnesse hath from time to time,
Obserued still this nations wandring thoughts,
And seene into their natures and their liues,
Who like yong colts and heifers loue to fling,
That without bits, and bridles, and strong hand,
Will not be held in peace or rest to stand.

The better therefore to instruct their liues,
As louing fathers vse vnto their sonnes,
To keepe them in a liking of good laws,
And to prouide them tutors of good life:
So did her Grace from time to time elect,
Graue and wise men this land for to direct.

Sussex was one worthie of such a charge,
Sidney another held of good account,
Fitz Williams had the like authoritie,
Lord *Gray* did also rule by like command:
Parret was chosen to the selfesame place,
And *Russell* held the sword another space.[3]

These stanzas start as if they mean to praise the wisdom and virtuous government of a sovereign who has the right to rule Ireland as
one of her kingdoms. However, almost immediately the poetry veers
towards a more anxious position. The queen has the ability to see what is
going wrong, represented most spectacularly in Marcus Gheeraerts the
Younger's Ditchley Portrait of 1592, in which Elizabeth is represented
standing on a map of England wearing a dress covered in eyes, a sign
of her ability to oversee everything happening throughout her realms.[4]
Unfortunately, as the second stanza makes clear, seeing is only part of
the solution. The queen detects the wandering thoughts of the Irish
rebels whose loyalty to her is compromised by their hot-headed, youthful
instability. They are, as Byrchensa applies a powerful – if hardly subtle –
simile, like unbroken colts that have no bits or bridles and so cannot
be made to stand still, controlled, and mounted. Byrchensa does not
spell out the implications of the comparison but he is surely referring
to the frequent use of the word halter, literally a bridle to control wayward animals, which was also a reference to the noose. The usage was
grimly euphemistic: in Edmund Spenser's *A View of the Present State of
Ireland*, the halter is contrasted to the more drastic action represented by

---

[3] Ralph Byrchensa, *A Discourse Occasioned Vpon The Late Defeat, Giuen To The Arch-Rebels,
Tyrone and Odonnell, by the right Honourable the Lord Mountioy* (London, 1602), sig.
C2v–C3r.

[4] Richard Helgerson, *Forms of nationhood: the Elizabethan writing of England* (Chicago,
1992), p. 112.

the sword.[5] The Irish people, like some powerful but wayward stallion, needed to be made to see sense so that they could serve the monarch as they should. The problem is, as the next stanza makes clear, that breaking horses is not work for women. Byrchensa argues that taming the Irish is the same as a father making his sons understand the value of obeying good laws. Accordingly the queen has transferred her authority to her deputies in Ireland, 'Graue and wise men', who have governed in her name and helped to transform the land so that it is finally brought to heel.

In providing a list of those who have governed in Ireland, Byrchensa carefully elides the fraught, fractious, and dangerous course of English attempts to rule Ireland through viceroys. He even has the gall to end his list with the last deputy before Charles Blount, Lord Mountjoy, to whom the poem is dedicated, neglecting to mention that Robert Devereux, 2nd earl of Essex, was not simply 'placed in the chaire of state' but used it to build up his power base in Ireland through the indiscriminate creation of knights, a manoeuvre that greatly angered the queen and led eventually to his execution.[6] Essex, who had once been so frustrated by the queen's authority over him that he had started to draw his sword on her, was simply the culmination of a long line of viceroys who, if they had not had a problematic relationship with the monarch before they went to Ireland, certainly did by the time they were installed in office.[7] Many had complicated relationships not only with the monarch and particular court factions, but also with each other. Of the list of names cited here we might note that Sir John Perrot died while under investigation for treason; Arthur Lord Grey de Wilton was recalled early because he was accused of corruption and perhaps had exceeded royal authority in punishing the Irish rebels; Sir Henry Sidney fell in and out of favour because he was thought to be guilty of similar abuses of power; he and Sussex were fierce court rivals who each felt they could correct the mistakes of the other; the same could be said of Fitzwilliam and Perrot; and Russell, poorly supported by his English masters, was extremely ineffective, and complained bitterly that he was denied access to the queen's presence on his return.[8] There was no straightforward relationship between the

---

[5] Eamon Grennan, 'Language and politics: a note on some metaphors in Spenser's *A View of the Present State of Ireland*', *Spenser Studies* 3 (1982), 99–110.

[6] Alexandra Gajda, *The earl of Essex and late Elizabethan political culture* (Oxford, 2012), pp. 58–60.

[7] Paul E. J. Hammer, 'Devereux, Robert, 2nd earl of Essex (1565–1601)', *ODNB*.

[8] See Hiram Morgan, 'The fall of Sir John Perrot', in Guy (ed.), *The reign of Elizabeth I*, pp. 109–25; Richard A. McCabe, *Spenser's monstrous regiment: Elizabethan Ireland and the poetics of difference* (Oxford, 2002), pp. 88–90; Sir Henry Sidney, *A viceroy's vindication? Sir*

crown and the viceroy, power flowing neatly from the queen to her men in the field who served her as grateful loyal subjects.[9] Rather, there was a complicated and fractious series of conflicts as the queen tried to govern a hostile land as cheaply as possible, and the men employed to implement her policies argued that they needed much better support and recognition of the dangers they faced in the field.

Byrchensa's poem was published by Matthew Lownes, the bookseller who had entered Spenser's *View* in the Stationers' Register in 1598 and who later acquired the rights to Spenser's works after the death of his major publisher, William Ponsonby, in 1604.[10] Spenser's writings certainly had an important influence on Byrchensa's poem, undoubtedly in part through Lownes.[11] Spenser, like Byrchensa, had represented Elizabeth and her court in an ambiguous manner and his defence of the colonists in Ireland and the military men who protected them was clear enough, especially in the second part of *The Faerie Queene* (1596). Book V, canto 9, is perhaps the central section of the Book of Justice, certainly in terms of historical allegory. The canto contains the description of the trial of Duessa, an easily decodable account of the events leading up to the execution of Mary Stuart, which so angered her son, James VI of Scotland, that he demanded that Spenser be punished.[12] It also included the disturbing image of the poet, Bonfont, with his tongue nailed to a post, and his name changed to Malfont, a prediction of what might be the author's fate when his verses were read, and a hostile comment on the silencing of political opposition in Elizabeth's England.[13] Spenser establishes an opposition between the effeminate values of the queen's court – which does not, of course, preclude the use of brutal violence – and the military values of her knights in the field, specifically in Ireland.

Henry Sidney's memoir of service in Ireland, 1556–1578, Ciaran Brady (ed.) (Cork, 2002); Steven G. Ellis, *Tudor Ireland: crown, community and the conflict of cultures, 1470–1603* (London, 1985), ch. 9.

[9] Hiram Morgan, '"Never any realm worse governed": Queen Elizabeth and Ireland', *Transactions of the Royal Historical Society*, 6th series, 14 (2004), 295–308; Willy Maley, *Salvaging Spenser: colonialism, culture and identity* (Basingstoke, 1997), ch. 5.

[10] Michael G. Brennan, 'William Ponsonby: Elizabethan stationer', *Analytical and Enumerative Bibliography* 7 (1984), 91–110; Stephen K. Galbraith, 'Edmund Spenser and the history of the book, 1569–1679' (PhD dissertation, Ohio State University, 2006).

[11] Andrew Hadfield, 'An allusion to Spenser's Irish writings: Matthew Lownes and Ralph Byrchensa's *A Discourse occasioned on the late defeat, given to the arch-rebels, Tyrone and O'Donnell* (1602)', *Notes & Queries* 242 (1997), 478–80.

[12] Richard A. McCabe, 'The masks of Duessa: Spenser, Mary Queen of Scots, and James VI', *English Literary Renaissance* 17 (1987), 224–42.

[13] M. Lindsay Kaplan, *The culture of slander in early modern England* (Cambridge, 1997), pp. 40, 120–1.

Artegall, the Knight of Justice, along with the iron man who accompanies him, Talus, head to the court of Mercilla to serve her after they learn of the threats that she faces from her aggressive foes. Mercilla is a figure of Elizabeth, as the first description of her in the poem indicates:

> Her name *Mercilla* most men vse to call;
> That is a mayden Queene of high renowne,
> For her great bounty knowen ouer all,
> And soueraine grace, with which her royall crowne
> She doth support, and strongly beateth downe
> The malice of her foes, which her enuy,
> And at her happinesse do fret and frowne:
> Yet she her selfe the more doth magnify,
> And euen to her foes her mercies multiply.
>
> Mongst many which maligne her happy state,
> There is a mighty man, which wonnes here by
> That with most fell despight and deadly hate,
> Seekes to subuert her Crowne and dignity,
> And all his powre doth thereunto apply:
> And her good Knights, of which so braue a band
> Serues her, as any Princesse vnder sky,
> He either spoiles, if they against him stand,
> Or to his part allures, and bribeth vnder hand.
>
> Ne him sufficeth all the wrong and ill,
> Which he vnto her people does each day,
> But that he seekes by traytrous traines to spill
> Her person, and her sacred selfe to slay:
> That O ye heauens defend, and turne away
> From her, vnto the miscreant him selfe,
> That neither hath religion nor fay,
> But makes his God of his vngodly pelfe,
> And Idols serues; so let his Idols serue the Elfe.[14]

The maiden queen is challenged by the furious and irrational Souldan, a tyrant who has been overcome by his passions, surrendered his masculine reason, and allowed his more womanly characteristics to overwhelm him – in other words, he has become effeminate, a point reinforced by his union with the equally rash and choleric Adicia.[15] The episode is an allegory of

---

[14] Edmund Spenser, *The Faerie Queene*, A. C. Hamilton (ed.) (London, 2001), V, viii, 17–19. All subsequent references to this edition appear in parentheses in the text.

[15] Rebecca Bushnell, *Tragedies of tyrants: political thought and theater in the English Renaissance* (Ithaca, NY, 1990); Sara Mendelson and Patricia Crawford, *Women in early modern England* (Oxford, 1998), pp. 19–20.

the defeat of the Spanish Armada.[16] Spenser makes the episode topical and hard-hitting, in line with the climate of fear that existed after the event that is too often seen as a high point of English military success.[17] Immediately after the Souldan is overthrown, torn to pieces by his own horses in a retelling of the myth of the foolish Phaeton who imagined that he had the ability to control the sun, Artegall and Talus have to face another dangerous foe, the elusive and devious Malengin, who can change his identity in order to evade capture and to threaten the stability of proper order and rule. The knights use the damsel, Samient, who has drawn their attention to the abuses of Malengin, to lure him out from his cave:

> The cry whereof entring the hollow caue,
> Eftsoones brought forth the villaine, as they ment,
> With hope of her some wishfull boot to haue.
> Full dreadfull wight he was, as euer went
> Vpon the earth, with hollow eyes deepe pent,
> And long curld locks, that downe his shoulders shagged,
> And on his backe an vncouth vestiment
> Made of straunge stuffe, but all to worne and ragged,
> And vnderneath his breech was all to torne and iagged (V.ix.20).

The description of Malengin links him to the Irish rebels described by Spenser in *A View of the Present State of Ireland*, written at about the same time.[18] Malengin's 'long curld locks' and 'vncouth vestiment' recalls the lengthy description of the glibs (long hair) and mantles (a woollen cloak designed as an all-purpose garment) that helped to foster rebellion in Ireland. Irenius, discussing the links between the Irish and the Scythians, the barbarians who inhabited Asia Minor north of Greece, notes that 'They have another custome from the Scythians, that is the wearing of Mantles, and long glibbes, which is a thicke curled bush of haire, hanging downe over their eyes, and monstrously disguising them, which are both very bad and hurtfull.'[19] The hairstyles and clothing of the Irish enable them to resist capture; provide them with a dangerous mobility (something that was carefully controlled in England); and allow them

[16] René Graziani, 'Philip II's Impressa and Spenser's Souldan', *Journal of the Warburg and Courtauld Institutes* 27 (1964), 322–4; Richard F. Hardin, 'Adicia, Souldan', in *The Spenser Encyclopaedia*, A. C. Hamilton (ed.) (London and Toronto, 1990), pp. 7–8.

[17] Carol Z. Weiner, 'The beleaguered isle: a study of Elizabethan and early Jacobean anti-Catholicism', *Past & Present* 51 (1971), 27–62.

[18] Andrew Hadfield, *Edmund Spenser: a life* (Oxford, 2012), ch. 10.

[19] Edmund Spenser, *A View of the State of Ireland*, Andrew Hadfield and Willy Maley (eds.) (Oxford, 1997), p. 56; see also Thomas Herron, *Spenser's Irish work: poetry, plantation and colonial Reformation* (Aldershot, 2007), pp. 77–8; McCabe, *Spenser's monstrous regiment*, pp. 111–12.

to subvert the established hierarchy and natural order of things, barbarian values undermining military and legal frameworks.[20] Specifically, the Irish lack the rooted order that masculine control provides. Malengin changes shape at will to escape Talus but eventually runs out of options:

> Into a Hedgehogge all vnwares it went,
> And prickt him so, that he away it threw.
> Then gan it runne away incontinent,
> Being returned to his former hew:
> But *Talus* soone him ouertooke, and backward drew.
>
> But when as he would to a snake againe
> Haue turn'd himselfe, he with his yron flayle
> Gan driue at him, with so huge might and maine,
> That all his bones, as small as sandy grayle
> He broke, and did his bowels disentrayle;
> Crying in vaine for helpe, when helpe was past.
> So did deceipt the selfe deceiuer fayle,
> There they him left a carrion outcast;
> For beasts and foules to feede vpon for their repast (18, lines 5–9, 19).

After the brief moment of comedy when Artegall drops the hedgehog, we witness a brutal description of the grisly end of Malengin, as Talus destroys him so thoroughly that he effectively disappears into the environment.[21] The fury that Talus unleashes mirrors that of the doomed Souldan and, although used to protect the realm, the balance points to a lack of equilibrium in the body politic that has a deeper cause. Malengin's time is up when he is described as 'incontinent', a sign that he has lost control and is now panicking, running wherever he can to escape the knight's weapons. Not only does this link the representation of Malengin as an Irish rebel as well as a Jesuit to the earlier extended discussion of temperance and continence as virtues in Book II, but it indicates that, like the Souldan and Adicia in their frenzied anger, Malengin has unmanned himself and become effeminate.[22]

Cantos viii and ix of *The Faerie Queene* establish that, for Spenser, opposition to the queen and attempts to overthrow her regime, in Ireland as elsewhere, were inspired by a lack of control and balance that was irrational and feminine. The problem is, as canto ix demonstrates,

---

[20] On the dangers posed by mobility and attempts to control the movement of people, see A. L. Beier, *Masterless men: the vagrancy problem in England, 1560–1640* (London, 1985).

[21] Andrew Hadfield, *Spenser's Irish experience: wilde fruit and salvage soyl* (Oxford, 1997), pp. 160–4.

[22] On Malengin as a Jesuit, see Harold Skulsky, 'Malengin', in *Spenser Encyclopedia*, Hamilton (ed.), p. 450.

that the same lack of manly rigour has infected the corridors of power and determined their character. Immediately after defeating Malengin, Artegall and Talus arrive at Mercilla's castle, enter the court chamber, and recognise the figure of Awe,

> by whom they passing in
> Went vp the hall, that was a large wyde roome,
> All full of people making troublous din,
> And wondrous noyse, as if that there were some,
> Which vnto them was dealing righteous doome.
> By whom they passing, through the thickest preasse,
> The marshall of the hall to them did come;
> His name hight *Order*, who commaunding peace,
> Them guyded through the throng, that did their clamors ceasse.
>
> They ceast their clamors vpon them to gaze;
> Whom seeing all in armour bright as day,
> Straunge there to see, it did them much amaze,
> And with vnwonted terror halfe affray,
> For neuer saw they there the like array.
> Ne euer was the name of warre there spoken,
> But ioyous peace and quietnesse alway,
> Dealing iust iudgements, that mote not be broken
> For any brybes, or threates of any to be wroken (23–4).

These are extraordinary stanzas, laced with excoriating sarcasm by way of conclusion, which start to place what we have read in the previous canto and a half in an even more disturbing and sinister context. The encounter is based on a misrecognition – the courtiers do not know who the knights are or what they do, indicating that there is a hard and fast separation between the knights in the field and those whose advancement had taken place at court, men who were generally contemptuously referred to as 'knights of the carpet'.[23] The courtiers debate matters in a conspicuously noisy manner, making an assumption that they are able to seek and understand justice, whereas the implication is that they just produce cacophony, empty words, and an excess of sound, which looks forward to the rather more sinister confusion generated by the Blatant Beast with his multitude of slanderous tongues at the end of Book VI, the last book published in Spenser's lifetime.[24] Spenser uses a characteristic device, the 'as if' construction, to undermine their right and authority. When

---

[23] H.S.G., 'Knight of the Carpet', *Notes and Queries*, 3rd series, 2 (15 Nov. 1862), 388–9. See Thomas Nashe, *Nashe's Lenten Stuffe* (1599), 'The epistle dedicatorie', in Thomas Nashe, *The works of Thomas Nashe*, R. B. McKerrow and F. P. Wilson (eds.), 5 vols. (Oxford, 1966), vol. III, p. 148.

[24] Hadfield, *Spenser's Irish experience*, pp. 170–4.

we read the first stanza we understand that what they do looks *as if* it has some connection with 'dealing righteous doome', the delivery of justice, and proper judgement. But, on a closer reading, that seems not to be the case, and what is happening is that they are shouting out as if someone was dealing *them* proper justice, which is probably not what they want at all and which would undoubtedly cause them to cry out in pain.

The last lines surely leave us in no doubt which way we are to interpret the division between the courtiers and the knights. The courtiers do not ever utter the word 'war', because they do not understand what it means. This indicates that the 'ioyous peace' they foster takes place in all ignorance of the conflicts that engage the knights on their way to the court. The clear implication is that the courtiers are isolated from the brutalities of the real world. They live in a soft world artificially isolated from warfare and deal out just judgements that cannot be undermined by bribes, threats, or any other hostile actions. The last lines of stanza 24 are ironic on two levels. First, Spenser's verse implies the opposite of its ostensible meaning. The court is taken at its own valuation, but set in a wider context of justice that the poet understands. Accordingly the lines pose a further question: how are these people able to make just judgements and deal out proper justice if they have no understanding of the conflict that exists outside the court, which constantly threatens to engulf it, and which the courtiers, being at the apex of society, are supposed to be solving? The irony is clear in terms of the narrative progress of the poem. It is even more pointed if we consider the time when the second edition of *The Faerie Queene* was published, as the Nine Years' War in Ireland was becoming ever more threatening to English settlers, revealing that the events of the late 1580s – the execution of Mary Stuart (1587) and the defeat of the Armada (1588) – were far more precarious triumphs than many had imagined. Many commentators on *A View* have pointed out that Spenser writes as an enthusiast for martial law in Ireland in his dialogue, and was a strong supporter of drastic measures in Ireland based on the need to re-establish authority through the use of military power.[25] Justice cannot work without the threat of the sword, which is why the courtiers' understanding of justice – they believe it is somehow protected from external pressure without the need to establish anything to ensure that this happens – is represented as inadequate and dangerous.

---

[25] David Edwards, 'Ideology and experience: Spenser's *View* and martial law in Ireland', in Hiram Morgan (ed.), *Political ideology in Ireland, 1541–1641* (Dublin, 1999), pp. 127–57; Herron, *Spenser's Irish work*, pp. 41–2.

Why do the courtiers behave as they do and why do they know so little about government and justice? The second half of the canto makes clear what many readers have realised already. It is because they are ruled by a queen, a monarch who is either unable, or who chooses not, to govern properly. Spenser revisits the trial and execution of Mary Stuart through his representation of the trial of Duessa. Mercilla is portrayed as a monarch who desires peace above all else, exactly what her courtiers have learned from her. She is described sitting in state holding her sceptre, 'The sacred pledge of peace and clemencie' (30, line 3), worthy and proper values for a monarch but not enough on their own to govern effectively in times of trouble. Around her feet sit 'A beuie of faire Virgins clad in white', daughters of Jove, whose task it is to wait by his judgement seat 'And when in wrath he threats the worlds decay, / They doe his anger calme, and cruell vengeance stay' (31, lines 8–9). Again, this sort of advice is exactly what a monarch needs to rule properly – at times, because at others more stringent advice and sterner action are required. The iconography that represents Mercilla indicates that her mode of government is partial, not comprehensive.[26] When she is called to preside over the trial of Duessa, 'She was about affaires of common wele, / Dealing of Iustice with indifferent grace' (36, lines 3–4), a sign that she is extremely effective in a familiar legal context. However, when confronted by a catastrophic series of events – the treasons of a fellow monarch – and the need to make a difficult decision which involves weighing the scales of justice to determine the right result from two equally painful options, Mercilla is found wanting.

The list of Duessa's crimes is lengthy and includes her plotting 'to depryue / *Mercilla* of her crowne, by her aspyred' (41, lines 6–7), a clear reminder of the Babington Plot, which eventually forced Elizabeth's hand.[27] A series of male courtiers urge the queen to act decisively and have Duessa/Mary executed in order to ensure the safety of the realm, culminating in the arguments of the Knight of Justice himself, but, even then, the queen is reluctant to make the decision:

> *Artegall* with constant firme intent,
> For zeale of Iustice was against her bent.
> So was she guiltie deemed of them all.
> Then *Zele* began to vrge her punishment,

---

[26] For a very different reading, see Jane Aptekar, *Icons of justice: iconography and thematic imagery in Book V of The Faerie Queene* (New York, 1969), who describes Mercilla as a great and entirely orthodox monarch... [and] inevitably, as a great judge' (p. 14).

[27] James E. Phillips, *Images of a queen: Mary Stuart in sixteenth-century literature* (Berkeley, CA, 1964), pp. 78–82, passim.

And to their Queene for iudgement loudly call,
Vnto *Mercilla* myld for Iustice gainst the thrall.

But she, whose Princely breast was touched nere
With piteous ruth of her so wretched plight,
Though plaine she saw by all, that she did heare,
That she of death was guiltie found by right,
Yet would not let iust vengeance on her light;
But rather let in stead thereof to fall
Few perling drops from her faire lampes of light;
The which she couering with her purple pall
Would haue the passion hid, and vp arose withal (49, lines 4–9, 50).

As Richard A. McCabe has pointed out, Artegall's representation as Arthur, Lord Grey de Wilton, Spenser's erstwhile patron, whose decisive actions at Smerwick in 1580 were defended so forcefully in *A View*, also served as a commissioner at Mary's trial.[28] Artegall, via his experience with Malengin, knows that justice can be achieved only if the enemies of the state are defeated. He also realises that the same logic applies to Duessa, who must also be treated harshly if she is not to undermine the good government that Mercilla/Elizabeth has established in England. Spenser is showing readers that a combined threat from Scotland and Ireland menaces England, one that the incumbent monarch fails to understand and which she can face only if she supports her knights and prevents her courtiers from dominating access to her presence. It is a new version of the familiar image of the good monarch undermined by bad counsel, one that reflects negatively on the incumbent ruler and her decision to surround herself with advisers who think too much about peace in times of war.[29] Mercilla, like the Souldan and Adicia, is afflicted by passion which threatens to cloud her judgement: here, pity, rather than anger. Even so, it is a weakness that she has to hide, as her sympathy for her fellow monarch is, in Spenser's eyes, compromising her ability to make the decisions that a ruler has to make. Her weak female government has led to her filling her court with advisers who cannot see how their security, and that of those they are responsible for, requires them to act decisively and harshly against dangerous enemies in Ireland and Scotland. In fact, they are all shocked by the appearance of men in

---

[28] Richard A. McCabe, 'The fate of Irena: Spenser and political violence', in Patricia Coughlan (ed.), *Spenser and Ireland: an interdisciplinary perspective* (Cork, 1989), pp. 109–25. On Spenser, Grey, and Smerwick, see also H. S. V. Jones, *Spenser's defense of Lord Grey* (Urbana, IL, 1919).

[29] John Guy, 'The rhetoric of counsel in early modern England', in Dale Hoak (ed.), *Tudor political culture* (Cambridge, 1995), pp. 292–310.

armour, so removed are they from the theatres of war and from a realisation that events in Ireland are actually more important than those which they oversee in England. Pity is an important component of the law, but one that needs to be balanced by harshness too. At Mercilla's court this equilibrium has been lost and the balance has tipped too far one way.

However, Mercilla has taken some decisive action when it suited her, and she has punished the poet who she thinks has transgressed against her laws, which Artegall and Talus witness after they have passed the throng of courtiers:

> There as they entred at the Scriene, they saw
> Some one, whose tongue was for his trespasse vyle
> Nayld to a post, adiudged so by law:
> For that therewith he falsely did reuyle,
> And foule blaspheme that Queene for forged guyle,
> Both with bold speaches, which he blazed had,
> And with lewd poems, which he did compyle;
> For the bold title of a Poet bad
> He on himselfe had ta'en, and rayling rymes had sprad.
>
> Thus there he stood, whylest high ouer his head,
> There written was the purport of his sin,
> In cyphers strange, that few could rightly read,
> BON FONT: but *bon* that once had written bin,
> Was raced out, and *Mal* was now put in.
> So now *Malfont* was plainely to be red;
> Eyther for th'euill, which he did therein,
> Or that he likened was to a welhed
> Of euill words, and wicked sclaunders by him shed (25–6).

The passage has rightly troubled commentators.[30] It is impossible to believe that Spenser was endorsing the behaviour of his fictional queen, given his own brushes with authority after the publication of *Mother Hubberds Tale* in 1591, or his involvement with the faction who were urging Elizabeth not to marry the duc d'Alençon in 1579–80.[31] Furthermore, there is a visual joke enshrined in the text. While the poet's original name may be razed out at Mercilla's court, it stands out here in capitals, whereas Malfont, which Spenser states was 'plainely to be red' there, is less visible in the poem as it is in standard type size. We do not know what Bonfont's crime of slandering the queen was, especially as it is written in cryptic ciphers. However, the accusation of 'forged guyle' suggests that

---

[30] David Norbrook, *Poetry and politics in the English Renaissance* (London, 1984), p. 133; Simon Shepherd, *Spenser* (Hemel Hempstead, 1989), p. 50.

[31] For the fullest treatment of the first episode, see Bruce Danner, *Edmund Spenser's war on Lord Burghley* (Basingstoke, 2011); for the second, see Hadfield, *Spenser: a life*, ch. 4.

the queen and her courtiers link him to the treason of Malengin, who is called 'Guyle' in the headnote to the canto. The 'BON FONT' that stands out here indicates that the poet should really preserve his original name and, therefore, that his purpose and aims are laudable, allying him with the knights who receive such a bemused and frosty reception at the court. He is 'likened' to a 'welhed / Of euill words, and wicked sclaunders', which suggests that this may not in fact be the case, just as the courtiers' links to justice turned out to be false a few lines earlier. Bonfont, presumably, asked serious and important questions about affairs of state in his poetry, which required proper answers, and that is why he is punished so forcefully and publicly at a court that has such a limited, dangerous, and misleading understanding of justice.

In a complex and carefully ordered allegory, Spenser has linked soldiers and poets against the monarch and the court, a connection made more explicit later by Ralph Byrchensa. Military and literary men carry out the real work of protecting the country from dangerous problems and proposing viable solutions: courtiers and the queen would do well to learn from the advice they provide and need to listen to what those out in the fields in the far-flung corners of the realm have to say to them. Of course, the two sides do not have to be at odds, but that would involve a more equitable and healthy balance in the body politic than currently Spenser imagines existed in the late 1590s.[32]

The queen and the court need to change more than the knights. It is a sign of this imbalance that Artegall kills the Giant with the Scales in canto v, leaving the Knight of Justice with only the sword to pursue his quest, perhaps a sign of a failure on his part, but more blame is surely attached to the monarch, who has failed to guide him properly.[33] It is also a sign of the need to move to this militarised culture that in *A View* Irenius describes what needs to be done to a diseased body politic:

the care of the soule and soule matters is to be preferred before the care of the body, in consideration of the worthynesse thereof, but not till the time of reformation; for if you should know a wicked person dangerously sicke, havinge now both soule and body greatly diseased, yet both recoverable, would you not thinke it evill advertizement to bring the preacher before the phisitian? for if his body were neglected, it is like that his languishing soule being disquieted by his diseasefull body, would utterly refuse and loath all sprituall comfort; but if his body were first recured, and broght to good frame, should there not then be found best tyme to recover his soule also? So it is in the state of a realme:

[32] Margaret Healy, *Fictions of disease in early modern England: bodies, plagues and politics* (Basingstoke, 2001), pp. 3, 189–91, passim.

[33] Michael O'Connell, 'Giant with the scales', in *Spenser Encyclopedia*, Hamilton (ed.), pp. 331–2.

Therefore (as I said) it is expedient, first to settle such a course of government there, as thereby both civill disorders and ecclesiasticall abuses may be reformed and amended, whereto needeth not any such great distance of times, as (you suppose) I require, but one joynte resolution for both, that each might second and confirm the other.[34]

Like so many passages in the dialogue, this is clearly designed to shock the reader, adapting the familiar analogy of the body politic in a disturbing way to suggest that things have gone so far and become so dangerous in Ireland that all concern for the soul must be abandoned. Clearly this is not an analogy that holds water: neglecting spiritual ministration when dealing with a gravely ill patient would not have been considered a legitimate strategy. What if the patient died without repenting for his or her sins? Of course, this was – formally at least – more important in the late medieval and contemporary Catholic church, with its need to apply extreme unction to the dying.[35] But Protestants also needed to witness the dying make peace with God and affirm their faith, so this description would have baffled readers on either side of the confessional divide and drawn their attention to the serious crisis that was engulfing Ireland, one which demanded an immediate, violent response, not the cautious vacillations of a prudent queen. The implication is that, if military action is not undertaken, then the disease may well spread to England, because a nation that fails to protect itself is already sick, part of the problem rather than the solution. The times are so far out of joint that what looks like a serious matter – thinking through ecclesiastical issues and getting religious policy right – is a distraction that should not be given a moment's thought.

Spenser's message was quite consistent after the advent of the Nine Years' War and the realisation that it was the most serious threat to English rule since the second Desmond Rebellion a decade earlier (1579–83), which had led to the mass land confiscation that had enabled Spenser to acquire his estate.[36] There is a marked change of tone after the *Amoretti* and *Epithalamion* (1594), celebrating the poet's second marriage, which see the English settlers living in a strange and often hostile land, but able to flourish in their everyday lives as farmers and merchants.[37] By the time of *Colin Clouts Come Home Againe* (1595), a poem undoubtedly revised from an earlier version written in 1591, the situation was much

[34] Spenser, *View*, pp. 85–6.
[35] Ralph Houlbrooke, *Death, religion and the family in England, 1480–1750* (Oxford, 1998), pp. 147–52; Philippe Ariès, *The hour of our death*, Helen Weaver (trans.) (New York, 1981), pp. 18–19, 23–4.
[36] Hadfield, *Spenser: a life*, chs. 5–6.
[37] Scott Wilson, *Cultural materialism: theory and practice* (Oxford, 1995), pp. 66–74.

more desperate and the need for the colonists to be protected was much more acute. But *Colin Clout* makes specific allegations against the queen and her court in line with the comments made in *The Faerie Queene*, Book V. It describes Colin's account of his journey over to England in 1589–90 given to his fellow English shepherds in Ireland.[38] Cuddy asks Colin, 'What land is that thou meanest.../ And is there other, then whereon we stand?', a blunt acknowledgement that the queen is not known to her subjects in Ireland, even though the first edition of *The Faerie Queene* had been dedicated to Elizabeth as 'Queen of England, France, and Ireland' (*Faerie Queene*, ed. Hamilton, p. 26).[39] Presumably her subjects in France may not know her, but for those in Ireland not to recognise Elizabeth indicates a serious failure of her government as well as a limited ability to rule a difficult kingdom. Colin praises England largely through a description of the dangers the shepherds/settlers experience in Ireland:

> Both heauen and heauenly graces do much more
> (Quoth he) abound in that same land, then this.
> For there all happie peace and plenteous store
> Conspire in one to make contented bliss:
> No wayling there nor wretchednesse is heard,
> No bloodie issues nor no leprosies,
> No griesly famine, nor no raging sweard,
> No nightly bodrags, nor no hue and cries;
> The shepheards there abroad may safely lie,
> On hills and downes, withouten dread or daunger:
> No rauenous wolues the good mans hope destroy,
> Nor outlawes fell affray the forest raunger (lines 308–19).

This is a powerful list of all the problems that afflict the English in Ireland. The shepherds have to witness suffering and misery, and are constantly ambushed by hostile natives (a bodrag is a 'hostile incursion, a raid': *Oxford English Dictionary*). There is always the danger of famine, the context making clear that such disasters are probably man-made rather than natural misfortunes. There is also the ever-present threat of disease, again, probably partly caused by human factors, both the threat of a contagious disease (leprosy) and the danger of blood leaving the body in life-threatening amounts (issues). Wild wolves, the natural enemy of the shepherd, whether taken literally as farmers fighting off predators or metaphorically as good Christians besieged by hostile

---

[38] For further analysis, see Hadfield, *Spenser's Irish experience*, pp. 13–16.
[39] *Colin Clouts Come Home Againe*, in Edmund Spenser, *The shorter poems*, R. A. McCabe (ed.) (Harmondsworth, 1999), lines 290–1 (all subsequent references to this edition in parentheses in the text).

Catholics, are a constant threat. Moreover, rural Ireland is noisy, not tranquil, the settlers constantly hearing threatening sounds. Most important for my argument here, the shepherds have to live with the constant accompaniment of the sword: the shepherds and their attendant poets are brought close to the military in ways that their counterparts in safe, rural England are not. Neither may really want this alliance – the shepherds would undoubtedly rather live as they would do in England, and clearly expect to be able to, and English soldiers were never happy in Ireland, living with the ever-present danger of ambush in a terrain they did not understand.[40]

Why then has Colin returned to Ireland if it is so violent and brutal and possesses so few of the advantages of life in England? Thesylis poses this question, and Colin explains that the problem in England is the court, which is corrupt beyond all measure, and that its falsehoods obscure the truth that concerned subjects tell:

> For sooth to say, it is no sort of life,
> For shepheard fit to lead in that same place,
> Where each one seeks with malice and with strife,
> To thrust downe other into foule disgrace,
> Himselfe to raise: and he doth soonest rise
> That best can handle his deceitfull wit,
> In subtil shifts, and finest sleights deuise,
> Either by slaundring his well deemed name,
> Through leasings lewd, and fained forgerie:
> Or else by breeding him some blot of blame,
> By creeping close into his secrecie;
> To which him needs, a guilefull hollow hart,
> Masked with faire dissembling curtesie,
> A filed toung furnisht with tearmes of art,
> No art of schoole, but Courtiers schoolery (lines 688–702).

Again, we note the pointed contrast between the effete and luxurious life of the courtiers and the hard life of soldiers and settlers. The description is surely designed to echo words used in *The Faerie Queene*, Book V (and Book VI).[41] The courtiers have guileful hearts, linking them to the Irish shape-shifting rebel, Malengin, and it is they who utter lies, slanders, and forgeries, filing their tongues to enable their speech to fit its purpose without regard for truth, not the poet who they punish so viciously. Read

---

[40] On English military experience in Ireland, see Cyril Falls, *Elizabeth's Irish wars* (London, 1950; 1970, reprint); Ciaran Brady, 'The captains' games: army and society in Elizabethan Ireland', in Thomas Bartlett and Keith Jeffrey (eds.), *A military history of Ireland* (Cambridge, 1996), pp. 136–59.

[41] See Hadfield, *Spenser's Irish experience*, ch. 5.

individually, Spenser's poems paint a dark picture of betrayal at the very heart of government, a theme that is repeated and revisited time and again. Put together they can be seen to go even further, asserting that there is a murderous imbalance in the body politic, the courtiers who advise the queen actually serving to undermine the state and place it in danger, so much so that they are far more akin to the most threatening rebels, the Jesuits and the wolves, who cause the leprosies, the famines, and the bloody issues, than they are to the good soldiers and colonists who wish to protect and expand the queen's legitimate dominions.

Spenser produced a disturbing, far-reaching, and coherent analysis of what was going wrong in Elizabethan Ireland, one that was not necessarily right, but that, as Nicholas Canny has argued about his prose dialogue, set the agenda for English thinking about Ireland in subsequent decades, as the case of Ralph Byrchensa demonstrates.[42] And Spenser was not alone. In particular, the group of intellectuals and soldier-poets who surrounded Arthur Lord Grey de Wilton, the lord deputy of Ireland from 1580 to 1582, were eager to foster a similar alliance between writers and military men. Spenser, who had travelled to Ireland as one of Grey's secretaries, was a key part of this group, and it is at least arguable that his understanding of Irish political distinctions owed much to this formative period, his first outside England. Within two months of his arrival Spenser witnessed the massacre at Smerwick harbour, when 600 Spanish and papal soldiers were executed by Lord Grey after they had surrendered, imagining that they would be shown mercy.[43] In *A View* Spenser defended Grey's actions, again blaming the opposition that developed against Grey on the bad faith of courtiers unable to understand how vital and defensible his actions had been. Spenser argues that Ireland was saved from worse calamities 'through the most wise and valiant handling of that right noble Lord', even though his detractors 'blotted [him] with the name of a bloody man'. Grey was 'gentle, affable, loving and temperate', all qualities that *The Faerie Queene* endorses and celebrates, 'but that the necessitie of that present state of things inforced him to that violence, and almost changed his naturall disposition'.[44]

Grey represents the noble soldier who is cultivated and reasonable, and who understands the brutal reality of war and the desperate effects it has on the men who wage it. George Gascoigne (1534/5–77), the soldier-poet

---

[42] Nicholas P. Canny, *Making Ireland British, 1580–1650* (Oxford, 2001), pp. 1–58.

[43] For more explanation and analysis, see Vincent P. Carey, 'Atrocity and history: Grey, Spenser and the slaughter at Smerwick (1580)', in David Edwards, Pádraig Lenihan, and Clodagh Tait (eds.), *Age of atrocity: violence and political conflict in early modern Ireland* (Dublin, 2007), pp. 79–94; Hadfield, *Spenser: a life*, ch. 5.

[44] Spenser, *View*, pp. 28, 103.

who served with Grey in the Low Countries (1572–4), wrote a long poem dedicated to Grey that was named after the most famous adage of Erasmus, 'Dulce bellum inexpertis' ('war is sweet to the ignorant').[45] Gascoigne transforms Erasmus's argument that enthusiasm for war would diminish if people actually realised its terrible effects to the understanding that only those who have experienced war can write properly about it:

> To write of Warre and wote not what it is,
> Nor ever yet could march where War was made,
> May well be thought a worke begonne amis,
> A rash attempt, in worthlesse verse to wade,
> To tell the trial, knowing not the trade:
> Yet such a vaine even nowe doth feede my Muse,
> That in this theame I must some labor use (lines 1–7).

Gascoigne was attempting to fashion himself as the soldier-poet, able to express the ancient arts of war in properly crafted and rhetorically constructed language, in the service of the most suitable patron, one who understood the ancient art of war, realising its powers and dangers.[46] The opening stanza makes it clear that one can write about war only if one has experienced it, an argument that excludes the court poetry of the 'carpet knights' excoriated by Spenser. Immediately after the description of the suffering and anxiety that characterise Ireland in *Colin Clout* the narrator states, 'There learned arts do flourish in great honor, / And Poets wits are had in peerlesse price' (lines 320–1). The adverb, 'There', is ambiguous: it looks as if it is England, but may well be the Ireland where the shepherds live and where the poem was written, the home of the title, as the dedicatory epistle to Sir Walter Raleigh makes clear. If it is England, given the descriptions of court culture, the link must surely be ironic, marking out a pointed contrast between the poem itself and the barren intellectual culture at the centre of the realm. If Ireland, then the suggestion is that, despite all the chaos and misery that afflicts the settlers, they can still produce marvellous and pointed poetry that is alive to the art and dangers of war, away from the court of Elizabeth.

Gascoigne did not serve in Ireland. Nevertheless, it is clear that others in the circle connected to Grey were also keen to promote writers sympathetic to military values and to highlight the links between soldiers

---

[45] George Gascoigne, 'Dulce bellum inexpertis', in George Gascoigne, *A Hundreth Sundrie Flowres*, G. W. Pigman III (ed.) (Oxford, 2000), pp. 398–439. Subsequent references to this edition in parentheses in the text.

[46] On martial poetry, see D. J. B. Trim, 'The art of war: martial poetics from Henry Howard to Philip Sidney', in Michael Pincombe and Cathy Shrank (eds.), *The Oxford handbook of Tudor literature, 1485–1603* (Oxford, 2009), pp. 587–605.

and poets.[47] A key work is Lodowick Bryskett's *A Discourse of Civill Life*, which was not published until 1606 but was originally written in the early 1580s, and dedicated to Lord Grey.[48] Bryskett's dialogue, an adaptation of Giambattista Giraldi Cinthio's *Tre dialoghi della vita civile* (1565), was designed to show off the lively and vibrant intellectual culture that thrived under Grey's leadership in Ireland, undoubtedly as a reminder to readers that such things were not simply the preserve of the court in London. The dialogue describes a real or imagined meeting of various intellectuals at Bryskett's house about a mile and a half from Dublin, possibly in the village of Rathfarnham, now a Dublin suburb, where Bryskett and, probably, Spenser lived.[49] As well as Spenser, described as 'late your Lordship's secretary', the nine friends present were John Long, the archbishop of Armagh (1547/8–89); Sir Robert Dillon (d. 1579), a judge, the only Old English member of the group, related to Bryskett by marriage; George Dormer, described as 'the Queenes sollicitor', probably working for the Irish judiciary under the lord justice; Sir William Pelham, the lord chief justice, whose second wife was the widow of Sir William Dormer, clearly a relative of George; Captain Christopher Carleill (1551?–93), a naval commander, who travelled to Russia, saw action in the Low Countries, and served in Drake's fleet in the West Indies; Sir Thomas Norris (1556–99), the fifth of the Norris brothers who, like Sir John Norris, spent considerable time in Ireland and later acted as Spenser's superior in Munster; Warham St Leger (1525?–97), sometime president of Munster, colonial adventurer in Ireland, who later became a neighbour of Spenser's on the Munster plantation; Captain Thomas Dawtrey; and Thomas Smith, an apothecary and the first medical practitioner in Dublin, according to Nicholas Malby (presumably the first English one).[50] All members of this group either definitely were or could have been in Dublin in 1582. The composition shows a neat balance of civil servants, poets, military commanders and soldiers, naval officers, and other civic officials. This group of diverse citizens from the civil service and the military has a wide range of interests from the conquest of Ireland and the establishment of colonies to treatises and poems on self-government and education (Spenser and Bryskett

---

[47] Some of the following three paragraphs have been adapted from my *Edmund Spenser: a life*, ch. 5.

[48] Henry R. Plomer and T. P. Cross, *The life and correspondence of Lodowick Bryskett* (Chicago, 1927), ch. 9.

[49] *Ibid.*, p. 80.

[50] See the *ODNB* entries: Henry Jeffries, 'Long, John'; Jon G. Crawford, 'Dillon, Sir Robert'; Hugh Hanley, 'Pelham, Dorothy'; D. J. B. Trim, 'Carleill, Christopher'; Judith Hudson Barry, 'Norris, Sir Thomas'; David Edwards, 'St Leger, Sir Warham'; Plomer and Cross, *Bryskett*, p. 82.

himself), all inter-related issues vital for the establishment of good government and the proper discussions that ensure its development and
maintenance.

Bryskett's purpose in recording those present at the debate was perhaps
a means of promoting and defending Grey – although the publication
more than a decade after Grey's death in 1593 suggests that this was now
a minor goal. But probably his real aim was to illustrate how civilised and
sophisticated Dubliners were in trying to establish culture in an island
best known to an English audience as a violent, savage outpost, and a
graveyard for the English forces there, and to show how long such efforts
had been taking place.[51] After all, although they are assigned speaking
parts in the dialogues, the group are not really required to further the
debate, which takes place over three days. The first day concerns the
ideal education of a young child; the second, the progress from youth to
adulthood; and the third, the proper activities and pursuits of a mature
man.[52] Bryskett's record of his symposium is probably a good guide to the
aspirations of the more educated and studious of the English in Ireland
in the late sixteenth century. More significantly still, there was a need not
only to stage such events but to make sure that they were recorded and
duly noted in England as well as Ireland.

War, and the need to train children for war, unsurprisingly enough,
plays a central role in the dialogue. On the first day, Captain Carleill
politely interrupts the speaker with a request that is perfectly in line with
the decorum of courtly speech, but which reminds those present of the
need to consider his chosen profession:

Whiles in this place I was pawsing a while, as to take some breath, Captaine
Carleil sayd in this sort: I hope your author giueth not ouer so this matter. For
howsoeuer his purpose was to discourse of the ciuill life of priuate men, yet the
declaring of the order which was held in the instructing and training vp of the
children of those Princes, cannot but be as well profitable as delightfull. Therefore
let vs (I pray you) heare what is sayd by him touching the same.[53]

The sub-text here is that civil life cannot thrive without an education
in the arts of war. Turning to Aristotle, Plato, and, most significantly,
Xenophon's *Cyropedia*, Bryskett provides a measured and inclusive
answer about the need for a child who is to rule to know the military arts:

---

[51] Bryskett was undoubtedly inspired by similar events in England that Spenser may well
have witnessed: see Anthony Grafton and Lisa Jardine, '"Studied for action": how
Gabriel Harvey read his Livy', *Past & Present* 129 (1990), 30–78.

[52] Thomas E. Wright, 'Bryskett, Lodowick', in *Spenser Encyclopedia*, Hamilton (ed.), p.
119.

[53] Lodowick Bryskett, *A Discourse of Ciuill Life Containing the Ethike Part of Morall Philosophie* (London, 1606), p. 61. All subsequent references in parentheses in the text.

His infancy being past, he was giuen in charge to others, that exercised him in handling his weapons, horse-manship, and feates of armes; and likewise in hunting, as a meet exercise to frame him fit for military discipline. And this the father did, because he was perswaded that the knowledge of warre was one of the surest foundations for the vpholding of a State or kingdome (p. 62).

The child will then continue to study religion, science, and other subjects vital for good government. The text makes clear that training in military discipline, strategy, and behaviour are vital components of the education of a prince, without which the courtier understands and possesses only a series of pointless and empty values. And, a few pages later, a vigorous defence of the universal right to train for war and to be prepared to wage war is outlined:

Furthermore, the vniuersal warre is allowed by the lawes of all those who haue bin founders of famous Common-weales, to take away seditions, and reduce such as were rebellious to obedience, and to maintaine temperance and order among all subiects. And God himselfe is called the God of hoasts, but not the God of combats: for they are none of his works, but of the diuell himselfe. Whereupon it is also sayd in the Scripture, that the strength of warre consisteth not in the multitude of souldiers, but that it commeth from heauen. And S. Augustine sayth, that warre is not vniust, vnlesse it be raised with purpose to vsurpe or to spoyle: and S. Ambrose in like sence affirmeth, that the valour of those men that defend their countrey from barbarous people, is full of iustice (pp. 72–3).

War as conflict is the work of the devil, but war designed to prevent conflict is holy. The definition provided here makes it clear to readers, especially as Bryskett's *Discourse*, like Byrchensa's *Discourse*, was published in the wake of the victory over the forces of O'Neill and O'Donnell that had ended the Nine Years' War in Ireland. According to Bryskett's reading of the Church Fathers, Augustine and Ambrose would have approved of English efforts to crush the Irish 'rebels'. God would have been on the side of the English to help end division and sedition, and to maintain balanced order.

Is Bryskett referring to Spenser's representation of Temperance, the subject of the second book of *The Faerie Queene*? Bryskett's *Discourse of Civil Life* contains one of the earliest discussions of Spenser's poem, and Bryskett was also the recipient of a sonnet from Spenser explaining to him why he had not yet finished his long work.[54] Bryskett is arguing that true temperance often requires the exercise of military virtue as well as control of the body itself. Indeed, proper and complete order involves a balanced consideration of every aspect of human life, a means of linking earthly and heavenly conduct, exactly what Spenser argued in *The Faerie*

[54] Hadfield, *Spenser: a life*, p. 179.

Queene.[55] And, just as Spenser was at pains to show how England under Elizabeth had lapsed into a dangerous and warped state that undermined the stable balance of good government, undervalued its true subjects, and failed to recognise the need for masculine as well as feminine values, so was Bryskett eager to remind readers that he was right, that he was not alone, and that good government and philosophy of government had flourished for a long time in Ireland despite the efforts of the queen.

Spenser died thinking that his worst fears were about to be realised and that the result of years of bad female rule would be the triumph of a pincer movement – or even an alliance – between the Stuarts and the Spanish to outflank and threaten the rump of England.[56] In fact, English military might reasserted itself under the astute command of Charles Blount, Lord Mountjoy, who defeated the Spanish at the Battle of Kinsale (24 December 1601).[57] This paved the way for the Ulster plantation and the transformation of Ireland in the seventeenth and eighteenth centuries to an English colony.[58] But the triumph was almost a disaster, and Elizabeth herself died before the Irish lords had finalised their surrender, a fact that was cunningly hidden from them during negotiations.[59] Of course, this phase of Anglo-Irish history is hardly a simple tale of male fortitude and female negligence: had Philip III of Spain supported his general, Don Juan del Águila with more troops, he might have been the victor in Ireland.

[55] Andrew Hadfield, 'Spenser and religion – yet again', *Studies in English Literature, 1500–1900* 51 (2011), 21–46.

[56] Andrew Hadfield, 'Spenser and the Stuart succession', *Literature and History* 13 (2004), 9–24.

[57] John J. Silke, *Kinsale: the Spanish intervention in Ireland at the end of the Elizabethan wars* (Liverpool, 1970; Dublin, 2000, reprint).

[58] Micheal O Siochru and Eamonn O Ciardha (eds.), *The plantation of Ulster: ideology and practice* (Manchester, 2012).

[59] Nicholas P. Canny, 'The *Treaty of Mellifont* and the re-organisation of Ulster, 1603', *Irish Sword* 9 (1969), 249–62.

12   Elizabeth on rebellion in Ireland and England: *semper eadem?*

Brendan Kane

On the 13th of November 1569, the earl of Sussex issued a proclamation against rebels to the crown. The leaders, he declared, had 'conspired to levy war against her Majesty'. Their motivations were, he noted, confused and changing: at times they claimed they were rising on the queen's orders to rid her court of evil counsellors; at other times that they acted in the name of religion; at still others in defence of the nobility against *arriviste* commoners at court. Sussex believed none of it. Rather than carrying out the queen's wishes, he declared, the rebels were attempting 'to bring the realm under the slavery of foreign powers'. As for religion, he thundered that most of those in the field had 'never respected any religion, but continued a dissolute life until driven to pretend to popish holiness, to put some false colour upon their treasons'. Nor did the claims about defending the nobility convince, for Sussex argued that 'not one of that stock has perished' under Elizabeth's reign. The rebel's true goals, he declared, were to sow sedition and threaten regime change through foreign assistance – an insidious set of treasons that required them to publish false declarations in order to trick the 'ignorant people' into joining them.[1]

For the student of Elizabethan English–Irish relations, Sussex's proclamation stands out for two reasons. The first is that the rebellion in question, the so-called Northern Rebellion of 1569, occurred *in England*. By the earl's description, the rising he was charged with suppressing bore all the chief characteristics familiar to historians of rebellion in Ireland: the raising of war, efforts at restoring Catholicism, threat of foreign invasion, and fear of new-made men undercutting traditional privilege. That Sussex himself served as lord lieutenant in Ireland lends this document further Irish resonance. However, as noted, the rising he described

I wish to thank Susannah Ottaway and Sarah Chambers for the generous invitation to test these ideas at Carleton College and the University of Minnesota, and Krista Kesselring and Steve Hindle for their close, careful, and immensely helpful readings of earlier versions.
[1] HMC, *Salisbury*, I, pp. 104–5.

occurred in England, and was undertaken by the heads of the ancient English noble houses of Northumberland and Westmorland. This raises the obvious question of just how similar, or different, were rebellions in the two realms. The second reason for the proclamation's significance is that it is evidence of Elizabeth's aggressive pursuit of rebels. Sussex did not initially approach this conflict with the muscular loyalty quoted above; he had to be pushed to it by the queen herself. Long described by historians as vacillating in matters martial, Elizabeth was anything but when it came to the transgressions of the northern earls. She sniffed treason and offence long before her noble servant Sussex did and hectored him to embody the power of crown and state against the disloyal. This, in turn, raises the question of the queen's responses to rebellion in her realms: if there were substantive similarities to insurrections in both kingdoms, did she take a similarly active role in their 'correction'?

This chapter tracks (if necessarily briefly) across Elizabeth I's long reign the two points raised above by Sussex's proclamation: the similarities between rebellious actions in the two kingdoms and the queen's role in effecting their suppression. Three suggestions will be offered as to how this exploration may add to our understanding of early modern English–Irish relations, the first and most significant being that the queen did not see rebellions in her realms as fundamentally different. This is not to say that she thought there were no dissimilarities, or that Ireland was merely an extension of England. However, it is to say that Elizabeth saw the actions of her rebellious subjects as exactly that: as the actions of 'unnatural' subjects, regardless of realm of origin. This prompts the second conclusion, namely that 'Tudor' rebellions occurred in both realms. According to the literature, there were on the one hand 'Tudor rebellions', which occurred in England, and on the other 'Irish rebellions'. This historiographical distinction – be it implicit or explicit – does not accord with the views of the monarch herself and as such serves to separate the queen's realms from one another and to drive an anachronistic wedge between the actions and motivations of their residents. Third and finally, then, Elizabeth's views highlight the domestic aspects of even the most violent of Irish affairs: they can be studied alongside other instances of unrest in the realms and, thus, they demonstrate the continuing phenomenon of internal rebellion throughout the entire Tudor period.

It is a historiographical commonplace, though not a historical fact, that Elizabeth's reign experienced fewer rebellions than did those of her predecessors. What is a matter of historical record, of course, is that the incidence of rebellion in England fell off dramatically during her monarchy, the only major episode being the Northern Rebellion (or

Rising, as it is sometimes called) of 1569. Much historical freight has been attached to this stunning *pax Elizabeth*, namely the triumph of the modernising/centralising state over the centripetal, local powers of a medieval aristocracy. Key to this interpretation was the work of Mervyn James, who saw in the Northern Rebellion the last of the regional risings that had characterised monarch–noble relations for centuries.[2] To James, however, the true 'end of an era' was the tragi-comic Essex Rebellion: the lack of popular support in London that it garnered, and the ease with which it was quashed and its principals punished, demonstrated clearly the inability of aristocratic principles to challenge a regnant, Protestant monarch for either practical power or the people's hearts and minds.[3] The end of rebellion, in short, meant the coming of the modern, an era in which the mobilisation of state forces was undertaken primarily for external theatres.

A difficulty with this interpretation, however, is that studies of Tudor rebellions invariably focus on England alone. Although the authority of the Tudor crown also embraced the kingdom of Ireland, rebellions there do not make the historiographical cut as 'Tudor rebellions'. The standard work on the subject, Anthony Fletcher and Diarmaid MacCulloch's *Tudor rebellions*, consigns Irish unrest to an epilogue in which explicit distinction is made between domestic risings of the 'Tudor' type and the 'overseas' imperial variants found in Ireland – a place which, the authors state, emerged as 'the first English colony; the beginning of a world empire; the first hint that England would be something more than a minor European power'. Whereas the 1596 Oxfordshire Rebellion was laughable and the state's reaction to it was overkill, and the Essex Rebellion was driven in part by the simple fact of the earl's mental 'instability', matters in Ireland 'turned into a genocidal conflict, in which English forces saw themselves as fighting a barbaric race who deserved no mercy'.[4] If the former were law-and-order problems, the latter were winner-take-all colonial wars.

This is not to claim that there has been no effort to see connections between rebellions in the two realms.[5] In his brilliant analysis of the

---

[2] Mervyn James, 'The concept of order and the Northern Rising, 1569', in Mervyn James, *Society, politics and culture: studies in early modern England* (Cambridge, 1986), pp. 308–415. More generally on his views of the collapse of traditional northern society, see James, *Family, lineage and civil society; a study of society, politics and mentality in the Durham region, 1500–1640* (Oxford, 1974).

[3] James, 'At a crossroads of the political culture: the Essex revolt, 1601', in James, *Society, politics and culture*, pp. 416–65.

[4] Anthony Fletcher and Diarmaid MacCulloch, *Tudor rebellions* (New York, 1997), pp. 112–14.

[5] The classic comparative approach is Steven G. Ellis, 'Henry VIII, rebellion, and the rule of law', *Historical Journal* 24 (1981), 513–31. The focus here, by obvious contrast, is on

Baltinglass Rebellion, Christopher Maginn asks explicitly whether this insurrection was a typical Tudor affair or something unique. While allowing that there were certain similarities – chiefly crown efforts to replace recalcitrant nobility with loyalists, a phenomenon seen in England throughout the sixteenth century – he concludes that the Baltinglass rising was preponderantly dissimilar on account of its Gaelic connection, Baltinglass having joined forces with the O'Byrnes and O'Tooles, who had decidedly anti-English intentions.[6] Anthony McCormack's authoritative handling of the Desmond Rebellions also addresses links between unrest in Ireland and England. In doing so he offers two classifications of armed threat faced by Tudor regimes – internal ones to which the state acted swiftly and with minimal planning, and external ones that required greater preparation and more money and materiel. Sensibly and persuasively, he characterises the Desmond Rebellions as hybrid phenomena bearing traits of both internal challenge and external threat, which elicited from the state both quick reaction and longer-term planning and investment. Nevertheless, in his final analysis the Desmond Rebellions rest chiefly in the 'foreign' threat category, given that the ultimate stakes concerned whether English rule would run through Ireland.[7] Even Krista Kesselring, who offers the most sophisticated comparative analysis of rebellious violence in England and Ireland, refers to the Northern Rebellion as the 'last great Tudor rebellion'.[8]

A case might be made for revisiting this historiographical convention and questioning the assumptions that undergird it. It is undoubtedly true, for instance, that rebellions in Ireland are different from English ones on account of their Gaelic elements. But this is in part an a priori demographic reality: rebellions in England would perforce lack a Gaelic component. Moreover, the Tudor polity was a diverse one, and it is not clear why being Gaelic would render one less a subject of the crown – and thus ineligible for participation in a proper Tudor rebellion – than would residing in some culturally distinct peripheral area of England itself. Gaelic cultural forms were, of course, deemed by many to be synonymous with rebelliousness, and the need to Anglicise Ireland constituted an effort to create cultural uniformity as the basis of loyalty that

---

the Elizabethan period. Nevertheless, some of the conclusions are the same, namely that Tudor monarchs were not so keen to differentiate rebellions by geographical setting as later historians have proven to be.

[6] Christopher Maginn, 'The Baltinglass Rebellion, 1580: English dissent or a Gaelic uprising?', *Historical Journal* 47 (2004), 205–32.

[7] Anthony McCormack, *The earldom of Desmond 1463–1583: the decline and crisis of a feudal lordship* (Dublin, 2005), pp. 145–92.

[8] Krista Kesselring, *The Northern Rebellion of 1569: faith, politics and protest in Elizabethan England* (Basingstoke, 2007), p. 9.

was tremendously more profound than that seen in the 'backward' north or even Wales.[9] Nevertheless, Elizabeth did have an interest in cultural difference – as some of the chapters collected in this book demonstrate – and it is a primary point of this chapter that she was more accepting of cultural diversity, as long as it was accompanied by loyalty, than were many of those below her. Again, Elizabeth's views and approaches are the quarry here, not those of the broader 'Elizabethan' regime.[10] Moving to a more strictly geographical perspective, we find that rebellions arising out of 'Celtic' Cornwall count in Fletcher and MacCulloch's working definition of 'Tudor rebellion'.[11] Nor is it clear that political intentions, and their implications, necessarily separated actors in the two kingdoms. On the one hand, the self-identifying 'English' earl of Desmond would have been horrified to learn that he was the point man of a new Irish identity predicated on separation from the monarchical centre. To his mind, the question in Munster concerned varieties of English rule rather than English versus 'other'. On the other hand, Northumberland no less than Tyrone played the game of seeking foreign assistance to settle internal matters. Why, then, do we cast the former as a typical 'Tudor rebellion' and the latter as a harbinger of uniquely modern imperial relations?

Focus on Elizabeth's views of rebellion may offer a means to see points of contact as well as of difference between late sixteenth-century rebellions in England and Ireland. There has been little work dedicated to the queen's personal commentary on, and reaction to, rebellion. Her role has, of course, found a place in studies of collective violence; copious examples are to be found in the secondary literature cited earlier, for instance. But it is never the central focus of analysis, hers being but one more – if very important – voice in explorations of events that are frequently cast in set categories. All actions that can bear the label of 'rebellion', however, were at their core challenges to the monarch by certain of her subjects. These could be directed towards any number of goals spanning a continuum from reform to regime change. Yet, in each case, the ultimate object was to move the monarch to some action favoured by the demonstrators, and the fundamental driving force was the dynamic relationship of rights and responsibilities linking subject and sovereign.

[9] Patricia Palmer, *Language and conquest in early modern Ireland: English Renaissance literature and Elizabethan imperial expansion* (Cambridge, 2001).

[10] One vital caveat here, however, is that I am aware of the impossibility of recovering the queen's 'true' thoughts, and such recovery is not my intention. Rather, I am interested to chart how she speaks of, and treats, rebels in both realms. Whatever the 'practicality' or 'authenticity' of her statements on subjects across the realms, their similarities and/or differences tell us much.

[11] Fletcher and MacCulloch, *Tudor rebellions*, pp. 6, 15–17.

The queen's perspective, then, was unique: everyone was her subject, and she no one's but God's. Whatever the views of even the highest members of her administration, for instance Lord Burghley, Elizabeth's personal take on rebellion was necessarily singular. Exploring that view, it will be argued here, allows a critically important insight into the close connection of rebellions across the realms and of sovereign–subject relations. In short, it allows us to look at rebellions unconcerned about their potential typology, classification, or utility in periodisation exercises, but rather as necessarily unique expressions of commonly shared notions of political right and responsibility found across the social hierarchy of both realms.

While this may seem a fairly straightforward undertaking, it faces three significant challenges in execution. The first involves the queen's practice of policy-making through 'proboleutic groups' (small bodies of confidants and informal councillors that were convened to discuss matters before broaching them to the full council).[12] Such an oral decision-making process among intimates necessarily leaves little trace in the written records. Consequently, we are cut off from much of the queen's thoughts on Ireland (and on all other subjects, too, of course). Nevertheless, the state papers alone contain a great number of documents in the queen's name related to violent protest in both realms. Yet therein lies the second problem: given that much of this material exists as drafts by her advisers, typically Burghley, it is unclear whether the opinions expressed are indeed hers. The third problem stems from the sheer number of rebellious events in Ireland compared to England. Space constraints preclude systematic analysis of Elizabeth's views on the many risings that plagued Ireland, those of Desmond, Baltinglass, Butler, Nugent, Shane O'Neill, the Burkes (Mac an Iarla), the O'Mores, and O'Neill and O'Donnell being merely the major ones. As such, comprehensive comparison with her views on risings in England is not feasible.

The strategy adopted here is to construct a (necessarily) impressionistic picture of Elizabeth's views on rebellion by triangulating among three types of sources. Actual autograph documents by the queen will, to the extent possible, drive the argument. Documents written in the queen's name will also be consulted, the thinking being that they could not have circulated without her approval, grudging as it may have been in some instances. (And even if these drafts did not become formal correspondence, they remain records of conciliar opinion as to her preferences and predilections.) Finally, letters addressed to the queen, or her council, will

---

[12] This is the term used by Natalie Mears in her *Queenship and political discourse in the Elizabethan realms* (Cambridge, 2005).

be used. As with the conciliar drafts noted above, these give a sense of contemporary understandings of Elizabeth's mindset. These understandings may often have been incorrect, but they will greatly increase our knowledge of how her subjects – rebellious or otherwise – perceived her actions and intentions in times of civil unrest. In terms of historical coverage, given the number of rebellious events in Ireland, particular attention will focus on the Desmond Rebellion and that of Hugh O'Neill, although gleanings from others will be presented where particularly illustrative.

We may start by demonstrating the queen's own role in precipitating rebellion. Elizabeth could be tough on her nobility. When the duke of Norfolk was requested to come to court to account for himself regarding intrigues concerning Mary Stuart, he threw numerous roadblocks in the queen's way. Having endured her considerable hectoring – including spectacularly the demand that sickness was no excuse and that if necessary she would send a litter to retrieve him – Norfolk finally set out for London. And a good thing it was, too, for as Elizabeth wrote Shrewsbury and Huntington in October 1569, 'otherwise the World shuld have seene some Effects of that Authoritie which God have given us'.[13] The threat of such 'Effects' may have helped push the duke fatally into conspiracy to press on with a match with the Scottish queen, a decision that cost him his life in 1572. It certainly seems to have done so in the case of Northumberland and Westmorland. In her fear over the challenge presented by Mary, queen of Scots', links to England's aristocracy, Elizabeth demanded an accounting of good behaviour from Northumberland. The latter was reluctant to come to court fearing that it would mean his destruction at the hands of court enemies, notably Burghley. Signs of recent monarchical disfavour had given him cause to fret: losing his post as lieutenant-general of the north and the wardenship of the Middle March, having no part in custody of the Scottish queen, and even the undercutting of his financial standing by rejection of his claims for rights over a copper mine. And so he declined Elizabeth's invitation, which in turn raised the stakes of the standoff to the point where the earl felt that his only chance for self-preservation came in armed demonstration flanked by his local affinity.[14]

Similarly, as Ciaran Brady has demonstrated, the earl of Desmond's fears about factional alignments against him, and despair over perception

---

[13] Samuel Haynes (ed.), *A collection of state papers, relating to affairs in the reigns of King Henry VIII... Queen Elizabeth, from the year 1542 to 1570* (London, 1740), p. 538 (consulted electronically through Eighteenth Century Collections Online).

[14] Elizabeth's role in undermining the earls' confidence, and thus helping push them to the desperation of armed rebellion, is more amply traced in Kesselring, *Northern Rebellion*, and Fletcher and MacCulloch, *Tudor rebellions*.

that the queen would not support him, pushed the earl to rebel.[15] In particular, it was her preference for his family's ancient enemy, the earl of Ormond, that helped convince him of his imminent destruction at crown hands.[16] This preference manifested itself in terms as practical as those affecting Northumberland. For instance, Elizabeth wrote to her lord deputy, Sir Henry Sidney, in August 1566 instructing him to transfer lands from Desmond to Ormond on account of the former's 'many great disorders against our peace'.[17] Nearly thirty years later Tyrone also found that his position with the government had deteriorated on account of monarchical choices. As Hiram Morgan writes, Elizabeth must bear blame for the drift to war by driving a harder bargain with O'Neill than those on the ground who knew the local situation, the earl of Essex principal among them.[18] Indeed, the Irish earl trotted out the same range of motivations given by his northern English predecessors: fear of low-born men whispering against him, defence of ancient privilege, and the like. Certainly, the same could be said about the genesis of the Essex Rebellion: a less aggressive reaction by the queen to his desperate return from Ireland to court might have precluded his fatal resort to arms.

Once rebellion proper had broken out, the dictates of personal politics continued to inform the queen's actions. As Natalie Mears has written, the key to Elizabethan politics was 'trust and personal intimacy with the monarch, backed by social and familial networks'.[19] Rebellions heightened the queen's concern for the defence of her personal honour, and here I wish to draw attention to two aspects of monarchical honour politics, deployed in times of emergency, which have as yet gone unremarked by scholars. The first is Elizabeth's manipulation of others' sense of their honour in order to have them do her bidding. In November 1569, the queen wrote to the earl of Cumberland urging him to assist against his neighbouring earls of Northumberland and Westmorland. As usual, and as the literature would tell us, she reminded him that her own honour was at stake. In addition, however, she stressed that he was bound to do so on account of the personal declaration of loyalty that the earl himself had recently made to her.[20] Implicating the earl's own sense of honour in

---

[15] Ciaran Brady, 'Faction and the origins of the Desmond Rebellion of 1579', *Irish Historical Studies* 22 (1981), 289–312.

[16] As Anthony McCormack notes, the queen's friendship with Ormond made arranging negotiations with Desmond difficult: McCormack, *Desmond*, p. 195.

[17] Sir Henry Sidney, 'Additional Sidney state papers', D. B. Quinn (ed.), *Analecta Hibernica* 26 (1970), 97.

[18] Hiram Morgan, *Tyrone's rebellion: the outbreak of the Nine Years War in Tudor Ireland* (Woodbridge, 1993), pp. 152, 176.

[19] Mears, *Queenship*, p. 71.   [20] Haynes (ed.), *State papers*, p. 553.

the defence of her administration was a clever, if deeply intrusive, strategy: whereas disloyalty was a sin of external relations, dishonour of the broken vow was one of internal worth. She used similar techniques on the rebels themselves, expressing pointed reminders of their given word of loyalty.[21]

But it was to potential, if foot-dragging, allies that such reminders were most intensely deployed. For example, the flawless loyalty of Northumberland's brother, Sir Henry Percy, was opposed against his brother the earl's transgressions which 'hazard[ed] the Overthrow of his Howse'. This praise was followed by the thinly veiled threat of her hope for the continuation of 'such a House in the Parson and Blood of so faithfull a Servant, as we trust to find you'.[22] Similarly, the earl of Shrewsbury was pointedly reminded of his recent, and face-to-face, profession of loyalty, and she trusted that he would conduct himself as 'duly representing the Truth and Honor of your Hous'.[23] The tactic of manipulating subjects' notions of individual and familial honour was also employed in Irish affairs. In reflecting on the rebellion of Desmond, Elizabeth expressed her incredulity at the earl's actions given how highly she esteemed him and that he had enjoyed great liberty on account of her favour.[24] Gaelic examples of such intimate declarations are more difficult to come by. In part this is because some of those raised at the court, say Donough O'Brien, 4th earl of Thomond, were committed loyalists (and in this case loyal to the state church, too) and thus needed no reminding. However, the sense of personal connection and of the reciprocal bonds of vertical honour linking monarch and subject pervades Elizabeth's remarks on Hugh O'Neill at the end of her reign. She never tired of mentioning that it was she who had brought O'Neill up, and thus that it was she who could bring him back down into obscurity once more. There even seems to have been an effort on her part to effect this manipulation of personal loyalties at a distance and through proxies. Morgan points out that Elizabeth believed that O'Neill 'could deal with O'Donnell on account of ties of marriage and dependence'.[25] In doing so, she reminded other potential allies of their loyalty, honourably proclaimed, as a means to wheedle them to her perspective.

A second notable aspect of how honour imperatives helped shape the queen's reaction to rebellion was her rhetorically powerful claim that they drove her to act against her otherwise merciful nature. Speaking of the

---

[21] See, for instance, her reminder to the rebellious earls of how they had recently, and in person, expressed their loyalty to her: *ibid.*, p. 533.

[22] *Ibid.*, p. 555.   [23] *Ibid.*, pp. 561–2.   [24] *CSPI*, 1571–5, p. 497.

[25] Morgan, *Tyrone's rebellion*, p. 160.

northern rebels, she expressed regret for having shown too much mercy since ascending the throne. This, she opined, had weakened the safety of both the state and her person. Consequently, she declared that in a 'Matter that toucheth us so nere, we can in no wyse fynd it convenient to grant Pardon or other shewe of Favor unto those, that doo not humblie and earnestly sue for the same'.[26] Her insistence on this point raised concerns with Sussex who cautioned that '[A]ll the wisest Protestants think that you should offer mercy before you try the sword.'[27] In Ireland, too, the queen feared that her merciful ways had proven detrimental to security. On the one hand, she had increasingly come to declare that her Irish subjects had abused her good will and tended to conduct themselves haughtily because of their trust in crown leniency.[28] On the other, executive mercy seemed to have encouraged those in Ireland to take to armed resistance if her officers did attempt to stamp their authority, this because they knew full well that the logistical difficulties of suppressing rebellion in Ireland frequently meant pardons would be forthcoming. As Elizabeth and her councillors complained, they often had to pardon rebel leaders and their followers because they had no practical means of cracking down on them all.[29] Consequently, once the queen decided to turn her face fully to suppression, defence of her honour put a quick end to her sense of mercy. To Sidney, she made clear her mind 'that we thynk it not for our honour, but rather to thincrease of the obstinate audacite of Shane Oneyle, to have you remove any treaty with him'.[30] Unsurprisingly, much of what got Sir John Perrot and the 2nd earl of Essex in trouble in Ireland was their willingness to negotiate with the rebels when the queen wished them unequivocally reduced to law, order, and obedience.[31]

As this last example suggests, Elizabeth took a hard-line attitude with her commanders be they in Ireland or England. To Sussex, who was not only reluctant at first to move against the earls but also referred to them in the early days of the commotion as those 'poor earls', she gave frequent epistolary tongue lashings. In October 1569, she expressed how she felt it 'strange' that her commander in the north had not sent news and that

---

[26] Haynes (ed.), *State papers*, p. 557. This letter also demonstrates nicely both the personal and official affront offered by the rebels' actions, for she commented how they had both 'offendyd us and our Lawes': *ibid.*

[27] *CSPD*, VII, p. 108.

[28] Krista Kesselring, *Mercy and authority in the Tudor state* (Cambridge, 2007), p. 194.

[29] *Ibid.*, pp. 195–6.   [30] SP 63/16/70.

[31] On the former, see Hiram Morgan, 'The fall of Sir John Perrot', in John Guy (ed.), *The reign of Elizabeth I: court and culture in the last decade* (Cambridge, 1995), pp. 109–25; on the latter, see Brendan Kane, *The politics and culture of honour in Britain and Ireland, 1541–1641* (Cambridge, 2010), ch. 3.

she wanted information as soon as possible.[32] The following February she again found it 'very strange' that he had not brought Lord Dacre to ground and then proceeded to berate him for tarrying, to belittle him for doing so little when such a strong force was at his disposal, and to offer her own thoughts on better courses of action.[33] What passed between contemporaries in speech is, of course, lost to history. But there are moments when we have insight into what was conveyed, and in the case of Elizabeth to Lord Scrope it was not positive. In the minute of her letter to him dated 7 December 1569, she expressed displeasure at how little support he had offered in her service, 'of which Matter we have somwhat more largely imparted our Mind to this Bearer'.[34]

And we do know that whatever their duties of loyalty, those charged to implement her orders were frequently exasperated with her lack of support and understanding for their actions. Lord Hunsdon vented his spleen spectacularly to Cecil in writing that the queen must be 'bewitched' to doubt those who do her best service.[35] Her Irish commanders faced similar displeasure, pressure, and second-guessing from the queen. A particularly telling example of the intrusiveness of her correction comes from her instructions to Sir Robert Gardiner in 1596 when she found how he had conducted negotiations 'dishonourable' and warned him not to meet in open fields with the rebels or use terms such as 'your loving friends' or 'your very good lord' when addressing them.[36] Elizabeth was so furious with Sir William Fitzwilliam's conduct during the Desmond unrest that at one point she offered Desmond himself the chance to come to London and explain himself because she severely doubted her lord deputy's 'impartiality'.[37] The tragic ends of Perrot and Essex are well enough known and require no extensive retelling here. Yet one noteworthy point for the present argument is how both affairs demonstrate Elizabeth's utter unwillingness to see her nobility make links between themselves that cut her out. In short, we might say that the fall of these two governors demonstrates the high stakes that were involved in not doing the queen's pleasure, and in a timely manner, when rebellion was afoot. Be it in Ireland or England, once Elizabeth was set on an objective she would brook no delay, and smile on no failure, from her subordinates. Long accused – and with some very good reason – of vacillating on policy matters, Elizabeth presented an unwavering sense of purpose in suppressing rebels.

---

[32] *CSPD*, VII, p. 89.
[33] In this case he should have gone first to York, and the letter commanded that he do so now: *ibid.*, p. 211.
[34] Haynes (ed.), *State papers*, p. 571.   [35] *CSPD*, VII, p. 195.
[36] Morgan, *Tyrone's rebellion*, p. 201.   [37] McCormack, *Desmond*, p. 133.

Not least in her mind was desire to quash rebel claims to religious justification. The role of continentally trained Catholic intellectuals in Irish
rebellions is well known; noteworthy here is the parallel reality of intense
involvement of Counter-Reformation zealots in the Northern Rebellion.
Two of the main allies, or agitators, of Northumberland and Westmorland were Nicholas Morton and his son-in-law, Thomas Markenfeld.
Morton was a 'Catholic ex-canon of Canterbury Cathedral'; both he and
Markenfeld had fled to the continent earlier in Elizabeth's reign and had
returned to England, fired up with Tridentine certainty, intending to win
all of England by first stirring the conservative north.[38] This does not
mean that the queen and her counsellors necessarily believed in the sincerity of the rebels' religious fervour. As we have already seen in Sussex's
proclamation against the northern earls, the regime's line was that religion was merely a pretence covering baser motives.[39] Nor were the claims
for holy war in Ireland, be they by Gall (Desmond) or Gael (O'Neill),
deemed credible. And, yet, for all of the queen's dismissive bravado
regarding her subjects' confessional motivations she harboured real fear
of the old religion. On hearing that the northern earls had overseen the
destruction of Bibles and other accoutrements of official worship, Elizabeth demanded to know if the local people joined in the sacrilege or
resisted it, whether they 'liked or misliked' this iconoclasm against the
state-sanctioned church. In spite of her expressed opinion that the rising
was 'grounded uppon an other Devise' than religion, she nevertheless
wished to forestall any possibility that the people would believe the earls'
rhetoric. To that end, Sussex was required to broadcast the speciousness
of the rebels' religious claims and make public what the regime held
to be their true desire, namely to bring England under the 'Yoke' of
foreign princes and, under 'Colour of Religion', make it 'the spoile of
Strangers'.[40] Writing from the field, in turn, Sussex warned his sovereign
that the peril of religious heterodoxy, even if born of Machiavellian cal-
culation rather than sincere attachment, was a 'peril that might grow by
toleration'.[41] And duly, as Kesselring has noted, that 'intense anti-papist
sentiment in the south demanded harsh, exemplary punishment' in the
rising's aftermath – and, as we shall see below, those demands were amply
satisfied.[42]

With links to co-religionists on the continent came monarchical fear
of foreign invasion in both kingdoms. This fact has largely been lost in

---

[38] Fletcher and MacCulloch, *Tudor rebellions*, pp. 105–6.
[39] Sussex, in fact, called it a 'pretence' in his letter to the queen of 13 November 1569:
   CSPD, VII, p. 103.
[40] Haynes (ed.), *State papers*, p. 556.   [41] *CSPD*, VII, p. 103.
[42] Kesselring, *Mercy*, p. 136.

a historiographical convention which considers that such talk of foreign assistance-in-arms in an English context to have been mere rhetoric, but that in Ireland it was demonstrative of shifting paradigms of political relations: whereas Northumberland was a pathetic character left behind by a modernising Protestant state and his foreign intrigues a slightly embarrassing bit of end-game desperation, Desmond and O'Neill were forward-looking warriors of faith-and-fatherland.[43] Conversely, however, it might be plausibly argued that foreign intrigues arising from England were the more threatening to the state and thus more likely to draw from the centralising state innovative forms of control and of rhetorical positions to justify them. This is to say that, whereas Desmond and O'Neill pursued the possibility of transferring Irish loyalties to a continental potentate and leaving England to its own devices, Northumberland and Westmorland toyed with regime change at home. And, indeed, the latter pair fled across the border to Scotland seeking foreign assistance. As a final speculation on this point, the fact that they considered linking up with sympathisers in Ireland (notably Turlough Luineach O'Neill) suggests that the clean break between Tudor and Irish rebellions, and the notion of a uniquely Irish context for foreign invasion, would not have made sense to those contemporaries who took up arms against Elizabeth. It certainly did not to Anthony de Gueras, whose Latin letter to the 'the rebels of Ireland' expressed his support and that of Philip II, the duke of Alva, Westmorland, Dacre and Northumberland's widow – all of whom he claimed to be in contact with and who desired their 'safety, honour, and splendor'.[44] Nor did it to Elizabeth herself, who publicly and vociferously accused rebels in both England and Ireland of wishing to bring the realms under foreign domination.[45]

Perhaps more curious than her tough stance with her commanders or her fear of foreigners was her ambivalent attitude towards the lower orders of both realms. Undoubtedly, Elizabeth expressed a great interest in the well-being of her English and Irish subjects. In her reactions to all rebellions, she often spoke in terms of lifting the scales from the eyes of

---

[43] As Mervyn James shows, the Northumberland tenantry was largely unmoved by '"neo-feudal" loyalties' and thus offered 'meager support' followed by surrender to crown forces after but 'token resistance': James, 'The concept of order', pp. 70–2. Kesselring, however, makes clear the Elizabethan regime's anxiety over foreign assistance in 1569, especially when the rebels took Hartlepool: Kesselring, *Northern Rebellion*, pp. 85–6. On faith-and-fatherland in Desmond's and O'Neill's rebellions, see McCormack, *Desmond*, and Morgan, *Tyrone's rebellion*.

[44] *Cal. Carew*, I, p. 333.

[45] See Sussex's proclamation, in HMC, *Salisbury*, i, pp. 104–5; for Irish instances, see William Palmer, *The problem of Ireland in Tudor foreign policy, 1485–1603* (Woodbridge, 1994) – a study dedicated to this very subject.

the commons, hoodwinked as they were by their traitorous, if ostensible, betters.[46] To Sussex, campaigning in the north of England, she expressed her wonder at his suspicion of the locals' loyalties. There are always a few bad apples, she conceded, but he was to trust that most knew their duty and would assist him:

The Doubt that you have conceyevd of the Stedfastnes of our Subjects of that Countie, that ar to goo with you in this Service, semeth somewhat strange unto us; for although wee doo well enough consider that emongst a great Multitude, sume may perhappes for privat Respects, forget theyr Duty toward us; yet doubt wee not but wee have a great Nomber of faythfull and trusty Subjects, both Gentlemen and others in that Countrie; and doo not mistrust but you will make Choyce of those that bee my reasonable Conjectures most lykely to contynue theyr Duty and Faythfullnes; towards our Service.[47]

Evidence also allowed her to imagine that those below the level of the nobility in Ireland were her allies. One of the issues that drove Desmond to violent desperation was his financial difficulty brought on as tenants sought to switch their allegiances, and thus tributary support, from the earldom to the crown.[48] During the rebellion itself, moreover, the crown enjoyed the loyalty of the cities.[49] As a general statement of the queen's publicly professed notions of her care for status-blind justice, we may turn to the following quote from a 1586 speech to Parliament in response to calls for Mary Stuart's execution: 'And for the course of justice, I protest that I never knew difference of persons – that I never set one before another but upon just cause, neither have preferred any to office or to other place of ruling for the preferrer's sake, but that I knew or was made believe he was worthy and fit for it.'[50]

Yet whatever the rhetoric, and occasional example, of loyal tenants bucking treasonous lords, Elizabeth's position vis-à-vis the lower orders in time of rebellion was more complex and fraught. Her correspondence and proclamations contain numerous denunciations of the people. These took a number of forms, the most basic being a general distrust of popularity. We tend to think of Elizabeth as a peerless manipulator and cultivator of her subjects' emotional attachments. That does not preclude, however, her harbouring a simultaneous and real fear of the people as many-headed monster (a fear she shared with perhaps all monarchs). To

---

[46] More broadly, Elizabeth's, and her regime's, rhetoric of paternalistic care for the people is demonstrated and parsed in Steve Hindle, 'Dearth, fasting and alms: the campaign for general hospitality in late Elizabethan England', *Past & Present* 172 (2001), 44–86.

[47] Haynes (ed.), *State papers*, p. 557.   [48] Brady, 'Faction', 294.

[49] McCormack, *Desmond*, p. 169.

[50] Elizabeth I, *Elizabeth I: collected works*, Leah Marcus, Janel Mueller, and Mary Beth Rose (eds.) (Chicago, 2000), p. 198.

the earl of Cumberland, she complained that the local people had done nothing to stop the rebels, an inactivity which brought 'Discredit of our good Subjects there'. In theory, then, they may have been good, but in practice less so.[51] Her concern about the old religion was not helped by her sense of the 'Hypocresy amongst the Vulgar gross People' and their 'lewd Collations' in favour of mass and pope.[52] Nor were hardship and want an excuse for disorder; in 1595 the privy council committed to print their and the queen's opinion that the people were 'to indure this scarsety with patience, and to beware how they give eare to any perwasyons or practices of discontented and ydle braynes to move them to repyne or swerve from the humble duties of good subjects'.[53] In Ireland, too, she fretted over how to deal with 'doubtful subjects'.[54] Rumour-spreading and news-mongering among the lower orders were a perceived problem in both realms. Crown distrust of the loose-lipped Irish is well known and traceable in law and policy enacted for Ireland under Elizabeth.[55] But this was also a feature of monarchical reaction to rebellion in England. Such anxiety was, of course, closely connected to the fear of vagabonds and masterless people, who bore much official opprobrium as creators of, as opposed to victims of, social problems.[56] Thus, the commons' presumed unregulated liberty, unleashed in times of unrest, spurred the crown to action in Ireland – as William Palmer has traced – and so in England, too.[57]

Elizabeth's distrust of the lesser-born – be they commoners or simply non-noble – also manifested itself in a repeated preference for the aristocracy, at least as a category. To take an Irish example, during the so-called Mac an Iarla uprising that raged over Connaught between 1567 and 1582, the queen was reluctant to see the earl of Clanricard himself as responsible.[58] Angrily, she demanded explanation from Sir Edward Fitton, the lord president of Connaught, as to why he had imprisoned the earl without informing her lord deputy, Sir William Fitzwilliam.[59]

---

[51] Haynes (ed.), *State papers*, p. 570.   [52] *Ibid.*, p. 558.

[53] Quoted in Hindle, 'Dearth, fasting and alms', 45.

[54] *Calendar of state papers, I, Tudor period 1571–1575*, Mary O'Dowd (ed.) (Dublin, 2000), p. 635.

[55] See Patricia Palmer, *Language and conquest*; T. F. O'Rahilly, 'Irish poets, historians, and judges in English documents, 1538–1615', *Proceedings of the Royal Irish Academy* 36 C 6 (1922), 86–120.

[56] Kesselring, *Northern Rebellion*, p. 15; see more generally J. A. Sharpe, *Crime in early modern England* (New York, 1984), and A. L. Beier, *Masterless men: the vagrancy problem in England, 1560–1640* (London, 1985).

[57] William Palmer, 'That insolent liberty: honor, rites of power, and persuasion in sixteenth-century Ireland', *Renaissance Quarterly* 46 (1993), 308–27.

[58] 'Mac an Iarla', meaning son of the earl, referred to Clanricard's eldest son.

[59] *CSPI, Tudor period, 1571–1575*, O'Dowd (ed.), p. 193.

Simultaneously, she wrote to Fitzwilliam making clear her intention that Clanricard should get a speedy trial and that it would have been wiser to inform her of the charges before imprisoning him.[60] Exasperated at his monarch's intrusion into affairs she could not know from such a distance, Fitton wrote back arguing 'why force was honourable and no way else would serve to good end' against both Clanricard's sons and the earl himself.[61] But to Fitzwilliam she expressed her satisfaction that the chief nobility of western Ireland, the earls of Thomond and Clanricard, recognised 'our sovereignty' and thus, in turn, her desire to ensure that their lands were not appropriated.[62]

In fact, she seems to have regularly blamed the lower-born for the transgressions of their betters. The very next year she opined that the foul play of evil counsel must be responsible for Desmond's insubordination, a thing she considered bizarre given her demonstrated esteem for him.[63] English examples of this status bias abound. Elizabeth believed, for instance, that the northern earls had been misled by their counsellors into believing that she sought their destruction.[64] This viewpoint meshed well with Sussex's own prejudices: writing to the queen in November 1569, he lamented that 'these simple Earles (thus, by false delusions, drawn on) be now with ther wicked Counsellors together at Bransby'.[65] This does not mean that she was unwilling to make them pay for their indiscretions (and as we have seen above, once she decided that punishment of her subjects was necessary she was relentless in its pursuit). But it does demonstrate her careful management of the situation so as to project a sense that the nobility as a category was not to blame, just a few misled souls.

Curiously, here, we see the language of evil counsel applied by the monarch towards her subjects. This rhetorical position is a well-known feature of the 'loyal rebellion' paradigm, and one engaged in by Northumberland, Desmond, O'Neill, and others. Evidently, the queen could use it in the reverse direction, too, demonstrating herself to be supportive of nobility generally, and even of the houses and families of those individuals who rose against her, while being firm in the destruction of the transgressive few. Might we consider there to have been a trope of loyal repression to complement that of loyal rebellion? As with the loyal rebellion, the real target was the 'evil councillors' themselves. In this case that meant those below the ranks of the nobility – the counsellors who misled their betters and, in turn, the people who forgot their natural duty

---

[60] *Ibid.*, p. 196.   [61] *Ibid.*, p. 207.   [62] *Ibid.*, pp. 243, 345.   [63] *Ibid.*, p. 497.
[64] Haynes (ed.), *State papers*, p. 589.
[65] Cuthbert Sharp, *Memorials of the rebellion of 1569* (Durham, 2009, reprint), p. 28.

as subjects in supporting their rebellious betters. Once elites declared themselves absolved of ties of unquestioning loyalty, Elizabeth claimed, they in turn fired up the people with hopes of new laws and rules 'as the ordinary High Way to all sensual and unruly Liberty, which commonly the ignorant covet, though it ever hath been will be most of all to their own Destruction'.[66]

And duly that destruction was forthcoming, both in England and Ireland. In the midst of rebellion, and in its aftermath, Elizabeth's fury was swift and terrible. Whatever her lingering reputation as 'Good Queen Bess', Elizabeth was a calculating ruler capable of severe repression, a fact explicitly revealed in a letter to Sussex.[67] If he were to find the rebels vulnerable, she wrote, he was to crush them. Should the disadvantage prove his own, she instructed that 'we wolde you used suche convenient means to intertayne the Rebells with Talk or and other Devices, as may best serve for the drawyng foorth of Tyme' until reinforcements (in this case, the expected support of troops under Hunsdon) could bolster his position. If the latter case, the rebels were not to know 'that this Delay groweth by lack of sufficient Power to meete with them, but for other Respects tending to theyr awne Benefit, for the pacifying of our Indignation towards them'.[68] Interestingly, this is the same letter noted above in which she chastised her field commander for his suspicion of the locals' loyalties. Be that as it may, Elizabeth concluded that Sussex would 'doo well, by the spedy Execution of two or three of them, to make an Example of Terror to others of their Nature and Qualitie'.[69]

In the final analysis, repression fell hardest on those 'evil councillors', the people. This, according to Kesselring, marked an innovation in Tudor policy: whereas tradition had it that the chief instigators primarily would bear the capital burden of guilt, under Elizabeth terminal punishment fell heavily on the rank and file as well.[70] In Ireland, of course, we see parallels. Yes, the 15th earl of Desmond was killed by bounty hunters for the state,[71] but Elizabeth spent a great deal of effort to install his son

---

[66] Haynes (ed.) *State papers*, p. 589.

[67] On the celebration of Elizabeth's agency and authority, see Leah Marcus's revealing comments at the opening of her essay in the present volume, p. 40. More generally, see Carole Levin, Jo Eldridge Carney and Debra Barrett-Graves, *Elizabeth I: always her own free woman* (Aldershot, 2003), and Julia M. Walker, *Dissing Elizabeth: negative representations of Gloriana* (Durham, NC, 1998), a collection that highlights the monarch's accomplishments in the face of startling levels of public opprobrium aimed in her direction.

[68] Haynes (ed.), *State papers*, p. 556.   [69] *Ibid.*, p. 557.

[70] Kesselring, *Northern Rebellion*, p. 90.

[71] Anthony J. Sheehan, 'The killing of the earl of Desmond', *Journal of the Cork Archaeological and Historical Society* 88 (1983), 106–10.

as the next earl and to prop up the earldom and preserve continuity of aristocratic governance in Ireland's south.[72] Meanwhile, she was happily receiving letters from officials detailing the hundreds of malefactors put to the sword or sent to the gallows.[73] In the north, while O'Neill and O'Donnell were pardoned and returned to elite status bearing earldoms, on the ground thousands died by force or famine.

In part this disproportionate destruction of the rebellious rank and file was driven by matters financial. The queen's fabled parsimony must be seen to have helped produce chilling consequences in the aftermath of rebellion. Concerns for the royal purse helped drive sweeping Irish land transfer, the most famous (or notorious) example being the Munster plantation – a massive social-engineering project founded upon the transplantation of English lords and labourers to southern Ireland and the lands expropriated from the rebellious earl of Desmond.[74] Land transferral also followed rebellion in England. The formal attainder of Westmorland saw his substantial holdings in Durham forfeit to the crown.[75] As Elizabeth wrote to the sheriffs of northern counties, Edward Dacre (brother of the rebellious Lord Dacre), on account of his own role in defying the queen and subsequent cross-border flight, stood to lose 'all his goods, chattels, and lands' which had been 'escheated to us'.[76] Such dispossession was a risk of rebellion and well understood by rebels and loyalists alike, who could not have been ignorant of the long history of attainder in such situations. Conversely, those who stood with the crown petitioned to take ownership of escheated rebel lands. As MacCulloch and Fletcher write of the Northern Rebellion, Cecil was beset by 'cravers' looking for the earls' estates.[77] Commanders, too, had their eyes on those lands as payment for their troops. As Sussex angrily commented to Cecil in early 1570, some of his subordinates' sharing of spoils without commission left him with nothing for his own men.[78] In the historiographical rush to see land transfer in Ireland from nobility to crown as the spoil of war and sign of modern imperial encounter, we should not lose sight of the mirror image of dispossession in England. From a queen's-eye view – and arguably more deeply down the social hierarchy – these seem

---

[72] See Kane, *Politics and culture of honour*, pp. 105–6.

[73] *CSPI, Tudor period, 1571–1575*, O'Dowd (ed.), p. 282.

[74] On the plantation generally, see Michael MacCarthy-Morrogh, *The Munster plantation: English migration to southern Ireland, 1583–1641* (Oxford, 1986); David Dickson, *Old world colony: Cork and South Munster, 1630–1830* (Cork, 2006); Nicholas Canny, *Making Ireland British, 1580–1650* (Oxford, 2001), ch. 3.

[75] Roger N. McDermott, 'Charles Neville, 6th earl of Westmorland', *ODNB*.

[76] *CSPD*, VII, p. 197.   [77] MacCulloch and Fletcher, *Tudor rebellions*, p. 101.

[78] *CSPD*, VII, pp. 205–6.

to be episodes separated by difference of degree (if, admittedly, quite profound) rather than kind.

As difficult as the loss of land may have been to its previous owners, the real victims in post-rebellion land scrambles were frequently the commons. In order to secure lands for crown ownership, elites among the rebels were typically spared. As Kesselring notes, those executed by martial law – which was imposed on much of the north during and following the rebellion – stood to lose only a third of their moveable property. Thus, to satisfy Elizabeth's demand for 700 executions, the state's noose came disproportionately to encircle the necks of the lower-born. In part this was by original design: Sussex wrote Cecil at the end of December 1569 that 'the worst disposed shall be executed for example. I guess the number will be 600 or 700 that shall be executed of the common sort, besides the prisoners taken in the field.'[79] In part it was driven by economic logic: the wealthy were proceeded against through more standard common-law process, which allowed for the escheating of land. To this story of manipulating the law's terror in the interest of real estate acquisition, we should add Robert Wood's disturbing observation that the better sort were frequently able to plea out of executions, a phenomenon he aptly describes as casting 'a revealing and unpleasant light on certain aspects of the Elizabethan attitude to human suffering'.[80]

More damning still is Kesselring's generalising comment that 'Elizabeth approached the resolution of the rising in a mercenary manner, determined not just to use fines and forfeitures as a form of punishment, but willing also to manipulate the principles of justice and mercy to extract a profit from protest.'[81] Mundane financial concerns also bore terminal consequences for the lower orders. For example, the Council of the North informed Elizabeth in May 1570 that among those executed was one for counterfeiting coin and others for 'sundry felonies',[82] and reports of capital punishment visited upon thieves in Ireland litter the correspondence to the queen, who presumably approved of this. The constant refrain of her subordinates to defend honour and profit in the realms – and her perpetual demand that they do so – was no mere rhetoric but rather a guide to frequently bloody action against the poor. This does not mean that no elites died for their actions. As already noted, the earl of Desmond met a violent end at the hands of state agents, and as Thomas Gargrave wrote to Cecil in April 1570, the queen's demand

---

[79] *Ibid.*, p. 169. I do not recall seeing in any of the secondary literature mention of prisoners' executions as having been *in addition* to the 700 demanded by the queen.
[80] Sharp, *Memorials*, p. xxix.   [81] Kesselring, *Northern Rebellion*, p. 140.
[82] *CSPD*, VII, p. 295.

to see some of the northern rebels punished was a decision 'most true' as local opinion held that the poor were 'both spoiled and executed, and the gentlemen and rich escape'.[83] Surveying rebellions in England over the Tudor period, Kesselring sees escalation in crown response to the 1569 rebellion relative to those of 1536 and 1549. The former witnessed less effort towards official mercy and pardon but rather a drive to 'invade, resist, repress, subdue, slay, kill, and put to execution of death by all ways and means'.[84] Given the work of Vincent Carey and, more recently, David Edwards, Ireland's population too experienced a dramatic uptick in state-sanctioned violence in the wake of rebellious activity.[85]

Perhaps the clearest example of similarity in Elizabeth's view of rebellions across the realms comes from the language she used to describe them. Be they in England or Ireland, rebels were simply 'rebels', occasionally 'enemies'. The conflicts themselves were frequently termed 'war' or, in a historically resonant term, as 'troubles'. While unsurprising in an English context, this usage was also in keeping with the tradition stretching back through centuries of English administrators and officials referring to the Irish as enemies. Of course, after 1541 all the Irish were subjects – Ireland having been made a kingdom under the Tudor crown by acts of the English and Irish parliaments. And, duly, Elizabeth typically referred to the disloyal in both realms as 'unnatural subjects' or as acting 'unnaturally'.[86] Equally, and as demonstrated above, she decried their wanton love and show of liberty. Moreover, her cross-border deployment of 'nature' and 'liberty' is noteworthy given that the literature on English–Irish relations continues to focus on a discourse of civility versus savagery. It is certainly the case that Elizabeth was largely ignorant of her second realm and its peoples, never having set foot there. In 1573 she enquired of the earl of Essex, '[W]hat kind of people inhabit these countries' of Ireland's north-east.[87] Nor was she entirely immune to the language of barbarousness and civility. Speaking of the 'horrible outrages' committed by Sir Barnabe Fitzpatrick upon the earl of Ormond's tenants, she found

---

[83] *Ibid.*, p. 272. Her decision was presumably in response to pressure from the field that the commons of the north were furious at preferential mercy for elites and thus were in danger of rising. See, for instance, *ibid.*, p. 223.

[84] Kesselring, *Northern Rebellion*, p. 81.

[85] The key text here is Vincent Carey, 'John Derricke's *Image of Irelande*, Sir Henry Sidney, and the massacre at Mullaghmast, 1578', *Irish Historical Studies* 31 (May 1999), 305–27. See now also David Edwards, 'The escalation of atrocity in sixteenth-century Ireland', in David Edwards, Pádraig Lenihan, and Clodagh Tait (eds.), *Age of atrocity: violence and political conflict in early modern Ireland* (Dublin, 2007), pp. 34–78.

[86] See for instance Haynes (ed.), *State papers*, pp. 554, 559.

[87] *CSPI, Tudor period, 1571–1575*, O'Dowd (ed.), p. 463.

it hard to believe he would have 'committed such barbarous acts' given that he had been 'civilly brought up' in England.[88]

Nevertheless, Elizabeth appears to have been no ethnographer and was evidently not engaged in 'othering' as a strategy to conquest. Although she complained that the earl of Desmond's answers to official interrogatories were 'rude and barbarous', this was to be understood as a product of nurture rather than of nature, for he was 'not seasoned with the reverent respect that a subject ought to have his sovereign'.[89] And, as noted earlier, even when dealing with the head of the O'Donnells, a kin group resident in arguably the most remote part of Ireland, she simply referred to him and his followers as 'doubtful subjects'.[90] Indeed, she made it known that the very person who should be charged with civilising the local inhabitants was none other than the O'Donnell himself.[91] Gaelic Ireland may have been considered 'rude partes' of the realms, but the queen also described the borderers of the north as 'lewd'.[92]

More so than over cultural difference, she seems to have fretted over the 'secret' character of rebel intention.[93] This seems a point worth considering, especially in light of the escalating sense of crisis that gripped the regime, reaching an apogee of panic in the 1590s. Whatever her thoughts on savagery – and, again, there are ample examples in her wider correspondence on Ireland of her noting the barbarousness of Irish customs[94] – it does appear that her abiding concern was not with cultural difference but with falsity. This was, after all, the great age of spy networks and of judicial torture.[95] In spite of her public assurances that loyal subjects should fear no examination of the 'secret opinions in their consciences', the category of 'loyal' seems to have been fluctuating enough to make very many fear exactly such examinations.[96] And, as she expressed to the

---

[88] *Ibid.*, pp. 581–2.   [89] *Ibid.*, pp. 643–4.   [90] *Ibid.*, p. 635.   [91] *Ibid.*, p. 463.

[92] *Ibid.*, p. 246. This is not to deny that the former required great efforts at Anglicisation, while the latter was more a law-and-order problem. Nevertheless, it is to suggest that Anglicisation and the imposition of law and order were processes deemed vital for all culturally suspicious parts of the realms. For a broader treatment of this point, see J. E. C. Hill, 'Puritans and "the dark corners of the land"', *Transactions of the Royal Historical Society*, 5th series, 13 (1962), 77–102; James, *Society, politics and culture*; and James, *Family, lineage and civil society.*

[93] Haynes (ed.), *State papers*, p. 589.

[94] See for instance her confidence in the 1st earl of Essex's ability to 'allure that rude and barbarous nation to civility rather by discreet handling than by force and shedding of blood'. It seems key here that her preference for 'discreet handling' did not hold in time of rebellion, for, as she continued, 'and yet, when necessity requires, you are ready to oppose yourself and your forces to the rebellious': *Cal. Carew*, I, p. 477.

[95] Paul Hammer, *The polarisation of Elizabethan politics: the political career of Robert Devereux, 2nd earl of Essex, 1585–1597* (Cambridge, 1999); John Langbein, *Torture and the law of proof* (Chicago, 1977), referred to in Kesselring, *Northern Rebellion*, p. 200.

[96] *Cal. Carew*, I, p. 592. This, of course, mirrors the famous line about not making windows into men's souls.

Scottish ambassador William Maitland in 1561, she had very little faith in her subjects' fundamental loyalty: 'I know the inconstancy of the people of England, how they ever mislike the present government and has their eyes fixed upon that person that is next to succeed; and naturally men be so disposed: *Plures adorant solem orientem quam occidentem.*'[97] Indeed, given Elizabeth's paranoia to distinguish natural from unnatural subjects in both realms, it might be worth considering the regime's actions in Ireland as more akin to inquisition than imperial cleansing.[98] Proto-racial language may have been on the rise, but it was not a hegemonic discourse, or one seemingly engaged in by the supreme authority in the realms.[99]

All of the above is not meant to suggest that there were no differences between rebellions arising from England and Ireland or in the means of their suppression. Yet many of them, it might be argued, were differences of degree rather than of kind: land seizure and redistribution, the garrisoning of soldiers, scorched-earth tactics, fear of foreign invasion, language of 'reduction to civility', use of martial law, destruction of local custom and jurisdiction, and the judicial or extra-judicial execution of hundreds being among the most prominent examples. Fletcher and Mac-Culloch's argument that Elizabeth in part experienced fewer rebellions than her predecessors precisely because they had witnessed so many may also provide some explanation for the greater unrest in Ireland: as the realities of a centralised, Protestant monarchy worked their way westward, so the protest so spectacularly demonstrated in earlier Tudor outbursts such as the Pilgrimage of Grace found expression in the second realm. It is perhaps worth considering, too, the prevalence of plotting in England that consistently unsettled the regime. Not all of these went off as rebellions, but fear of them led the regime to quite extraordinary measures of societal repression – here we need only remember the Bond of Association, an extraordinary phenomenon referred to by one historian as 'Elizabethan lynch law'.[100] Seen from this perspective, the regime's lightning-swift and draconian punishment of the Oxfordshire rebels is not so bizarre as Fletcher and MacCulloch suggest.[101] Rather, it seems in keeping with the

---

[97] She is quoting Petrarch, 'More do adore the rising than the setting sun'. Elizabeth I, *Works*, Marcus *et al.* (eds.), p. 66.

[98] The regime's concern over true and false is, of course, readily apparent in its fear over outwardly conforming religious dissenters, be they to the doctrinal left or right. Consider, for instance, the hysteria over 'church papists' and the Family of Love.

[99] Moreover, it should be pointed out that even that great theorist of violent colonialism, Edmund Spenser, feared the Old English more than the Gaelic Irish on account of their outward appearance of civility masking an internal degeneration.

[100] Patrick Collinson, 'The monarchical republic of Queen Elizabeth I', in Collinson, *Elizabethan essays* (London, 1994), p. 48.

[101] For enlightening discussion of the government's reaction, see John Walter, 'A "rising of the people"? The Oxfordshire rising of 1596', *Past & Present* 107 (1985), 90–143.

sense of the 1590s as a time of panic and perceived crisis.[102] Moreover, differences in the queen's own reactions to rebellion did not necessarily speak to preferential treatment of the English. Whereas she ultimately raged over the killing of 600 on Rathlin Island and the same number in Smerwick – the latter of which may have contributed to the commanding officer Arthur Lord Grey de Wilton's fall from monarchical favour – she fumed in England as to why more executions against the lower orders had not been carried out. In February 1570 Gargrave expressed to Cecil his misgivings over Elizabeth's expectations for the commission of oyer and terminer in the north. Were it to attaint all offenders, he fretted, 'we shall leave many places naked of inhabitants. I think a number should be chosen, chiefly papists, and the rest pardoned, except some chief people who are abroad. The poor husbandmen may become good subjects, and 500 of the poor sort are already executed.'[103] This was not, however, a position likely to placate Elizabeth, who noted that in spite of 'our natural and private Dulcenes' she had never shied from bringing justice to malefactors 'wherewith this Age generally in all Countries aboundeth; in such sort as by Records may appere that the Judges criminal of our realm have in no Time given fewer bloody judgments'.[104] And, thus, writing to Sussex in January 1570 she 'marvel[led] that we have heard of no execution by martial law, as was appointed, of the meaner sort of rebels in the North'. He was thus instructed to follow the order 'for the terror of others' and to inform her of its doing.[105] This particular difference, in fact, suggests a further point of similarity: in both realms she seems to have been keen to check the excesses of her commanders – too bloodthirsty in Ireland, too lenient in England – and in doing so failed to express the supposed Elizabethan-era mindset of intrinsic Irish difference and a need to brutally erase it.[106]

---

[102] John Guy (ed.), *The reign of Elizabeth I: court and culture in the last decade* (Cambridge, 1995). Instructive in understanding the historical condescension towards the 1596 rebels are Steve Hindle's comments on periodisation and its effects on historians' attention to and classification of armed risings. In speaking of another largely ignored, if chronologically later, disturbance, he writes: 'It is, indeed, arguable that this attack of historiographical amnesia is structural, a deliberate relegation of an episode which contradicts the widely accepted meta-narrative whereby the dying tradition of disorder was killed off by skilful political management' (Hindle, 'Imagining insurrection in seventeenth-century England: representations of the Midland Rising of 1607', *History Workshop Journal* 66 (2008), 24).

[103] *CSPD*, VII, p. 221.   [104] Haynes (ed.), *State papers*, p. 590.

[105] *CSPD*, VII, p. 188.

[106] Here it is worth considering Steven Ellis's claim that Elizabeth's harsher vengeance against the English rebels of 1569 than that exacted by Henry VIII in the wake of the widespread unrest of the 1530s was a product of the greater traction of the rule of law by the time of her reign. By that reading, Elizabeth would have been less harsh in Ireland because the full force (and fury) of the law could not be mobilised there and negotiation was necessary. See Ellis, 'Henry VIII, rebellion', 531.

The material presented here is not intended to deny the frequent brutality of English–Irish relations but simply to suggest that a queen's-eye view on rebellion in the Tudor realms may complicate our notions of subjects' violent resistance against the state in the late sixteenth century. Looking from the perspective of a commander in the field – say a Nicholas Bagenal – or from a settler colonialist such as Edmund Spenser, it is clear that there was a strain of English thought towards Ireland and the Irish that was as savage as any found in the 'new world'. The immense, and still growing, literature on the 'modern' colonial horrors of Ireland in this period amply describes this. But it does not describe adequately an 'Elizabethan' mindset, for it does not take into account the monarch's own outlook. Again, as sovereign, she was in the unique position of seeing all below her as merely subjects, be they a Burghley, a Northumberland, a Desmond, or an O'Donnell. Indeed, she was at pains to point out that the suppression of Hugh O'Neill had nothing to do with conquest but was simply a matter of law and order.[107] More revealing of her position on the Irish as subjects was her assurance to Lord Deputy Fitzwilliam that the rumour that the earl of Essex's arrival in the north was intended to 'dispossess the nobility and gentlemen of the Irishry of their ancient patrimonies by way of conquest' was false and her declaration that he was merely there to 'drive out rebels'.[108] The language of 'nobility and gentlemen' and 'rebels' is emphatically not that of savages and barbarians.

The notion that 'Tudor' and 'Irish' rebellions were two separate phenomena, I suspect, would have made little impression on the queen, the differences between them having been magnified from ones of degree to ones of kind on account of our knowledge of the *longue durée* of what was then merely nascent, albeit very real, faith-and-fatherland national consciousness. Moreover, separating the two phenomena does some violence to the intentions and agency of the actors themselves: as noted earlier, why do we think of Northumberland as a hopeless 'medieval' whose fatal blunder was misreading the times, and yet we think of Fitzmaurice, O'Neill, and Baltinglass (to take but three Irish examples) as forerunners of modernity? Should we not also take seriously that the actions of the latter three were as much variations of the loyal rebellion as those of the former?[109] And, conversely, that Northumberland was just as capable of imagining innovative post-Reformation political relations

---

[107] 'Declaring reason for sending Army into Ireland', in *Tudor royal proclamations*, P. L. Hughes and J. F. Larkin (eds.), 3 vols. (New Haven, 1969), vol. III, *1588–1603*, pp. 200–2.

[108] *Cal. Carew*, I, p. 453.

[109] On Irish national imaginings that stressed conservative notions of aristocratic right to rule, see Brendan Kane, 'A dynastic nation? Rethinking national consciousness in early

as were his Irish fellow subjects? Indeed, bearing in mind what Steve Pincus has argued regarding the 'modernity' of 1688, we may in fact here be witnessing not so much a battle of the old against the new but of variations of the new versus new, or perhaps more accurately (or at least less categorically) a series of political manoeuvres and positions that emerged and evolved largely on account of their interactions with one another.[110]

As a final comparison, where Elizabeth may truly have understood rebellions to be different was when they occurred in foreign territories. Although the rebellious Protestants of the Low Countries looked with desperation to England for help against Spain, Elizabeth was extremely reluctant to intercede. Famously, she grew furious at Leicester for imagining that he could accept some form of executive authority (as governor) over another sovereign territory. Similarly, she was averse to meddling too strongly in Scotland. To take one dramatic example, her cold feet in 1560 prior to signature of the Treaty of Berwick seem to have played a role in spurring Burghley and others to clandestine military organisation. Moreover, her prolonged hand-wringing over the fate of Mary, queen of Scots, provides ample demonstration of her reluctance to interfere with a regnant and legitimate, thus divinely ordained, monarch – her acceptance of the conventions of the 'hot trod' across the border in pursuit of the northern rebels in 1570 notwithstanding. But in Ireland as well as England, she believed herself the sole bearer of sovereign authority. That being the case, few means were too extraordinary to ensure that that authority was not weakened or that the social hierarchy which flowed from it was shaken. As Elizabeth herself may have said it, when reacting to rebellion, be it in her English or Irish realm, she remained *semper eadem*.

seventeenth-century Ireland', in David Finnegan, Marie-Claire Harrigan, and Eamonn Ó Ciardha (eds.), *Imeacht na n-Iarlaí: the flight of the earls* (Derry, 2010), pp. 124–31.
[110] Steve Pincus, *1688: the first modern revolution* (New Haven, 2009).

13   Print, Protestantism, and cultural authority in Elizabethan Ireland

Marc Caball

I

The use of print in the Irish language is arguably both the most enduring and most positive inheritance that derived from Queen Elizabeth's
opaque and still imperfectly delineated encounter with Gaelic society
and culture. Although the monarch was essentially a benign if remote
patron of print's debut in Gaelic Ireland, this fascinating process of cultural interchange was nonetheless enabled and facilitated by her evan-
gelically inspired commitment to inaugurating a new departure in Gaelic
communicative practice.[1] From the mid fifteenth century onwards, the
technology of print spread rapidly from Mainz through the cities of the
German empire, southwards beyond the Alps to Italy, and westwards and
eastwards to France, the Low Countries, England, Poland, and Bohemia.
By 1490, printing presses had been established in more than 200 cities
across Europe.

Given the close link between the early expansion of print and large
urban centres of trade and commerce, it is perhaps not surprising that
the first Gaelic book printed in Ireland was published in Dublin as late
as June 1571.[2] The reformer Seaán Ó Cearnaigh compiled a primer of
religion entitled *Aibidil Gaoidheilge & Caiticiosma* ('Gaelic alphabet and
catechism') with a view to presenting the central tenets of the established
church to the Gaelic Irish. However, this work was not the first printed
book in the Irish language. Several years previously in April 1567, John
Carswell (*c.* 1522–72), superintendent of Argyll and bishop of the Isles,

I am indebted to the Irish Research Council for the Humanities and Social Sciences
and the Department of the Taoiseach for the award of a Project Grant in Theology and
Religious Studies which has enabled me to undertake research for this chapter.

[1] Uilliam Ó Domhnuill (ed. and trans.), *Tiomna nuadh ar dtighearna agus ar slanaightheora
Iosa Criosd* (Dublin, 1602), p. 1v; *Calendar of the patent and close rolls of chancery in Ireland*,
James Morrin (ed.), 2 vols. (Dublin and London, 1861–2), vol. II, p. 401; *Acts of the privy
council of England, 1532–1631*, new series, J. R. Dasent *et al.* (eds.), 46 vols. (London,
1890–1964), vol. XXII, p. 26.

[2] Andrew Pettegree, *The book in the Renaissance* (New Haven, 2010), pp. xiii–xiv.

published a classical Gaelic translation of the Calvinist Book of Common Order.[3] Significantly, classical Gaelic was a standardised literary form of the language used by literary scholars, jurists, and physicians throughout the Gaelic realms and as such constituted a *lingua franca* among the educated elites. Therefore, the publication of an evangelical primer for use by adherents of the established church in Ireland relatively shortly after the appearance of a Calvinist work in Gaelic is unlikely to be a coincidence. It has been suggested that the appearance of Carswell's translation, which was explicitly intended for dissemination in Ireland as well as in Gaelic Scotland, implied the unwelcome prospect of the circulation of Calvinist doctrine in Ireland.[4]

In this chapter, it is proposed to discuss the 1571 Irish primer of religion with a view to elucidating aspects of the promulgation of the message of reform in Elizabethan Ireland. If this primer has received scant attention from cultural or ecclesiastical historians, it has been recognised by philologists as a landmark in the Gaelic tradition from the viewpoint both of the history of the book and of the first adaptation in Ireland of a codified and prescriptive literary dialect to the medium of print in the context of communicative practices historically defined by orality and script.[5] In the main, Brian Ó Cuív's exemplary edition of the work is centred on a linguistic analysis of the text.[6] However, it is arguable that what has generally been depicted as a somewhat modest engagement with print on the part of a Gaelic reformer is considerably more nuanced and ambitious in terms of content and strategic intent.[7] This apparently purely functional text is far from inert in cultural and political terms. It is suggested in this chapter that Ó Cearnaigh's primer of religion aimed to address the cultural and political ambivalence that informed the actual and occasionally purely rhetorical evangelisation of Gaelic Ireland on the part of the Elizabethan state and its established church. In order to understand better the cultural and political tensions inherent in the incremental colonial focus of the Protestant Reformation in Ireland, it is necessary to review briefly the nature and

---

[3] John Carswell, *Foirm na n-urrnuidheadh: John Carswell's Gaelic translation of the Book of Common Order*, R. L. Thomson (ed.) (Edinburgh, 1970), pp. lix–lxiv.

[4] Nicholas Williams, *I bprionta i leabhar: na protastúin agus prós na Gaeilge 1567–1724* (Dublin, 1986), p. 21.

[5] Niall Ó Ciosáin, 'Print and Irish, 1570–1900: an exception among Celtic languages?', *Radharc: A Journal of Irish and Irish-American Studies* 5–7 (2004–6), 73–106.

[6] Brian Ó Cuív (ed.), *Aibidil Gaoidheilge & Caiticiosma: Seaán Ó Cearnaigh's Irish primer of religion published in 1571* (Dublin, 1994, reprint).

[7] Henry Jefferies has described the 1571 primer as an 'anaemic affair' that 'was not likely to inspire evangelical zeal in many of its readers': *The Irish church and the Tudor Reformations* (Dublin, 2010), p. 201.

context of its insular implantation by the Tudor regime and its agents in Ireland.

II

There was no Reformation from below in Ireland and, unlike England, there was no Reformation from above either. Rather, Reformation was externally imposed in Ireland.[8] The establishment of a programme of reform in Ireland was essentially driven by the Reformation in England, which was inaugurated formally by the recognition of Henry VIII as head of the church in England by the 1534 Act of Supremacy. The parallel Irish Act of Supremacy enacted by the Lords and Commons of the Irish parliament in 1536 similarly acknowledged the English monarch as supreme head of the church in the kingdom of Ireland. If the Reformation in England was inspired in many key respects by political and dynastic considerations, its episodic and contested trajectory in Ireland was no less influenced by political factors. In this regard, a fundamental tension arose from the perception that the authority of the English monarch on the island derived its legitimacy from the papal bull Laudabiliter. Promulgated in 1155, this bull had authorised Henry II to conquer the island with the objective of reforming religion.[9] Ironically, Henry's rejection of papal suzerainty unintentionally weakened a potent foundational premise of the English monarchy's claim to jurisdiction in Ireland. Additionally, the question of religious change became embroiled in a broader *Kulturkampf* entailed in the expansion and consolidation of Tudor imperium in sixteenth-century Ireland. For example, the crown policy of surrender and regrant in the early 1540s – by which Irish noblemen submitted to and acknowledged formally the authority of the crown in exchange for official confirmation of the lands held by them – also prioritised a process of Anglicisation among the newly acquiescent. The latter committed themselves to the adoption of English dress and agricultural practices and the education of their children in English civility and language.[10]

Importantly, the Protestant Reformation in England involved not just a process of ecclesiastical, theological, and liturgical renewal and

---

[8] Karl S. Bottigheimer and Ute Lotz-Heumann, 'The Irish Reformation in European perspective', *Archive for Reformation History* 89 (1998), 269. For the historiography of the reformation in sixteenth-century Ireland, see James Murray, *Enforcing the English Reformation in Ireland: clerical resistance and political conflict in the diocese of Dublin, 1534–1590* (Cambridge, 2009), pp. 1–19.

[9] S. J. Connolly, *Contested island: Ireland 1460–1630* (Oxford, 2007), p. 92.

[10] *Ibid.*, p. 106.

reconfiguration; it also served to enhance the prestige of the English language through its use as a medium of worship and theological discussion and argument. Although conservative English clergy in the mid sixteenth century continued to champion Latin as the language of religious expression in opposition to English, considered the language of the vulgar masses, the standing of the vernacular was inexorably in the ascendant.[11] Concurrently, the more frequent appearance of English in print further consolidated the political and cultural status of the language.[12] Increasingly, English was considered to articulate and even shape national character.[13] Ironically, however, as Felicity Heal has argued in her study of language and dialects in the British and Irish Reformations, the translation of Protestant devotional material into the Celtic languages often conflicted with the commitment of Tudor and Stuart governments to English as an instrument of political and cultural authority.[14]

A form of linguistic colonialism was informed by a close association between Protestantism and English national identity. However, the implicit cultural ascendancy of English enshrined in evangelical liturgical practice and worship generated considerable potential for tension in a Gaelic Irish context where a highly self-conscious and elaborate notion of linguistic, literary, and cultural sovereignty pertained. Gaelic Ireland, although lacking centralised political and judicial structures and composed of a mosaic of lordships of varying degrees of magnitude and power, was characterised by a high degree of homogeneity in at least one highly influential respect. The Gaelic septs and Gaelicised descendants of the medieval Anglo-Norman colonists shared a common literary culture. A vibrant manuscript tradition facilitated the transmission, dissemination, and reception of a rich corpus of poetic, legendary, historical, devotional, legal, and medical material. As was the case throughout early modern Europe, a protean oral culture was also integral to the expression of shared values, beliefs, and lore. Additionally, the remarkable success of the Franciscan Observant reform movement in Gaelic areas in the fifteenth century and the continued importance of Franciscan monasteries as centres for both worship and civic interaction provided another layer of common religious and cultural reference.[15]

---

[11] Gillian Brennan, 'Patriotism, language and power: English translations of the Bible, 1520–1580', *History Workshop* 27 (1989), 18.

[12] Cathy Shrank, *Writing the nation in Reformation England 1530–1580* (Oxford, 2004), p. 153.

[13] *Ibid.*, p. 153.

[14] Felicity Heal, 'Mediating the word: language and dialects in the British and Irish Reformations', *Journal of Ecclesiastical History* 56 (2005), 261–86.

[15] Colmán N. Ó Clabaigh, *The Franciscans in Ireland, 1400–1534: from reform to Reformation* (Dublin, 2002); Salvador Ryan, '"The most contentious of terms": towards a new

Complementary to an emphasis on the vernacular as a medium for evangelisation, Protestant reformers also recognised the need to engage actively with the religious instruction of all groups within society. The laity in medieval Europe received no formal religious education and were little acquainted with church doctrine. Such ignorance was possibly not problematic in a context where uniformity of faith essentially prevailed.[16] Catechesis was widely perceived in England as God's wish, as evidenced by Scripture and by the example of the early church and other Protestant churches in the wake of the Reformation. A lack of knowledge of the basic doctrines of the Christian religion prevented the espousal of faith, and a want of faith negated the possibility of salvation.[17] Andrew Pettegree has highlighted that basic instruction in reading and writing across sixteenth-century Europe, in both reformed and Catholic regions, was closely linked to the inculcation of the fundamental tenets of religion. The *ABC with Catechism* and the more elaborate *Primer with Catechism* were approved by the state authorities in Elizabethan England as reading primers.[18] Ironically, although such inexpensive works were printed in large numbers, few have survived heavy usage consequent on their instrumentalist function.[19] Ian Green has highlighted the importance generally accorded catechisms by both the Protestant and the Catholic church in early modern Ireland. He identified on a preliminary basis over a hundred catechetical works with an Irish connection published between approximately 1560 and 1800.[20] In the case of Protestants in Ireland, Green argued that, although some catechetical activity had been undertaken at an early stage, it was only from the 1680s that first Presbyterians and then Episcopalians systematically provided for the supply of catechetical material. Aside from being the first book in Irish printed in Ireland, the 1571 primer was also the first Protestant catechism printed in Ireland. Green suggested that the primer was otherwise unremarkable on the basis that in its combination of an alphabet with the official short

---

understanding of late medieval "popular religion"', *Irish Theological Quarterly* 68 (2003), 281–90.

[16] Benjamin J. Kaplan, *Divided by faith: religious conflict and the practice of toleration in early modern Europe* (Cambridge, MA, 2007), p. 30.

[17] Ian Green, *The Christian's ABC: catechisms and catechizing in England c. 1530–1740* (Oxford, 1996), pp. 25–6.

[18] Pettegree, *The book in the Renaissance*, pp. 188–9. See also H. Anders, 'The Elizabethan ABC with catechism', *The Library*, 4th series, 16 (1936), 32–48.

[19] Pettegree, *The book in the Renaissance*, p. 189; William St Clair, *The reading nation in the romantic period* (Cambridge, 2004), p. 27.

[20] Ian Green, '"The necessary knowledge of the principles of religion": catechisms and catechizing in Ireland, c. 1560–1800', in Alan Ford, James McGuire, and Kenneth Milne (eds.), *As by law established: the Church of Ireland since the Reformation* (Dublin, 1995), p. 69.

catechism it was 'in fact a direct copy of a standard English work called *The ABC with the catechism*' that was printed in very large quantities during Elizabeth's reign.[21] However, the Irish primer is considerably more than an uninspired derivative imitation of its English counterparts in so far as its Gaelic cultural inflection is both deliberate and strategic.

Actuality would more often than not belie rhetoric during the course of various efforts to effect reformation in an island whose populace largely remained fixed in its allegiance to the old faith. Appropriately enough, the Henrician reformation in Ireland inaugurated no dramatic changes either in liturgy or doctrine. The implementation of ecclesiastical reform was protracted during Edward VI's reign, and liturgical change encountered a mixture of indifference and hostility. The first Book of Common Prayer was introduced to Ireland in 1549 subsequent to an act of uniformity passed in the English Parliament and applicable to all the king's dominions. Importantly, Lord Deputy Sir Anthony St Leger made provision for circulation of the text through the establishment of a printing press in Dublin which enabled its publication in 1551.[22] St Leger also obtained permission to make the Prayer Book available in a Latin version which appears to have circulated in manuscript format. Not unmindful of the linguistic realities of Ireland, the English council also reluctantly authorised the translation of divine service to Irish and the usage of such translations where a majority of the congregation did not understand English.[23] The Elizabethan Act of Uniformity (1560) stipulated that clergy use an amended version of the 1552 English Prayer Book although the legislation recognised the impracticality of the use of English in Irish-speaking districts, while also alluding by way of implicit mitigation of slow progress to what was described as a difficulty in having material printed in Irish and the apparently low levels of literacy in that language. As a concession to these particular considerations, it allowed for the public use of a conservative Latin Prayer Book in Irish parishes where English was not commonly understood.[24]

Explicit admission of protracted delay in the provision of printed Protestant translations to Irish is clear from an exasperated official demand to two prelates in 1567 for repayment of funds previously

[21] *Ibid.*, pp. 71–2.

[22] E. R. McClintock Dix, *The earliest Dublin printing* (Dublin, 1901), p. 5.

[23] Evelyn Philip Shirley (ed.), *Original letters and papers in illustration of the history of the church in Ireland, during the reigns of Edward VI, Mary, and Elizabeth* (London, 1851), pp. 39–40; Brendan Bradshaw, 'The Edwardian Reformation in Ireland, 1547–1553', *Archivium Hibernicum* 34 (1976–7), 90.

[24] Myles V. Ronan, *The Reformation in Ireland under Elizabeth 1558–1580* (London, 1930), pp. 27–9; Henry A. Jefferies, 'The Irish parliament of 1560: the Anglican reforms authorised', *Irish Historical Studies* 26 (1988), 128–41.

disbursed for the manufacture of type for a projected New Testament in Irish. Some time previously – it is not known precisely when – the authorities had authorised the payment of £66 12s 4d to Adam Loftus, the archbishop of Armagh, and Hugh Brady, the bishop of Meath. Finally, by 1567 the dilatory prelates were threatened with the obligation to refund the monies expended unless publication of the New Testament was imminent.[25] Eight years later, Elizabeth was publicly reminded of the continuing failure to provide an Irish translation of the Bible in an oration by Laurence Humphrey at Woodstock during her 1575 progress. Praying that the divine word might strengthen the English and tame the 'wild Irish', Humphrey, the staunchly Puritan president of Magdalen College, Oxford, presented her with a manuscript translation to Irish of the Scriptures apparently by the eminent fourteenth-century archbishop of Armagh, Richard Fitzralph.[26] Elizabeth, sphinx-like in terms of her personal religious disposition and no doubt inured to sustained admonition by the godly, might well have conceded Humphrey's case had she known then that the Gaelic New Testament would not be published until 1602/3.[27]

III

In effect, the 1571 primer of religion was published against a backdrop of generally sceptical English evangelical attitudes to the Gaelic Irish.[28] In light of this unpromising approach to evangelisation in the vernacular, Seaán Ó Cearnaigh's career assumes particular significance

[25] Brady, an Irish-speaker born in Dunboyne around 1527, was appointed bishop of Meath in 1563. He had previously served as rector of a London parish. In light of his competence in Irish and impeccable evangelical credentials, it seems likely that Brady, who enjoyed the patronage of William Cecil, was commissioned to procure the manufacture of an Irish type while resident in London where he had access to the technical skills of the city's book trade. In respect of Brady's career, see Helen Coburn Walshe, 'Enforcing the Elizabethan settlement: the vicissitudes of Hugh Brady, Bishop of Meath, 1563–1584', *Irish Historical Studies* 26 (1989), 352–76.

[26] John Nichols (ed.), *The progresses and public processions of Queen Elizabeth*, 3 vols. (London, 1823), vol. I, p. 598; Heal, 'Mediating the word', 277–8. Humphrey's emphasis on vernacular evangelisation may have influenced the Munster planter, Sir William Herbert, who had the Lord's Prayer, Articles of the Creed, and the Ten Commandments translated to Irish in the late 1580s for the benefit of Irish-speakers in mid Kerry. Humphrey was reputedly Herbert's tutor at Oxford. See Sir William Herbert, *Croftus sive de Hibernia Liber*, Arthur Keaveney and John A. Madden (eds.) (Dublin, 1992), p. ix; Williams, *I bprionta i leabhar*, p. 26.

[27] Fearghus Ó Fearghail, *The Irish testament of 1602* (Dublin, 2004).

[28] Colm Lennon and Ciaran Diamond, 'The ministry of the church of Ireland, 1536–1636', in T. C. Barnard and W. G. Neely (eds.), *The clergy of the church of Ireland 1000–2000: messengers, watchmen and stewards* (Dublin, 2006), p. 46.

in better understanding the opaque encounter between the Reformation and Gaelic Ireland in the sixteenth century. A dearth of evidence allows only an outline reconstruction of his biography.[29] Both in the record of his matriculation at Cambridge in 1561 and in a letter written in 1572 from the Dublin administration to the royal minister William Cecil, Lord Burghley, Ó Cearnaigh was described as being of Connaught birth.[30] Although there is no extant evidence to substantiate the claim, it has been suggested that he was a native of the barony of Leyney in Sligo.[31] However, it is known that a branch of the Ó Cearnaigh family was settled in Leyney in the late medieval period. It seems also that clerics in the local church were drawn from this family.[32] References to churchmen bearing the surname Ó Cearnaigh in the parish of Kilmactigue in the barony of Leyney and elsewhere in the diocese of Achonry in the fifteenth century strongly suggest that Seaán Ó Cearnaigh was born to a family traditionally linked to the church.[33] Katharine Simms has argued that the Protestant Reformation by virtue of the new bishops' control of church lands and the validation of clerical marriage may well have proved attractive for some traditional Gaelic church families.[34] Certainly, a traditional church family lineage would partly explain Ó Cearnaigh's decision to pursue a clerical career.[35] Moreover, the Protestantism of the Ó Domhnalláin learned family of Galway indicates

[29] M. Pollard, *A dictionary of members of the Dublin book trade 1550–1800* (London, 2000), pp. 329–30.

[30] *Alumni Cantabrigienses: a biographical list of all known students, graduates and holders of office at the University of Cambridge, from the earliest times to 1900,* John Venn and J. A. Venn (eds.), 4 vols. (Cambridge, part 1; 1922–7), vol. I, p. 294; *Calendar of state papers, Ireland, Tudor period 1571–1575,* Mary O'Dowd (ed.) (Dublin, 2000), p. 204. Ó Cuív suggested Ó Cearnaigh was born around 1545 on the basis of his 1561 matriculation at Cambridge: Ó Cuív, *Aibidil,* p. 4.

[31] Nollaig Ó Muraíle, 'The Carneys of Connacht', in Donnchadh Ó Corráin, Liam Breatnach, and Kim McCone (eds.), *Sages, saints and storytellers: Celtic studies in honour of Professor James Carney* (Maynooth, 1989), p. 347; Ó Cuív (ed.), *Aibidil,* p. 3; N. J. A. Williams, 'Kearney [Carney], John [Seán Ó Cearnaigh] (b. *c.* 1545, d. after 1572)', *ODNB.*

[32] Ó Muraíle, 'The Carneys of Connacht', pp. 346–7.

[33] Representative Church Body Library, Dublin, MS 61/2/9 (J. B. Leslie, 'Biographical succession list of the clergy of Killala & Achonry'), pp. 53, 54, 62, 66, 67, 68 (under Achonry).

[34] Katharine Simms, 'Frontiers in the Irish church – regional and cultural', in T. B. Barry, Robin Frame, and Katharine Simms (eds.), *Colony and frontier in medieval Ireland: essays presented to J. F. Lydon* (London, 1995), p. 199.

[35] However, the family may not have taken a common approach to the new church. Continued loyalty to Catholicism is evident from the Gaelic obituary of Uilliam Ó Cearnaigh (d. 1586), a member of the Franciscan community of Moyne, near Killala, in the diocese adjacent to that of Achonry, where he was described as the best preaching friar in Ireland. See Aubrey Gwynn and R. Neville Hadcock, *Medieval religious houses: Ireland* (Dublin, 1988), p. 255.

that Ó Cearnaigh was not unique in contemporary Connaught.[36] On the basis of the short section on Irish letters included in the primer, Brian Ó Cuív has speculated that he was partly educated in a bardic school.[37] If this was the case, it is quite likely that he received his early education from the local Ó hUiginn bardic sept.[38] In a move which was surely crucial to his future career advancement and status, he enrolled as a student at Magdalene College in Cambridge where he matriculated in 1561. He graduated from the university with a BA degree in 1565.[39]

Ó Cearnaigh's attendance at Cambridge raises questions to which surviving evidence provides no definite answers. Unlike Catholicism, which stressed the sacrificial role of the priest in saying mass, the preaching and pastoral emphasis of the reformed ministry required the provision of educated and trained clerics. In response to this need, there was an increased emphasis on a graduate ministry during Elizabeth's reign. In 1560 the crown made available theology scholarships to encourage young men to pursue a university education with a view to ordination to the ministry.[40] It was perhaps through some such scholarship arrangement that Ó Cearnaigh was enabled to study at Cambridge. It is recorded that he was a sizar at Magdalene, and this form of scholarship intended for students from poorer backgrounds would certainly have partly subsidised his studies.[41] Given his birth in the west of Ireland, it is almost certain that his first language was Irish and that he would have learned English as a second language perhaps in Dublin or England before proceeding to university. There is no record of when he took holy orders in the established church. However, by late 1570 Ó Cearnaigh was treasurer of St Patrick's Cathedral in Dublin.[42] His knowledge of canon law was possibly a key factor in his rapid promotion so soon after graduation.[43] In October 1570, he was reimbursed by the authorities for expenses (£22 13s 4d)

---

[36] Nicholas Canny, 'Why the Reformation failed in Ireland: *une question mal posée*', *Journal of Ecclesiastical History* 30 (1979), 442.

[37] Ó Cuív (ed.), *Aibidil*, pp. 3–4.

[38] Eleanor Knott (ed. and trans.), *The bardic poems of Tadhg Dall Ó hUiginn (1550–1591)*, 2 vols. (London, 1922–6), vol. I, pp. xxxi–xxxii.

[39] James Ware, *De scriptoribus Hiberniae* (Dublin, 1639), p. 86; *Alumni Cantabrigienses*, vol. I, p. 294.

[40] Rosemary O'Day, *The English clergy: the emergence and consolidation of a profession 1558–1642* (Leicester, 1979), pp. 126–7, 133.

[41] *Alumni Cantabrigienses*, vol. I, p. 294.

[42] Hugh Jackson Lawlor, *The fasti of St Patrick's, Dublin* (Dundalk, 1930), p. 70; Raymond Gillespie, 'Reform and decay, 1500–1598', in John Crawford and Raymond Gillespie (eds.), *St Patrick's Cathedral, Dublin: a history* (Dublin, 2009), p. 166.

[43] *The Irish fiants of the Tudor sovereigns during the reigns of Henry VIII, Edward VI, Philip & Mary, and Elizabeth I*, 4 vols. (Dublin, 1994, reprint), vol. II, nos. 2375, 2384, 2386, 3030, 3394, 3511.

defrayed by him in relation to the acquisition and manufacture of an Irish type and the printing of 200 catechisms in Irish.[44] As the financial prospects of the reformed clergy were generally unpromising at this period, it is possible that Ó Cearnaigh was advanced monies for the manufacture of the Gaelic type in the first instance by alderman John Ussher, a member of a long-established Dublin merchant family and a devout Protestant.[45] The title page of the primer of religion declares that it was printed at Ussher's expense. The background to Ó Cearnaigh's appointment at St Patrick's and what is known of his subsequent career indicates that he was well regarded by the political and ecclesiastical authorities in Dublin. The archbishop of Dublin, Adam Loftus, writing to Lord Burghley, in September 1571 recommended Ó Cearnaigh as a possible new dean of St Patrick's.[46] That Loftus, a leading reformer who had been advanced to the archbishopric of Dublin from the archdiocese of Armagh in 1567, considered him suitable for such a prestigious position at quite an early stage in his career suggests that he was a capable administrator, an effective preacher, and a sound evangelical.

Ó Cearnaigh was appointed to St Patrick's in succession to Patrick Barnewall, who had been deprived of the treasurership early in 1570 on foot of his failure to produce papers of dispensation for prebendal non-residence during the course of a visitation of the cathedral initiated by Loftus and by Lord Chancellor Robert Weston, an English ecclesiastical lawyer and fervent Protestant who was invited from England to fill the chancellor's position in 1567.[47] As the main bulwark of the old faith in Dublin, a city in which most parishes remained indifferent to the practices and doctrines of the reformed church, the conservative Catholic clerical interest in Dublin had been centred on the city's secular cathedral of St Patrick from the time of Queen Mary's restoration of the church.[48] James Murray has argued persuasively that Loftus, conscious of the government's disinclination, for strategic political reasons, to enforce a punitive regime of religious conformity, tempered the harsher aspects of his reforming zeal during this period with a view to eliciting loyalty to the established church through a less coercive approach to conformity and through the use of the traditional administrative structures of the cathedral to legitimate his mission.[49] Invoking the time-honoured

---

[44] Ó Cuív (ed.), *Aibidil*, p. 5.

[45] William Ball Wright, *The Ussher memoirs; or, genealogical memoirs of the Ussher families in Ireland* (Dublin, 1889), pp. 121–6; Colm Lennon, *The lords of Dublin in the age of Reformation* (Dublin, 1989), p. 137.

[46] *CSPI, Tudor period, 1571–1575*, O'Dowd (ed.), p. 83.

[47] Murray, *Enforcing the Reformation*, pp. 261–71.   [48] *Ibid.*, pp. 261–2.

[49] *Ibid.*, p. 263.

sanction and orthodox lineage of canon law, Loftus and Weston inaugurated a visitation of the cathedral in April 1569 with a view to negating the influence of its traditionalist clerical hierarchy. During the course of an especially rigorous visitation, the non-resident treasurer, John Barnewall, connected to an old Pale family and possibly a religious conservative, was deprived of his office for failure to present documentary evidence of dispensation.[50] The deprivation of Barnewall and others enabled their replacement by clergymen with attested Protestant credentials.[51]

The appointment of Ó Cearnaigh to the chapter of St Patrick's against the backdrop of the Loftus/Weston visitation indicates that he was regarded as a reliable and orthodox Protestant by Loftus and Weston. Indeed, the irony of the intrusion within the cathedral of a Cambridge-educated Gaelic Irish Protestant by English reformers was surely not lost on the erstwhile and remaining members of this venerable ecclesiastical and cultural bastion of the English Pale. Ciaran Brady and James Murray have stressed the challenge posed to the legitimacy and prestige of the English-Irish church by the sixteenth-century state church. Given that the twelfth-century conquest of Ireland had been predicated on the basis of reform of Gaelic Ireland in line with the canonical norms and customs of the medieval English church, the new religious dispensation fundamentally undermined the ideological, devotional, and cultural role of the English Irish clergy.[52] Ó Cearnaigh's succession to the deprived Barnewall radically subverted the ideological and ethnic ethos of the traditional religion of the medieval colonial community. Evidently, Ó Cearnaigh's career was in the ascendant, for in 1572 he was proposed to Lord Burghley for the archbishopric of Tuam, no doubt partly on the grounds of his primer and his stated commitment to the translation of the New Testament to Irish.[53] However, he declined the appointment because of the apparently unsettled state of the country.[54] No doubt, the relatively modest income of the archbishopric of Tuam also informed his decision to remain in the richer and more lucrative diocese of Dublin.[55] His appointment in 1577 to the commission for ecclesiastical causes, the body charged with enforcing religious conformity across the realm

---

[50] *Ibid.*, pp. 270–71.   [51] *Ibid.*, p. 274.

[52] Ciaran Brady and James Murray, 'Sir Henry Sidney and the Reformation in Ireland', in Elizabethanne Boran and Crawford Gribben (eds.), *Enforcing Reformation in Ireland and Scotland, 1550–1700* (Aldershot, 2006), p. 28.

[53] Ó Domhnuill (ed. and trans.), *Tiomna nuadh ar dtighearna agus ar slanaightheora Iosa Criosd*, p. 1v.

[54] *CSPI, Tudor period, 1571–1575*, O'Dowd (ed.), pp. 204, 224.

[55] Hubert Thomas Knox, *Notes on the early history of the dioceses of Tuam Killala and Achonry* (Dublin, 1904), p. 220; Steven G. Ellis, 'Economic problems of the church: why the Reformation failed in Ireland', *Journal of Ecclesiastical History* 41 (1990), 257.

by means of fine or imprisonment, indicates that he continued to enjoy the esteem of the Tudor authorities in Dublin.[56] Uniquely for a Gaelic Irishman, Ó Cearnaigh was at the heart of the English establishment in Ireland in the 1570s. He continued to occupy the position of treasurer of St Patrick's until at least as late as 1578, although the office was occupied by Richard Thomson from 1581 onwards.[57]

IV

The Irish primer of religion is a relatively short work consisting of 28 leaves resulting in 56 pages. The primer comprises five principal sections: an opening address to the reader or epistle; an introduction to the Irish alphabet and orthography; a catechism including articles of the creed, the Ten Commandments, duties towards God and neighbourly obligations, and the Lord's Prayer and a discussion of it; a section containing ten prayers; a translation of a declaration on the Articles of Religion first proclaimed at Dublin in 1566/7 by Lord Deputy Sir Henry Sidney (viceroy of Ireland in the periods 1565–71 and 1575–8).[58] The inclusion in the primer of these Articles of Religion is significant in that they represent an early manifestation of local autonomy on the part of the Irish church.[59] Unlike Elizabethan England, where the Thirty-Nine Articles (1563) defined the theology of the state church, the legislative foundation of the Irish church remained centred on the Acts of Supremacy and Uniformity. The Twelve Articles, issued on the authority of the lord deputy, bishops, and the Irish ecclesiastical commissioners, constituted the Church of Ireland's confession of faith during Elizabeth's reign and were formally superseded only by the 105 articles of 1615.[60] Based on Archbishop Matthew Parker's Eleven Articles of 1561, drawn up by him as an interim measure in advance of the Thirty-Nine Articles, Alan Ford has described the Twelve Articles as a 'bland and unexceptional statement of essential reformation principles'.[61] Their uncontroversial character was, perhaps, also important in ensuring their acceptability

---

[56] *Irish fiants*, vol. II, no. 3047; Murray, *Enforcing the Reformation*, p. 298.

[57] Lawlor, *Fasti*, p. 70; Ó Cuív (ed.), *Aibidil*, pp. 5–6.   [58] Ó Cuív (ed.), *Aibidil*, p. 11.

[59] Aidan Clarke, 'Varieties of uniformity: the first century of the Church of Ireland', in W. J. Sheils and Diana Wood (eds.), *The churches, Ireland and the Irish* (Oxford, 1989), p. 107; Alan Ford, 'Dependent or independent? The Church of Ireland and its colonial context, 1536–1649', *Seventeenth Century* 10 (1995), 168.

[60] Jefferies, *The Irish church and the Tudor Reformations*, pp. 159–61.

[61] Charles Hardwick, *A history of the Articles of Religion* (Cambridge, 1859), pp. 120–3; Alan Ford, 'The Church of Ireland, 1558–1634: a Puritan church?', in Alan Ford, James McGuire, and Kenneth Milne (eds.), *As by law established: the Church of Ireland since the Reformation* (Dublin, 1995), p. 57.

to the diverse clerical personnel of the sixteenth-century church in Ireland. Brady and Murray have argued convincingly that, while the Twelve Articles are evidently mild in stipulating subscription by the clergy and laity to the Church of Ireland on the basis of general conformity to royal supremacy and the prayer book services, the real significance of the articles is best understand in the context of Sidney's broader ecclesiastical programme.[62] In fact, the Twelve Articles form part of a larger reformation strategy that was focused on propaganda, diocesan reorganisation, clerical reform, restoration of churches, and the proposed foundation of a university.[63]

Although he was largely unsuccessful in his plan to construct a coherent reformed national church, it is arguable that the 1571 primer of religion is the most lasting product of Sidney's subtle but ambitious religious agenda.[64] The inclusion of the Irish translation of the Twelve Articles suggests that Ó Cearnaigh was entrusted by the lord deputy with the task of enticing the Gaelic Irish within the fold of his envisaged national church. In any case, the translation of this confession of faith to Irish evidences a serious commitment on Ó Cearnaigh's part to engagement with the Gaelic Irish through dialogue and instruction rather than by crude coercion.

V

At first glance, the 1571 primer seems transparent and wholly instrumentalist in terms of its application. Its sole element of innovation derived from its canonical status as the first book in Irish printed in Ireland.[65] Apart from Ó Cuív's meticulous edition of the text and Nicholas Williams's discussion of the volume in his study of Protestant translations to the Irish language in the early modern period, this apparently unremarkable publication has attracted no extended discussion of its political or cultural significance. Such historiographical neglect and indifference suggest an assumption that the text is without broader ideological relevance. In fact, Ó Cearnaigh's text on closer enquiry reveals a versatile and adept negotiation of the predicament confronting Gaelic reformers in their allegiance to a variety of Protestantism intimately linked to

---

[62] Brady and Murray, 'Sidney and the Reformation in Ireland', p. 18.
[63] *Ibid.*, p. 21.   [64] *Ibid.*, pp. 21–3.
[65] Richard Stanihurst, *The historie of Irelande from the first inhabitation thereof, unto the yeare 1509. Collected by Raphaell Holinshed and continued till the yeare 1547 by Richarde Stanyhurst* (London, 1577), p. 25v; John Richardson, *A short history of the attempts that have been made to convert the Popish natives of Ireland, to the establish'd religion: with a proposal for their conversion* (London, 1712), pp. 13–14.

the expansion of English political authority and cultural sovereignty. In essence, this challenge centred on how to accommodate the autonomy of Gaelic culture and language to the requirements of a reform movement which constituted a component in the Elizabethan state's programme of consolidation in Ireland. The Irish primer of religion operates on at least two textual levels. First, it obviously functions as an introduction to the basic precepts of Protestantism. Second, the text manifests a blend of conformity and agency in its articulation of Tudor dominion while concurrently validating Gaelic culture in the context of print. In making the case for this argument, it is proposed to focus on the text in so far as it concerns questions of print and of political and cultural authority.

Projection of a sense of cultural integrity is discussed in terms of the materiality of print and a complementary articulation of identity in the primer's epistle and orthographical section. Although the primer of religion was not the first printed book in Irish, it was the first book to be printed in a Gaelic-style type. In contrast, Carswell's translation had been printed in roman type, possibly reflecting more fluid scribal practices in Gaelic Scotland and a certain intellectual distance from the elite Gaelic culture of Ireland. However, Ó Cearnaigh's work is printed in a fount evidently designed by someone familiar with Irish scribal conventions.[66] As Ó Cearnaigh had been specifically reimbursed in 1570 for the provision of 'stamps, forms and matrices' in conjunction with the printing of an Irish catechism, it is quite possible that he was responsible for the decision to base the design largely on historic practice.[67] While bibliographical scholars traditionally argued that the Irish characters in the primer of religion derived ultimately from the famous Elizabethan printer John Day's Anglo-Saxon fount created at the behest of the antiquarian archbishop of Canterbury, Matthew Parker, it has been demonstrated by Dermot McGuinne that Ó Cearnaigh's Gaelic fount was cut independently.[68] Moreover, Ó Cuív has noted that, while many of the letters, both capitals and lower-case, are effectively standard roman type, others are distinctive in design. These are the capital and lower-case a, which are italic in appearance, and the letters d, e, f, g, i, m, n, r, s, t, and u, in addition to capital B and lower-case p. Ó Cuív concluded that 'all of these are reminiscent of letters found in Irish manuscripts'.[69]

This hybrid fount was also used in 1571 to print a single broadsheet containing a religious bardic poem ('Tuar feirge foighide Dhé' or 'God's

---

[66] Ó Cuív (ed.), *Aibidil*, p. 4.

[67] Dermot McGuinne, *Irish type design: a history of printing types in the Irish character* (Dublin, 1992), p. 7.

[68] *Ibid.*, pp. 7–8.   [69] Ó Cuív (ed.), *Aibidil*, p. 10.

patience is an omen of anger') by the fifteenth-century Franciscan poet, Pilib Bocht Ó hUiginn (d. 1487).[70] It has been assumed by scholars that this work was printed as a trial-piece in advance of the larger and more exacting task of producing the primer of religion. However, it is also quite possible that the publication of such a broadsheet containing devotional material was envisaged as an expedient and inexpensive way of promoting popular piety. It is probably no coincidence that the first generation of reformers in England had deployed godly ballads as an instrument of evangelisation. It seems likely that Ó Cearnaigh would have been familiar with such ballads from his time at Cambridge in the early 1560s. However, Tessa Watt has noted that the composition of these ballads was on the decline by the middle of Elizabeth's reign.[71] Significantly, the sole extant copy of the broadsheet survives in Archbishop Parker's magnificent library which he bequeathed to Corpus Christi College, Cambridge.[72] It contains an inscription possibly in the hand of Parker's son John, which noted that 'this Irishe balade printed in Irelande who belike use the olde Saxon carecte'.[73] It is possible that the Gaelic broadsheet was sent to Parker, who in the 1560s and 1570s was at the centre of a nexus of historians seeking to articulate an ancient English ecclesiastical lineage for reformed practices, for ideological as well as antiquarian reasons.[74] The Anglo-Saxon church was viewed benignly in the sixteenth century as largely unblemished by overt or excessive Roman influence and, in his preface to the 1540 official Bible, Archbishop Cranmer noted approvingly that Anglo-Saxon clerics had translated Scripture into the vernacular.[75] As the first Anglo-Saxon fount had been cast by John Day in 1566 on behalf of Parker for the publication of the sermons of Aelfric (*A testimonie of antiquity*) and a second Anglo-Saxon fount was cast at some point before 1570, it surely is no coincidence that an explicit association was made contemporaneously and well into the eighteenth century between Gaelic and Anglo-Saxon characters.[76] Fifteen years after the

---

[70] Bruce Dickins, 'The Irish broadside of 1571 and Queen Elizabeth's types', *Transactions of the Cambridge Bibliographical Society* 1 (1949), 48–60.

[71] Tessa Watt, *Cheap print and popular piety, 1550–1640* (Cambridge, 1991), p. 41.

[72] V. J. K. Brook, *A life of Archbishop Parker* (Oxford, 1962), p. 341.

[73] McGuinne, *Irish type design*, p. 12.

[74] Benedict Scott Robinson, '"Darke speech": Matthew Parker and the reforming of history', *Sixteenth Century Journal* 29 (1998), 1061–83; Felicity Heal, 'Appropriating history: Catholic and Protestant polemics and the national past', *Huntington Library Quarterly* 68 (2005), 113–14.

[75] Diarmaid MacCulloch, *Tudor church militant: Edward VI and the Protestant Reformation* (London, 1999), pp. 137–8.

[76] John N. King, 'John Day: master printer of the English Reformation', in Peter Marshall and Alec Ryrie (eds.), *The beginnings of English Protestantism* (Cambridge, 2002), pp. 180–208.

appearance of the Irish primer, the influential English historian and antiquarian, William Camden (1551–1623), in his seminal and frequently
republished work *Britannia* (1586), stated that the Anglo-Saxons had
acquired their characters from the Irish.[77] Notwithstanding Camden's
attribution of the Anglo-Saxon script to an Irish exemplar, the question
of who borrowed from whom remained a matter of contention down
to the early eighteenth century.[78] The Gaelic antiquarian Conall Mac
Eochagáin, in his 1627 translation to English of the 'Annals of Clonmac-
noise', boasted in his dedication to the work of how the ancient Irish provided both the Welsh and Anglo-Saxons with their respective alphabets.[79]
Geoffrey Keating, in the polemical introduction to his highly influential
history of Ireland titled *Foras feasa ar Éirinn* completed *c.* 1634/5, noted
Spenser's remarks on apparent Anglo-Saxon cultural borrowing in this
regard. Keating concluded tartly that the English must likewise have
acquired their knowledge of literature from the Irish.[80] In the late seventeenth century, the virulently anti-Catholic Richard Cox in his *Hibernia
Anglicana* (1689), arguing against the linguistic purity and distinctiveness
of the Irish language, declared that 'the Irish use the Saxon character to
this day'.[81] On the other hand, Irish Catholic writers such as Peter Walsh,
Mathew Kennedy, and Hugh Mac Curtin, or the Protestant champion of
Gaelic culture, John Keogh, articulated the case for English indebtedness
to the ancient Irish.[82] In the longer term, Edward Lhuyd's emphasis on an

---

[77] 'And from thence it may seeme our forefathers the ancient English learned the maner of
framing their letters, and of writing; considering that they used the selfesame character,
which the Irish commonly use at this day': William Camden, *Britain... written first in
Latine by William Camden... translated newly into English by Philémon Holland* (London,
1610), p. 68.

[78] Edmund Spenser in his *A View of the State of Ireland*, written *c.* 1596 but first printed
in 1633, has Irenius remark to Eudoxus that 'the Saxons of England are said to have
their letters, and learning, and learned men from the Irish, and that also appeareth by
the likenesse of the character, for the Saxons character is the same with the Irish'. See
Edmund Spenser, *A View of the State of Ireland*, Andrew Hadfield and Willy Maley (eds.)
(Oxford, 1997), p. 47.

[79] BL Additional MS, 4817, fol. 4r.

[80] Geoffrey Keating, *Foras feasa ar Éirinn le Seathrún Céitinn, DD*, David Comyn and Patrick
S. Dinneen (eds. and trans.), 4 vols. (London, 1902–13), vol. I, pp. 65–7.

[81] Richard Cox, *Hibernia Anglicana: or, the history of Ireland from the conquest thereof by the
English, to this present time with an introductory discourse touching the ancient state of the
kingdom*, 2 pts (London, 1689–90), pt 1, sig. fv.

[82] Peter Walsh, *A prospect of the state of Ireland* (London, 1682), p. 58; Mathew Kennedy, *A
chronological genealogical and historical dissertation of the royal family of the Stuarts* (Paris,
1705), p. 33; Hugh Mac Curtin, *A brief discourse in vindication of the antiquity of Ireland*
(Dublin, 1717), p. 291; John Keogh, *A vindication of the antiquities of Ireland* (Dublin,
1748), pp. 8–9, 65. The broader historiographical environment in which these historians
worked is discussed in Toby Barnard, *Improving Ireland? Projectors, prophets and profiteers,
1641–1786* (Dublin, 2008), pp. 89–119.

ancient British provenance for Anglo-Saxon characters in his pioneering work of Celtic philology, *Archaeologia Britannica* (1707), seems to have inaugurated the beginning of the end for this long-standing controversy.[83]

Given its subsequent potential to inform rival claims to ancient cultural primacy, Ó Cearnaigh's deployment of a Gaelic-style script is surely an example of the 'expressive function' of typography.[84] A similar contemporary example of the ideological dimension of typography is evident in the use of black letter in sixteenth-century England for civil or divine texts which enshrined state authority and which sought to instil obedience and acquiescence.[85] Ó Cearnaigh may well have attempted simultaneously to assert for the benefit of an influential English audience a distinctive Irish cultural heritage which was reassuringly aligned at some remote point in antiquity with the Anglo-Saxon world.[86] The visual and representational impact of the printed primer was no doubt significant in communicative terms in a world where literacy was the preserve of social and learned elites. The decoration of the parish church of St Werburgh in Dublin in the early 1590s with the royal arms and the Ten Commandments serves as a reminder that early modern churches, even of the reformed variety, facilitated performance and instruction through visual as much as oral and script media.[87] However, such was the contested nature of royal supremacy in matters of faith in Ireland that even its visual embodiment was liable to elicit opposition. The case of the Cork children who systematically ripped the image of the monarch from their school books in the mid 1590s but continued to use the books themselves also highlights the discretionary and strategic use of printed material.[88]

Given Ó Cearnaigh's educational and professional trajectory, it would seem unlikely that he played any part in the technical aspects of the production of the Gaelic characters often called 'Queen Elizabeth's type'. However, if as seems probable Ó Cearnaigh exercised an oversight or supervisory function in the design of the fount, it is arguable that his

[83] Edward Lhuyd, *Archaeologia Britannica* (Oxford, 1707), p. 225; David Malcolme, *An essay on the antiquities of Great Britain and Ireland* (Edinburgh, 1738), pp. 5–6 ('A compleat translation of the Welsh preface to Mr Lhuyd's glossography, or his *Archeologia Britannica*').

[84] D. F. McKenzie, *Bibliography and the sociology of texts* (London, 1986), pp. 8–10; Mark Bland, *A guide to early printed books and manuscripts* (Oxford, 2010), p. 9.

[85] Sabrina Alcorn Baron, 'Red ink and black letter: reading early modern authority', in Sabrina Alcorn Baron with Elizabeth Walsh and Susan Scola (ed.), *The reader revealed* (Washington, DC, 2001), p. 25.

[86] Robinson, 'Matthew Parker', p. 1061.

[87] Adrian Empey (ed.), *The proctors' accounts of the parish church of St Werburgh, Dublin, 1481–1627* (Dublin, 2009), pp. 130, 132.

[88] *CSPI*, VI, p. 17.

contribution evidences a high degree of cultural agency.[89] It is not known who precisely designed and cut the hybrid Gaelic type used to print the 1571 primer which was subsequently used for the Irish New Testament in 1602/3, the Irish Book of Common Prayer in 1608, and other texts in Irish printed as late as 1652. A possible candidate for this work is William Kearney.[90] Apart from Humphrey Powell, Kearney is the only other printer known to have worked in Dublin in the sixteenth century. Describing him as a kinsman of Seaán Ó Cearnaigh, the privy council, in a letter dated 1587 to the lord deputy and council in Dublin, reported that he had in his possession a copy of an Irish translation of the New Testament made by Ó Cearnaigh and Nicholas Walsh.[91] He was said to have mastered the art of printing over the previous fourteen years both in London and on the continent. It is also stated that the New Testament remained unprinted because of a lack of suitable Irish characters and for want of skilled printers versed in the Irish language. However, Kearney, subject to the provision of funding, was willing to use his knowledge of Irish and printing to print the New Testament. In 1591 Kearney was issued with a warrant by the privy council to enable him to travel with his letters, presses, and books to Ireland unhindered by crown officials, and the latter were requested to provide assistance to him where necessary, to facilitate the printing of Irish Bibles. By the mid 1590s, he was working as a printer at the newly founded Trinity College in Dublin, and by 1597 he is presumed to have printed the Irish gospels as far the sixth chapter of St Luke.[92] It is not possible to speak with certainty as to the craftsman who created Queen Elizabeth's Irish type. However, the fact that a kinsman of Ó Cearnaigh had mastered the art of printing in London is significant and demonstrates engagement with technology in the service of evangelisation in a manner that underpinned Gaelic cultural integrity.

VI

A striking degree of cultural agency is discernible in the primer's epistle and orthographical section. Ó Cearnaigh opens his brief address to the reader by describing how he had laboured for a long time on a work

[89] McGuinne, *Irish type design*, p. 9.

[90] R. B. McKerrow, *A dictionary of printers and booksellers in England, Scotland and Ireland, and of foreign printers of English books 1557–1640* (London, 1910), p. 162.

[91] Cosslett Quin, 'Nicholas Walsh and his friends: a forgotten chapter in the Irish Reformation', *Journal of the Butler Society* 2 (1984), 294–8.

[92] E. R. McClintock Dix, 'William Kearney, the second earliest known printer in Dublin', *Proceedings of the Royal Irish Academy* 28 C 7 (1910), 157–61.

in the Irish language which would open a pathway previously closed to speakers of that language. Speaking inclusively in the first person plural, he states that 'we' (i.e. the Gaelic Irish) were mired in ignorance and darkness lacking the rule of God and of the world up to that time ('bheith báite a ndaille, 7 a ndíth eóluis, d'uireasbhuigh reachda Dé, 7 an tsaoghail gus á nossa'). Dramatically, he claims, again in the first person plural, that in customs and habits 'we' were the most untamed and barbarous of all the peoples in the western part of Europe ('7 ní is barbartha ann ar modhuibh 7 ann ar mbhésuibh, in á aon chineól daoine, dá bhfuil ann sa rann iartharach so na Eúrópa'). Having emphasised the need for comprehensive religious and secular reform on the part of the Gaelic Irish, he proceeds to distance them from responsibility for their predicament by attributing it to the want of provision of the law of God and the state. The present work, he says, enables them to access both divine and secular law in their own language printed in its appropriate format. In effect, the Gaelic Irish were now empowered to attain temporal and divine redemption via their own language. Remarking that, although he had brought the work to completion as nobody else had been prepared to do so, he had done so with financial support from the all-powerful Elizabeth ('ar chosdas ar n-árd-phrionnsa dhiagha mórchumhachdaigh Elízabed'). Moreover, he had also acted with the consent of Lord Deputy Sir Henry Sidney and the most honourable council members of the queen's sovereignty in the island of Ireland ('7 na coda ele de chomhairle ro-onóraighe fhlaitheasa na bannríoghna ann sa n-oílén so na hÉireann'). It is interesting that in acknowledging the authority of the queen that Ó Cearnaigh does so in a strictly insular jurisdictional context with no reference made to England. He proceeds in a formulaic manner to ask his readers to overlook any errors in the present work which was undertaken for the glory of God and the public good ('do chúm glóire Dé do chur a mach, 7 do chúm an mhaitheasa phuiblidhe so'). The alignment of Reformation with the public or common good, which was to prove a recurrent element in Protestant arguments for the conversion of Irish Catholics down to the nineteenth century, underlines Ó Cearnaigh's emphasis on the beneficial civic impact of the new faith.[93] Moreover, Breandán Ó Buachalla's claim that *maitheas poiblí* ('common good') was 'one of the new politico-religious concepts introduced into Irish discourse in the seventeenth century by the agents of the

---

[93] Richard Cox, *An essay for the conversion of the Irish* (Dublin, 1698); John Richardson, *The true interest of the Irish nation* (Dublin, 1716); Robert Daly, *A sermon, preached in St Anne's church, Dublin, on Sunday, the 27th of May, 1821, in aid of the Irish Society* (Dublin, 1821).

Counter-Reformation' highlights again previously unremarked innovation in Ó Cearnaigh's catechism.[94] Drawing to a close, Ó Cearnaigh declares that, should his efforts meet with approbation and endorsement, he promises to produce more material in this vein.[95] Aside from the requisite avowal of Tudor dominion in Ireland, this epistle is remarkable for its sense of focus and inclusiveness. Reformation is advocated not from an intruded external perspective. On the contrary, Ó Cearnaigh makes the case for reform from a purely Gaelic point of view and in terms of its potential for beneficial religious and civic transformation.

A similar sense of cultural self-confidence is manifest in the orthographical section, simply headed *Aibghitir* or alphabet in Irish. In his commentary on this section of the primer, Ó Cuív proposed that its contents derived from the teaching of contemporary bardic schools as reflected in extant linguistic tracts. Rather curiously, in light of the fact that Ó Cearnaigh's epistle was clearly directed at his fellow *Gaoidhil*, this section seems intended to assist readers unfamiliar with the characters and pronunciation of the language. Another possible target audience may have been native speakers of Irish with limited literacy skills. In any case, Ó Cearnaigh gives the letters of the alphabet along with their Irish names, called after trees as defined in the Ogham system of writing, which originated in pre-Christian Ireland. This exposition is followed by details of abbreviations used commonly in scribal practice and now replicated in the printed text. Details follow on the division of sounds as manifest by the letters of the alphabet presented as vowels and consonants. A brief account is provided on the use of h as a marker of lenition and a table is presented giving an overview of seventeen diphthongs found in Gaelic orthography.[96] The section concludes by advising those readers anxious to deepen their knowledge of the language to address themselves to the praise poets whose function it was to discuss such matters expertly ('fághbhadh fóghluim óna fileaghuibh. Oír is lé na n-ealádhain bheanas sin do thráchdadh go hínntleachdach éolusách'). For his part, Ó Cearnaigh insists that his primary purpose centres not on matters of linguistic usage. In fact, he is simply seeking to open a pathway previously closed and to print Irish in its own appropriate character like every language in Christendom ('in teanguidh ghaóidhelge do chur ann a cló dhíleas fén mar tá gach teanguidh ele sa chríosduigheachd').[97] Given the

---

[94] Breandán Ó Buachalla, 'The making of a Cork Jacobite', in Patrick O'Flanagan and Cornelius G. Buttimer (eds.), *Cork history and society* (Dublin, 1993), p. 493 n. 28. Regarding the medieval concept of the 'common good' in early modern England, see Phil Withington, *Society in early modern England: the vernacular origins of some powerful ideas* (Cambridge, 2010), pp. 138–52.

[95] Ó Cuív (ed.), *Aibidil*, pp. 52–7.   [96] *Ibid.*, pp. 13–14.   [97] *Ibid.*, p. 67.

intermittent but sustained hostility of the Tudor regime to Gaelic praise poets as perceived agents of political and cultural dissension, it is remarkable that Ó Cearnaigh should defer to bardic linguistic and cultural authority. Indeed, it is quite probable that in acknowledging the superior literary scholarship of the praise poets that Ó Cearnaigh hoped to secure their influential endorsement both of his pioneering print initiative and of Gaelic evangelisation. However, it is also possible that concurrently he aimed to deflect hostility to his use of print from a venerable learned elite that relied exclusively on script and the verbal as communicative media. Comments written in 1620 by an anonymous scribe who recorded in manuscript format praise poetry composed for members of the O'Reilly family of east Bréifne provide an important reminder of how a dynamic interchange between orality and script informed the communication and transmission of Gaelic scholarship and literature. In this instance, the scribe sought the indulgence of readers in respect of the poems copied, as his only source for them was an old man who had committed them to memory thirty years previously.[98] The advent of print fundamentally challenged the dominance of the bardic elite whose capacity to exercise cultural and political influence was enabled by the complementary media of script and orality. The advent of an alternative and transformative mode of dissemination and transmission of material operating outside the remit of the literati signalled an implicit challenge to their professional status and political power. Therefore, it is also possible that by deferring explicitly to the praise poets in the matter of linguistic usage Ó Cearnaigh was aware of the degree to which print had the potential to expand cultural and literary creativity significantly beyond the sanctioned parameters of bardic tradition. More particularly, print's capacity to engender innovation is evident in the primer's unambiguous validation of Gaelic language and culture as an instrument to communicate the message of reform and to advocate Gaelic political docility.[99]

VII

By way of conclusion, it is proposed briefly to review how Ó Cearnaigh, in addition to validating Gaelic cultural autonomy in his primer, concurrently sought to communicate a message of acquiescence in Elizabethan

---

[98] James Carney (ed.), *Poems on the O'Reillys* (Dublin, 1950), p. xiii. For another early seventeenth-century example of the interplay between oral tradition and script in Gaelic culture, see Alan Bruford, *Gaelic folk-tales and mediaeval romances* (Dublin, 1969), p. 46.

[99] Keith Thomas, 'The meaning of literacy in early modern England', in Gerd Baumann (ed.), *The written word: literacy in transition* (Oxford, 1986), p. 118.

political authority.[100] In fact, advocacy of submission to the queen and her agents is explicit and pervasive in the text. This is made clear on the title page of the primer when it is declared that its teaching is mandatory for all who wish to observe divine law and the queen's rule in the kingdom of Ireland ('is ínghabhtha, dá gach aon dá mbhé fómánta do reachd Día 7 na bannríoghan sa ríghe').[101] In other words, acceptance of religious reform and acknowledgement of the monarch's authority are indivisible. In the catechism section, framed around a question-and-answer format and drawn from the equivalent text in the 1559 Book of Common Prayer, the master ('An Maighister') queries the learner ('An Fóghluínnthíghe') as to his neighbourly obligations. Among the requisite traits and behaviour is the demonstration of obedience and honour to the monarchy and its officers ('onóir 7 úmhla, do thabhairt dom Rígh 7 dá mhiniostráláibh') and submission to one's teachers and spiritual pastors. In short, appropriate respect and reverence are due to all deemed socially superior.[102] Ó Cearnaigh's overt Protestantism arguably complements and reinforces his message of temporal conformity. For instance, Ó Cearnaigh's inclusion of the doxology in the Pater Noster has been adduced as evidence of Calvinist inclinations on his part.[103] Moreover, contemporary English anti-Catholic rhetoric is replicated in the text. In the morning prayer, divine intercession is sought in the battle to defeat Satan, Antichrist, their sundry agents, and the Papists who have deserted God ('Claoi Satan, 7 an Anticríosd maille ré na uile luchd tuarosdoil, lé na phápánachuibh, a tá agad tréigeansa').[104] In the prayer for the state of Christ's universal church, the seamless interconnection between allegiance to Queen Elizabeth and conformity to reformed religion is presented unambiguously.[105] Ó Cearnaigh's translation of the 1566 Dublin-printed articles of religion constitutes the final section of the primer.[106] In this ultimate avowal of political and religious orthodoxy, conformity is adumbrated not simply by virtue of persuasion and argument as in the preceding texts but also on the incontrovertible basis of official ordinance.

VIII

In summary, the 1571 Irish primer of religion represents a dynamic and ideologically inflected text. Ó Cearnaigh's work constitutes considerably more than a pallid provincial redaction of an English Protestant ur-text.

---

[100] Cf. J. P. D. Cooper, *Propaganda and the Tudor state: political culture in the Westcountry* (Oxford, 2003), pp. 3–4.
[101] Ó Cuív, *Aibidil, ibid.*, p. 51.   [102] *Ibid.*, pp. 15, 83.   [103] *Ibid.*, p. 167 n. 20.
[104] *Ibid.*, p. 97.   [105] *Ibid.*, p. 121.   [106] *Ibid.*, pp. 185–9.

His ideological objectives were twofold. In aiming his publication at a Gaelic audience, he presented his material in a manner that was culturally sensitive to an Irish environment. In fact, it was not simply a case of accommodation of Gaelic values and mores to an evangelical message. Ó Cearnaigh envisaged engagement with Protestantism within an autonomous cultural sphere not subject to the intrusion of English intellectual dominance. His text is an example of cultural hybridity in so far as it translates an English language exemplar to a linguistic and cultural Gaelic idiom. Peter Burke has described translations as essentially hybrid given that in their quest for 'equivalent effect' they introduce words and ideas known to new readers but unfamiliar to the original culture and language.[107] Burke has drawn on the concept of the 'ecotype' articulated by the Swedish folklorist Carl Wilhelm von Sydow to contextualise such cultural hybridity. Von Sydow deployed the term ecotype (or oicotype) to describe folktales that were adapted to their host cultures and, as such, were variants on original forms with their own internal rules.[108] In a similar vein, Ó Cearnaigh's text is hybrid in its presentation of the message of Elizabethan reform in a vivid Gaelic guise. In matters of faith and political allegiance, however, there seems to be no reason to question his commitment to Elizabeth's aspiration to political consolidation and religious reformation in Ireland. Ironically, it was perhaps the sophistication of Ó Cearnaigh's vision of a vibrant Gaelic Irish Protestantism accommodated within a benign Tudor state that ensured its rapid negation by the primal but potent influences of sectarianism, colonialism, and nationalism.

---

[107] Peter Burke, *Cultural hybridity* (Cambridge, 2009), p. 17.
[108] *Ibid.*, p. 51. See also C. W. von Sydow, *Selected papers on folklore* (Copenhagen, 1948), pp. 52–3.

Bibliography

MANUSCRIPTS

BODLEIAN LIBRARY, OXFORD

Laud MS (Miscellaneous) 612
Willis MS 58
Tanner MS 76

BRITISH LIBRARY

Additional MSS 4817, 34313, 72407
Cotton MSS Titus BX
Harleian MS 6996
Lansdowne MS 23, no. 4.
Royal MS 19.B.VIII
Vespasian MS F IX, no. 22

LAMBETH PALACE LIBRARY

MSS 601, 607, 612, 623, 628, 632, 692, 2002
Fairhurst MS 3470

LONGLEAT, WILTSHIRE

Devereux MSS, Box 6, Commissions and legal instruments, 1577–1603

THE NATIONAL ARCHIVES, LONDON

SP 12 State papers, domestic, Elizabeth I
SP 63 State papers, Ireland
SP 78 State papers, foreign, France
C 66 Chancery, patent rolls
E 351 Exchequer, pipe office
PRO 31 Transcripts . . . of manuscripts relating to Great Britain and Ireland from the National Archives, Paris.

REPRESENTATIVE CHURCH BODY LIBRARY, DUBLIN.

MS 61/2/9

SALISBURY HOUSE, HERTFORDSHIRE, CECIL PAPERS

CP 28, 47, 72, 80, 82, 177, 179, 186

TRINITY COLLEGE, DUBLIN

MS 1440

UNIVERSITY LIBRARY CAMBRIDGE

Additional MSS
Ee 3 56, no. 32
Kk 1 15, no. 17

PRINTED PRIMARY SOURCES

Acts of the privy council of England, 1532–1631, new series, J. R. Dasent *et al.*
(eds.), 46 vols. (London, 1890–1964).
*Alumni Cantabrigienses: a biographical list of all known students, graduates and holders
of office at the University of Cambridge, from the earliest times to 1900,* John Venn
and J. A. Venn (eds.), 4 vols. (Cambridge, 1922–7).
Ancient Irish poetry, Kuno Meyer (trans.) (London, 1994, reprint).
Bacon, Francis. 'Sir Francis Bacon's MSS relating to Ireland', www.ucc.ie/celt/
published/E600001-015/, docs. 3 and 4.
Beacon, Richard. *Solon his Follie, or a Politique Discourse touching the Reformation
of Common-weales conquered, declined or corrupted,* Clare Carroll and Vincent
Carey (eds.) (Binghamton, NY, 1996).
Bellings, Richard. *History of the Irish Confederation and the War in Ireland, 1641–
1643,* J. T. Gilbert (ed.), 10 vols. (Dublin, 1882).
Bergin, Osborn. *Irish bardic poetry: texts and translations* (Dublin, 1970).
Birch, Thomas (ed.). *Memoirs of the reign of Queen Elizabeth,* 2 vols. (London,
1754).
Breatnach, Pádraig (ed. and trans.). 'Metamorphoses 1603: dán le Eochaidh Ó
hEodhasa', *Éigse* 17 (1977–8), 169–80.
Bryskett, Lodowick. *A Discourse of Ciuill Life Containing the Ethike Part of Morall
Philosophie* (London, 1606).
Byrchensa, Ralph. *A Discourse Occasioned Vpon The Late Defeat, Giuen To The
Arch-Rebels, Tyrone and Odonnell, by the right Honourable the Lord Mountioy*
(London, 1602).
*Calendar of letters and state papers, relating to English affairs, preserved principally in
the archives of Simancas, Elizabeth,* M. A. S. Hume (ed.), 4 vols. (London,
1896–1947).
*Calendar of state papers and manuscripts relating to English affairs, existing in the
archives and collections of Venice, and in other libraries of northern Italy,* G. C.
Bentinck *et al.* (eds.), 38 vols. (London, 1864–1947).
Calendar of state papers, domestic, R. Lemon and M. A. E. Green (eds.), 12 vols.
(London, 1856–72).
Calendar of state papers, Ireland, Tudor period 1571–1575, Mary O'Dowd (ed.)
(Dublin, 2000).

Calendar of the Carew manuscripts preserved in the archiepiscopal library at Lambeth, 1515–1642, J. S. Brewer and William Bullen (eds.), 6 vols. (London, 1867–73).

Calendar of the patent and close rolls of chancery in Ireland in the reigns of Henry VIII, Edward VI, Mary and Elizabeth, James Morrin (ed.), 2 vols. (Dublin and London, 1861–2).

Calendar of the state papers relating to Ireland of the reigns of Henry VIII, Edward VI, Mary, and Elizabeth I, 1509–1603, H. C. Hamilton, E. G. Atkinson, and R. P. Mahaffy (eds.), 11 vols. (London, 1860–1912).

Calvin, John. *Institutes of the Christian religion*, Henry Beveridge (trans.) (Peabody, MA, 2008).

Camden, William. *Annales Rerum Gestarum Angliae et Hiberniae Regnante Elizabetha* (London, 1615–25), Dana F. Sutton, online edn, www.philological.bham.ac.uk/camden/.

Britain . . . written first in Latine by William Camden . . . translated newly into English by Philemon Holland (London, 1610).

Campion, Edmund. *Two Bokes of the Histories of Ireland (1571)*, A. F. Vossen (ed.) (Assen, 1963).

Carney, James (ed.). *Poems on the Butlers of Ormond, Cahir, and Dunboyne* (Dublin, 1945).

Poems on the O'Reillys (Dublin, 1950).

Carswell, John. *Foirm na n-urrnuidheadh: John Carswell's Gaelic translation of the Book of Common Order*, R. L. Thomson (ed.) (Edinburgh, 1970).

Castiglione, Baldessare. *The Book of the Courtier*, Charles Singleton (trans.) (New York, 1959).

Chamberlain, John. *The letters of John Chamberlain*, N. E. McLure (ed.), 2 vols. (Philadelphia, 1939).

Churchyard, Thomas. *A Generall Rehearsal of Warres* (London, 1579).

The miserie of Flanders, calamitie of Fraunce, missfortune of Portugall, unquietnes of Irelande, troubles of Scotlande: and the blessed state of Englande (London, 1579).

Clark, Andrew. *The Shirburn ballads, 1585–1616* (Oxford, 1907).

Cokayne, George E. *The complete peerage of England, Scotland, Ireland, Great Britain, and the United Kingdom*, 8 vols. (London, 1887–98).

Collins, Arthur. *Letters and memorials of state, in the reigns of Queen Mary, Queen Elizabeth, King James, King Charles the First, part of the reign of King Charles the Second, and Oliver's usurpation*, 2 vols. (London, 1746).

Cox, Richard. *An essay for the conversion of the Irish* (Dublin, 1698).

Hibernia Anglicana: or, the history of Ireland from the conquest thereof by the English, to this present time with an introductory discourse touching the ancient state of the kingdom, 2 pts (London, 1689–90).

Daly, Robert. *A sermon, preached in St Anne's church, Dublin, on Sunday, the 27th of May, 1821, in aid of the Irish Society* (Dublin, 1821).

Davies, Sir John. *A Discoverie of the True Causes why Ireland was neuer entirely Subdued nor brought vnder Obedience of the Crowne of England, vntill the Beginning of his Maiesties happie Raigne* (London, 1612); also published as *A discovery of the true causes why Ireland was never entirely subdued and brought under the obedience of the crown of England until the beginning of His Majesty's happy reign* (1612), James P. Myers Jnr (ed.) (Washington, DC, 1988).

Dawson, Jane E. A. and L. K. Glassey, 'Some unpublished letters from John Knox to Christopher Goodman', *Scottish Historical Review* 84 (2005), 183–5.

Derricke, John. *The Image of Irelande with a Discoverie of the Woodkarne* (1581), David B. Quinn (ed.) (Belfast, 1985).

Devereux, Robert, 2nd earl of Essex. *An apologie of the earle of Essex against those which jealously and maliciously tax him to be the onely hinderer of peace and quiet of his countrey. Penned by himself in anno 1598* (London, 1603).

Dictionary of the Irish language: compact edition (Dublin, 1983).

E.C.S. *The Government of Ireland under the honourable, iust, and wise governor Sir John Perrot, 1584–1588* (London, 1626).

Elizabeth I. *Elizabeth I: collected works*, Leah S. Marcus, Janel Mueller, and Mary Beth Rose (eds.) (Chicago, 2000).

Empey, Adrian (ed.). *The proctors' accounts of the parish church of St Werburgh, Dublin, 1481–1627* (Dublin, 2009).

Falkiner, C. L. 'William Farmer's chronicles of Ireland from 1594 to 1613', *English Historical Review* 22 (1907), 104–30 and 527–52.

Finglas, Patrick. 'Breviate of the getting of Ireland and the decay of the same', in Walter Harris (ed.), *Hibernica, or some ancient pieces relating to Ireland*, 2 vols. (Dublin, 1770), vol. I, pp. 79–103.

Fitzwilliam accounts, 1560–1565, A. K. Longfield (ed.) (Dublin, 1965).

Gascoigne, George. 'Dulce bellum inexpertis', in George Gascoigne, *A Hundreth Sundrie Flowres*, G. W. Pigman III (ed.) (Oxford, 2000), pp. 398–439.

Gawdy, Philip. *Letters of Philip Gawdy of West Harling, Norfolk, and of London to various members of his family, 1579–1616*, I. H. Jeayes (ed.) (London, 1906).

Gildas. *De Excidio Britanniae*, M. Winterbottom (trans.) (Totowa, NJ, 1978).

Gilbert, J. T. (ed.). *A contemporary history of affairs in Ireland from AD 1641 to 1652*, 3 vols. (Dublin, 1879).

Facsimiles of the National Manuscripts of Ireland, 4 pts in 5 vols. (London, 1882).

Goodman, Christopher. *How superior powers oght to be obeyd of their subjects* (Geneva, 1558).

The Great Parchment Book of Waterford: liber Antiquissimus Civitatis Waterfordiae, Niall J. Byrne (ed.) (Dublin, 2007).

Harington, Sir John. *The letters and epigrams of Sir John Harington, together with The prayse of private life*, N. E. McLure (ed.) (Philadelphia, 1930).

Nugae Antiquae, Henry Harington (ed.), 3 vols. (1779; Hildersheim, 1968, reprint).

Haynes, Samuel (ed.). *A collection of state papers, relating to affairs in the reigns of Henry VIII . . . Queen Elizabeth, from the year 1542 to 1570* (London, 1740).

Herbert, Sir William. *Croftus sive de Hibernia Liber*, Arthur Keaveney and John A. Madden (eds.) (Dublin, 1992).

Historical Manuscripts Commission (London). *Calendar of manuscripts of the . . . marquess of Salisbury preserved at Hatfield House*, 24 vols. (London, 1883–1976).

The manuscripts of the Marquess of Bath preserved at Longleat, Wiltshire, G. Dynfault Owen (ed.), 5 vols. (London, 1904–80).

Report on the manuscripts of Lord de l'Isle and Dudley preserved at Penshurst Place, 6 vols. (London, 1925–66).

Holinshed, Raphael. *Holinshed's chronicles: England, Scotland and Ireland...*, 6 vols. (London, 1587; London, 1808).

The Irish fiants of the Tudor sovereigns during the reigns of Henry VIII, Edward VI, Philip & Mary, and Elizabeth I, 4 vols. (Dublin, 1994, reprint).

Keating, Geoffrey. *Foras feasa ar Eirinn le Seathrún Céitinn, DD*, David Comyn and P. S. Dinneen (eds. and trans.), 4 vols. (London, 1902–13).

Kennedy, Mathew. *A chronological genealogical and historical dissertation of the royal family of the Stuarts* (Paris, 1705).

Keogh, John. *A vindication of the antiquities of Ireland* (Dublin, 1748).

Knott, Eleanor (ed. and trans.). *The bardic poems of Tadhg Dall Ó hUiginn (1550–1591)*, 2 vols. (London, 1922–6).

Lee, Thomas. 'Brief declaration of the government of Ireland... 1594', in *Desiderata Curiosa Hibernica*, John Lodge (ed.), 2 vols. (Dublin, 1772), vol. I, pp. 87–150.

Letters and papers, foreign and domestic of the reign of Henry VIII, J. S. Brewer *et al.* (eds.), 21 vols in 32 pts, and addenda (London, 1862–1932).

The letters of Queen Elizabeth, G. B. Harrison (ed.) (London, 1968).

Lhuyd, Edward. *Archaeologia Britannica* (Oxford, 1707).

Lombard, Peter. *The Irish war of defence 1598–1600: extracts from the 'De Hibernia insula commentarius'*, M. J. Byrne (ed. and trans.) (Cork, 1930).

Luther, Martin. *The bondage of the will*, Henry Cole (trans.) (Peabody, MA, 2008).

Mac an Bhaird, Fearghal Óg. 'Teasda Éire san Easbáinn', in Pádraig Breatnach, 'Marbhna Aodha Ruaidh Uí Dhomhnaill (1602)', *Éigse* 15 (1) (1973), 31–50.

Mac Cionnaith, Láimhbheartach (ed.). *Dioghlium dána* (Baile Átha Cliath, 1938).

Mac Curtin, Hugh. *A brief discourse in vindication of the antiquity of Ireland* (Dublin, 1717).

MacErlean, John C. (ed. and trans.). *Duanaire Dhábhidh Uí Bhruadair: the poems of David O Bruadair*, 3 vols. (London, 1910–17).

Malcolme, David. *An essay on the antiquities of Great Britain and Ireland* (Edinburgh, 1738).

Memorials of affairs of state in the reigns of Q. Elizabeth and K. James I. Collected (chiefly) from the original papers of... Sir Ralph Wiunwood, E. Sawyer (ed.), 3 vols. (London, 1725).

Moryson, Fynes. *An History of Ireland from the Year 1599, to 1603* (Dublin, 1735).

An itinerary, containing his ten yeeres travell through the twelve dominions of Germany, Bohmerland, Sweitzerland, Netherland, Denmarke, Poland, Italy, Turky, France, England, Scotland & Ireland, 4 vols. (Glasgow, 1907–8).

Shakespeare's Europe: unpublished chapters of Fynes Morysons's Itinerary, Charles Hughes (ed.) (London, 1903).

Murphy, Gerard (ed.). 'Poems of exile of Uilliam Nuinseann, mac Baruin Dealbhna', *Éigse* 6 (1948–52, pt 1), 8–13.

Nashe, Thomas. *Nashe's Lenten Stuffe* (1599), 'The epistle dedicatorie', in Thomas Nashe, *The works of Thomas Nashe*, R. B. McKerrow and F. P. Wilson (eds.), 5 vols. (Oxford, 1966).

Naunton, Sir Robert. *Fragmenta regalia*, Edward Arber (ed.) (1870; New York, 1966, reprint).

Ó Cuív, Brian (ed.). *Aibidil Gaoidheilge & Caiticiosma: Seaán Ó Cearnaigh's Irish primer of religion published in 1571* (Dublin, 1994, reprint).

Ó Domhnuill, Uilliam (ed. and trans.). *Tiomna nuadh ar dtighearna agus ar slanaightheora Iosa Criosd* (Dublin, 1602).

O'Donovan, John (ed. and trans.). *Annála Ríoghachta Éireann: Annals of the Kingdom of Ireland by the Four Masters*, 7 vols. (Dublin, 1851; 2nd edn, Dublin, 1856); also published as *Annála Ríoghachta Éireann*... ucc.ie/celt/published/G100005F/index.html.

(ed.). 'The Irish correspondence of James fitz Maurice of Desmond', *Journal of the Royal Society of Antiquaries of Ireland* 5 (1859), 354–69.

O'Flaherty, Roderick. *A chorographical description of West –Connaught or Iar – Connacht, 1684*, James Hardiman (ed.) (Dublin, 1846).

O'Hart, John. *Irish pedigrees*, 2 vols. (Dublin, 1892).

O'Rahilly, Cecile (ed.). *Five seventeenth-century political poems* (Dublin, 1977).

O'Sullivan Beare, Philip. *Ireland under Elizabeth: chapters towards a history of Ireland in the reign of Elizabeth... by Don Philip O'Sullivan Beare*, Matthew J. Byrne (ed. and trans.) (Dublin, 1903).

Ó Tuama, Sean and Thomas Kinsella (eds. and trans.). *An duanaire 1600–1900: poems of the dispossessed* (Dublin, 1981).

Perrot, Sir James. *The Chronicle of Ireland 1548–1608*, Herbert Wood (ed.) (Dublin, 1933).

The history of that most eminent statesman, Sir John Perrot, R. Rawlinson (ed.) (London, 1728).

Plowden, E. 'Treatise on Mary, Queen of Scots' (1566), in Robert S. Miola (ed.), *Early modern Catholicism: an anthology of primary sources* (Oxford, 2007), pp. 55–7.

'Prayer for the good success of her Maiesties forces in Ireland' (London, 1599), STC 16530.

Puttenham, George. *The art of English poesy by George Puttenham: a critical edition*, Frank Whigham and Wayne A. Rebhorn (eds.) (Ithaca, NY, 2007).

The Records of the Honorable Society of Lincoln's Inn: The Black Books. Volume 1 from AD 1422 to AD 1586 (London, 1897).

Richardson, John. *A short history of the attempts that have been made to convert the Popish natives of Ireland, to the establish'd religion: with a proposal for their conversion* (London, 1712).

The true interest of the Irish nation (Dublin, 1716).

Rymer, Thomas. *Foedera, conventiones, literae, et cujuscunque generis acta publica inter reges Angliae et alios quosvis imperatores, reges, pontifices, principes vel communitates*, 20 vols. (London, 1704–35).

Sander, Nicholas. *Rise and growth of the Anglican schism*, David Lewis (ed. and trans.) (London, 1877).

Savile, Henry. *The ende of Nero and the beginning of Galba. Fower books of the Histories of Cornelius Tacitus. The life of Agricola* (London, 1591).

Sawyer, Edmund (ed.). *Memorials of affairs of state in the reigns of Q. Elizabeth and K. James I. Collected (chiefly) from the original papers of... Sir Ralph Winwood*, 3 vols. (London, 1725).

Seanchus Búrcach, T. Ó Raghallaigh [Thomas O' Reilly] (ed. and trans.), *Journal of the Galway Archaeological and Historical Society* 13 (1926–7), 50–60 and 101–37; 14 (1928–9), 30–51 and 142–67.

Shirley, Evelyn Philip (ed.). *Original letters and papers in illustration of the history of the church in Ireland, during the reigns of Edward VI, Mary, and Elizabeth* (London, 1851).

Sidney, Sir Henry. 'Additional Sidney state papers', D. B. Quinn (ed.), *Analecta Hibernica* 26 (1970), 89–102.

Sidney state papers, 1565–1570, Tomás Ó Laidhin (ed.) (Dublin, 1962).

A viceroy's vindication? Sir Henry Sidney's memoir of service in Ireland, 1556–1578, Ciaran Brady (ed.) (Cork, 2002).

Spenser, Edmund. *Edmund Spenser: the shorter poems,* R. A. McCabe (ed.) (Harmondsworth, 1999).

The Faerie Queene, A. C. Hamilton (ed.) (London, 2001).

A View of the State of Ireland, Andrew Hadfield and Willy Maley (eds.) (Oxford, 1997); also published as *A View of the Present State of Ireland* (1596), Risa S. Bear (ed.) (Eugene, OR, 1997), scholarsbank.uoregon.edu/xmlui/handle/1794/825.

The works of Edmund Spenser, Edwin Greenlaw *et al.* (eds.), Variorum Edition, 11 vols. (Baltimore, 1932–58).

Stanihurst, Richard. *The historie of Irelande from the first inhabitation thereof, unto the yeare 1509. Collected by Raphaell Holinshed and continued till the yeare 1547 by Richarde Stanyhurst* (London, 1577).

Staphylus, Fridericus. *The apologie of Fridericus Staphylus counseller to the late Emperour Ferdinandus . . . Of disagreement in doctrine amonge the protestants . . . ,* Thomas Stapleton (trans.) (Antwerp, 1565).

State papers concerning the Church of Ireland in the time of Queen Elizabeth, W. M. Brady (ed.) (London, 1868).

Statutes at large, passed in the parliaments held in Ireland, 1310–1800, 20 vols. (Dublin, 1786–1801).

Strype, John. *The Annals of the Reformation . . . during . . . Queen Elizabeth's Happy Reign,* 4 vols. (London, 1709).

'The supplication of the blood of the English most lamentably murdered in Ireland, cryeng out of the yearth for revenge (1598)', Willy Maley (ed.), *Analecta Hibernica* 36 (1995), 3–77.

Sutcliffe, Matthew. *The practice, proceedings and lawes of armes* (London, 1593).

The Tain: translated from the Irish epic, Tain Bo Cuailnge, Thomas Kinsella (ed. and trans.) (Oxford, 2002).

Tudor royal proclamations, P. L. Hughes and J. F. Larkin (eds.), 3 vols. (New Haven, 1969).

Verstegan, Richard. *Letters and despatches of Richard Verstegan (c. 1550–1640),* Anthony G. Petti (ed.) (London, 1959).

Verse in English from Tudor and Stuart Ireland, Andrew Carpenter (ed.) (Cork, 2003).

Walsh, Paul (ed. and trans.). *Beatha Aodha Ruaidh Uí Dhomhnaill: the life of Aodh Ruadh O Domhnaill,* 2 vols. (London, 1948–57).

Gleanings from Irish manuscripts, 2nd edn (Dublin, 1933).

Walsh, Peter. *A prospect of the state of Ireland* (London, 1682).

The Walsingham letter-book, James Hogan and N. McNeil O'Farrell (eds.) (Dublin, 1959).

Ware, James. *De scriptoribus Hiberniae* (Dublin, 1639).

White, Rowland. 'Rowland White's "Discors touching Ireland, *c.* 1569"', Nicholas Canny (ed.), *Irish Historical Studies* 20 (1977), 439–63.

Winter, Ernest F. (ed. and trans.). *Discourse on free will: Erasmus and Luther* (London, 2005).

SECONDARY SOURCES

Adams, Simon. *Leicester and the court: essays on Elizabethan politics* (Manchester, 2002).

Alford, Stephen. *The early Elizabethan polity: William Cecil and the British succession crisis, 1558–1569* (Cambridge, 2002).

Alter, Robert and Frank Kermode (eds.). *The literary guide to the Bible* (Cambridge, MA, 1990).

Anders, H. 'The Elizabethan ABC with catechism', *The Library*, 4th series, 16 (1936), 32–48.

Anon. 'An account of Gran Uile's castle – with an engraving', *Anthologia Hibernica* 2 (Jul.–Dec. 1793), 2–3.

Anon. 'The earl of Essex (1598–1601)', *Notes & Queries for Somerset and Dorset*, 24 (221) (Jun. 1944), 110–12.

Anon. 'Grainne O'Malley: she pirate', *Dublin University Magazine* 50 (1870), 385–400.

Aptekar, Jane. *Icons of justice: iconography and thematic imagery in Book V of The Faerie Queene* (New York, 1969).

Arditi, Jorge. *A genealogy of manners: transformations of social relations in France and England from the fourteenth to the eighteenth century* (Chicago, 1998).

Ariès, Philippe. *The hour of our death*, Helen Weaver (trans.) (New York, 1981).

Armstrong, Megan. *The politics of piety: Franciscan preachers during the wars of religion* (New York, 2004).

Bagenal, P. H. *Vicissitudes of an Anglo-Irish family, 1530–1800* (London, 1925).

Bagwell, Richard. *Ireland under the Tudors*, 3 vols. (1885–90; London, 1963, reprint).

Ball, F. E. *The judges in Ireland*, 2 vols. (London, 1926).

Barnard, Toby. *Improving Ireland? Projectors, prophets and profiteers, 1641–1786* (Dublin, 2008).

Baron, Sabrina Alcorn. 'Red ink and black letter: reading early modern authority', in Sabrina Alcorn Baron with Elizabeth Walsh and Susan Scola (eds.), *The reader revealed* (Washington, DC, 2001), pp. 19–30.

Barry, John and Hiram Morgan (eds.). *Great deeds in Ireland: Richard Stanihurst's De rebus in Hibernia gestis* (Cork, 2013).

Beem, Charles (ed.). *The foreign relations of Elizabeth I* (Basingstoke, 2011).

Beem, Charles and Dennis Moore (eds.). *The name of a queen: William Fleetwood's Itinerarium ad Windsor* (Basingstoke, 2013).

Beier, A. L. *Masterless men: the vagrancy problem in England, 1560–1640* (London, 1985).

Bell, Ilona. *Elizabeth I: the voice of a monarch* (Basingstoke, 2010).

Benedict, M. *A presence in the age of turmoil: English, Irish and Scottish Augustinians in the Reformation and Counter-Reformation* (Villanova, PA, 2002).

Bernard, G. W. *Power and politics in Tudor England* (Aldershot, 2000).

'The Tudor nobility in perspective', in G. W. Bernard (ed.), *The Tudor nobility* (New York, 1992), pp. 1–48.

Bland, Mark. *A guide to early printed books and manuscripts* (Oxford, 2010).

Bostock, D. 'Aristotle, Zeno, and the potential infinite', *Proceedings of the Aristotelian Society*, new series, 73 (1972–3), 37–51.

Bottigheimer, Karl. 'The failure of the Reformation in Ireland: *une question bien posée*', *Journal of Ecclesiastical History* 36 (1985), 196–207.

Bottigheimer, Karl and Ute Lotz-Heumann, 'The Irish Reformation in European perspective', *Archive for Reformation History* 89 (1998), 268–309.

Braddick, Michael and John Walter (eds.). *Negotiating power in early modern society: order, hierarchy and subordination in Britain and Ireland* (Cambridge, 2011).

Bradshaw, Brendan. *The dissolution of the religious orders in Ireland under Henry VIII* (Cambridge, 1974).

'The Edwardian reformation in Ireland, 1547–1553', *Archivium Hibernicum* 34 (1976–7), 83–99.

The Irish constitutional revolution of the sixteenth century (Cambridge, 1979).

'Nationalism and historical scholarship in modern Ireland', *Irish Historical Studies* 26 (1989), 329–51.

'Native reactions to the westward enterprise: a case-study in Gaelic ideology', in K. R. Andrews, N. P. Canny, and P. E. H. Hair (eds.), *The westward enterprise: English activities in Ireland, the Atlantic, and America 1480–1650* (Detroit, 1979), pp. 65–80.

'Sword, word and strategy in the Reformation in Ireland', *Historical Journal* 21 (1978), 475–502.

Bradshaw, Brendan, Andrew Hadfield, and Willy Maley (eds.). *Representing Ireland: literature and the origins of conflict, 1534–1660* (Cambridge, 1993).

Brady, Ciaran. 'The attainder of Shane O'Neill, Sir Henry Sidney and the problems of Tudor state-building in Ireland', in Brady and Ohlmeyer (eds.), *British interventions in early modern Ireland*, pp. 28–48.

'The captains' games: army and society in Elizabethan Ireland', in Thomas Bartlett and Keith Jeffrey (eds.), *A military history of Ireland* (Cambridge, 1996), pp. 136–59.

The chief governors: the rise and fall of reform government in Tudor Ireland, 1536–1588 (Cambridge, 1994).

'Conservative subversives: the community of the Pale and the Dublin administration, 1556–1586', in Patrick J. Corish (ed.), *Radicals, rebels and establishments* (Belfast, 1985), pp. 11–32.

'Court, castle and country: the framework of government in Tudor Ireland', in Ciaran Brady and Ray Gillespie (eds.), *Natives and newcomers: essays on the making of Irish colonial society, 1534–1641* (Dublin, 1986), pp. 22–49.

'The decline of the Irish kingdom', in Mark Greengrass (ed.), *Conquest and coalescence: the shaping of the state in early modern Europe* (London, 1991), pp. 94–115.

'England's defence and Ireland's reform: the dilemma of the Irish viceroys, 1541–1641', in Brendan Bradshaw and John Morrill (eds.), *The British problem*, c. *1534–1707: state formation in the Atlantic archipelago* (Cambridge, 1996), pp. 89–117.

'Faction and the origins of the Desmond Rebellion of 1579', *Irish Historical Studies* 22 (1981), 289–312.

Shane O'Neill (Dundalk, 1996).

'Shane O'Neill departs from the court of Elizabeth: Irish, English, Scottish perspectives and the paralysis of policy, July 1559 to April 1562', in S. J. Connolly (ed.), *Kingdoms united? Great Britain and Ireland since 1500: integration and diversity* (Dublin, 1999), pp. 13–28.

'Spenser, plantation and government policy', in Richard A. McCabe (ed.), *The Oxford handbook of Edmund Spenser* (Oxford, 2011), pp. 86–105.

(ed.). *Worsted in the game: losers in Irish history* (Dublin, 1989).

Brady, Ciaran and James Murray. 'Sir Henry Sidney and the Reformation in Ireland', in Elizabethanne Boran and Crawford Gribben (eds.), *Enforcing the Reformation in Ireland and Scotland, 1550–1700* (Aldershot, 2006), pp. 14–39.

Brady, Ciaran and Jane Ohlmeyer (eds.). *British interventions in early modern Ireland* (Cambridge, 2005).

Breatnach, Pádraig A. 'The chief's poet', *Proceedings of the Royal Irish Academy* 83 C (1983), 37–79.

'Moladh na féile; téama i bhfilíocht na scol', *Léachtaí Cholm Cille XXIV: an dán díreach* (Maigh Nuad, 1994), pp. 61–76.

Téamaí taighde Nua-Ghaeilge (Dublin, 1997).

Brennan, Gillian. 'Patriotism, language and power: English translations of the Bible, 1520–1580', *History Workshop* 27 (1989), 18–36.

Brennan, Michael G. 'William Ponsonby: Elizabethan stationer', *Analytical and Enumerative Bibliography* 7 (1984), 91–110.

Brigden, Susan. *New worlds, lost worlds: the rule of the Tudors, 1485–1603* (New York, 2000).

Brook, V. J. K. *A life of Archbishop Parker* (Oxford, 1962).

Brooke, Tucher. 'Queen Elizabeth's prayers', *Huntington Library Quarterly* 2 (1938), 69–77.

Bruford, Alan. *Gaelic folk-tales and mediaeval romances* (Dublin, 1969).

Bryson, Anna. *From courtesy to civility: changing codes of conduct in early modern England* (Oxford, 1998).

Bushnell, Rebecca. *Tragedies of tyrants: political thought and theater in the English Renaissance* (Ithaca, NY, 1990).

Burke, Peter. *Cultural hybridity* (Cambridge, 2009).

The fortunes of The Courtier: the European reception of Castiglione's Cortegiano (State College, PA, 1995).

Caball, Marc. *Poets and politics: reaction and continuity in Irish poetry, 1558–1625* (Notre Dame and Cork, 1998).

Canny, Nicholas. *The Elizabethan conquest of Ireland: a pattern established, 1565–1576* (Hassocks, 1976).

'The formation of the Irish mind: religion, politics and Gaelic Irish literature 1580–1750', *Past & Present* 95 (1982), 91–116.

The formation of the Old English elite in Ireland (Dublin, 1975).

Making Ireland British, 1580–1650 (Oxford, 2001).

'The *Treaty of Mellifont* and the re-organisation of Ulster, 1603', *Irish Sword* 9 (1969), 249–62.

'Why the Reformation failed in Ireland: *une question mal posée*', *Journal of Ecclesiastical History* 30 (1979), 423–50.

'Writing early modern history: Ireland, Britain and the wider world', *Historical Journal* 46 (3) (2003), 723–47.

Carey, Vincent. 'Atrocity and history: Grey, Spenser and the slaughter at Smerwick (1580)', in Edwards, Lenihan, and Tait (eds.), *Age of atrocity*, pp. 79–94.

'A "dubious loyalty": Richard Stanihurst, the "wizard" earl of Kildare, and English-Irish identity', in Carey and Lotz-Heumann (eds.), *Taking sides?*, pp. 61–77.

'Elizabeth I and state terror in sixteenth-century Ireland', in Donald Stump, Linda Shenk, and Carole Levin (eds.), *Elizabeth I and the 'sovereign arts': essays in literature, history, and culture* (Tempe, AZ, 2011), pp. 201–16.

'The Irish face of Machiavelli: Richard Beacon's *Solon his Follie* (1594) and republican ideology in the conquest of Ireland', in Morgan (ed.), *Political ideology in Ireland*, pp. 83–109.

'John Derricke's *Image of Irelande*, Sir Henry Sidney, and the massacre at Mullaghmast, 1578', *Irish Historical Studies* 31 (1999), 305–27.

'"Neither Good English nor Good Irish": bi-lingualism and identity formation in sixteenth-century Ireland', in Morgan (ed.), *Political ideology in Ireland*, pp. 45–61.

Surviving the Tudors: the 'wizard' earl of Kildare and English rule in Ireland, 1537–1586 (Dublin, 2002).

Carey, Vincent and Ute Lotz-Heumann (eds.), *Taking sides? Colonial and confessional mentalities in early modern Ireland* (Dublin, 2003).

Carroll, Clare. 'The Janus face of Machiavelli, adapting *The Prince* and the *Discourses* in early modern Ireland', in Clare Carroll, *Circe's cup* (Cork, 2001), pp. 91–103.

Cathcart, Alison. 'James V King of Scotland – and Ireland?', in Sean Duffy (ed.), *The world of the galloglass: kings, warlords and warriors in Ireland and Scotland* (Dublin, 2007), pp. 124–43.

Chambers, Anne. *Granuaile: the life and times of Grace O'Malley*, 2nd edn (Dublin, 1998).

Clark, Peter. *English provincial society from the Reformation to the Revolution* (Hassocks, 1977).

Clarke, Aidan. 'Varieties of uniformity: the first century of the Church of Ireland', in W. J. Sheils and Diana Wood (eds.), *The churches, Ireland and the Irish* (Oxford, 1989), pp. 105–22.

Coburn Walshe, Helen. 'Enforcing the Elizabethan settlement: the vicissitudes of Hugh Brady, Bishop of Meath, 1563–1584', *Irish Historical Studies* 26 (1989), 352–76.

'The rebellion of William Nugent, 1581', in R. V. Comerford, Mary Cullen, Jacqueline R. Hill, and Colm Lennon (eds.), *Religion, conflict and coexistence in Ireland: essays presented to Monsignor Patrick J. Corish* (Dublin, 1990), pp. 26–52.

Collinson, Patrick. *Archbishop Grindal, 1519–1583: the struggle for a reformed church* (London, 1979).
    Elizabethan essays (London, 1994).
    The Elizabethan Puritan movement (Oxford, 1967).
Connolly, S. J. *Contested island: Ireland 1460–1630* (Oxford, 2007).
Conrad, F. W. 'The problem of counsel reconsidered: the case of Sir Thomas Elyot', in Paul A. Fideler and T. F. Mayer (eds.), *Political thought and the Tudor commonwealth* (London, 1992), pp. 75–107.
Cooper, J. P. D. *Propaganda and the Tudor state: political culture in the Westcountry* (Oxford, 2003).
Coughlan, Patricia (ed.). *Spenser and Ireland: an interdisciplinary perspective* (Cork, 1989).
Crane, Mary. '"*Video et taceo*": Elizabeth I and the rhetoric of counsel', *Studies in English Literature* 28 (1988), 1–15.
Crawford, Jon. *Anglicizing the government of Ireland: the Irish privy council and the expansion of Tudor rule, 1556–1578* (Dublin, 1993).
Cross, Claire. *The royal supremacy and the Elizabethan church* (London, 1969).
Crowley, Tony. *War of words: the politics of language in Ireland 1537–2004* (London, 2005).
Cunningham, Bernadette. 'Illustrations of the Passion of Christ in the *Seanchas Búrcach* manuscript', in Rachel Moss, Colman O'Clabaigh, and Salvador Ryan (eds.), *Art and devotion in late medieval Dublin* (Dublin, 2006), pp. 16–32.
    'Native culture and political change in Ireland, 1580–1640', in Ciaran Brady and Raymond Gillespie (eds.), *Natives and newcomers: essays on the making of Irish colonial society, 1534–1641* (Dublin, 1986), pp. 148–70.
    'Politics and power in sixteenth-century Connaught', *Irish Arts Review* 21 (2004), 116–21.
Danner, Bruce. *Edmund Spenser's war on Lord Burghley* (Basingstoke, 2011).
Dawson, Jane E. A. 'John Knox, Goodman and the example of Geneva', in Polly Ha and Patrick Collinson (eds.), *The reception of the continental reformation in Britain* (Oxford, 2010), pp. 107–35.
Dean, David M. *Law-making and society in late Elizabethan England: the parliament of England, 1584–1601* (Cambridge, 1996).
Devereux, W. B. (ed.). *Lives and letters of the Devereux earls of Essex*, 2 vols. (London, 1853).
Dickens, Bruce. 'The Irish broadside of 1571 and Queen Elizabeth's types', *Transactions of the Cambridge Bibliographical Society* 1 (1949), 48–60.
Dickson, David. *Old world colony: Cork and South Munster, 1630–1830* (Cork, 2006).
Dix, E. R. McClintock. *The earliest Dublin printing* (Dublin, 1901).
    'William Kearney, the second earliest known printer in Dublin', *Proceedings of the Royal Irish Academy* 28 C 7 (1910), 157–61.
Dobson, Michael and Nicola J. Watson. *England's Elizabeth: an afterlife in fame and fantasy* (Oxford, 2002).
Doran, Susan. *Elizabeth I and foreign policy* (New York, 2000).

'Elizabeth I's religion: the evidence from Elizabeth's letters', *Journal of Ecclesiastical History* 51 (2000), 699–720.

Monarchy and matrimony: the courtships of Elizabeth I (London, 1996).

Queen Elizabeth I (New York, 2003).

Doran, Susan and Thomas S. Freeman (eds.). *The myth of Elizabeth* (Basingstoke, 2003).

Dudley Edwards, Robert. *Church and state in Tudor Ireland: a history of penal laws against Irish Catholics 1534–1603* (Dublin, 1934).

Duffy, Eamon. *The stripping of the altars: traditional religion in England 1400–1580*, 2nd edn (New Haven, 2005).

'William, Cardinal Allen, 1532–1594', *Recusant History* 22 (3) (1995), 265–90.

Dunne, T. J. 'The Gaelic response to conquest and colonisation: the evidence of the poetry', *Studia Hibernica* 20 (1980), 7–30.

Edwards, David. 'The Butler revolt of 1569', *Irish Historical Studies* 28 (1993), 228–55.

'The escalation of atrocity in sixteenth-century Ireland', in Edwards, Lenihan, and Tait (eds.), *Age of atrocity*, pp. 34–78.

'Ideology and experience: Spenser's *View* and martial law in Ireland', in Morgan (ed.), *Political ideology in Ireland*, pp. 127–57.

The Ormond lordship in County Kilkenny, 1515–1642: the rise and fall of Butler feudal power (Dublin, 2003).

(ed.). *Regions and rulers in Ireland, 1100–1650* (Dublin, 2004).

Edwards, David, Pádraig Lenihan, and Clodagh Tait (eds.), *Age of atrocity: violence and political conflict in early modern Ireland* (Dublin, 2007).

Edwards, David and Keith Sidwell (eds.). *The Tipperary hero: Dermot O'Meara's Ormonius* (Turnhout, Belgium, 2012).

Ellis, Steven G. 'Economic problems of the church: why the Reformation failed in Ireland', *Journal of Ecclesiastical History* 41 (1990), 239–65.

'Henry VIII, rebellion, and the rule of law', *Historical Journal* 24 (1981), 513–31.

'More Irish than the Irish themselves? The "Anglo-Irish" in Tudor Ireland', *History Ireland* 7 (1) (1999), 22–6.

Tudor Ireland: crown, community and the conflict of cultures, 1470–1603 (London, 1985).

Tudor frontiers and noble power: the making of the British state (Oxford, 1995).

Ephraim, Michelle. 'Jewish matriarchs and the staging of Elizabeth I in *The History of Jacob and Esau*', *Studies in English Literature 1500–1900* 43 (2003), 301–21.

Elton, G. R. *The parliament of England: 1559–1581* (Cambridge, 1989).

'Tudor government: the points of contact, III: the court', *Transactions of the Royal Historical Society*, 5th series, 26 (1976), 211–28.

Falls, Cyril. *Elizabeth's Irish wars* (London, 1950; 1970, reprint).

Felch, Susan and Donald Stump (eds.). *Elizabeth I and her age* (New York, 2009).

Fenlon, Jane. *Caisleán Urmhumhan* (Dublin, 1996).

'The decorative plasterwork at Ormond Castle – a unique survival', *Architectural History* 41 (1998), 67–81.

Fissell, M. C. *English warfare, 1511–1642* (London and New York, 2001).

Fitzsimons, Fiona. 'Fosterage and gossiprid in late medieval Ireland: some new evidence', in Patrick J. Duffy, David Edwards, and Elizabeth FitzPatrick (eds.), *Gaelic Ireland c. 1250–c. 1650: land, lordship and settlement* (Dublin, 2001), pp. 138–49.

Fletcher, Anthony and Diarmaid MacCulloch. *Tudor rebellions* (New York, 1997).

Ford, Alan. 'The Church of Ireland, 1558–1634: a Puritan church?', in Alan Ford, James McGuire, and Kenneth Milne (eds.), *As by law established: the Church of Ireland since the Reformation* (Dublin, 1995), pp. 52–68.

'Dependent or independent? The Church of Ireland and its colonial context, 1536–1649', *Seventeenth Century* 10 (1995), 163–87.

Gajda, Alexandra. 'Debating war and peace in late Elizabethan England', *Historical Journal* 52 (2009), 851–78.

The earl of Essex and late Elizabethan political culture (Oxford, 2012).

Galloway, Daniel. 'Brian of the Ramparts O'Rourke', *Breifne* 2 (1962), 50–79.

Galwey, Hubert. *The Wall family in Ireland, 1170–1970* (Cork, 1970).

Gillespie, Raymond. 'Print culture, 1550–1700', in Raymond Gillespie and Andrew Hadfield (eds.), *The Irish book in English 1550–1800* (Oxford, 2006), pp. 17–33.

'Reform and decay, 1500–1598', in John Crawford and Raymond Gillespie (eds.), *St Patrick's Cathedral, Dublin: a history* (Dublin, 2009), pp. 151–73.

Gilman, Ernest B. *Iconoclasm and poetry in the English Reformation: down went Dagon* (Chicago, 1986).

Grafton, Anthony and Lisa Jardine, '"Studied for action": how Gabriel Harvey read his Livy', *Past & Present* 129 (1990), 30–78.

Graham, Andrew. 'The Picardy companies, 1598–1599: an Elizabethan regiment in Ireland', *Irish Sword* 21 (1998), 43–50.

Graves, Michael A. R. *Elizabethan parliaments 1559–1601* (London, 1996).

Graziani, René. 'Phillip II's Impressa and Spenser's Souldan', *Journal of the Warburg and Courtauld Institutes* 27 (1964), 322–4.

Green, Ian. *The Christian's ABC: catechisms and catechizing in England c. 1530–1740* (Oxford, 1996).

'"The necessary knowledge of the principles of religion": catechisms and catechizing in Ireland, *c.* 1560–1800', in Alan Ford, James McGuire, and Kenneth Milne (eds.), *As by law established: the Church of Ireland since the Reformation* (Dublin, 1995), pp. 69–88.

Grennan, Eamon. 'Language and politics: a note on some metaphors in Spenser's *A view of the present state of Ireland*', *Spenser Studies* 3 (1982), 99–110.

Gunn, Steven. 'The structures of politics in early Tudor England', *Transactions of the Royal Historical Society*, 6th series, 5 (1995), 59–90.

Guy, John. 'The 1590s: the second reign of Elizabeth I?', in Guy (ed.), *The reign of Elizabeth I*, pp. 1–19.

(ed.). *The reign of Elizabeth I: court and culture in the last decade* (Cambridge, 1995).

'The rhetoric of counsel in early modern England', in Hoak (ed.), *Tudor political culture*, pp. 292–310.

Tudor England (Oxford, 1988).

The Tudor monarchy (London, 1997).

Gwynn, Aubrey and R. Neville Hadcock. *Medieval religious houses: Ireland* (Dublin, 1988).

Hackett, Helen. *Virgin mother, maiden queen: Elizabeth I and the cult of the Virgin Mary* (Basingtoke, 1995).

Hadfield, Andrew. 'An allusion to Spenser's Irish writings: Matthew Lownes and Ralph Byrchensa's *A Discourse occasioned on the late defeat, given to the arch-rebels, Tyrone and O'Donnell* (1602)', *Notes & Queries* 242 (1997), 478–80.

Edmund Spenser: a life (Oxford, 2012).

Shakespeare, Spenser and the matter of Britain (New York, 2004).

'Spenser and religion – yet again', *Studies in English Literature, 1500–1900* 51 (2011), 21–46.

'Spenser and the Stuart succession', *Literature and History* 13 (2004), 9–24.

Spenser's Irish experience: wilde fruit and salvage soyl (Oxford, 1997).

Haigh, Christopher. *Elizabeth I* (London, 1988; 2nd edn, 1998).

English reformations: religion, politics and society under the Tudors (Oxford, 1993).

Hammer, P. E. J. *Elizabeth's wars: war, government and society in Tudor England, 1544–1604* (Basingstoke, 2003).

'Letters from Sir Robert Cecil to Sir Christopher Hatton, 1590–1591', in Ian Archer (ed.), *Religion, politics and society in sixteenth-century England* (Cambridge, 2003), pp. 197–267.

'Myth-making: politics, propaganda and the capture of Cadiz in 1596', *Historical Journal* 40 (1997), 621–42.

The polarisation of Elizabethan politics: the political career of Robert Devereux, 2nd earl of Essex, 1585–1597 (Cambridge, 1999).

Hanning, Robert W. and David Rosand (eds.). *Castiglione: the ideal and the real in Renaissance culture* (New Haven, 1983).

Hardwick, Charles. *A history of the Articles of Religion* (Cambridge, 1859).

Harris, Jason and Keith Sidwell (eds.). *Making Ireland Roman: Irish neo-Latin writers and the republic of letters* (Cork, 2009).

Harris Sacks, David. 'The countervailing of benefits: monopoly, liberty and benevolence in Elizabethan England', in Hoak (ed.), *Tudor political culture*, pp. 272–91.

Harrison, G. B. *The life and death of Robert Devereux earl of Essex* (London, 1937; Bath, 1970, reprint).

Hasler, P. W. (ed.). *The history of Parliament: the House of Commons, 1558–1603*, 3 vols. (London, 1981).

Haugaard, William P. 'Elizabeth Tudor's book of devotions: a neglected clue to the queen's life and character', *Sixteenth Century Journal* 12 (1981), 79–106.

Heal, Felicity. 'Appropriating history: Catholic and Protestant polemics and the national past', *Huntington Library Quarterly* 68 (2005), 109–32.

'Mediating the word: language and dialects in the British and Irish Reformations', *Journal of Ecclesiastical History* 56 (2005), 261–86.

Healy, Margaret. *Fictions of disease in early modern England: bodies, plagues and politics* (Basingstoke, 2001).

Helgerson, Richard. *Forms of nationhood: the Elizabethan writing of England* (Chicago, 1992).

Herron, Thomas. *Spenser's Irish work: poetry, plantation and colonial Reformation* (Aldershot, 2007).

Highley, Christopher. 'The royal image in Elizabethan Ireland', in Walker (ed.), *Dissing Elizabeth*, pp. 60–76.

Shakespeare, Spenser, and the crisis in Ireland (Cambridge, 1997).

Hill, J. E. C. 'Puritans and "the dark corners of the land"', *Transactions of the Royal Historical Society*, 5th series, 13 (1962), 77–102.

Hindle, Steve. 'Dearth, fasting and alms: the campaign for general hospitality in late Elizabethan England', *Past & Present* 172 (2001), 44–86.

'Imagining insurrection in seventeenth-century England: representations of the Midland Rising of 1607', *History Workshop Journal* 66 (2008), 22–61.

Hoak, Dale (ed.). *Tudor political culture* (Cambridge, 1995).

Hogan, James. 'Shane O'Neill comes to the court of Elizabeth', in Séamus Pender (ed.), *Féilscríbhinn Torna: essays and studies presented to Professor Tadhg Ua Donnchadha* (Cork, 1947), pp. 154–70.

Houlbrooke, Ralph. *Death, religion and the family in England, 1480–1750* (Oxford, 1998).

H.S.G. 'Knight of the Carpet', *Notes and Queries*, 3rd series, 2 (15 Nov. 1862), 388–9.

Hulbert, V. P. 'Spenser's relation to certain documents in Ireland', *Modern Philology* 34 (1937), 345–53.

Hunt, Arnold. 'Tuning the pulpits: the religious context of the Essex revolt', in Lori Ann Ferrell and Peter McCullough (eds.), *The English sermon revisited: religion, literature and history 1600–1750* (Manchester, 2000), pp. 86–114.

Hutchinson, Mark A. 'Reformed Protestantism and the government of Ireland, *c.* 1565 to 1580: the lord deputyships of Henry Sidney and Arthur Grey', *Sidney Journal* 29 (2011), 71–104.

Jackson, Donald. *Intermarriage in Ireland, 1550–1650* (Montreal, 1970).

James, Mervyn. 'The concept of order and the Northern Rising, 1569', *Past & Present* 60 (1973), 49–83; also published in James, *Society, politics and culture*, pp. 308–415.

Family, lineage and civil society: a study of society, politics and mentality in the Durham region, 1500–1640 (Oxford, 1974).

Society, politics and culture: studies in early modern England (Cambridge, 1986).

Jansen, Sharon L. *The monstrous regiment of women: female rulers in early modern Europe* (London, 2002).

Jaski, Bart. *Early Irish kingship and succession* (Dublin, 2000).

Javitch, Daniel. '*Il Cortegiano* and the constraints of despotism', in Hanning and Rosand (eds.), *Castiglione: the ideal*, pp. 17–28.

Poetry and courtliness in Renaissance England (Princeton, 1978).

Jefferies, Henry. 'The early Tudor reformations in the Irish Pale', *Journal of Ecclesiastical History* 52 (2001), 34–62.

The Irish church and the Tudor Reformations (Dublin, 2010).

'The Irish parliament of 1560: the Anglican reforms authorised', *Irish Historical Studies* 26 (1988), 128–41.

Priests and prelates of Armagh in the age of reformations, 1518–1558 (Dublin, 1997).

Johnson, Paul. *Elizabeth I: a biography* (New York, 1974).

Jones, H. S. V. *Spenser's defense of Lord Grey* (Urbana, IL, 1919).

Jones, Norman. *The birth of the Elizabethan age: England in the 1560s* (London, 1995).

Jordan, Constance. 'Women's rule in sixteenth-century British political thought', *Renaissance Quarterly* 40 (1987), 421–51.

Jowitt, C. 'Political allegory in late Elizabethan and early Jacobean "Turk" plays: *Lust's dominion* and *The Turke'*, *Comparative Drama* 36 (2003), 411–33.

Kane, Brendan. 'A dynastic nation? Rethinking national consciousness in early seventeenth-century Ireland', in David Finnegan, Marie-Claire Harrigan, and Eamonn Ó Ciardha (eds.), *Imeacht na n-Iarlaí: the flight of the earls* (Derry, 2010), pp. 124–31.

'Languages of legitimacy? *An Ghaeilge*, the earl of Thomond and British politics in the Renaissance Pale, 1600–1624', in Michael Potterton and Thomas Herron (eds.), *Dublin and the Pale in the Renaissance, c. 1540–1660* (Dublin, 2011), pp. 267–79.

The politics and culture of honour in Britain and Ireland, 1541–1641 (Cambridge, 2010).

Kaplan, Benjamin J. *Divided by faith: religious conflict and the practice of toleration in early modern Europe* (Cambridge, MA, 2007).

Kaplan, M. Lindsay. *The culture of slander in early modern England* (Cambridge, 1997).

Kelly, David. 'Medieval Augustinian foundations in Britain and Ireland', *Institutum Historicum* 70 (2007), 187–204.

Kelly, Fergus. *A guide to early Irish law* (Dublin, 1988; 1995, reprint).

Kelly, James and Ciarán Mac Murchaidh (eds.). *Irish and English: essays on the Irish linguistic and cultural frontier, 1600–1900* (Dublin, 2012).

Kesselring, Krista. *Mercy and authority in the Tudor state* (Cambridge, 2007).

The Northern Rebellion of 1569: faith, politics, and protest in Elizabethan England (Basingstoke, 2007).

Kiberd, Declan. 'Bardic poetry: the loss of aura', in Declan Kiberd, *Irish classics* (Cambridge, MA, 2001), pp. 13–24.

Kinealy, Christine. *A new history of Ireland* (Stroud, UK, 2004).

King, John N. 'John Day: master printer of the English Reformation', in Peter Marshall and Alec Ryrie (eds.), *The beginnings of English Protestantism* (Cambridge, 2002), pp. 180–208.

Knox, Hubert Thomas. *Notes on the early history of the dioceses of Tuam Killala and Achonry* (Dublin, 1904).

König, Ekkehard. 'Conditionals, concessive conditionals and concessives: areas of contrast, overlap and neutralization', in Elizabeth Traugott, Alice Ter Meulen, Judy Snitzer Reilly, and Charles A. Ferguson (eds.), *On conditionals* (Cambridge, 1986), pp. 229–46.

Lake, Peter. *Anglicans and Puritans? Presbyterianism and English conformist thought from Whitgift to Hooker* (London, 1988).

Langbein, John. *Torture and the law of proof* (Chicago, 1977).

Lawlor, Hugh Jackson. *The fasti of St Patrick's, Dublin* (Dublin, 1930).

Leerssen, J. 'For a post-Foucaldian literary history: a test case from the Gaelic tradition', *Configurations* 7 (1999), 227–45.

Mere Irish and fíor-Ghael: studies in the idea of Irish nationality, its development and literary expression prior to the nineteenth century (Notre Dame, 1997).

Lennon, Colm. 'Edmund Campion's *Histories of Ireland* and reform in Tudor Ireland', in Thomas M. McCoog, SJ (ed.), *The reckoned expense: Edmund Campion and the early English Jesuits* (Woodbridge, 1996), pp. 67–83.

The lords of Dublin in the age of Reformation (Dublin, 1989).

'Mass in the manor house: the Counter-Reformation in Dublin, 1560–1630', in James Kelly and Daire Keogh (eds.), *History of the Catholic diocese of Dublin* (Dublin, 2000), pp. 112–26.

'Richard Stanihurst (1547–1618) and Old English identity', *Irish Historical Studies* 21 (1978), 121–43.

Richard Stanihurst, the Dubliner, 1547–1618 (Dublin, 1981).

'Taking sides: the emergence of Irish Catholic ideology', in Carey and Lotz-Heumann (eds.), *Taking sides?*, pp. 78–93.

Lennon, Colm and Ciaran Diamond, 'The ministry of the church of Ireland, 1536–1636', in T. C. Barnard and W. G. Neely (eds.), *The clergy of the church of Ireland 1000–2000: messengers, watchmen and stewards* (Dublin, 2006), pp. 44–58.

Levin, Carole. *The heart and stomach of a king: Elizabeth I and the politics of sex and power* (Philadephia, 1994).

'Queens and claimants: political insecurity in sixteenth-century England', in Janet Sharistanian (ed.), *Gender, ideology, and action: historical perspectives on women's public lives* (New York, 1986), pp. 41–66.

Levin, Carole, Jo Eldridge Carney, and Debra Barrett-Graves (eds.), *Elizabeth I: always her own free woman* (Aldershot, 2003).

Levy Peck, Linda. 'Peers, patronage and the politics of history', in John Guy (ed.), *The reign of Elizabeth I: court and culture in the last decade* (Cambridge, 1995), pp. 87–108.

Loades, David. *Elizabeth I* (London, 2003).

Lyall, Andrew. *Land law in Ireland* (Dublin, 1994).

Lyons, Mary Ann. *Franco-Irish relations, 1500–1610: politics, migration and trade* (Woodbridge, 2003).

MacCaffrey, Wallace. *Elizabeth I* (London, 1993).

Elizabeth I: war and politics, 1588–1603 (Princeton, 1992).

'Place and patronage in Elizabethan politics', in S. T. Bindoff *et al.* (eds.), *Elizabethan government and society: essays presented to Sir John Neale* (London, 1961), pp. 95–126.

The shaping of the Elizabethan regime (London, 1969).

MacCarthy, D. F. *The book of Irish ballads* (Dublin, 1846).

MacCarthy-Morrogh, Michael. *The Munster plantation: English migration to southern Ireland 1583–1641* (Oxford, 1986).

Mac Craith, Mícheál, 'Eochaidh Ó hEoghasa agus an freagra fileata', in Pádraigín Riggs, Breandán Conchúir, and Seán Ó Coileáin (eds.), *Saoi na hÉigse: aistí in ómós do Sheán Ó Tuama* (Baile Átha Cliath, 2000), pp. 23–33.

'From the Elizabethan settlement to the Battle of the Boyne: literature in Irish 1560–1690', in Margaret Kelleher and Philip O'Leary (eds.), *The Cambridge history of Irish literature*, 2 vols. (Cambridge, 2006), vol. I, pp. 191–231.

Lorg na hIasachta ar na dánta grá (Baile Átha Cliath, 1989).

MacCulloch, Diarmaid. *Thomas Cranmer: a life* (New Haven, 1996).

Tudor church militant: Edward VI and the Protestant Reformation (London, 1999).

Maginn, Christopher. 'The Baltinglass Rebellion, 1580: English dissent or Gaelic uprising?', *Historical Journal* 47 (2004), 205–32.

'The Gaelic peers, the Tudor sovereigns, and English multiple monarchy', *Journal of British Studies* 50 (2011), 566–86.

Maley, Willy. *Salvaging Spenser: colonialism, culture and identity* (Basingstoke, 1997).

Mannaerts, P. 'Creations: medieval rituals, the arts, and the concept of creation', *Music and Letters* 90 (2009), 480–3.

Marcus, Leah S. *Childhood and cultural despair: a theme and variations in seventeenth-century literature* (Pittsburgh, 1978).

'Elizabeth on Elizabeth: underexamined episodes in an overexamined life', in Kevin Sharpe and Steven N. Zwicker (eds.), *Writing lives: biography and textuality, identity and representation in early modern England* (Oxford, 2008), pp. 209–32.

'Erasing the stigma of daughterhood: Mary I, Elizabeth I, and Henry VIII', in Lynda Boose and Betty S. Flowers (eds.), *Daughters and fathers* (Baltimore, 1989), pp. 400–17.

'Shakespeare's comic heroines, Queen Elizabeth I, and the political uses of androgyny', in Mary Beth Rose (ed.), *Women in the Middle Ages and the Renaissance: literary and historical perspectives* (Syracuse, NY, 1985), pp. 135–53.

Martin, F. X. 'The Irish Augustinian friaries in pre-Reformation Ireland', *Augustiniana* 6 (1956), 346–84.

Mattimoe, Cyril M. 'The Battle of the Curlieus, 15th August, 1599', *Journal of the Roscommon Historical and Archaeological Society* 1 (1986), 47–51.

Mattingly, Garret. 'William Allen and Catholic propaganda in England', *Travaux d'Humanisme et Renaissance* 28 (1957), 325–39.

McCabe, Richard. 'Edmund Spenser: poet of exile', British Academy Chatterton Lecture on Poetry, in '1991 Lectures and Memoirs', *Proceedings of the British Academy* 80 (1993), 73–103.

'The fate of Irena: Spenser and political violence', in Patricia Coughlan (ed.), *Spenser and Ireland: an interdisciplinary perspective* (Cork, 1989), pp. 109–25.

'Fighting words: writing the "Nine Years' War"', in Thomas Herron and Michael Potterton (eds.), *Ireland in the Renaissance, c. 1540–1660* (Dublin, 2007), pp. 105–21.

'Making history: Holinshed's Irish *Chronicles*, 1577 and 1587', in David J. Baker and Willy Maley (eds.), *British identities and English Renaissance literature* (Cambridge, 2002), pp. 51–67.

'The masks of Duessa: Spenser, Mary Queen of Scots, and James VI', *English Literary Renaissance* 17 (1987), 224–42.

The pillars of eternity: time and providence in The Faerie Queene (Dublin, 1989).

Spenser's monstrous regiment: Elizabethan Ireland and the poetics of difference (Oxford, 2002).

McCavitt, John. *The flight of the earls* (Dublin, 2002).

McCormack, Anthony. *The earldom of Desmond 1463–1583: the decline and crisis of a feudal lordship* (Dublin, 2005).

McDiarmid, John F. (ed.). *The monarchical republic of early modern England: essays in response to Patrick Collinson* (Aldershot, 2007).

McGettigan, Darren. 'The political community of the lordship of Tír Chonaill', in Robert Armstrong and Tadhg Ó hAnnracháin (eds.), *Community in early modern Ireland* (Dublin, 2006), pp. 91–102.

McGlynn, Margaret. *The royal prerogative and the learning of the Inns of Court* (Cambridge, 2003).

McGowan-Doyle, Valerie. *The Book of Howth: Elizabethan conquest and the Old English* (Cork, 2011).

'"Spent blood": Christopher St Lawrence and Pale loyalism', in Morgan (ed.), *The Battle of Kinsale*, pp. 179–91.

McGuinne, Dermot. *Irish type design: a history of printing types in the Irish character* (Dublin, 1992).

McGurk, John. *Sir Henry Docwra, 1541–1631: Derry's second founder* (Dublin, 2006).

McKenzie, D. F. *Bibliography and the sociology of texts* (London, 1986).

McKerrow, R. B. *A dictionary of printers and booksellers in England, Scotland and Ireland, and of foreign printers of English books 1557–1640* (London, 1910).

McKibben, Sarah. *Endangered masculinities in Irish poetry: 1540–1780* (Dublin, 2011).

McLaren, A. N. 'Delineating the Elizabethan body politic: Knox, Aylmer and the definition of counsel 1558–1588', *History of Political Thought* 17 (1996), 224–52.

Political culture in the reign of Elizabeth I: queen and commonwealth, 1558–1585 (Cambridge, 1999).

Mears, Natalie. 'Counsel, public debate, and queenship: John Stubbs's "The Discoverie of a Gaping Gulf", 1579', *Historical Journal* 44 (2001), 629–50.

'Courts, courtiers, and culture in Tudor England', *Historical Journal* 46 (2003), 703–22.

Queenship and political discourse in the Elizabethan realms (Cambridge, 2005).

Mendelson, Sara and Patricia Crawford. *Women in early modern England* (Oxford, 1998).

Meyer, Kuno. 'The expulsion of the Déssi', *Y Cymmrodor* 14 (1902), 101–35.

Montano, John. *The roots of English colonialism* (Cambridge, 2011).

Morgan, Hiram (ed.). *The Battle of Kinsale* (Bray, 2004).

'The colonial venture of Sir Thomas Smith', *Historical Journal* 28 (1985), 261–78.

'Faith and fatherland in sixteenth-century Ireland', *History Ireland* 3 (1995), 13–20

'Faith and fatherland or queen and country? An unpublished exchange between O'Neill and the state at the height of the Nine Years' War', *Duiche Neill: Journal of the O'Neill Country Historical Society* 9 (1994), 9–65.

'The fall of Sir John Perrot', in Guy (ed.), *The reign of Elizabeth I*, pp. 109–25.

'Hugh O'Neill and the Nine Years War in Tudor Ireland', *Historical Journal* 36 (1993), 21–37.

'Hugh O'Neill – not guilty', *Dúiche Néill: Journal of the O'Neill Country Historical Society* 18 (2010), 29–34.

'"Never any realm worse governed": Queen Elizabeth and Ireland', *Transactions of the Royal Historical Society*, 6th series, 14 (2004), 295–308.

'Overmighty officers: the Irish lord deputyship in the early modern British state', *History Ireland* 7 (1999), 17–21.

(ed.). *Political ideology in Ireland, 1541–1641* (Dublin, 1999).

Tyrone's rebellion: the outbreak of the Nine Years War in Tudor Ireland (Woodbridge, 1993).

Morrissey, Thomas J. *James Archer of Kilkenny, an Elizabethan Jesuit* (Kilkenny, 1979).

Murphy, James J. *Rhetoric in the Middle Ages: a history of rhetorical theory from Saint Augustine to the Renaissance* (Berkeley, CA, 1974).

Murphy, Virginia. 'The literature and propaganda of Henry's divorce', in Diarmaid MacCulloch (ed.), *The reign of Henry VIII: politics, policy and piety* (Basingstoke, 1995), pp. 135–58.

Murray, James. *Enforcing the English Reformation in Ireland: clerical resistance and political conflict in the diocese of Dublin, 1534–1590* (Cambridge, 2009).

'St Patrick's Cathedral and the university question in Ireland *c.* 1547–1585', in Helga Robinson-Hammerstein (ed.), *European universities in the age of Reformation and Counter-Reformation* (Dublin, 1998), pp. 1–21.

Neale, J. E. *Elizabeth I and her parliaments, 1559–1581*, 2 vols. (London, 1953–7).

Nicholls, K. W. *Gaelic and Gaelicized Ireland in the Middle Ages* (Dublin, 2003).

'Irishwomen and property in the sixteenth century', in Margaret MacCurtain and Mary O'Dowd (eds.), *Women in early modern Ireland* (Edinburgh, 1991), pp. 17–31.

'Worlds apart? The Ellis two-nation theory on late medieval Ireland', *History Ireland* 7 (2) (1999), 22–6.

Nicholls, Mark. 'Sir Charles Percy', *Recusant History* 18 (1986–7), 237–50.

Nichols, John (ed.). *The progresses and public procession of Queen Elizabeth*, 3 vols. (London, 1823).

Ní Chuilleanáin, Eiléan. 'Forged and fabulous chronicles: reading Spenser as an Irish writer', *Irish University Review* 26 (1996), 237–51.

Norbrook, David. *Poetry and politics in the English Renaissance* (London, 1984).

Ó Buachalla, Breandán. 'James our true king: the ideology of Irish royalism in the seventeenth century', in D. G. Boyce, Robert Eccleshall, and Vincent Geoghegan (eds.), *Political thought in Ireland since the seventeenth century* (London, 1993), pp. 7–35.

'The making of a Cork Jacobite', in Patrick O'Flanagan and Cornelius G. Buttimer (eds.), *Cork history and society* (Dublin, 1993), pp. 469–98.

'Na Stíobhartaigh agus an t-aos léinn: king Séamus', *Proceedings of the Royal Irish Academy* 93 C 4 (1983), 81–134.

'Poetry and politics in early modern Ireland', *Eighteenth-Century Ireland* 7 (1992), 149–75.

O'Byrne, Emmet. *War, politics, and the Irish of Leinster, 1156–1606* (Dublin, 2003).

Ó Ciosáin, Niall, 'Print and Irish, 1570–1900: an exception among Celtic languages?', *Radharc: A Journal of Irish and Irish-American Studies* 5–7 (2004–6), 73–106.

Ó Clabaigh, Colmán N. *The Franciscans in Ireland, 1400–1534: from reform to Reformation* (Dublin, 2002).

Ó Cuív, B. *The Irish bardic duanaire or 'poem book'* (Dublin, 1973).

O'Day, Rosemary. *The English clergy: the emergence and consolidation of a profession 1558–1642* (Leicester, 1979).

Ó Fearghail, Fearghus. *The Irish testament of 1602* (Dublin, 2004).

Ó Grady, Standish. *Early bardic literature* (New York, 1970, reprint).

Ó Háinle, Cathal G. 'Flattery rejected: two seventeenth-century Irish poems', *Hermathena* 138 (1985), 5–27.

Ohlmeyer, Jane. 'Making Ireland English: the early seventeenth-century Irish peerage', in Brian Mac Cuarta (ed.), *Reshaping Ireland 1550–1700. Colonization and its consequences: essays presented to Nicholas Canny* (Dublin, 2011), pp. 131–47.

Making Ireland English: the Irish aristocracy in the seventeenth century (New Haven, 2012).

Ó Muraíle, Nollaig. 'The Carneys of Connacht', in Donnchadh Ó Corráin, Liam Breatnach, and Kim McCone (eds.), *Sages, saints and storytellers: Celtic studies in honour of Professor James Carney* (Maynooth, 1989), pp. 342–57.

O'Rahilly, R. F. 'Irish poets, historians, and judges in English documents, 1538–1615', *Proceedings of the Royal Irish Academy* 36 C 6 (1922), 86–120.

O Riordan, Michelle. *The Gaelic mind and the collapse of the Gaelic world* (Cork, 1987).

Irish bardic poetry and rhetorical reality (Cork, 2007).

O Siochru, Micheal and Eamonn O Ciardha (eds.). *The plantation of Ulster: ideology and practice* (Manchester, 2012).

Pagden, Anthony. *Lords of all the world: ideologies of empire in Spain, Britain and France c. 1500–c. 1800* (New Haven, 1995).

Palmer, Patricia. *Language and conquest in early modern Ireland: English Renaissance literature and Elizabethan imperial expansion* (Cambridge, 2001).

Palmer, William. *The problem of Ireland in Tudor foreign policy, 1485–1603* (Woodbridge, 1994).

'That insolent liberty: honor, rites of power, and persuasion in sixteenth-century Ireland', *Renaissance Quarterly* 46 (1993), 308–27.

Peden, Joseph R. 'Property rights in Celtic Irish law', *Journal of Libertarian Studies* 1 (1977), 81–95.

Peltonen, Markku. 'Rhetoric and citizenship in the monarchical republic of Queen Elizabeth I', in McDiarmid (ed.), *The monarchical republic of early modern England*, pp. 109–28.

Pettegree, Andrew. *The book in the Renaissance* (New Haven, 2010).

Phillips, James E. *Images of a queen: Mary Stuart in sixteenth-century literature* (Berkeley, CA, 1964).

Pincus, Steve. *1688: the first modern revolution* (New Haven, 2009).

Plomer, Henry R. and T. P. Cross. *The life and correspondence of Lodowick Bryskett* (Chicago, 1972).

Pollard, M. *A dictionary of members of the Dublin book trade 1550–1800* (London, 2000).

Poppe, Erich. 'The pragmatics of complex sentences', *Journal of Celtic Linguistics* 3 (1994), 1–34.

Power, Gerald. *A European elite: the nobility of the English Pale in Ireland, 1450–1566* (Hanover, 2011).

Pritchard, Arnold. *Catholic loyalism in Elizabethan England* (London, 1979).

Questier, Michael. *Catholicism and community in early modern England: politics, aristocratic patronage and religion*, c. *1550–1640* (Cambridge, 2006).

Quiggin, E. C. *Prologomena to the study of the later Irish bards, 1200–1500* (Oxford, 1911).

Quin, Cosslett. 'Nicholas Walsh and his friends: a forgotten chapter in the Irish Reformation', *Journal of the Butler Society* 2 (1984), 294–8.

Quinn, D. B. *The Elizabethans and the Irish* (New York, 1966).

'Parliaments and great councils in Ireland, 1461–1586', *Irish Historical Studies* 3 (1943), 60–77.

Rabb, Theodore K. *The last days of the Renaissance: the march to modernity* (New York, 2006).

Rankin, Deanna. *Between Spenser and Swift: English writing in seventeenth-century Ireland* (Cambridge, 2005).

Rapple, Rory. *Martial power and Elizabethan political culture: military men in England and Ireland, 1558–1594* (Cambridge, 2009).

Rebhorn, Wayne A. *The emperor of men's minds: literature and the Renaissance discourse of rhetoric* (Ithaca, NY, 1995).

Richards, Judith M. '"To promote a woman to beare Rule": talking of queens in mid-Tudor England', *Sixteenth Century Journal* 28 (1997), 101–21.

Ridley, Jasper. *Elizabeth I* (London, 1981).

Robinson, Benedict Scott. '"Darke speech": Matthew Parker and the reforming of history', *Sixteenth Century Journal* 29 (1998), 1061–83.

Ronan, Myles V. *The Reformation in Ireland under Elizabeth 1558–1580* (London, 1930).

Rose, Jacqueline. 'Kingship and counsel in early modern England', *Historical Journal* 54 (2011), 47–71.

Ryan, Salvador. 'Creation and recreation in Irish bardic poetry', in Sven R. Havsteen, Nils H. Petersen, Heinrich W. Schwab, and Eyolf Østrem (eds.), *Creations, medieval rituals, the arts, and the concept of creation* (Brepols, 2001), pp. 65–85.

'"The most contentious of terms": towards a new understanding of late medieval "popular religion"', *Irish Theological Quarterly* 68 (2003), 281–90.

'"New wine in old bottles": implementing Trent in early modern Ireland', in Thomas Herron and Michael Potterton (eds.), *Ireland in the Renaissance, c. 1540–1660* (Dublin, 2007), pp. 122–37.

Saccone, Eduardo. '*Grazia, sprezzatura, affettazione* in *The Courtier*', in Hanning and Rosand (eds.), *Castiglione: the ideal*, pp. 45–68.

Sharp, Cuthbert. *Memorials of the rebellion of 1569* (Durham, 2009, reprint).

Sharpe, J. A. *Crime in early modern England* (New York, 1984).

Sharpe, Kevin. *Selling the Tudor monarchy: authority and image in sixteenth-century England* (New Haven, 2009).

Shaw, K. *The knights of England*, 2 vols. (London, 1906).

Sheehan, Anthony J. 'The killing of the earl of Desmond', *Journal of the Cork Archaeological and Historical Society* 88 (1983), 106–10.

'Official reaction to native land claims in the plantation of Munster', *Irish Historical Studies* 23 (1983), 297–318.

'The overthrow of the Plantation of Munster in October 1598', *Irish Sword* 15 (1982), 11–22.

Shepherd, Simon. *Spenser* (Hemel Hempstead, 1989).

Shirley, E. P. *The history of the County of Monaghan* (London, 1879).

Shrank, Cathy. *Writing the nation in Reformation England 1530–1580* (Oxford, 2004).

Sidwell, Keith and David Edwards, 'The Tipperary hero: Dermot O'Meara's *Ormonius* (1615)', in Harris and Sidwell (eds.), *Making Ireland Roman*, pp. 59–85.

Siegfried, B. R. 'Wrestling with the angel: the typology of Israel in John Derricke's *The image of Ireland*', in Thomas Herron and Michael Potterton (eds.), *Dublin and the Pale in the Renaissance, c. 1540–1660* (Dublin, 2011), pp. 319–51.

Silke, John J. 'The Irish appeal of 1593 to Spain: some light on the genesis of the Nine Years' War', *Irish Ecclesiastical Record*, 5th series, 92 (1959), 279–90.

   Kinsale: the Spanish intervention in Ireland at the end of the Elizabethan wars (Liverpool, 1970; Dublin, 2000, reprint).

Simms, Katharine. 'Bardic poetry as a historical source', in T. J. Dunne (ed.), *The writer as witness: historical studies* (Cork, 1987), pp. 58–75.

   'Frontiers in the Irish church – regional and cultural', in T. B. Barry, Robin Frame, and Katharine Simms (eds.), *Colony and frontier in medieval Ireland: essays presented to J. F. Lydon* (London, 1995), pp. 177–200.

   'Native sources for Gaelic settlement: the house poems', in P. J. Duffy, D. Edwards, and E. Fitzpatrick (eds.), *Gaelic Ireland, c. 1250–c. 1650: land, lordship and settlement* (Dublin, 2001), pp. 246–67.

Smith, A. Hassell. *County and court: government and politics in Norfolk, 1558–1603* (Oxford, 1974).

Smith, James M. 'Effaced history: facing the colonial contexts of Ben Jonson's "Irish Masque at Court"', *English Literary History* 65 (1998), 297–321.

The Spenser encyclopaedia, A. C. Hamilton (ed.) (London and Toronto, 1990).

St Clair, William. *The reading nation in the romantic period* (Cambridge, 2004).

Stallybrass, Peter. 'Patriarchal territories: the body enclosed', in Margaret W. Ferguson, Maureen Quilligan, and Nancy J. Vickers (eds.), *Rewriting the Renaissance: the discourse of sexual difference in early modern Europe* (Chicago, 1986), pp. 123–42.

Stevenson, Jane. 'The court culture of England under Elizabeth I', in Martin Gosman *et al.* (eds.), *Princes and princely culture, 1450–1650*, 2 vols. (Leiden, 2005), vol. II, pp. 191–212.

Stone, Lawrence. *The crisis of the aristocracy 1558–1641* (Oxford, 1965).

Strong, Sir Roy. *Gloriana: the portraits of Queen Elizabeth I* (London, 1987).

Sutherland, N. M. *The Huguenot struggle for recognition* (New Haven, 1980).

Tait, Clodagh. 'Art and the cult of the Virgin Mary in Ireland', in Rachel Moss, Colmán Ó Clabaigh, and Salvador Ryan (eds.), *Art and devotion in late medieval Ireland* (Dublin, 2006), pp. 163–83.

Teague, Frances. 'Queen Elizabeth in her speeches', in S. P. Cerasano and M. Wynne-Davies (eds.), *Gloriana's face: women, public and private, in the English Renaissance* (Detroit, 1992), pp. 63–78.

Tenison, E. M. *Elizabethan England: being the history of this country 'in relation to all foreign princes'*, 14 vols. (Leamington Spa, 1933–61).

Thomas, Keith. 'The meaning of literacy in early modern England', in Gerd Baumann (ed.), *The written word: literacy in transition* (Oxford, 1986), pp. 97–131.

Thrush, A. and J. P. Ferris (eds.), *The history of Parliament: the House of Commons, 1604–1629*, 6 vols. (Cambridge, 2010).

Treadwell, Victor. 'The Irish parliament of 1569–1571', *Proceedings of the Royal Irish Academy* 65 C (1966–7), 55–89.

'Sir John Perrot and the Irish parliament of 1585–1586', *Proceedings of the Royal Irish Academy* 85 C (1985), 259–308.

Trim, D. J. B. 'The art of war: martial poetics from Henry Howard to Philip Sidney', in Michael Pincombe and Cathy Shrank (eds.), *The Oxford handbook of Tudor literature, 1485–1603* (Oxford, 2009), pp. 587–605.

Tristram, H. J. C. (ed.). *Text und Zeittiefe* (Tübingen, 1994).

Turvey, Roger. *The treason and trial of Sir John Perrot* (Cardiff, 2005).

Ullmann, Walter. 'This realm of England is an empire', *Journal of Ecclesiastical History* 30 (1979), 175–203.

von Sydow, C. W. *Selected papers on folklore* (Copenhagen, 1948).

Walker, Julia (ed.). *Dissing Elizabeth: negative representations of Gloriana* (Durham, NC, 1998).

Walsh, Micheline Kerney . 'Archbishop Magauran and his return to Ireland, October 1592', *Seanchas Ardmhacha* 14 (1990), 68–79.

Walsham, Alexandra. *Church papists: Catholicism, conformity, and confessional polemic in early modern England* (Woodbridge, 1993).

Walter, John. 'A "rising of the people"? The Oxfordshire rising of 1596', *Past & Present* 107 (1985), 90–143.

Watt, Tessa. *Cheap print and popular piety, 1550–1640* (Cambridge, 1991).

Weiner, Carol Z. 'The beleaguered isle: a study of Elizabethan and early Jacobean anti-Catholicism', *Past & Present* 51 (1971), 27–62.

Wernham, R. B. *After the Armada: Elizabethan England and the struggle for Western Europe, 1588–1595* (Oxford, 1984).

Williams, Nicholas. *I bprionta i leabhar: na protastúin agus prós na Gaeilge 1567–1724* (Dublin, 1986).

Williams, Penry. *The later Tudors* (Oxford, 1995).

Wilson, Derek. *Sweet Robin: a biography of Robert Dudley earl of Leicester 1533–1588* (London, 1981).

Wilson, Elkin Calhoun. *England's Eliza* (New York, 1966 [1939], reprint)

Wilson, Scott. *Cultural materialism: theory and practice* (Oxford, 1995).

Withington, Phil. *Society in early modern England: the vernacular origins of some powerful ideas* (Cambridge, 2010).

Wood, Andy. *The 1549 rebellions and the making of early modern England* (Cambridge, 2010).

Wright, Pam. 'A change of direction: the ramifications of a female household', in David Starkey *et al.* (eds.), *The English court from the wars of the roses to the civil war* (London, 1987), pp. 147–72.

Wright, William Ball. *The Ussher memoirs: or, genealogical memoirs of the Ussher families in Ireland* (Dublin, 1889).

UNPUBLISHED THESES AND DISSERTATIONS

Canning, Ruth. 'War, identity and the Pale: the Old English and the 1590s crisis', PhD thesis, University College Cork (2012).

Galbraith, Stephen K. 'Edmund Spenser and the history of the book, 1569–1679', PhD thesis, Ohio State University (2006).

Hutchinson, Mark A. 'Sir Henry Sidney and his legacy: reformed Protestantism and the Government of Ireland and England, c. 1558–1580', PhD thesis, University of Kent (2010).

Leonard, H. 'Knights and knighthood in Tudor England', PhD thesis, University of London (1970).

McGowan-Doyle, Valerie. '"Ancient English gentlemen": the Old English communities of Tudor Ireland in Edmund Campion's *Two Bokes of the Histories of Ireland (1571)*', MA thesis, John Carroll University (1999).

O'Connor, Elizabeth Ann. 'The rebellion of James Eustace, Viscount Baltinglass III, 1580–1581', MA thesis, National University of Ireland, Maynooth (1989).

Trim, D. J. B. 'Fighting "Jacob's wars": the employment of English and Welsh mercenaries in the European Wars of Religion: France and the Netherlands, 1562–1610', PhD thesis, University of London (2002).

UNPUBLISHED LECTURES

Lake, Peter. 'Bad Queen Bess? Libelous politics and secret histories in an age of confessional conflict (University of Oxford, Mar.–Apr. 2011).

Moyeart, Paul. 'Icons as relics: touching God in his image' (Brigham Young University, 3 Nov. 2009).

Ó Macháin, Pádraig. 'In search of Tadhg Dall Ó hUiginn' (Sligo Field Club, 9 May 2009).

Index

CPSIA information can be obtained
at www.ICGtesting.com
Printed in the USA
LVOW01*1923140416

483639LV00015B/222/P

9 781107 040878